Heartland

Heartland

Neil Cross

Scribner

First published in Great Britain by Scribner, 2005
This edition published by Scribner, 2006
An imprint of Simon & Schuster UK Ltd
A Viacom Company

3 5 7 9 10 8 6 4 2

Simon & Schuster UK Ltd
Africa House
64–78 Kingsway
London WC2B 6AH

www.simonsays.co.uk

Simon & Schuster Australia
Sydney

A CIP catalogue record for this book is available from the
British Library

ISBN 0-7432-6374-X
EAN 9780743263740

Typeset in Granjon by M Rules
Printed and bound in Great Britain by
Cox & Wyman Ltd, Reading, Berkshire

Heartland

To Caroline

1

When I was very young, my mother suffered a prolonged melancholy. Her post-natal depression was compounded by grief for dead children and the sorrow of a long, unhappy marriage.

In photographs taken around this time, she's always smiling, wearing the short skirts and clunky shoes of the early 1970s, the plastic macs. Her hair is permed, dyed a harsh black. She stands on the seafront at Weston-super-Mare. I'm in the pram, a Victorian-looking thing, and I'm wearing a white, knitted cardigan with pearly buttons. My mother is either smiling or squinting into the sun. Behind the smile, she was thinking about killing us both.

One day, she positioned herself at the edge of a busy road in Bristol. She watched the traffic bludgeon past. She thought, *Just one step*.

The way she told it, it was a disconnected moment in a dark day, the clouds rolling over Bristol. Just one step. But suicide isn't one step: she went to that hectic road having decided to do it.

She woke in the morning and brushed her teeth and put on her shoes and coat and changed my nappy and put me in the pram with the intention of deleting us both.

And there she stood, at the side of the road, with mirrors behind her eyes. She looked down at me, in the pram. I was tiny and helpless, she said, a baby with my name and my eyes, wriggling, wearing clothes she had knitted, and she couldn't kill me. So she wheeled me home, and we lived.

Five years later, she went out and didn't come back.

My oldest sister and I went to look for her. We went to the local shops, to Parker's Bakery where she worked, serving jam doughnuts and pasties and crusty bread. We went there to see if she was late. But she wasn't; she hadn't shown up that day. Nobody knew where she was.

My sister and I walked round the shops. We wondered if Mum had gone to get some bread and milk, or perhaps some lamb chops for tea. But she wasn't down the shops. She'd run away. I thought of her, clasping her handbag, tottering in her shoes. Running and running and running.

After she left, I was sitting up in Dad's bed. It was morning; Dad was on his way to work. He crossed the bedroom in white underpants and a vest. He was carrying a towel. He wasn't tall, my dad, and he was stocky. He had a big, solid belly and a big, solid nose. He was a quiet and gentle man.

His hair was white: all the colour had drained from it when Mum left. You could see it in photographs. There we are, on a see-saw – him at one end, me at the other. My hair is long and blond, cut into a fringe. His is short, dark, neatly parted. He's wearing a suit and tie; his trousers have hiked around his shins and you can see his socks. He has one hand raised in salute, bent at the elbow. A year later and he's still smiling in photographs, but the colour has gone from his hair.

I said, 'Dad.'

He was distracted, getting ready for work.

He said, 'What?'

I told him: 'When you love somebody, really it's just their face you love.'

He stopped. He turned to look at me. His face became unfamiliar. He still had the towel in his hand.

He said, 'Sometimes, Sonner.'

Sonner was one of his names for me. Nipper was another. He hardly ever used my real name.

He put down the towel and began to dress. He wore a grey suit, a white shirt, a tie, aftershave. He worked for the Post Office. Had since he was a boy.

To most people, my dad seemed very jolly. At Christmas he put on the Rolf Harris LP and he danced around the room to 'Six White Boomers', a song in which Santa was forced by the Australian heat to use kangaroos instead of reindeer. We lined up and followed him. He did silly moves and we copied them. He sang loudly. He grew pink in the face. He laughed.

He never went to the pub. He socialized at the Post Office club on weekend afternoons, and often he took me along with him. He wore whites to play crown-green bowling; a white-haired man, bowling a heavy black ball down a tended lawn. The ball was called a wood.

Crown-green bowling was tedious. The players maintained their posture long after the wood had left their hand; balancing on one leg with an arm extended, like elderly ice-skaters. In the air was a soft, Bristolian cackle and when the wood closed on the jack, there was the slow clapping of appreciative, wrinkled hands.

Usually, I took a box of Swan Vestas from a green-side table and followed the hedges that outlined the green, hunting ants. When I located a caravan of them – a dotted line undulating over the soil, carrying crumbs of cheese and onion crisps and pork scratchings – I lit a match. I enjoyed the sulphurous wink, sharp in my nose, then touched the burning head to an ant. Quick as burning cellophane, it curled into a husk, leaving a chitinous hollow that resembled a burnt match-head.

Sometimes, I singled out an individual. The train would halt, as if shocked by this arbitrary retribution, then hastily jerk into motion, moving round the smoking corpse. Sometimes I eliminated five or six of them in rapid and random succession. The train scattered like soldiers escaping an air-raid. Some of them still carried crumbs in their mandibles. I wondered if I was so big the ants couldn't conceive of my existence.

Dad liked football. Once, he took me to see Bristol City play at Ashton Gate. The rain bit cold and horizontal. We wore anoraks. The crowd was disconsolate and few. The players were more disconsolate still, and even fewer. They hobbled round the muddy field.

It lasted for ever. Football felt like damnation. My hands were chapped and the wind burned my ears. I was proud, because I was there with my dad. But I never went to a football match again.

Because I'd been a mummy's boy, there had always been a distance between me and Dad. But he tried to bridge it. He worked hard to make me laugh, even though his heart was shattered like a land-mine. He kept me close, tried to pull me closer. I orbited him like a moon.

But we didn't talk about love again, not even the day I was taken away from him. He was trying not to cry. His jaw was trembling. He just made sure my anorak was zipped to the throat. He said, 'Take care of yourself, Nipper.'

And I said, 'Okay.'

And that was that.

My maternal grandparents were named Claude and Rose. They ran a tobacconist called The Sweet Basket. My mother, when she was still a schoolgirl, worked behind the counter.

Alan Gadd was a telegram boy. He rode a GPO motorcycle and wore his helmet at a cheeky angle. Girls liked him.

They met in 1947, two years after the great tribulation. These children in Box Brownie black and white. My mother wore her fringe backcombed over her school beret, because that's the way girls wore their hair. Alan's hair was dark, brilliantined. He smoked Players cigarettes. He had a girlfriend called Connie Stevens, but on school mornings he walked my mother to the bus-stop, wheeling his motorcycle. And in the afternoon, he was waiting at the same bus-stop, to walk her home again.

My mother's two best friends were called Sheila and June,

and they liked Alan, too. So when he took his girlfriend to the cinema, poor Connie Stevens, my mother and her friends followed them. First, they went to the cinema. Then they shadowed Alan and Connie to her doorstep. They watched as Alan kissed her goodnight and waited until she went inside. Then Alan met them and walked them home, too. My mother's friends each got a goodnight kiss. My mother, the last and his favourite, got two.

Her name was Edna. That's not a name for incautious youth, not even what passed for it in 1947, five years before the end of rationing and ten before Elvis Presley rolled his hips on 9-inch television screens, thick as cider bottles.

I have heard her called Eddie, sometimes Ed. That sounds better. It's easier to imagine a besotted girl with backcombed fringe and a school beret who's called Ed or Eddie. So that's who Alan loved: a girl called Ed, who worked at The Sweet Basket.

On their first date, they went to see *Easter Parade*. Alan did his National Service in the RAF. They married at St Gregory's Church in Horfield, in 1951. Before that decade ended, they had three children: Clive, Linda and Caroline. And that's almost as much as I know about Alan and Ed.

I know he loved her. He loved her when that Box Brownie boy and girl were long gone, bloomed into Polaroids and middle-age and unhappiness. I know he loved her, because she made his hair turn white.

Alan and Edna, troubled and sorrowful, remembered when their children were small. Perhaps more children would restore that lost happiness.

I was born in 1969, when Ed was thirty-nine years old. Before me came a number of miscarriages. Others followed.

I wasn't unwanted. The children who almost followed me were to provide me with companionship, a brother or sister my own age. But they died, and whatever needed fixing in the marriage did not get fixed.

My mother hadn't been faithful to my father, nor he to her. But those stories aren't mine to tell. I only saw their consequence.

One day, when I was four years old, the wife and daughters of my mother's lover rang the doorbell. When my grandmother answered, they forced their way inside. They kicked my grandmother to the floor. She was in her seventies. They grabbed fistfuls of her hair and dragged her along the hallway. My sister was eight months pregnant. They punched her in the swollen belly. When she fell to the floor, they kicked her. They grabbed my mother. They kicked her and clawed her and punched her. They ripped and tore at her clothes. They tore hanks of hair from her scalp.

One of the women shoved me into a room. I screamed and punched the door. Outside were terrible noises, like the excited howling in the monkey house.

When it was over, I let myself out. My sister, my mother and my grandmother were sitting on the stairs, on different levels. They seemed drowsy, pulling out wispy handfuls of hair.

Not long after that, my mother's lover attacked my father in his own living room. He was much bigger than my dad. This time, there was no room in which to lock me away, nor any time to do it. I cowered in the far corner, behind the TV.

I screamed into my hands. I watched the strange man punching my dad.

When we visited Dad in hospital, he was in a wheelchair. He said, 'Don't worry, Sonner: I'm all right,' and he patted my hand. My sister was crying and so was I.

A spray of Dad's blood dried high on the living-room wall, near the comic statuette of a knight with a drooping sword. On the base of it was inscribed: *Once a King, Always a King, but Once a Knight is Enough.*

I don't know what kind of husband Alan was. He worked for the Post Office until he retired. Notoriously, he was careful with his money, but Mum always used to laugh about that, even years after she left him. Perhaps he was dull, but all husbands are dull – and, anyway, it wasn't adventure that Ed craved. It was a certain kind of love, the kind that doesn't last four children and twenty-five years.

Being in love, being loved, made her feel good. It inoculated her against unhappiness. Even when their marriage was long dead, she often talked about that telegram boy in his cheeky hat, his GPO motorcycle, about poor Connie Stevens and cheeky kisses on doorsteps. Thinking about those children, young and in love, made her happy for a while. But the seeds of unhappiness multiplied inside her like a virus. It always came back.

So when I think of them together, I choose to think of them as teenagers, waltzing at the Locarno, or at the Empire, dancing past the stage where a young Archie Leach once stood, spellbound by an image of his coming transmutation. I think of

Alan and Ed as tentative, as excited and shy: no more than avatars of the parents they became. Fireflies in a bottle. Full of the future.

Their marriage has evaporated, all twenty-five years of it. It ended more years ago than it lasted. They're old now. Those years have dissolved into a ghost haze, through which walk their grandchildren and great-grandchildren.

But sometimes I can't help but think of that black-haired woman at the roadside, thinking, Just one step. Or of the soul-broken man that Alan became, straightening my anorak, zipping it to my throat while my mother, an outlander, waited at the door of a hired car, flanked by police officers. She was waiting to take me away, to a different city, a different world.

Dad swallowed and he said, 'Take care of yourself then, Nipper. Take care of yourself.'

And I said, 'Okay.'

All these things braid in the telling. Become one.

2

Stockwood is a windy plateau with steep slopes descending on three sides. It stands on the south-east edge of Bristol, where the city bleeds into countryside. The Domesday Book lists it as hunting woodland. During the Second World War it was a Starfish site.

Starfish sites were developed in 1940, after the Luftwaffe laid waste to Coventry. They were designed to attract enemy bombs away from positions of strategic importance. By December, the Stockwood fields were piled high with incendiary materials; great heaps of anything that would burn. In a single air-raid, the site drew fifty-nine high-explosive bombs. It must have looked impressive, all that tonnage, blazing away in those empty fields.

After the war, they built a housing estate where the bombs had fallen. The estate was typical of post-war architecture. Pebble-dashed council houses ran up the steep hills; on the plateau were semis and detached houses designed by builders called Wimpey, Laing's, Federated.

We lived at 63 Bifield Road. It was a Federated Avon model, complete with 'feature-built serving hatch with mahogany laminate finish'. Stockwood was a working-class dream of suburbia.

Dad rented from a housing association. In the house lived my mum, my dad, my sisters and my brother. I was a nervous child, scared of the dark, and I was an irksome mummy's boy.

The younger of my sisters was called Caroline. She was ten years older than me, a pupil at Brislington Comprehensive School. She wore knee-length, stripy socks and a butterfly clip in her hair. She liked David Cassidy and David Essex.

Sometimes in the afternoon she came home with a few friends and they took me upstairs and used me as a doll, dressing me in girls' clothes and putting ribbons in my hair. They wheeled me round in a pram. To ensure my cooperation, Caroline confided in a grave whisper that the Daleks were downstairs. They had killed Mum and Dad and everybody else. So I had to be quiet or they'd hear me. The Daleks were shrieking pepper-pots who appeared on *Dr Who*. They sought the destruction of planet Earth but lacked a technology enabling them to climb stairs. So I was safe, as long as I stayed up there, with ribbon in my hair.

I knew Caroline was lying. I hadn't heard any zapping lasers or agonized death screams. But it was quiet downstairs. It was easy to imagine the Daleks wheeling themselves into position, round the corner, ready to surprise me.

Sometimes, Caroline was my babysitter. We watched *The Incredible Shrinking Man*. At the end, after a terrible battle with a giant spider, the dwindling hero grew so tiny he popped out of existence. My horror was vertiginous.

When the credits had faded, it was intensified by Caroline's whispered confidence: we were shrinking, too.

It was night, and we had become tiny. We were trapped in a dolls' house at the dark end of the garden. Outside, the night was rich with giant spiders and monstrous ants.

In the concrete toilet-block of a holiday camp outside Dawlish Warren, a wasp stung my arse. I stumbled back to the caravan, shorts round my knees. My face and T-shirt were smeared with tears and ice cream and fragments of Cadbury's Flake. The wasp followed me. It stung me twice more on the exposed arse, and once on my neck.

During the same holiday, I joined my parents, Caroline and a large group of holidaymakers in the 'Hokey Cokey'. We screamed and ran, hands joined, to the centre of the room. And we screamed and ran, half-stumbling back again.

My brother, Clive, clashed with my father about his motor-cycle and his long hair. Caroline listened to David Cassidy in her room and sulked about boys. Lin, my other sister, got pregnant.

And Ed had a lover. He forced his way into the house and attacked my dad as I grovelled in the corner.

Even with Dad in a hospital bed, Mum denied having an affair. She swore it wasn't true. And Dad believed her. He had no choice but to believe her. So he sued the man for assault.

It was only under under cross-examination that Mum admitted adultery. It hadn't been a fling; it hadn't even been an affair. The man had been her lover for a decade.

Dad sat there and listened while those ten years rushed out of him like air.

When it was all over, Mum promised to make it better. And Dad loved her. So he crammed it all inside him – the lies, the adultery, the beating at the hands of a man who had cuckolded him for a decade; he packed it inside him like wadding, and he took her back. I don't know if it took courage to do that, or weakness; I don't know if it took pride or self-hatred. I do know that it took love.

But something secret bubbled inside my mother, like mud in a pool. And, a few months later, she met another man. No one knew who. Someone from work.

Whoever he was, she very quickly left us for him. She left her family – her husband, her four children, her first grand-child, a boy – without a forwarding address or a goodbye. Without even a note.

She faded from the empty house like an apparition, as if she had never really been there at all.

3

Dad swam through the months that followed like a fish in a tank. He was jovial, laughing, gulping for air.

One lunchtime, my teacher asked why I was crying. I was crying because lunch was cheese flan. I hated cheese flan: it made me feel sick. But the rules were that you had to clear your plate. (Once I'd been caught trying to sneak the skin of a baked potato into the bin. It seemed obvious to me that potato skins were deadly poison.)

The teacher didn't believe I was crying because of the cheese flan: not even when she followed me to the lavatory at a half-jog and saw me vomiting in the sink. She kneeled at my side in the lavatory. She made the fittings look tiny. She dabbed at my mouth with a coarse paper towel, moistened under the tap.

She said, 'Is everything okay?'

I said, 'I don't like cheese flan.'

'I know,' she said. 'But apart from not liking the cheese flan, is everything all right?'

'Yes.'

'Are you sure?'

'Yes.'

Lin came to pick me up from school. She was pushing a pram. In it was her young son. Sometimes when Lin and I went to the Top Shops, people thought she was my mum. We thought it was funny. I told them, 'She's my sister!', and people laughed and said, 'I'm ever so sorry, my love.'

I lived with Dad, my two sisters and my baby nephew. Our brother had married his girlfriend, Jackie. She and Clive lived in Pucklechurch. They too had a baby son.

Lin looked after us, because she was the oldest. She got me up and dressed in the morning. She buckled my sandals. She said, 'Lift your arms!' and helped me into my jumper. She kneeled to pull up my socks.

In the afternoon, she cooked tea for Caroline and me. But she also had her baby to look after. He was a lot of work; she had to make his food and keep him in nappies and clean clothes. She never complained, but looking after all of us made Lin very tired.

Most afternoons, we had eggs on toast for tea. I didn't mind. I liked eggs on toast, especially when the toast was a bit over-done. You added a bit of Heinz Tomato Ketchup to the egg, banging on the base of the bottle until it came out in a red dollop. Then you broke the yolk: it mixed with the cold ketchup and the melted butter, and it was lovely.

Then, after a few months, Dad met Margaret. She worked in a café at Temple Meads, the railway station. Dad met her there. Perhaps she'd served him a scone or a cup of milky tea.

Margaret wasn't like Mum. She was a broad woman with pale, fat arms and legs. And she had enormous breasts, from which draped her floral smocks in a way that made them look too short. She walked flat-footed in Scholl sandals. Her hair was dark and curly, shot through with threads of grey. Her voice was raucous, hard-edged, sometimes strident. She swore a lot.

She was younger than Dad. He was fifty, she was thirty-five. She was divorced – the marriage hadn't been a good one – and had two sons, Gary and Wayne.

One day, I was introduced to them. Gary was a year older than me, Wayne a couple of months younger. Each had a smirking, moon face and an impudent cowlick. They were dressed identically.

Dad told me it was a happy day, because Margaret, Gary and Wayne were coming to live with us.

On Saturdays, Dad drove Margaret to Bath, so she could do the shopping. She liked to buy food from Marks and Spencer; she called it Marks and Sparks. She cooked salmon and new potatoes or lamb chops with peas and mash.

But she only cooked it for Dad and her sons. They ate together at the table, and later they had dessert: trifle or ice-cream or Arctic roll. Whatever was left of the salmon and the trifle, or the chops and the ice-cream, Margaret scraped into the bin.

Lin still cooked for Caroline and me. But Dad didn't give her enough money to buy our food at Marks and Spencer, and anyway she had no way of getting there. So Caroline and I kept eating eggs on toast, and Margaret continued to scrape

into the kitchen bin salmon steaks and lamb chops and roast
beef on Sundays. The bin was a better place for it than
Caroline's plate, or mine.

Dad didn't mind. He was scared of making Margaret
unhappy. It was because he was scared of being alone; but it was
also because she could be terrifying. Sometimes she beat Gary
and Wayne. She slapped them hard across the face with her
open palm; or sometimes she hit them with something she
picked up, a slipper or – once – a length of bamboo she brought
in from the garden. It didn't matter which of them was being
beaten, Gary and Wayne both wept, bent before the screeching
onslaught.

I could feel Margaret's gaze passing across my skin. She
never beat me, never even threatened to. She just wished I
wasn't there and let me know it with her eyes. She wanted me
gone from the house, and my sisters too, because from now on
it belonged to her.

Gary and Wayne needed new clothes. But Dad wasn't paid
enough to keep buying new things for everyone. So he and
Margaret decided to give the old clothing to me. They dressed
me in the old anoraks and the torn jeans and the washed-out
underpants that were no longer good enough for my stepbrothers. And Margaret came back from town with carrier
bags of jeans, T-shirts, jumpers, jackets, trainers.

Once, I cried. She'd bought a new Action Man uniform for
each of her boys. They were very excited: the uniforms were
extra special ones, with all kinds of accessories. Gary had the
Escape From Colditz costume: Wayne had *Field Marshal*.

Margaret saw me trying not to cry.

She said, 'What's wrong *now*?'

I didn't want to tell her. But I couldn't help crying as she stood there, waiting, glaring at me. My words came out all snotty and broken.

Margaret listened. Then she said, 'Oh, pissing hell.'

She stomped out. I heard the front door slam. She was gone a long time, because she stomped all the way to the Top Shops. But I waited in the chair until she came back, because I was scared to move.

Then she came back. She slammed the door behind her. She stomped into the living room and threw a box into my lap. It was a new Action Man uniform.

She said: 'There. All right?'

Dad and Margaret married on New Year's Day, 1976. Gary, Wayne and I wore identical clothes; brown corduroy jackets with furry collars, and brown corduroy trousers. I am there, in a photograph, sitting on Dad's knee. Wayne stands to our right. Gary is behind us. I cannot read the expression on Dad's face.

We moved to a new house, at the other end of Stockwood. It was modern suburbia, a place for the aspirant working class. It stood on the edge of the countryside.

It was a bigger house, designed and built in the early 1960s, which stood in a block of four. There was a patch of unfenced front garden. As you entered, there was a small lavatory to your left. Dad put a wooden plaque above the cistern which read: *We aim to please. Would you aim too, please?*

I looked at it every time I went for a wee. I read it over and over. I knew the extra O and the comma changed things. But I couldn't quite make sense of what the plaque was trying to say: I didn't understand what it meant, to *aim to please*. It was like a riddle. It circled through my head like the words of a trapped song.

The house had a fitted kitchen with a service hatch that opened on to the living room. The living room was a big square, with a swirly carpet. At the back, Dad and Margaret put a table. And there was a sofa: on Sundays, Dad liked to take forty winks on it. He kicked off his soft shoes and lay out with the newspaper on his belly and soon he was snoring.

In the far wall of the living room, double glass doors gave on to a long garden. At the end of it, a wooden gate opened on to a track. It was dry and cracked in summer, muddy in winter. On the other side of the track were some hedges. Behind the hedges were fields that belonged to the local farmer.

The first few days in 92 Bifield Road were busy. Margaret was angry because the kitchen cupboards smelled of the previous occupants. She was a very clean woman. She scrubbed the cupboards over and over, until the smell was gone and the cupboards smelled like Marks and Spencer.

She was glad to be gone from the old place. It had been difficult, living in the house my mother had left, with the man and the children she'd deserted. It made her feel like second best. It filled her with jealousy and fury. But now she lived in a new house: like my Dad, it belonged to her and to her sons.

At first, it was a close-walled and unhappy house, full of bitterness and rivalry. But soon my sisters would be gone from it. Lin and her boyfriend were due to marry. And anyone could see that Caroline was desperate to leave: soon enough, she would. Then it would be only me; an unfledged squatter, an unwanted and gaping mouth to feed.

But I was the most timid of trespassers, one who kept to empty corners. I longed to go unnoticed, to become invisible. The longer I lived with Margaret, the more I felt myself growing silent. The more I felt myself vanishing.

Two years is a long time, when you're very small.

One day I was walking home from school. I wore grey shorts and carried a satchel over my shoulder. I was with Clive Petrie. He was a clever, flat-footed boy with whom I painted model soldiers. I had once trodden dog-shit deep into his house. We were pupils at Stockwood Primary School. I was six years old.

The school was a few minutes' walk from our house on Bifield Road. It was a low-rise, open-plan building in the modern style. There were no classrooms, just different segments, nooks and alcoves that ran off the main corridor. All day I sat, cross-legged, listening to the teacher. At the book sale they held in the gymnasium, I bought the *Ladybird Book of Dinosaurs*.

As Clive Petrie and I walked home, a black-haired woman materialized in the corner of my eye. Clive and I knew we should be careful of strangers, so we kept walking. My legs started to shake. They felt funny beneath the knees.

The woman smiled. She half-squatted. She put her hands on her knees.

She said, 'Hello, Neil.'

I stopped. It couldn't be a stranger if she knew your name.

She said, 'Do you know who I am?'

I said, 'You're my mum.'

She said, 'That's right. I'm your mummy.'

She came up to me and gave me a cuddle. Her coat was cold. She smelled unfamiliar. She asked how I was. I told her I was okay. I had an Action Man. She said that was nice. She gave me a present; a wrapped-up box. Then she began to cry because my legs looked thin.

I said goodbye to Clive Petrie, who had to walk home alone. Then Mum and I went to my nan's flat, which was in St Jude's, in the centre of Bristol.

I hadn't seen my nan for a long time. She and Dad didn't get on; there was something about money. But the smell of her flat was familiar; the thin, blue perfume of Calor gas. There was a plastic tablecloth in the little kitchen, brightly floral. And there was her Yorkshire terrier, Tiny.

Over her bed hung a small, white crucifix. It was a single bed. My grandfather had died shortly before I was born. I played on the bed with my present, a box of American Civil War soldiers. Mum watched me playing. She asked how I was. Did I like school? Did I have lots of friends? Nan made me drinks and gave me slices of cake.

In the evening I went home again. When I got there, I went inside. I shut the door on an afternoon that already did not seem real. It felt like a brilliant dream, fading. As soon as I took off my coat and sandals, it seemed to have happened a long time ago. The woman had been my mum, but she was someone else, too. She was spectral, shifting. She was two people at once.

Neither Dad nor Margaret asked me how my afternoon had gone. They didn't mention it; it was like it hadn't happened.

I kept the soldiers on the window-sill, ranked according to colour, their rifles pointed at me and away from me, at the windows and doors. I never played with them. I just kept them there, neat and unchanging.

4

I knew something was going on because, not long after Mum came to see me, Caroline gave me a present. It was a Roman helmet, short sword and breastplate. They were a bit small. Whenever I turned my head, the helmet scratched the top of my nose and the breastplate dug into my armpits the way new shoes cut into your heel. But I understood the present to have some weird significance. In some way, it was connected with the brief reappearance of my mother.

To show I appreciated its unspoken gravity, I wore the helmet and the breastplate for days and walked around the house ostentatiously swishing the sword, smiting invisible foes.

Then, one night, the whole family came round – my brother and sisters, their partners, their children. They stood in groups and talked, like it was Christmas. It grew late, past bedtime, but I was allowed to stay up.

The living-room door opened and Dad came in. He was singing a nonsense song and dancing a lop-sided samba. In his hands was a gift-wrapped box – another present. He sambaed up to me and gave me the box.

He said, 'Here you go, Nipper.'

Everyone gathered round. They were eager to see what was in the box. I ripped off the paper. It was an Action Man armoured personnel carrier. With it came an Action Man Commando. Gary and Wayne got presents too: a tank and a helicopter. But nobody found their toys as fascinating as mine.

I pushed the armoured personnel carrier up and down. But I didn't like to be watched: I liked it when people ignored me. Then Dad came up to me and kneeled. The room went quiet and seemed to change size. Dad stuck out his hand.

He said, 'Come with me a minute, Nipper.'

I stood up, put my hand in his and went with him. Silence followed us like the wake of a boat. Everyone watched us leave.

I followed him to his bedroom. We went inside and he turned on the light, then closed the door. He squatted there, with his back to the door. I could feel the emptiness of the room behind me, the made-up bed and the wardrobe: their shapes were a coolness on the back of my neck. Dad squatted on his haunches. His eyes were level with mine. He touched my collar. Straightened it.

He said, 'Nip, I've got something to tell you.'

He took my collar in both hands and straightened it again. He brushed it down.

I said, 'What?'

He said, 'Well. You're not going to be living with me any more. Tomorrow, you're going to live with your mum.'

A rush of memory. The spectral woman. The thin blue smell of my nan's flat; the white crucifix above the single bed.

I said, 'Why?'

'Because a judge decided it was best for you.'

He looked away. He kept straightening something on my shirt, some smudge or wrinkle or fold.

I said, 'I want to stay with you.'

He tried to smile. He still wasn't looking at me. There was birdy flutter of panic inside me. It was like when the bad dog on Coape Road launched itself at the garden gate.

He said, 'I want you to stay with us, too.'

I said, 'I don't even know where she lives.'

'She lives in Edinburgh.'

'Where's that?'

'In Scotland.'

He tugged down on my collars.

My feet were cold and my hands were cold.

'She's got a nice house. You've got your own bedroom. There's a park across the road.'

I said, 'Please.'

He wrapped his arms around me and he pulled me into him, into his neck. It was a bit bristly. I could smell his aftershave. Beneath it was the smell of his skin, like no one else's. Something had hitched in his chest. Then he finished hugging me. We went downstairs. We were holding hands.

In the morning I got dressed. Then Dad carried my suitcase downstairs. We waited. After we had waited, there was a knock at the front door.

We went to the front door. Dad opened it. On the other side of the door stood my mother. Her handbag was on her shoulder, hung by a thin strap. She was book-ended by two policemen. They seemed monumental and unreal.

Behind Mum and the policemen, a red Morris Marina was parked at the kerb. A man sat at the wheel. I could only see the back of his head and the reflection of his eyes. He was watching everything in the rear-view mirror, like a spy. He had tilted the mirror so the angles were right.

My family came to the door. They stood behind us. They stood on the little patch of front garden in front of the kitchen window.

Nobody spoke to my mother.

It was like an anxiety dream, the kind where I pissed myself. The police had steady eyes. They didn't look at anyone or at anything.

Dad kneeled, to make sure my anorak was zipped to the neck. It wasn't raining. He cupped my face.

He said, 'You look after yourself, Nipper.'

I said, 'Okay.'

And that was that.

I walked away. I took my suitcase to the car and got in. It smelled new because it was a hire car; after you handed it in, they washed it. I said hello to the man at the wheel. Then Mum got in the front passenger seat. She closed the door. She was looking through the windscreen.

The man at the wheel started the engine. The car pulled away from the kerb. I turned in my seat. My family stood on the doorstep of 92 Bifield Road. They waved. I waved back.

I saw that the policemen had relaxed. One had already taken off his hat, and the other was saying something into his radio. They got smaller and then we turned a corner and they were gone.

The first few minutes of the journey were silent. Mum and the man stared through the windscreen. Bristol went past. Then Mum turned in her seat. She smiled. It was shaky at the corners.

She said, 'Neil, this is Derek.'

He looked over his shoulder and he smiled too. His eyes narrowed and crinkled at the edges. It was a nice smile.

He said, 'Hello, Neil.'

His voice was posh.

I said, 'Hello.'

He returned his attention to the road.

He said, 'What's that in your lap?'

'A book.'

'A book? Do you like books?'

'Yes.'

He drove for a bit.

He said, 'Well, then. We'll have to stop off on the way and buy you some.'

That was good. I watched Bristol go by.

I said, 'How far is it?'

He said, 'About four hundred miles.'

'How long will it take?'

'About eight hours.'

'Is that further than Dawlish?'

A silence.

'A little bit further,' said Derek. 'Yes.'

Mum began to tell me about our new house, about the lovely park across the street and the lovely school a little way up the road. It sounded all right, but I would rather stay at Stockwood Primary School. At break time, Clive Petrie and I would clamber and hang on the multicoloured climbing frames that we called the apps, short for apparatus. And later we would walk home past the fierce dog on Coape Road, which came lumbering and barking and slavering to the flimsy gate whenever a frightened child walked by.

On the back seat of the car, I nodded. I said, 'Okay.'

On the way, we pulled in at the motorway services. The sun had shone pleasantly hot through the car windows and the wheels had hissed a rhythm and I'd fallen asleep. Saliva had dried to a flaky crust between the corner of my mouth and my chin. It was like rice paper.

We parked at the services and got out of the car. It was here, with the wind cooling my sleep-sweat, that I properly met Derek Cross. Until then he'd been a posh voice, the back of a dark head, some twinkling chestnut eyes in the rear-view mirror.

He was short and portly, but elegant in a way that made me think of a field marshal. He wore fawn slacks and a green, ribbed sweater with epaulettes and patches on the elbows. His hair was very dark, combed into a parting that fell in a lick across his broad forehead. His smile was transforming. When he smiled, I thought he was very handsome.

He took me – just me and him – to the little newsagent inside the service station. We approached the magazine rack.

He stood at my side, looking at the magazines. He said, 'What sort of books do you like?'

'I like dinosaurs and pirates.'

'Ah. Dinosaurs.'

He scanned the ranks of magazines. I could feel his concentration. He stared at the shelves. Then he selected the closest he could find to a book on dinosaurs: a glossy-covered magazine about cavemen. It was full of words, and on every second page was a line-drawing of a big-jawed Neanderthal, dressed in raggedy deerskins. There were Neanderthal families in caves, sitting round fires; Neanderthal men surrounding a rearing woolly mammoth, prodding at it with spears. The blades were bound to the shafts with strips of leather. It was a big boy's book. All those words.

Derek looked at me.

I told him it was just the thing. I felt him relax.

I cast yearning glances at the rack of comics.

He smiled, like someone might at a dog who has returned a stick. He said, 'You like these, too?'

I nodded and blushed. I was ashamed.

'Which ones? *The Beano*?'

I nodded. He stooped to take *The Beano* from the low shelf.

'*The Dandy*?'

I nodded. He took *The Dandy* too.

'*Whizzer and Chips*?'

'Okay.'

He tucked them under his arm like a swagger-stick. He turned to face me. He smiled.

He said, 'I'll tell you what; when we get home, we'll sub-
scribe to these. Then you'll get them every week. How do you
feel about that?'

I nodded, not sure. I walked with him to the checkout. He
bought a bag of barley sugars for the glove compartment.

We went out again. We joined Mum on the grass verge. She
had gone for a walk to stretch her legs, but now she was back.
She had brought some drinks from the café. They were on a
tray.

Cars bucketed by on the motorway. They seemed much
faster when I was standing still, watching them. Mum gave
me a glass of Coca-Cola.

I took the glass and swigged. I bit down on the rim and the
glass shattered in my mouth.

Coke frothed between my lips and jetted through my nostrils. It splashed as a pale foam on the ground, like at the edge
of the dirty sea. I stood with my shoulders hunched and my
head projected forwards. My mouth was crammed with sharp
ends. They poked my gums and my tongue and the roof of my
mouth. I could hear them. I was scared to breathe.

Derek kneeled. We were beside the car. He put his hand to
my mouth. He inserted a thumb and finger between my upper
and lower jaw. He exerted pressure, like a tyre jack. He kept
my mouth open as far as it would go.

He said, 'For God's sake, don't swallow.'

He tilted his head and looked inside. Then he began to pick
broken glass from my mouth, shard by shard. His hand was
steady. When all the big pieces were gone, he said, calm but
urgent, that there were still tiny bits of glass inside my mouth.

If I swallowed them, they might cut up my insides and that would be very bad. So I kept my mouth open. It flooded with saliva. It gathered at the top of my throat. It kept trying to swallow.

Derek led me to the public lavatory. My mouth was agape and my head was projected forward like a caveman. The floor of the lavatory was tiled white and pooled with grey water. There were soggy scraps of toilet paper.

Derek took me to the sink and ran the cold tap. He stood at my shoulder and made me use the water like mouthwash, rinsing and spitting. He didn't let me swallow until I'd spat clean a hundred times. Even then, he crouched and put his hands on my shoulders and watched my face as I let my throat work. He waited to see if blood came gurgling up from inside me, but none did. I hadn't even cut my tongue.

Derek didn't want me to dry my face on the loop of filthy towel that hung from the dispenser, so he led me through the swinging door with my hands and my mouth wet. Outside, the air made them cold. As we walked, he lay a hand across the base of my neck, the way a doctor might. He wasn't angry.

We rejoined Mum at the car. Derek told her I was fine. They looked at each other. Then he clapped his hands, once.

He said, 'Right. Chop chop.'

We got into the Morris Marina and drove on to the motorway, headed north. I lay *The Beano,* the *Whizzer and Chips* and *The Dandy* on the seat next to me and opened the book about cavemen. I looked at all those words on the page, crowding the line drawings, bracketing the colour spreads.

'You'll get a headache,' said Derek. 'Reading in the car.'

I said, 'I'm okay. This is interesting.'

Mum said, 'Your teacher told me you were a good reader.'

I said, 'I read *The Purple Pirate* in one go.'

But I wasn't really reading the book about cavemen. I was looking at the pictures. I hoped Derek could see me in the mirror. Every time I looked up, he was looking at the road. But I could tell by a feeling in my scalp that he kept looking back, and that he and Mum kept looking at each other, and I furrowed my brow and looked studious. I turned the pages, flicked back as if to check something, turned the page again, and my eyes grew tired and it was warm in the car and I fell asleep.

Mum woke me to celebrate passing the sign that read 'Welcome to Scotland' but I didn't stay awake for long. I only woke when we entered the Edinburgh city limits.

I sat up in the back seat, gummy mouthed, and looked at it. It was different from the butter-yellow and concrete city I knew. It was lower and darker, and it rose higher and stonier. The air smelled different, biscuity.

We passed the Haymarket railway station and went down Dalry Road. Grey-black buildings lined the road. There were shops on the ground floor, flats above.

'That's your new school,' said Mum, as we turned.

I looked at its strange, lowering brow, its metal gates, its concrete playground. I missed Clive Petrie.

We turned right at the school, on to a cobbled street. On either side rose high Georgian terraces. They were grey stone, gone black with age. Some stood dignified and austere, others

were shabby, with weeds growing in cracks. At the bottom of
the street, we turned right again, on to Duff Street.

We parked outside number 30. The block across the way,
where two terraces had met on a corner, had long gone: once
again, the Luftwaffe had mistaken a place I'd one day live for
a target of strategic importance. This time, the bomb had
missed the Leith docks. The shattered blocks had never been
rebuilt; instead, some climbing frames and a spinning globe
had been erected. The paint was peeling and they were psori-
atic with rust. The ground was sprinkled with broken glass
and half-bricks. There was graffiti on the walls.

I stared at it as Derek took my stuff from the boot, a suitcase.
At my feet, faded caramel pats of horseshit melded with the
polished cobbles. The pats were imprinted with tyre-tracks.

Derek took my bag and we stepped through the main door.
The stone hallway was painted two tone, cream above and
chocolate below. It smelled of chip fat and old piss. On a mat
outside the ground floor flat cowered a black and white
mongrel. As we passed, she bared her teeth – a pointy mesh
basket.

Mum said, 'That's Suzie. She's harmless.'

I paused to look. Suzie cowered still lower and growled from
the root of her throat. As I took the stairs, I could feel her fearful eyes on my back.

The stairs were bare stone. A pale grey hemisphere was
worn into the edge of each by the passage of many feet over
many years. The banister stood on metal rails, and was made of
cracked, dark, varnished wood. The stairwell looked up to a
great glass roof, metal ribbed.

Our flat was on the third floor, behind a blue door. Beneath the letterbox was a plaque, about the size of a cigarette packet. It read CROSS, white letters etched into a glossy blue background.

The door opened on to a hallway. It ran to a narrow bathroom with an opaque glass door. The first internal door, on my right, led to my new bedroom. The second door on the right was the living room and kitchenette. At the bottom of the hallway on the left was Mum's bedroom. The flat had a funny smell, not unfriendly or unwelcoming, but vegetal and old, undercut with gas and hairspray.

We bustled through to the living room. Derek set down my bag in the corner. I put my coat on a chair. It was a stripy deckchair, like you saw at the beach. It was a strange thing to have in a room. The other furniture was normal. At the end of the room, under the windows, was the kitchenette. It was a strip of linoleum, a sink, a cooker and a fridge.

I looked around the room. Nobody knew what to do. Mum gave me a hug. But it felt stiff. I asked if I could watch TV. I was tired.

Derek said, 'You can do what you want. This is your home.'

I said, 'Do I have to go to school tomorrow?'

Something passed between them. It was anticlimactic. Two years in court, fighting for this. And now here I was, just a little boy they didn't know, asking to watch TV.

Derek stood in front of the TV. He put his hands in his pockets and stood there, rocking on the balls of his feet.

He said, 'We thought you'd like to spend a few days settling down, first. Get to know the place.'

I said, 'Okay.'

He said, 'Okay, then,' and turned on the TV.

They watched me, watching TV. I could feel them.

Mum said, 'You get some funny words here.'

I looked at her.

'When I first got here,' she said, 'I was on my way to the shops. And an old lady said to me, "Are you away for your messages, hen?" And I thought, *"who are you calling hen? You old cow."*'

I kept looking at her.

'"Messages" means shopping,' said Derek. 'It took us a while to work that one out.'

I looked at him.

'And they call each other "hen", like we call each other "love",' said Mum.

'And they don't say "yes",' said Derek. 'They say "aye".'

I began to sob.

Mum kneeled.

She said, 'Love, whatever's wrong?'

I said, 'Do I have to say it?'

'Say what?'

'Aye.'

'Not if you don't want to,' said Derek. 'Not if you don't want to.'

I nodded. I wiped my nose. I thought about my bedroom. It was eight hours away, four hundred miles, down a winding road then a long motorway. Past glass-in-the-mouth services, past the edge of Bristol. Through Broadmead, along the Wells Road: up Sturminster Road, past the Top Shops, past

Stockwood Primary, where the red and yellow apps stood in the playground.

I tried to stop crying. There was just the sound of the TV.

The room was half-lit. It was dark outside. The window-panes were black mirrors. And I could still smell the flat. The scent of it hadn't faded the way the smell of strange houses usually did. It was in the walls and carpet.

Mum said, 'Would you like to see your room?'

She led me by the hand down the hallway, to the box room. She was excited and nervous. In the room were a bed and a wardrobe. On the walls, Mum and Derek had hung some pictures. They were proud of them. The pictures showed animals; swans, deer, ponies. They were girls' pictures.

They had gone to the shops, because they were looking forward to me coming to live with them. They had selected these proud stags and pretty kittens. Then they'd walked home with the pictures in a carrier bag, and they'd talked about me as they hung the pictures on the walls of my new bedroom. Mum told Derek how much he was going to like me. And now here I was. The pictures made me sad for them.

High on the wall above the bed was a small, square window. It looked on to the stairwell and admitted some light, second-hand, via the massive glass ceiling. The window was frosted, so nobody could see in. Mum had hung an orange curtain there, and a square of net. It looked naked, an orange square set high on the wall.

I told them I liked the room. I was very tired. I got my comics and my book about cavemen. Mum found some pyjamas in my bag. She tutted and made a fuss about the state

of them, as she had tutted and fussed about the state of my
anorak, torn with all the white padding spilling from inside it,
short at the wrist and tight under the armpits.

I changed and got into bed. They said goodnight. I kissed
them. Mum tucked me up. She kissed me on the head. Then
she waited in the doorway for a while. She said goodnight
again. Very quietly, she began to cry. Then she left.

Under the noise of the TV, I could hear their voices. They
were murmuring. I couldn't hear what they were saying. I lay
face down on my caveman book and pretended to sleep.

After a while, they sneaked into my room. Mum moved
closer to the edge of the bed. Her voice sounded different.

She said, 'Look at him. Asleep on his book.'

She lifted my head and Derek slipped the book from under
my cheek. I could tell that I had dribbled on it. Mum and
Derek laughed, softly. Derek closed the book and lay it on the
floor, next to the bed. Then they left the room again.

That night, I had a dream. It was a dream that came back
again and again until I grew up. In the dream, I was lost and
alone in a vast forest. I knew a witch was somewhere in the
trees, hunting me. She could smell me, just like the Child
Catcher. Sometimes, I could hear her feet, breaking dry twigs.
The forest was still. No birds sang.

Eventually, I found a clearing and in the clearing was a
cottage. It was made of Battenburg cake. I knew I would be
safe inside. So I crept down the garden path – it was full of
dead grass and black twigs that poked out of the soil. I let
myself in through the door. The cottage had a low ceiling. It

smelled like an old, empty cake tin. In the kitchen there was a rough wooden table. On it were haphazardly piled hundreds of rusty knives.

I knew I would be safe in the house. I put boards on the windows and a giant mousetrap at the door. In the dream, I stayed in the cottage for months and months.

I woke on my first morning in Edinburgh believing that I'd been gone for a long time. I looked at my new bedroom, the new hallway, with a strange nostalgia, as if I was seeing them for the first time in many years. I walked, barefoot, to the living room. The radio was on: Jimmy Young.

Mum was doing something in the kitchenette. She heard me. She jumped and turned round and screamed. I thought she was surprised to see me, because I'd been gone so long. But it was just that she didn't hear me get up, because Jimmy Young was on the radio.

She hugged me very tight. She kissed the crown of my head. She made me some breakfast; fried eggs on toast and bacon and a cup of tea. She took a little table from a nest of three and I ate my breakfast on that. The room was too small for a proper table.

Later that day, she went through my suitcase, tutting and muttering under her breath. She separated my clothes into piles: those that could be worn for a while, those which had to be thrown away. I played with Action Man. He swung from the sofa. Dived into deep pools. Flew.

Then I got dressed. Mum and I went for a walk. On Dalry Road, we caught a maroon and cream bus. I watched the stony buildings go past. We got off the bus at Princes Street.

It was a long, straight road. Along one side were large shops. The other side took an oceanic plunge into the gardens, then rushed up again to the craggy, volcanic plug on top of which squatted Edinburgh Castle. It looked as if it had been carved from a single, ancient meteorite. Clouds rushed behind it.

We took a walk in the gardens. We went to a little playground. I swung on the swings. The castle glowered like a god. Mum sat on a bench and watched me, her bag on her lap.

5

Evenings in the flat on Duff Street were always the same. Derek came home from work and we ate tea from the little tables that nested in the corner.

We watched TV. But we were only half-watching it, because we spent our time in conversation. Usually, it was Derek who decided on the subject. Mum and I waited expectantly, wondering what he'd be in the mood to discuss.

Sometimes he was funny, and the three of us sat with our knees jammed under the little tables, laughing as we ate. Or he might talk about his day at work, problems with staff or stupid things some customer had said. He might comment on the day's big news story, or tell us what he called a yarn from his boyhood. He knew everything. There was nothing he couldn't talk about.

On the nights when I wasn't in the mood to talk, he'd be quiet too. He liked to watch me as I read. It seemed to make him happy, just to have me in the room.

Usually, I didn't like being looked at. It made me drop things or bump into furniture. Sometimes, it made my speech come out strangely. A word hooked in my throat and I had to wait until it came unstuck, like the stylus on a record player. If I was walking down the street and someone glanced at me, my legs went numb. Feeling drained from them. It was like I'd forgotten how to walk, the way I forgot how to breathe when I noticed I was doing it. But when Derek watched me, I didn't feel like that. It was relaxing.

Sometimes, he said, 'How many times are you going to read that bloody thing?'

I'd look up from the comic and feel pleased and embarrassed at the same time. I shrugged, and we both began to laugh.

But mostly we sat and watched TV. Derek liked wildlife programmes with David Attenborough, and so did I. And he liked programmes about the Roman Empire, and so did I.

I told him that I wanted to be an archaeologist. He said he'd wanted to be an archaeologist, too, when he was my age. He said we could go camping along Hadrian's Wall, if I liked. He'd show me some Roman sites. There were good Viking sites, too; I liked Vikings.

Mum didn't quite know what to say to me. Sometimes she spoke to me as if I was still five, the age I'd been when she left us. But it didn't matter, because Derek was there. We never ran out of things to talk about.

After I'd read and re-read my comics many times, Derek took me to Bobby's Book Shop. It stood on Dalry Road, not far from the cobbled corner with Duff Street. It was just across the road from Dalry Primary School.

One side of the shop was packed high with second-hand paperbacks. Most of them were science fiction and spy books. And there were war books by Sven Hassel, the covers of which made my stomach pitch. One showed an unshaven German soldier staring into the middle distance, while behind him stretched snow and endless battle carnage: burning half-tracks and tanks. And there were many slim cowboy books by a man called Louis L'Amour.

Derek took one of these from the shelf.

I said, 'Do you like cowboys?'

'Louis L'Amour is very good,' he said, and I was flattered by the gravity of his confidence. He put the book back. He said, 'What are you looking at?'

'*Wheels of Terror*. It's about German tanks.'

It was subtitled *The book no German publisher dared print*! Derek took it and flicked through the yellowing, musty pages, a good smell. He scanned them.

He said, 'I think this might be a tiny bit old for you. Why not have a look round the corner?'

The other half of the shop was given over to second-hand American comic books. They were pinned to the walls, ranked in cardboard boxes on the floor, packed face-forward on shelves. Everything was there: Spiderman, the Fantastic Four, the Avengers, and some I'd never seen before: Deathlok, Manwolf. Each of the comics had the top, right-hand corner of its cover neatly snipped off. A price was marked in felt-tip on its front page.

Derek gave me 50p. And he waited with something like pleasure while I searched through the hundreds of comics.

They were priced 6p. I built a pile of possibles, then sat on the
floor sorting further. Finally, I made my selection. I was aware
of Derek watching me. Sometimes, he idly flicked through a
chapter of Louis L'Amour, rocking on the balls of his little feet.
He wasn't impatient. He'd have waited all afternoon, if need
be.

I was tempted to see if that was true. But I was too excited by
the pile of comics, of Spider Man grappling with Doctor
Octopus, Dr Strange weaving psychedelic spatters round the
lightbulb-head of the Dread Dormammu. So I passed the
comics I'd chosen to the unsmiling man behind the counter,
who perhaps was Bobby.

Derek bought a cowboy novel and we walked home
together. Outside, the light had changed, had moved through
several notches towards darkness. I hadn't noticed. I didn't
think Derek had, either. But Mum was anxious because we'd
been gone so long.

Derek sat in his deckchair and flicked through what I'd
bought. The attention made me tense. I watched him. In
the end, he passed me the comics spread in his hands like
playing cards. He said, 'Goodness gracious me', and that was
good.

He opened his book and read while Mum made the tea, and
I read my comics and the TV was on in the background. We sat
there like that until it was time to eat. It was my job to separate
the three little tables from their nest. We had a table each; they
were teak.

I watched Derek salt his food. He would not allow me to
read while we ate, but the TV stayed on, so I watched that

instead, and we talked as we ate. I was always careful not to speak with my mouth full. I wasn't allowed.

You could tell when Derek was due home, because Mum became more animated. She laughed more easily. She moved more quickly. When Derek walked in, it was like a flare had ignited inside her, which shone out through her eyes and teeth.

But he always took care to say hello to me first: before he'd even taken off his camel-coloured coat and sometimes – when it rained – his little Homburg hat, made of greyish tweed.

He didn't ask where I'd been or what school had been like. Adults who asked that question were never interested in the answer. He just kissed my forehead and patted my shoulder and said, 'How are you?'

I said, 'Good,' and he ruffled my hair. He went to give Mum a kiss and a cuddle, then took off his overcoat. He draped it over his forearm and went to the bedroom, to hang it. Mum began to sing. She always sang when Derek came home.

One Friday afternoon, I ran to the door when his key scraped in the lock. It was the weekend and I was excited to see him. He stood in the open doorway, surprised by the speed of my approach. I ran into his arms. He was still cold with the outside and the prickly wet strands of his coat tickled my face. He'd set his briefcase down on the cold stone floor. There was a carrier bag next to it. It was lumpy with corners.

I said, 'What's that?'

He said, 'Go on inside and I might show you.'

I hesitated.

He said, 'Go on. Chop, chop.'

So I ran to the front room, where Mum was waiting.

Derek came in. He was carrying his briefcase and the carrier bag. He said hello to Mum and then he sat down. He was still wearing his coat. He sat on the sofa, not on the deckchair, and patted the seat next to him. I sat.

Mum stayed in the kitchenette behind us. I looked at the bag.

I said, 'What is it?'

'Well,' said Derek, 'it's a present.'

I'd already guessed that. I said, 'What sort of present?'

He opened the bag. One by one, he began to remove books from it: *The Three Musketeers*, *Treasure Island*, *Kidnapped*, *Little Men*, *The Adventures of Tom Sawyer*.

He passed them into my hands. I looked at the covers. I flipped them over and scan-read the back cover. I piled the books next to me.

Derek was grinning.

He said, 'Well? What do you think?'

I hugged him, a quick hug because I wanted to get back to the books. He sat there, laughing at the slapdash haste of it. It was a good laugh, happy for my happiness.

I picked up a book and began to flick through. It was all words. Page after page of them. Sometimes there was a sketchy ink drawing.

He said, 'Comics are all very well and good. But I think you'll find you enjoy these just as much.'

I said, 'There's a lot of words.'

He said, 'Yes. I think perhaps they're a bit too much for you to tackle on your own. So, how would you like it I were to read to you? Just a little bit, every night. A chapter or two.'

I said, 'Yes, please.'

It started the same evening. He perched on a little stool next to my bed. He sat very still and upright. His voice was precise and clipped, but unhurried and relaxing: it made me think of the voice doctors used when they looked in your ear. It made the stories real. The first book Derek read to me was *Tom Sawyer*.

He did all the voices. Even Becky Thatcher and Injun Joe. But Tom and Huck were his favourites: Tom and Huck Finn, those best, most adventurous of friends.

On Saturday night, he bought himself six little cans of lager. He sipped from them as we watched TV: *The Two Ronnies*, *The Generation Game*, *Saturday Night at the Movies*. The lager made him talk. While we were watching the Saturday film, he told me he came from a place called South Africa.

I turned away from the TV.

I said, 'Have you seen lions and tigers? Not in the zoo. In the garden.'

'I've seen lions, yes,' he said. 'But not so many of them in the garden.'

He glanced at Mum.

'What about tigers?' I said.

'You don't get tigers in Africa. Tigers live in India.'

'Then how come Tarzan fights them?'

'I'm not sure he does.'

'He does, I seen him.'

"'I saw him.'"

'I saw him. He was fighting a tiger and it was in the jungle.'

He told me it was just a film. Tarzan was played by a man called Johnny Weissmuller, who was the best swimmer in the world. Derek always knew who'd been the best at things. The Romans had been best at civilization. Elvis had been best at singing. Johnny Weissmuller had been best at swimming and diving.

Then he stood up and made a little groan. He always groaned when he stood up, and grimaced and dug his knuckles into his lower back. Then he put his hands in his pockets and smiled. He had a very wide smile, like a child's drawing. And brown eyes that crinkled nicely at the corners.

He went for a wee. Sometimes when he did that, he paused in the doorway – his hands were still in his pockets – and he lifted one leg off the floor and farted. It made him laugh every time, and it made me laugh, too.

When he came back, he was carrying a tiny guitar. He sat in his stripy deckchair and put the guitar on his lap. He strummed it.

He said, 'This is called a ukulele.'

I leaned close, to watch his fingers.

He said, 'And this is called a chord.'

He moved his finger-tips, then strummed another chord. It took fierce concentration because it was such a tiny guitar. It made me sad, to see him bent over it. Then he began to sing;

Irene, goodnight Irene.
Irene, goodnight

Goodnight Irene, goodnight Irene.
I'll see you in my dreams.

An old feeling swelled up inside me. It was a memory of before I was born. It was a sad song and I was sad for the man in it. When I joined in, singing a melancholy goodnight to Irene, I felt myself becoming the man in the song. I felt weary and beaten by the world and I felt the weight of all that heartbreak and all those years.

It grew darker. The blackness pressed in from the corners of the room. We were sitting in a shrinking bubble of blue light that sometimes flexed, shuddering in time with the silent pictures on the TV screen.

As Derek and I sang our long goodnight to Irene, wherever she had gone, Mum watched, smiling. Then a mouse poked its head under the pantry door. It watched us. Mum threw her slipper. The mouse whipped its head inside so quickly it seemed to disappear.

Mum said, 'Cheeky bugger.'

She looked at me. She had tears in her eyes.

She said, 'He's a cheeky bugger, that one.'

On Sunday, the three of us went walking in the Pentland Hills. On the bus, Derek pointed out a practice ski-slope, like a milk-spill down the side of a hill. Up close, you could see it was a thick plastic waffle, a carpet laid over grass.

Derek wore a rucksack and hiking boots in caramel brown, with knee-length socks. Along the way, he picked up a sturdy stick to walk with. I copied him. I found a fallen branch, nearly as tall as me. It made a difference. We walked a long way, like shepherds.

I felt different, walking up the hill. We passed free-grazing sheep. They were unperturbed by our presence and by the corpse of one of their flock. It lay eviscerated and mummifying in a dip, close by a loose-hung, barbed-wire fence. Bits of fleece fluttered in the barbs like cotton wool. The sheep's legs were stiff and wide and its belly cavity was open and empty. An eyeless skull protruding from the fleece. There was no smell. A few flies crawled over it, but there were no maggots. I stared at it for a long time, leaning on my stick.

I said, 'What killed it?'

Derek leaned on his stick, next to me.

He said, 'A dog, probably. Some people can't control their dogs.'

It was a sunny day but the wind was cold and I shivered. I leaned more heavily on my own stick. I felt old and wise, like a man in a song.

I said, 'Are there wolves?'

'There used to be. But not any more. All the wolves have gone.'

'Where?'

'People killed them. Farmers. Because they killed sheep.'

'And boys and girls.'

'Sometimes, I expect. But if they did that, it was a long time ago.'

I nodded.

We trudged up the hill. At the top we sat down and looked at Edinburgh. It was the colour of the moon, thunderhead grey, even under the bright sun. Derek opened his rucksack and took out the little picnic Mum had packed: egg sandwiches, made with Heinz Salad Cream, some biscuits, tea in a tartan flask. I watched the clouds race over the city, the play of sunlight on the Firth of Forth. I strained to see the bridges which spanned it, passing into the kingdom of Fife.

I ate the sandwiches and the biscuits, but I didn't want the milky tea. It tasted of the plastic cup that screwed to the top of the flask. It wasn't an unpleasant taste, but a few metres downhill was a spring, a braided rope of clear water spilling from some black rocks. It was as if, many years ago, a wizard had struck this point with his staff. And that was what I wanted to drink, water from the wizard's spring.

'It's called a burn,' said Derek, and he rolled his R's and tried to sound Scottish. But he sounded like a man from a war film, a Spitfire pilot. Not the hero, who was a decent man played by John Mills, but the hero's friend. And that thought made me ache for him, that if Derek was in a film, he wouldn't be the hero of it.

The way the water gobbeted from the split rock, undeviating, was hypnotic. I kneeled and prodded the water with the tip of my finger. I watched it run over my knuckles. Then I stuck in my hand. It was shockingly cold, and it made my hand look pale. I watched the flux of light reflecting on the egg-shaped pebbles at the bottom.

I cupped my hands and lifted them to my mouth, to drink. Most of the water spilled, wetting my shirt and thighs. I looked up. Mum and Derek were laughing. There was a spike inside me. I blushed for being clumsy and strange. But they were just happy.

I lay flat on my stomach. I got muddy. I scooped the water

into my mouth with both hands. It was good water, and the effort of getting it made it better. I drank until my stomach cramped.

I sat next to the burn until the sick feeling passed. I was looking down on the city. It spread like mould round the green node of Arthur's Seat and the black crag of Castle Mount. It sent out questing tendrils, Edinburgh's roads.

I watched birds and wandering sheep. When the sickness had gone I stood, feeling the miles walked behind my knees and in my thighs, and we gathered our things and walked down the hill, past the fake ski-slope, and we waited at the bus-stop. On the bus my head nodded and I fell asleep, resting on Derek's shoulder, and the mud dried on the front of my shirt. At home I brushed it away; it had turned to dust.

Derek showed me how gentlemen looked after their finger-nails. They cut them off square and used a file to round the edges: a gentleman should always have square, clean finger-nails.

That was one sign of being a real man. There were many others. You were always polite. You were always clean and tidy. If you wore a tie, you made sure it was straight. Even more importantly, your shoes should always be clean. The only way to get them clean was spit and polish and good old elbow grease. ('To get a really good shine,' said Derek, 'you set fire to the polish. But I'll show you how to do that a bit later on.') You looked someone in the eye when they were speaking to you: not out of the window or at your shoes. You always said please and thank-you. You never started eating until everybody was seated, and you never left the table without seeking permission. On buses, you offered your seat to old people and pregnant women. If they thanked you, you replied, 'You're very welcome.'

These were some of the things that made you a gentleman. If you weren't a gentleman, you were a yob.

I cut my nails like he told me, but he didn't like my hair. It was too long and girlish. What I needed was a man's haircut. So he took me on the bus to see his barber. It felt like a long way. It was near the supermarket in Corstorphine, where Derek worked. He liked his staff to call him Mr Cross. Being respected was another part of being a gentleman.

The barber shop was around the corner from the supermarket. The barber was an old man in a white coat. And he was bald, which I thought was a funny thing for a barber to be.

He greeted Derek fondly – 'Well, hello there, Mr Cross' – and I was proud that Derek was a man who was known.

The barber said, 'And who's this?'

'This is Neil,' said Derek.

'Well, hello to you, Neil. And has your dad brought you in before?'

I should have been embarrassed by the mistake. I waited for Derek to correct it, but he didn't.

So I said, 'No, he hasn't.'

It wasn't really a lie; not technically.

'You see?' said the barber. 'I thought we'd not met before. I'm sure I'd have remembered such a handsome lad.'

I blushed and he smiled. Then, from the far corner of the shop, he retrieved a board and lay it across the arm-rests of the cracked leather chair. He said, 'All aboard,' and helped me up.

I could see Derek in the mirror, sitting in the row of chairs next to the empty coat-rack in the corner. On the floor were curls of brown and black and grey hair.

The barber tied a gown around my neck and tucked tissues into the gap. He snipped the scissors close to my ear. They hovered impatient and hungry, like hummingbirds.

He said, 'And what are we doing for you today, young man?'

Derek spoke for me. He stood up. He put his hands behind his back and rocked on the balls of his feet.

He said, 'Short back and sides, please.'

The barber hesitated. He lifted the side of my hair with the comb. Then he half-turned, facing Derek. The scissors kept snipping the air at waist height.

He said, 'Oh, man, surely not?'

'Short back and sides,' said Derek. His smile widened. His eyes went narrow, wrinkled at the corners. He rocked on his feet.

The barber ruffled my head.

He said, 'Och, it's such a shame.'

I looked at Derek, reversed in the mirror.

'Don't be in a hurry to grow him up,' said the barber.

There was a long moment. Derek kept smiling, rocking.

Then the barber said, 'It's no good. I can't do it.'

He took the gown from round my neck and helped me climb down to the floor.

Derek's smile was the same shape: beaming and broad. And his eyes were crinkled in exactly the same way. But something had gone from it; something you couldn't see. When I looked at him, I felt strange.

He said, 'Very well, then.'

We said a hurried goodbye to the barber. Outside the shop, Derek zipped me into my anorak. Then we caught the bus home. All the way, Derek didn't speak. I looked out the window: Edinburgh, going past.

We got off the bus at Dalry Road. Derek took me to a barber called Koolcutz. Mr Koolcutz was younger and skinny and he too was almost completely bald, with hairy arms and blue-grey lenses in his spectacles.

He passed the electric clippers over my head. Blonde curls fell on to my lap and on to my shoulders. I closed my eyes when he cut my fringe. The scissors were cold and they tickled my forehead.

When he was finished, I looked at myself. I had short hair. It looked darker. My neck was long and my ears were big and red.

'That's better,' said Derek, 'that's much more like it.'

We walked home together.

Derek said, 'And how does it feel, to have a proper haircut?'

He rubbed the back of my neck, where the hair was bristly. I said, 'Ace.'

When Mum saw it, she ran all ten fingers through my shorter, darker hair. I could tell she was about to cry. Her hand went to her throat.

But then Derek told her about the first barber. He said, 'Can you believe the bloody *cheek* of the man?'

'So what did you do?'

'Well,' said Derek. 'I told him what was what.'

I looked up at that bit. I hadn't heard Derek letting the barber know what was what. I'd seen him grinning and nodding with all the humour gone out of it, like a red apple that only looks good on the outside. Then I remembered him hurrying us from the shop, helping me into my anorak only when we were back on the street, in the drizzle.

'I told him,' said Derek. 'I said, *"Don't be expecting my continued custom. Because I'm telling you right now: you're not getting it."*'

'Oh, Derek,' said Mum. 'Did you have to be so hard on him?'

You could tell by the way she said it that Derek was forever letting people know what was what.

Then she looked at me, happy sad, and ruffled my hair. She told me it was lovely. She was lying. She wanted me to look like a baby.

I said, 'It's a proper man's haircut.'

'It is,' she said. 'It's very grown up.'

I went to the bathroom and for a long time I stared into the mirror. I looked at my long neck and my big, red ears. And I thought about Derek, smiling at the barber and leaving the shop, zipping up my anorak outside in the rain. Then sitting silent and angry on the bus, all the way back to Dalry Road.

Derek wasn't his real name; not his real first name anyway. He'd been baptized Winston Derek Cross. But he didn't like to be called Winston. He never told me why, but Winston was a funny name: the children at school had probably laughed at him for it. They probably chanted 'Winston Churchill' and danced round him in a circle. I'd have laughed, too, at a boy called Winston.

Back in Bristol, he'd been regional manager for Parker's, the chain of bakeries that employed my mum. That's how they met. Their eyes locked over the jam doughnuts and the hot Cornish pasties and the French sticks. They flirted with one another. Then they fell in love and ran away together.

But he wasn't from Bristol. He was a white man from South Africa who'd lived in Britain for many years: 'Many years,' he said, 'many, many years.'

He never told me why he had chosen Bristol as a place to live.

He'd already been married four or five times. He told me this with a certain resigned sadness, as if being married to all those women had been necessary but regrettable. He talked about his wives as he might a childhood friend who had died young, of a rare and incurable disease.

But I asked him to tell me more about them, these other wives – where had they lived, what had been their names? He counted them off on his fingers, the way he might have checked Roman emperors or the greatest films of Yul Brynner. Their names were just information, like a timetable. Because of that, I couldn't imagine their faces: and because I couldn't imagine their faces, I couldn't remember their names. Each of them flashed once in my imagination, like sheet lightning, and then was gone. They left the vaguest after-image: a shifting, composite, woman.

He also had a son. His name was Richard. Richard lived in another city with his mother. Derek told me her name once and didn't use it again. She was just 'Richard's mother'.

When Mum talked about Caroline or Lin or Clive, her children, she had a certain look on her face. It was a mixture of cheerfulness and sorrow. But when Derek told me about Richard, his voice and his face remained perfectly neutral. Richard Cross was just more information, another entry on the timetable.

We only talked about him once, and soon I forgot that he existed. He was a failure of my imagination. I never wondered if Derek had read to him *The Adventures of Tom Sawyer*, doing all the voices, even Becky Thatcher, or if they had gone camping along Hadrian's Wall. It didn't matter to Derek, so it didn't matter to me, either.

Derek liked ballroom dancing. A real man could dance, he said. Every Wednesday, he and Mum went for lessons. I went with them. Derek told me I'd thank him one day, and gave me a peculiar smile.

He and Mum were in the advanced class. They danced very well together; they could do the rhumba. I was in the juniors, the only boy in the class and in some demand as a partner. The girls wore their best dresses and shiny black shoes with buckles. I wore a collar and tie and a brown blazer. I learned to waltz and to cha-cha-cha. The teacher told me I had wonderful rhythm. I couldn't wait to tell Derek.

He liked Laurel and Hardy. He had most of their silent movies on reels of Super 8 film. Sometimes, he set up the white screen and projector he kept in the pantry. It was a delicate operation, spooling on a Laurel and Hardy movie. When it was done, we turned off all the lights. The only sound came from the unspooling tape. The room smelled of dust, burning on the hot bulb of the projector.

On screen, Laurel and Hardy slipped and slid. Derek laughed until he wept, and I did too. The way we laughed made Mum laugh, even though she wasn't watching. You could hear her, laughing in the bedroom as she folded clothes or ran the carpet sweeper over the floor.

He also had a Super-8 cine camera which he took on trips to the zoo and the botanical gardens. He was always behind the lens, recording. He and Mum liked to watch the films he'd taken.

Once, long before I arrived, my nan had been to visit them. Derek had filmed their coach holiday to the Isle of Skye. Mum always cried when the camera closed up on my nan's embarrassed, grinning face and her silly, nervous wave.

My sister Caroline and her boyfriend Tony had also been to visit. There was film of them, too: Caroline and Tony in their denim flares and platform shoes, walking arm-in-arm and laughing, trying to pretend the camera wasn't there. During that visit, Caroline became pregnant with her first child.

And Derek liked music. There was a record-player in the living room, under the TV. He squatted down there and showed me his records. He liked Johnny Cash and Jim Reeves and Hank Williams. And he liked Bill Haley and the Comets, and Eddie Cochran, whose final concert, he said, had been at the Bristol Hippodrome: Eddie Cochran had played "Summertime Blues' and 'Three Steps to Heaven'. Then on his way to the airport – he was flying home for Easter – his car blew a tyre and hit a lamp-post. Eddie Cochran sailed through the windscreen and smashed up his head. He died the next day, in hospital.

Derek also liked Fats Domino and Little Richard and Chuck Berry. He told me that Chuck Berry and Little Richard and Fats Domino had helped to invent the music known as rock 'n' roll, but that it had taken white men like Elvis and Bill Haley to make it famous.

Often, we listened to *Live at San Quentin*, because Johnny Cash was my favourite. Soon I knew all the words to all the songs. Derek put the stylus to the vinyl and we listened to the rumbling hiss then, at just the right time, we made deep voices and looked at each other and said: 'Hello, I'm Johnny Cash'.

It was because of back pain that he sat in the stripy deckchair. He'd once passed a kidney stone. Passing a kidney stone was the most painful experience a human being could endure, he told me. It made him scream with pain.

And he hated niggers.

He lay a hand on my shoulder, a soft hand with a gold band on the third finger, not a wedding ring. He looked me in the eye. A dark, glossy lock of fringe fell across his pale brow.

He said, 'I don't have many rules in my house. But one of those rules is, you never, ever bring a nigger through my door. If you bring a nigger into my house, then you're out on the street. And you will never be welcome under my roof ever again. Do you understand that?'

I said, 'Yes.'

'Good,' he said, 'good boy.'

He gave me a hug. He kissed me on the forehead.

I hugged him back.

He took me to the cinema. All the way, he wore an expression of rueful endurance and he laughed at himself when he bought the tickets.

I was excited; I loved going to the pictures. When the lights went down and the adverts began, I was happy.

Halfway through the film, I turned to whisper something and saw that Derek was asleep. His head was thrown back on the port-red velvet chair and his mouth was open.

There was a slow, fond sunburst inside me.

I thought about how Mum began to sing when Derek came home – and how the anticipation of his arrival even made her move more energetically, as if he was battery that recharged her. I thought about Derek waiting for me in Bobby's Book Shop, how he was amused and pleased by the frankness of my awe. And later, he had passed me those books, one by one from the bulging carrier bag: *Kidnapped*, *Tom Sawyer*, *Treasure Island*. And I thought what an immense burden it was that he carried: not to love, but to be loved.

In that cinema, watching him sleep, I came to understand that adoration requires a kind of pity. I looked at him, and I wanted nothing bad ever to happen to him. I wanted to protect him. I wanted him always to be happy, because when he was happy I was happy too.

I had not by then been in Edinburgh for many months. But time has a different quality in the solemn heart of a seven-year-old boy.

By now, when we went walking in the hills, Mum used to hang behind Derek and me – not because she was tired, but because I'd begun to walk just like him. She liked to watch us, walking together: Stan and Ollie. Eric and Ernie.

Tom and Huck.

6

On my final weekend before starting at my new school, we'd gone walking again in the Pentland Hills. Once more, I'd looked down upon the city. I knew the school was there. It was a very old school. It sat still and empty, like an old lady in an empty room. The passing of a single weekend meant nothing to it.

During the ascent, I found a sheep skull. It was lying in the grass by a grey-brown fencepost that was weighed down by sagging barbed wire. The skull was bare. The blunt teeth were loose, and they clattered when I shook the skull in my hand. It was difficult to believe it had once been a sheep's face, packed out with wary eyes. I asked if I could keep it. Derek said yes. Mum said no. She didn't want dead animals in the house.

I looked at Derek and he looked at me. He made a face, but he said nothing, and we walked along, laughing. For dinner we were having roast leg of lamb.

In the evening, I had my bath and changed into my pyjamas. I watched some TV. Then I was sent to clean my teeth.

The hallway frightened me. It had no windows and it was dark and straight. When I stood at the sink, it seemed to telescope into the darkness, like a hallway in dreams and I sensed something rushing towards me from the far end of it. The thought of it loosened my bowels. I cleaned my teeth, two or three scrubs, then hurried to the living room. I watched TV until my heart had slowed. Then Mum came with me to bed, to tuck me up.

She sat on the edge of the bed.

She said, 'Big day tomorrow.'

I nodded.

We said goodnight. Then Derek came to read to me. It was a short chapter – the one where Tom Sawyer cons his friends into whitewashing the fence. It was my favourite. I'd already heard it two or three times. I liked that one of Tom's friends swapped him a dead rat and a string to swing it with.

It was Derek's favourite bit, too. He thought it was hilarious, the way Tom fooled his friends: *If he hadn't run out of whitewash, he'd have bankrupted every boy in the village.*

When he'd finished the chapter, I asked him to leave the light on and the door a tiny bit ajar. Only a tiny bit. And he said what he always said: 'There are no spooks here.' But he did as I asked.

I tried to stay awake, to keep tomorrow away. I read comics until I felt myself drifting and knew I couldn't stop it. I hoped I'd have the Hansel dream, of the cottage in the woods. That would keep tomorrow away for many months.

But I slept and didn't have the Hansel dream. I was woken by Mum, calling me out of bed. Derek was ready to leave for work. He had to get there early, because he opened up. He was in charge of the money. He was all clean and dressed, carrying his briefcase. He ruffled my hair, and that made me feel a better, like I was brave. But when he left, my bravery diminished with every metre he put between us.

When I tried to clean my teeth, I vomited green bile, the colour of a bad apple. It hurt coming out, and when it was gone my stomach kept trying to squeeze out more, like toothpaste through an empty tube.

Mum made me breakfast. I tried to eat it. But the thought of food was horrible and the knife and fork felt wrong in my hands. So I put on my school clothes. Mum wet my hair and combed it into a parting. She got her handbag and put on her boots and walked me to school.

The walls of the school were high and stone-built. They were lower by the main gates, and dotted with black metal nubs, like decayed teeth. Once, they'd been railings, but they were cut down and melted during the war, to make tanks and aeroplanes. Derek told me that.

The school looked like a church. It had a concrete playground where the graveyard would be, with football and netball pitches marked out in different coloured paint. Children teemed through the gates. Some of their mothers stood in small groups at the gate, talking. The infants went through a big blue door. The bigger children had a separate entrance.

At the gates, Mum kneeled. I was aware of the current of

children rippling past us. As they passed, they nudged each other and nodded. Some of the smaller ones just stared. I was embarrassed by Mum's attention. I told her I was okay. Then I turned and went inside. I could feel that she was still there, at the gates.

The corridor smelled of school; of floor wax and old milk and chalk dust and cheesy feet. The floor was polished parquet, much scarred and indented. The classroom doors were of solid wood, half-glazed with wired-glass.

The bell went. It was hand-rung by the headmaster, a lanky man who went out into the playground to ring it. It was big, wood-handled. And suddenly the corridor was full of children and noise. Then they were gone and it was quiet and the corridors were empty.

My new teacher came to get me. She was small and old and she wore spectacles on a chain round her neck. She ushered me inside. She closed the door behind her, and asked me to stand by her desk. The class looked at me. Blue eyes and brown eyes and lazy eyes and glasses. White knee socks and flared corduroys.

The little teacher said, 'This is Neil. He'll be joining our class from today.'

She showed me to a desk with an empty chair. The class watched. My legs felt strange, so I went to the desk with exaggerated caution. I sat in the chair, facing the blackboard.

The kid next to me wore an orange tank-top with a blue zigzag across the chest. He was pale, with transparent eyebrows and clumpy orange hair that stuck up. He smelled of piss. He smiled. He said, 'Hiya.'

I said, 'All right?'

Then the teacher called the register. We got on with the lesson. I watched her write on the board. I was watching myself from high in the corner. I could see myself, bent over the little desk.

During morning break, I loitered in the doorway as children spilled into the playground. It was a rule that everyone had to be out of the building. So I walked as slowly as I could, and went outside and sat on the stone steps.

An older boy came up. He stood over me. His friends stood behind him.

He said, 'Are you a Yank?'

I looked at him. The sun heliographing behind his head.

I said, 'English.'

'Oooh,' he said, 'English.'

They laughed and walked away.

Back in the classroom, we studied hundreds, tens and units. The little teacher approached me. She asked what was wrong. I hadn't done hundreds, tens and units. She kneeled and helped me. She smelled like lavender. I started to cry.

When she'd gone, I wiped snot on the back of my hand.

'It doesn't matter,' said Billy Flockart, the boy with the ginger hair. He said it: 'Disnae matter'.

After school, mothers gathered at the gates to meet the younger children. Some had prams or held the hands of fat toddlers. They stood in twos and threes. None of them was alone, except my mum. She stood there smiling.

We walked home together. It wasn't far. She asked how it had been. I told her I'd learned hundreds, tens and units and sat next to a boy who smelled of wee; he was nice, though.

In the flat, Mum made me Noodle Doodles on toast. They were spaghetti shapes, and I liked them because the advert was funny. I liked Campbell's soup for the same reason. The Campbell's soup advert had a superhero in it, in an armchair, wearing slippers, which I thought was the funniest idea in the world.

She passed me the plate. I looked down at shapes meant to be cars, boats, trees, dogs, little men with hats.

She said, 'Did you make any new friends?'

'A few. Mum?'

'Yes?'

'What's a cunt?'

She went to the kitchen and busied herself, her back to me.

She said, 'Why, love?'

'People keep calling me an English cunt.'

'What people?'

'Just kids.'

She put the kettle on. Rinsed out the pan in which she'd heated the Noodle Doodles.

She said, 'Never mind.'

I turned in my chair. She was looking at me, drying the saucepan.

I said, 'But what does it mean?'

'It's a horrible word,' she said.

She made a disgusted face. It transformed her.

I turned away and ate my tea. I worried about being a cunt.

It might have something to do with the way I walked or the colour of my hair or the way I smelled. Perhaps I smelled of wee too, and that is what it meant to be a cunt.

I decided to ask Derek. I waited for him to come home. When the key turned in the lock, my heart quickened. He walked in, grinning. He was happy to see us: just me and Mum.

I could feel her joy. It shone behind me like a lighthouse.

Derek didn't take off his coat or even put down his briefcase.

He said, 'Well? How did it go?'

I wanted to say, 'What does "cunt" mean?'

But I didn't want to see that disgusted look on Mum's face again. It had reminded me of candlelight flickering on a gargoyle. And Derek looked so keen to hear good news.

I said, 'It was nice.'

'Did you make friends?'

'A few.'

He stood there, the briefcase in his fist.

'It won't take long,' he said. 'You'll settle in.'

On Wednesdays, Mum didn't meet me at school because she was having her hair set. The hairdresser was two or three doors along from Bobby's Bookshop. So that was my favourite afternoon.

After school, I ran across the road, and walked to the hairdresser. Inside, a sharp-edged fug of setting lotion and hair lacquer hung in the air and gave the light an ancient, varnished quality.

The same women got their hair done at the same time every week, and quickly they learned to recognize me. Most of them were elderly; they were attentive and kind and knew about small boys. They asked me to fetch their bag and then dug around inside and gave me a barley sugar or a Murray Mint. Then Mum gave me 20p to spend at Bobby's.

Paying for the comics was always a silent transaction, except when I said thank you. Then I took the comics to the hairdresser and read them while Mum and the old women sat under the big hair dryers. The old women took obscure, smiling pleasure in the fact of my existence, of any child's existence.

On Friday, I got a parcel from Dad. It was wrapped in brown paper and secured with parcel tape. Mum had to cut it open with a bread knife. Inside was a letter:

Dear Nip
Hope you are still well and enjoying your new school.

At the top was sellotaped a 50p piece. And the parcel contained *Battle!* and *Action!* comics. British comics were still printed largely in black and white, and mostly concerned the Second World War. Each featured several stories, told in episodes. They featured maverick protagonists, each of whom was his own man, unfettered by structures of command. By far my favourite story was *Darkie's Mob*. It was about *a hard cruel son of Satan* who turned his rag-tag team into *the most savage fighting force the Japs had ever known*.

Darkie's Mob finished in tragedy so total I wept myself to sleep. For weeks I carried the thought of them around with me: Darkie and Flyboy, Smiley and Shorty, dead in the Burmese jungle.

*

Although the extermination of *Darkie's Mob* was the worst pain I had ever endured, most of my entertainment pivoted on violent death. But normally it was the violent death of Germans.

One blustery Sunday, Derek and I sat down to watch *The Dam Busters*. He told me it was a good film. As soon as it started, I knew he was right. I loved the music. It was martial and triumphant, but undershot with melancholy. It made me feel English. And I liked Barnes Wallis, a boffin in spectacles who invented bombs that skipped like flat stones across the surface of a lake, in order to destroy some vital German dams. In films, German dams were always vital. So, for some reason, were ball-bearing factories.

When the dams burst, I cheered. But then, at the end of the film, Barnes Wallis removed his spectacles, weighed down by his triumph.

I said, 'What's wrong with him?'

'He's just a scientist,' said Derek. 'Not a soldier. The bouncing bomb was just an idea. Now it's worked, thousands of people have been killed. So imagine how he feels.'

'But they were baddies.'

'Not all Germans were baddies. And not all the people who died were Germans. Imagine what it must be like, having a wall of water a mile high slam down on top of your house.'

He clapped his hands once, loudly.

I imagined it.

I said, 'Then why did the Dambusters do it?'

'Because there was a war on.'

I gave him a blank look.

He hesitated. Then he said, 'There was a man called Robert

Oppenheimer. In America. During the war, he was boss of the
Manhattan Project. It was a secret project to build an atomic
bomb, before the Germans did. It was very important. But in
the end, they dropped the bombs on two Japanese cities. They
were called Hiroshima and Nagasaki.

'Thousands of people were destroyed. Hundreds of thousands. Burned to death. Atomized. There was nothing left of
them, except their shadows: they'd been burned into the walls.
The ones who lived, their eyes melted in their face. And they
died over years: of burns, of horrible cancers. They gave birth
to deformed children: babies born without brains, without eyes.

'And Robert Oppenheimer was like Barnes Wallis. He was
just a scientist. One day, they asked how he felt, about what his
invention had done. And do you know what his answer was?'

I said, 'No.'

'His answer was: "I am become death, destroyer of worlds."'

Derek had grown heavy in his chair. The rainy light had
become slow and oppressive.

Mum stepped out of the kitchenette, a tea-towel over her
forearm. The smell and sound of roasting lamb.

She said: 'Der-ek.'

He snapped out of it.

He gave her an innocent look.

He said, 'What?' and flashed me a grin.

'You know what,' Mum said. 'He's seven years old.'

'Going on twenty-seven,' said Derek.

I basked in that like sunshine.

But then Derek stood up and said, 'Come on. Dinner time.'

I tarried, sitting on my hands. I wanted to talk some more

about the war. I was close to knowing something. But Derek clapped his hands, twice.

'Come on now,' he said. 'Chop chop.'

I went to wash my hands. It was one of the things he made me do. I turned on the cold tap and drizzled water over my fingertips. Then I dried them on a towel and went to help set out the little tables.

After dinner, we watched the news. The local bulletin reported on a house fire. The newsreader was grave. But then she announced that only one person had died.

I said: 'One's not many, is it?'

Derek lay the palm of his hand on the crown of my head. It felt good. I could still feel it there, when he took it away.

He said, 'Well, it's an awful lot to that person.'

I thought about that all night. I thought about it until I went to bed, and I thought about it as I tried to sleep. I chewed it in my dreams.

The saddest part of *The Dam Busters* had been when, on the eve of the mission, Wing Commander Guy Gibson's dog was run over and killed. The dog was called Nigger, and Wing Commander Guy Gibson loved him. He was a good dog. And that is what I dreamed about: not about burning in chip fat, or about thousands of screaming Germans smashed and drowned by a wall of water; nor even about Robert Oppenheimer, turned by his own genius into a monster.

I dreamed about Nigger the dog, and the sorrow of the brave wing commander, the very day before his most important battle.

*

It was several weeks before someone at school actually hit me. The escalation towards it was incremental. An older boy and his friends backed me into a quiet corner in the playground. The boy twisted my ear, spat in my face. He contorted his mouth, called me a cunt. Soon, there was another corner, another boy from the same group. He slapped me and pulled my hair and punched me. Then he too delivered the mysteries: I was a cunt, a fenian, a radge. He rounded it off with a dead-leg. A dead-leg was more bemusing than painful.

It was always one boy showing off to a group. There was at least one group for each year above me, but the oldest ones were the worst. An older boy would shove my shoulder and say 'Hey, you'. He took a handful of my hair and twisted it in his fist. He pulled down on my hair so that I bent at the waist. He tried to punch my face, but it was awkward because I was bent double and most of the punches hurt the side of my head and my ears. He kicked me in the guts. He tried to knee me in the balls. His friend laughed and shoved. A few of them kicked at my shins and thighs and arse.

Then he pushed me to the ground and spat on my face. He called me some more names and wandered off. I lay on the concrete.

I got up and went to class. I saw the little teacher's face and her eyes followed me as I walked to my desk, next to the boy who smelled of wee, and opened my jotter.

I walked home with holes in my jeans and scabs on my knees. My collar had been torn from my shirt.

When I came home with ripped and bloodied clothes, Mum was angry. She wore the disgusted face that I feared so much to

7

Long before I went to live with them, Mum and Derek had been to see a film called *The Exorcist*. Even now, they discussed it often, in subdued voices, the way people discussed a family secret. When I paid attention to what they were saying, Mum hushed Derek. It was as if 'Exorcist' was another word too bad to be uttered.

I said, 'What's *The Exorcist*?'

Mum gave me a look, the look she wore when she was lying. She said, 'Nothing. It's a film. A horrible film. That's all.'

I thought of the Hansel dream: the Battenburg-cake cottage, the witch outside in the forest, rushing through the trees. The stained wooden table and the long, rusty knives.

Now, when I ran out to clean my teeth, it was *The Exorcist* I was scared of, although I couldn't give shape to it. It was *The Exorcist* at my heels when I went to bed. It was *The Exorcist* who leaned over me at night, peering through the thin skin of my eyelids. It was *The Exorcist* on the other side of the bedroom wall, scratching.

Eventually, I could no longer stand it, to have this thing stalking at my heels, leaning over me at night. On Saturday, when Derek had drunk some lager, I asked him to tell me about it. Mum tried to stop him. She put her hand on his knee. But he squeezed her hand and leaned forward in his deckchair.

He said, 'It's a very, very frightening film. When your Mum and I went to see it, there were ambulance men in the cinema, waiting to take out the people who fainted.'

I said, 'What, grown-ups?'

To think of a grown-up fainting in horror was terrible to me.

'Grown-ups. They carried them out on stretchers. One man was so frightened, he had a heart attack. Right there in the cinema. Right in front of us.'

I didn't want to know any more.

I said, 'What's it about?'

Derek said, 'It's about a young girl, a little bit older than you, who becomes possessed by the devil.'

'Derek,' said Mum.

He made an innocent face.

'What?'

'He's too young.'

I said, 'I want to know.'

Mum looked at Derek. He was sitting back in his deckchair with his hands knitted in his lap. He was smiling.

I said, 'What does it mean, "possessed"?'

'It means the devil gets inside you and takes over your body.'

Mum said, 'Derek. That's enough. Look at him.'

I said, 'I'm all right. Can that really happen?'

'Can what happen?'

'Can the devil get inside you?'

A long silence.

'Oh, yes,' said Derek.

It was cold. I could feel the dark windows.

I said, 'But it can't really happen.'

'Of course not,' said Mum, 'there's no such thing.'

But she had the same face on, that same look of disgust, and I knew she was lying.

'Actually,' said Derek, '*The Exorcist* is based on a true story. It really happened. Except it happened to a young boy. He was a little bit older than you.'

'Derek,' said Mum, 'you're frightening him.'

'I am not,' he said.

'He isn't, Mum,' I said.

'He's talking rubbish,' said Mum, 'don't listen to him. It's just a film.'

Resigned, Derek picked up the ukulele. But I wasn't in the mood for singing. So he put the ukulele down and, instead, he told me a story.

It happened when he was a boy, about my age. They lived on a farm in South Africa. His father had occasion to sack one of the farm workers, who was surly and lazy and dishonest. That night a monkey came by the farmhouse and did terrible damage. It broke windows, lit fires. And it came back the next night, and the night after that.

Eventually, Derek's father was advised by a local witch doctor to set a trap for the monkey. He told him what kind of trap it should be, and where they should set it, and all this they did. When the monkey came back, it fell into the pit they'd dug, and into the net with which they'd lined it. They hauled it out, and – as the witch doctor had instructed – they poured petrol on it and set it alight. It was a terrible sight, Derek said, the way the monkey writhed and burned. It screamed liked a baby even when the fire was out and it lay in the dirt, not yet dead. And that was the end of their monkey problems.

But the story didn't end there, because the next day, the man who had been sacked was found dead in his bed. His hut was perfectly unmarked, inside and out. But the man had burned to death. Only his blackened skull was left in the clean bed, grinning at the ceiling.

When Derek had told me this story, I decided I would not go to bed for some time.

I said, 'That's not true.'

He strummed the ukulele. Gave me a look.

He said, 'A lot of strange things happen in Africa. They're primitive people. They have access to spirits and demons.'

'Derek,' said Mum.

He strummed the ukulele. He began to sing. It was 'You Are My Sunshine'. It had become one of our favourites.

I sang with him for a while, but the shadows in the room were oppressive and the air seemed heavy, like the silence after a bell has been struck. Eventually, I was sent to clean my teeth. In the cold, narrow bathroom my legs shook and I dared not look in the mirror, in case the devil should be looking back at me: chop-licking, grinning.

Derek didn't read to me that night. I was up too late. Instead, he sat on the edge of the bed, smiling, and patted my knee. Then he said goodnight. He hesitated in the doorway. He asked if he should leave the door open, and I said no. I didn't like to see the hallway at night. He closed the door, and he left the hallway light on.

In bed, I waited for the devil. I wondered if he was already inside me, like the presence in a haunted house, lingering before he showed himself.

The bedroom door snicked open.

I got out of bed and closed it. Then I went back to bed. I pulled the blankets over my head. My heart was loud. When I peeked out from under the blankets, the door was open again.

I didn't stay for long in the little teacher's class; perhaps a term and a half. The summer holiday came, an infinite stretch of six weeks. It began with my first return to Bristol.

Mum packed my suitcase and Derek inventoried the contents. He made a note that read: 5 × sox, 1 × kagoul, 3 × jeans. Then the suitcase was zipped shut, with the note inside.

We took a bus to the airport. My suitcase jostled on Derek's knee. We passed the supermarket where he worked, in Corstorphine, and I pointed it out to him and he smiled.

I had never been to an airport. At the desk, the woman smiled and said: 'Are you travelling by yourself?'

I said, 'Yes.'

I was proud.

My suitcase jerked along the conveyor belt. Mum took me to one side and poked the ticket and boarding pass into my pocket. She told me not to lose them. I said goodbye at the gate. They stood there with their arms linked, smiling and waving.

On the other side, I was met by a woman with an orange face who smelled of perfume. She took my hand and led me to the front of the queue, so that I was first down the gangway. I was elated by the ascending whine of engines and the smell of aviation fuel. The aircraft was a Vickers Viscount. It had four propellers.

The woman took me to a seat in the front row and showed me how to use the seatbelt. I sat there, reading, while the other passengers boarded.

When the plane taxied to the runway, I lay the comic in my lap. The acceleration pressed me into my seat and made me laugh. I watched the ground slip away.

When she had served some drinks, the woman asked me to unlock my seatbelt and come with her. She held out her hand. Her nails were red. I stood. The plane shifted like a boat beneath me. She went to a heavy door at the front and rapped on it with her knuckles. Then she pushed the door open.

Behind it was the cockpit. The pilots wore shirts and hats. Clouds came at us through the windscreen.

One of the pilots turned in his big seat and smiled and offered his hand. I shook it. Derek had shown me how to shake hands properly. Nice and firm. Three times. Let go.

The pilot said, 'Hello there.'

I said, 'Hello.'

I smiled.

I said, 'Who's flying the plane?'

He pointed to something. 'Right now, it's the automatic pilot.'

I said, 'Have you got bombs?'

He looked at the other pilot. They grinned.

'Not on this plane, no.'

I pointed to something else. 'Is this the ejector seat?'

He looked at where I was pointing.

'We don't have ejector seats on this kind of aeroplane.'

'But what if it crashes?'

'Well, we don't have crashes.'

'But what if it does?'

'Look at this,' he said. 'This measures our airspeed. Do you see how fast we're going?'

I looked. We were going fast. I could see the clouds being ripped apart.

The pilot said goodbye and turned again to face the front. The woman led me back to my seat. She gave me a small can of Coca-Cola and a little bag of peanuts. Later, she told me to hold my nose and blow if my ears started to hurt. I was still blowing when the wheels shrieked on the runway of Birmingham airport. There were no planes from Edinburgh to Bristol.

I was first off the plane. The woman led me down the steps on to the tarmac and she walked with me to the airport building. She held my hand. It was windy and she kept stooping and pressing her little hat on her head.

Before we reached the building, I spotted a group of smiling, waving figures: Gary, Wayne, Margaret and Dad. I waved back. I was embarrassed that the woman was holding my hand.

When we were inside, she let go. She said to Dad, 'I assume

this one's for you?' and Dad thanked her. She said goodbye and walked off.

It was strange, seeing Dad and Margaret in an airport. The bright lights made them seem not quite real.

Dad said, 'Hello, Sonner.'

I said, 'Hello, Dad.'

He said, 'Who was that holding your hand, then?'

He looked at Margaret.

He said, 'Who do you think that was, Marg, holding our Nipper's hand? I reckon that was Miss Lushbody.'

He looked at me.

He said, 'Nipper, was that Miss Lushbody?'

Everyone laughed, and I laughed too. Miss Lushbody was one of Dad's jokes. All teachers were called Miss Lushbody, even the really old and ugly ones.

I wanted to tell him about meeting the pilot, but he was busy joking. I finally got to mention it when we were waiting at the luggage carousel. I stood next to Dad. I told him that I'd been taken into the cockpit and I'd met the pilot and I'd seen clouds coming at us at a hundred miles an hour.

He seemed distracted, concentrating on all the jostling suit-cases. I realized that he thought I was lying.

I said, 'Honest. They showed me the ejector seat and every-thing.'

He said, 'That's nice, Nip.'

We waited for the bags. My face burned.

I decided to wait until I got back to Edinburgh. Then I'd tell Derek about meeting the pilots. Derek would ask for the details. When I told him I'd seen the ejector seat, he would smile and say, 'Well, it probably looked like an ejector seat, but I expect it was actually something else.'

Then he would tell me how impressive it was that I even knew what an ejector seat was, at seven years old. And all my disgrace would evaporate and I would be happy.

Outside, it was dark, and the sky was high with aircraft noise and lights and the smell of fuel, and everything was unfamiliar.

We walked to Dad's car. It was a dark-blue Hillman Minx with canary yellow hubcaps. I called it the Yellow-Wheeled Speed.

We got in. Everyone had been excited, now everyone was tired. We drove off.

Lights pulsed overhead, like alien spacecraft in precise formation. Margaret turned in her seat. She asked me how I was, and how was Scotland, and how was my new school? I told her I was well, that Scotland was nice.

She turned again to face the front. She said, 'Your Dad wishes you'd write more often, Nipper.'

I'd tried to write. But when finally I sat down to do it, Derek stood at my shoulder, hands in pockets, rocking on the balls of his feet. He dictated to me:

Dear dad how are you i am well my new school is nice we went to the zoo they have monkeys and there is a caslte. Wen it is sunnie we go to the hills we climb a long way i like to drink from bursn they are like streams

He made me write our address in the top right-hand corner,

which was stupid, because Dad knew where I lived. He sent me parcels.

It was boring, writing what I was told, and it felt dishonest and it took ages, and it made my hand ache.

Dad looked at me in the rear-view mirror.

He said, 'Just a few words, Nip. Just to let us know how you are.'

Just a few words, is what he always asked for in his letters, before ending them: *Love, Your Dad*.

I said, 'Sorry, Dad.'

I spent the rest of the journey in silence. I watched the darkness broken by the swelling headlamps of passing cars. Then I saw Bristol, multi-lit in its basin, like a landed UFO.

We arrived at 92 Bifield Road. The house seemed very big, and – when they turned on the light – too bright. We walked into the front room. There was the table and the swirly carpet. There was the big storage heater you sat on when it was cold: it made your bum feel nice and warm. There was the sofa on which Dad lay on for forty winks. He slept with the newspaper on his belly: if you tried to lift it off, ever so gently, he woke up and said 'Get off with you' shooing you away like a fly.

There was the double door that gave on to to the long, skinny garden. The smell of the house was familiar but different. I supposed it was just the old smell of it, with the smell of me taken away.

I was tired. Dad took my suitcase upstairs to my old bedroom. He put the suitcase on the bed and opened it for me, to get some pyjamas. Inside, he found Derek's inventory. His face went blank, then dark, then jolly. I thought of the shadow of clouds, passing over the sunny city while I looked down from a high hill.

He showed me the piece of paper.

He said, 'What's this, then?'

I shrugged.

'I don't know.'

He said, 'It's a list of your bloody clothes. What does she think? That I want to keep them?'

I wanted to tell him it was Derek who wrote the list. But I knew that would make things worse. Seeing Dad looking at the list made me homesick. I felt like I was betraying someone. I was not sure who.

A bit later, we said good-night. I lay in bed. My old bedroom was washed in ambient light; there was a streetlight outside the window. It was different from the darkness of the little box room in the flat on Duff Street. I listened to the creaking of the house, a couple of late-night voices wandering by on the pavement outside. They spoke in an accent that was familiar and strange. It was an accent I'd never heard before leaving Bristol: I'd been surrounded by it, the way you're surrounded by air.

The next day was Saturday. I had a fried breakfast with Gary and Wayne and Dad and Margaret. The light shone in. The radio was on. Margaret liked the radio. She was always listening to it, always singing. She liked a band called Showaddywaddy. She would do the vacuuming and sing 'Three Steps to Heaven', which was one of their hit singles. Sometimes Dad would take her arm and they'd waltz to it. It was their song. They had danced to it at their wedding. They sang:

Step one: You find a girl to love
Step two: She falls in love with you
Step three: You kiss and hold her tightly
Well it sure feels like heaven to me

And Margaret would say that Dad was a bloody nutcase, and I could see they were happy together.

I wondered if they knew about Eddie Cochran; that 'Three Steps to Heaven' was his song, and the last place he ever sang it was the Bristol Hippodrome, because that was the last place he ever sang anything.

I had a shower. Dad came in while I was drying off. He cleaned his teeth in warm water, then he stood at the toilet to have a wee. He seemed to wee for a long time. He weed and weed. I passed through the weird normality of it, then I went to get dressed.

Because the Scottish educational year was slightly different, Gary and Wayne had another week of school. On Monday morning, the house was frantic for half an hour. Then they were gone and so was Margaret and it was quiet.

Dad told me to go and get dressed and then we went out. In the morning sunshine, Stockwood didn't seem real. The roads were wide and grey: the houses big and pale. They had front gardens, with bikes parked in them. It was so quiet, you could walk down the middle of the road.

We got into Dad's car. I sat in the front seat.

He said, 'Strapped in, Nip?'

I said, 'Yes.'

He drove me to Stockwood Primary School. It looked very

strange, sitting low and modern in its playground, with the same old apparatus out in front, by the gates.

I had a feeling in my belly that was like descending in a lift.

I said, 'Where are we going?'

Dad yanked up the handbrake.

'We're just going to pop inside.'

My legs went funny.

I said, 'Why?'

He looked at me. He'd already taken the keys from the ignition. They were in his hand.

He said, 'Don't you want to see your friends?'

I got out of the car and I followed him through the gates and through the doors and into the school. It seemed odd now, that classes gathered in different nooks down the length of one long room. As I followed Dad, children fell silent and looked at me.

We stopped when we found my old class. They were sitting cross-legged on the floor with their backs to us. The teacher looked up. She saw Dad and me. She stopped talking.

She said, 'Look who's come to see us, everyone!'

The class turned its many heads.

I stood there.

Dad rubbed my crown.

He said, 'Say hello, Nipper.'

I said, 'Hello.'

Wayne was there, smiling. And so was Clive Petrie. But Clive Petrie didn't want to look at me. He sat looking at his knees.

The teacher said, 'Say hello, everyone.'

The class said, 'Hello.'

Some of them started speaking earlier than others, making the word long and jumbled, like *Amen* at the end of the Lord's Prayer.

The teacher said, 'And how are you getting on?'

I said, 'Fine, thank you.'

'That's nice. Are you still enjoying your reading?'

'Yes, thank you.'

'Good.'

Dad stood there, playing with the hair on the crown of my head.

'Well,' said the teacher. 'It's ever so nice to see you.'

Dad said, 'Say goodbye to everyone, Nipper.'

I said, 'Bye.'

They looked at me.

The teacher said, 'Say goodbye.'

They said, 'Goodbye.'

Dad smiled at the teacher and said thanks. She smiled back. Then we turned and walked back down the corridor. It was very long. We walked into the sunshine and went back to the blue car with yellow wheels. We got in and put on our seatbelts.

Dad said, 'So how was that, Nip?'

I said, 'Good.'

'Was it nice to see your friends?'

'Yes.'

'There you are, then.'

He drove us to the Top Shops. We went to the bakery (not the one where Mum used to work, it had shut down). We went inside and he asked what I wanted. I looked at all the cakes.

I said, 'Can I have a jam doughnut?'

Dad laughed.

He said, 'Are you sure? You can have a cream slice if you like.'

I said, 'A doughnut's okay.'

You couldn't get proper jam doughnuts in Edinburgh. So Dad bought me two. The lady put them in a white paper bag with scalloping round the top.

She said, 'Here you are, love,' and passed the bag over the counter.

Dad took me to see my old class twice a year until I was ten years old. He wanted me to stay friends with everyone, in case one day I should come back to Bristol. It would be as if nothing had happened.

But eventually the silence and embarrassment that greeted our visits became intolerable to everyone involved. Quietly, he gave up the idea.

He'd taken the week off work. I spent most of it at the edge of a bowling green. There were the same cheery exhortations, the soft echo of kissing balls. The same held pose, like a slowly deflating discus thrower.

I dissected cigarette butts left piled in alfresco ashtrays. I peeled off the fake cork paper and unpacked the yellow wadding, staining my fingers and making them smell. I left the ashtray full of something that looked like chaff, something that might have blown from the boughs of a spring-laden tree. When all the butts were taken apart I took some matches and punished ants for my boredom.

Then, at the end of the first week, we went on holiday. The Yellow-Wheeled Speed cleaved to the slow lane. Even the dawdling cars behind lurched into the middle lane to pass before dumping themselves back down in front of us.

In my imagined commentary, the Yellow-Wheeled Speed was lapping everyone. Gary and Wayne's own, louder narration seemed more disrespectful and hurtful. During it, they called my dad Alan, sometimes Al. Nobody ever called him that.

Margaret joined in, too. Her voice was joyous and hectoring and it set me on edge. She said, 'Come on, Al, stop pissing around.'

Excited, Gary and Wayne described cars that went past: better cars, red cars, more expensive. Dad seemed unconcerned. But I was hurt on his behalf. I liked the Yellow-Wheeled Speed and I presumed that Dad liked it, too, because he'd kept it for so many years.

But he said nothing. Eventually, I realized that his feelings weren't being hurt at all. He knew they were only joking and he didn't mind. He might even have been enjoying it, all the happy noise in the car.

Clive and Linda and Caroline had gone. They were all married, with children of their own. And I was gone too. I lived in a flat he'd never seen in a city he'd never visited.

In my absence, Dad and Margaret and Gary and Wayne had become a proper new family. I still belonged to it, but only at a shallow and glancing angle. I was like a comet: orbiting the same sun, but in a distant, elliptical orbit.

Sometimes, when they were laughing together, Margaret looked at me through narrow eyes and I felt awkward and ashamed.

Because of me, they were on edge. I was a subject Margaret and her sons couldn't discuss, like the meaning of a bad word. It passed between them, transmitted by eye-contact and small expressions of irritation. When I did something stupid, which was often – I fell down or forgot to bring my coat or asked if I could stay in to read while they went to play Crazy Golf – they made small, hateful faces that I was supposed to see but Dad was not, and never did.

When I was alone, Gary and Wayne's irritation spilled over and they hit me or pinned me to the floor and pressed a pillow on to my face, to stop me breathing. I panicked, but didn't cry, and never told.

Margaret made no pretence of including me in her jokes or her conversation. It was between her and her husband and her sons. It wasn't her fault or responsibility that I happened to be there, too.

She cooked my meals, but set them down with distracted contempt. When I told her the food was nice – they still went shopping at Marks and Spencer – she looked at her son and said, 'We always have this on a Tuesday, don't we, Gary?'

She didn't voice her dislike, not even when Dad wasn't around. It was coded in certain gestures, and coded in the lack of certain others. It was in the furtive hiss of her endless, private wrath.

Dad liked one-armed bandits, and so did Margaret. He whiled away the Great Yarmouth afternoons by pumping fistfuls of five-pence pieces into the slots and slapping at agitated *Nudge* and *Hold* buttons. He gave Gary, Wayne and me 10p each.

I wandered the sandy-smelling arcade. I stopped to get change in two-pence pieces from a bored man in a tubular booth. I loved the arcade, the smell of sand and candy-floss and rubber and suntan lotion. Eventually I bumped into Gary and Wayne, or they bumped into me, and I spent the money and we went to loiter around Dad.

We waited for a win. When that happened, he'd scoop coins from the steel pot riveted to the bandit's belly and he'd dispense one or two to each of us. Otherwise, he remained oblivious of our presence. If a payout was too long coming, Gary and Wayne moved to the next machine, where Margaret stood, yanking down the ratcheted arm. When Margaret gave them money, she gave them some for me, too.

In the evening we had fish and chips and ate them on the sea wall as the sun went down, and sometimes we went to the camp-site bar and I drank lemonade shandy from a blue and gold can. Sometimes Dad and Gary and Wayne played darts.

On the beach, I made high sandcastles and demolished them with the aid of miniature, invisible armies equipped with pebbles for siege equipment. There came a moment when the castle, having withstood the early assault, began at last to crumble, and that was the best bit.

Dad and Gary and Wayne and sometimes Margaret played cricket on the beach, with wooden stumps and a tennis ball. When Dad caught Gary or Wayne's ball, he threw it in the air and shouted *Howzat*.

At night, in the narrow caravan bed, I longed to be home.

At the end of my two weeks, Dad and Margaret drove me to

Birmingham airport. I said goodbye to them at the gate. They stood there, waiting.

When another woman with red nails and a little hat took my hand, I looked over my shoulder and Dad called out, 'Go on, Nip!', and raised his thumb. Then he looked at Margaret and they laughed. The woman led me on to another plane, the same as the first.

When we arrived at Edinburgh, the woman led me off the plane and on to the tarmac. In the airport, Mum and Derek were waiting for me. This time, it was they who were flattened by the airport lights. Their smiles of greeting were bright and unreal. Looking at them, I missed my dad.

We caught the bus home. The smell of the two-tone hallway was cruder than I had remembered. And all the time I'd been away, in the arcades and at the beach and by the side of the bowling green, Suzie the dog had cowered on the same mat in the same semi-darkness, snarling at whoever passed. That made me feel funny; sad inside my stomach, like I wanted to be sick.

Mum unpacked the suitcase. Margaret had washed and pressed my clothes, so Mum put them straight into the wardrobe and the chest of drawers. They smelled liked Dad's house.

I ate some tea, an egg sandwich, and drank some lemon squash. Mum and Derek didn't have a telephone and neither did Dad, so we hadn't spoken in two weeks. Now they wanted to know everything. They leaned in towards me and asked how my trip had been.

I said, 'All right.'

I thought how stupid I'd been, to lay in that bed in Bifield Road – on the bedroom door was a little plaque with a vintage car on it, and the words *Neil's Room* – longing so desperately to be home. It had only been fourteen days, and those days had gone and they would never come again.

And now I was back home, thinking about Bristol. I wished I'd joined in the games of beach cricket instead of poking round rock pools and building castles to destroy. I wished I'd shrieked and squabbled when Gary and Wayne teased me or hit me, because Gary and Wayne shrieked and squabbled when they hit each other. I wished I hadn't submitted silently to their blows and their scorn. I wished I'd gone running to Dad. I wished I'd told.

But I didn't say any of that to Mum and Derek. I told them it had been a nice holiday, that the bowls had been a bit boring.

When all the other questions had been asked, Mum said, 'And how's your dad?'

I knew she was asking because, once upon a time, he'd been a telegram boy in a jaunty hat, who wheeled his motorcycle to the bus-stop when she was on her way to school. She wanted me to say he was happy. I told her he was.

It was true.

8

During the summer break, I sometimes went to work with Derek. He was the manager of a St Cuthbert's supermarket in Corstorphine.

On my first visit, he introduced me as his son. But he didn't like me going with him, not really; it made him uncomfortable.

Sometimes we wandered the shop floor together. I clasped my hands at the small of my back, just like him. He liked to inspect the shelves, to make sure they were neat, tidy and well-stocked. If a popular product wasn't being moved speedily enough from the stockroom, it made him furious. Several times, I saw him curtly summon a shelf-stacker to the back, where he bellowed at them for leaving the Heinz Tomato Soup half-empty, or for not properly mopping up a spillage of milk.

'For God's sake, man,' he shouted, 'what do you think you're *here* for?'

His staff didn't like him. They made faces behind his back, like he was a strict headmaster.

But he always smiled for the customers, even when he was angry with one of his workers. If an old lady couldn't find her brand of cat-food, Derek gave her a big smile and called her 'Madam' and asked if she'd be so kind as to wait, just a moment. Then he marched off and promptly returned, a tin of Whiskas clasped like a baton in his right hand.

When the customer thanked him, he always said, 'You're very welcome', and kept smiling until they turned away. Then he turned pointedly to whichever of his staff might be watching and gave them the cold, dead eye. Finally he looked at me. Silently and secretly, he arched an ironic eyebrow and we moved on.

But I didn't go to work with Derek very often. Mostly, I went with mum, because it was easier. She also worked for St Cuthbert's, part-time at a much smaller branch on Nicholson Street.

It was a bus ride away, along Princes Street and across the Bridges; past the museum and the ABC. It was a small supermarket, antique, with a staff of five or six. Mum worked 10.30 a.m. until 3 p.m. on the check-out, the busy period.

Her boss was Bob Cruickshank. He was an old man with brushy white hair. One of his eyes was gluey. The other was fierce blue. But he was a kind man, and he let me work to pass the time.

At the back of the shop – at the end of the aisle where you found tins of beans and stewing steak – a pile of Tate & Lyle sugar stood on a rough wooden pallet. When the pile grew low, I restocked it, carefully cross-hatching the hard-packed pouches. They leaked small landslides of sugar from their folds, and sugar was ground into the splintery wood of the palette. I pretended the bags of sugar were sand-bags, and I was on a D-Day beach. When the sugar was stacked, I took the price gun and labelled the cans of beans and the cans of tomatoes and the cans of soup. Then I restocked the shelves, neat and tidy, labels forward.

Sometimes, an old lady asked me to fetch her a half tin of Whiskas from a low shelf, and she told me I was doing a grand job and that made me happy. It was fun, working in the shop. But behind the shop was better.

First, you passed through a fringed plastic curtain; then you were in the back room. Back there, it was perpetual twilight: the only window was set high in the wall and was opaque with dust and cobwebs, admitting light the colour of cider. The back room was full of cardboard boxes in lilting piles; they were filled with fast-moving lines brought up from the stockroom. There were wooden shelves, once rough, now waxed and darkened by time, on which lay box knives and curls of plastic wrapping and half-filled, cold mugs of tea. In one corner was the cash office, a tiny room which I never entered.

In the corner was a stairwell. The banister was dotted with ancient nails, around which had been tied plastic tags and fraying bits of coarse string. The stairs were noisy and loose. Halfway down, they took a sharp turn, to the basement.

It was built of stone and low-ceilinged, and had a smell which incorporated soil and wood and cardboard and plumbing. A high, wired window stood at ground level, but it too had grown a milky cataract with age. In one corner was a square table of unfinished wood. It was set out with old tea-making things on a tray, and pushed to it were some stools polished by generations of arses.

Down a short, dim passage were two stockrooms. Each was windowless and wet-walled, piled with damp boxes on wooden pallets. There were trolleys to move the pallets, and there were rat-traps. The bulbs were naked and cobwebbed.

Down there, as you sat at the table, drinking a can of Cresta, it was easy to convince yourself there had been sudden, secretive movement in one of the stockrooms; that something was preparing to rush at you, moving so quickly you couldn't reach the stairs in time. It would grab at your flailing ankles, as you clambered towards the daylight and the safety of those bent old women in headscarves, buying half tins of beans for themselves and tinned steak in gravy for their cat.

Mum's best friend in the shop was a woman called Ida. They sat on the two checkouts, in blue-checked nylon overalls, and when the shop was quiet they talked. Mum also liked Mike and Rab, because they were cheeky. Rab was big and blonde and ruddy. Mike looked like a scrivener; an intense brow, eyes in shadow. His hair was curly and monkish. They wore white coats, just like Bob Cruickshank's, but not as white. Rab's strained at the buttons.

They spent as much time as they could in the stockrooms, talking quietly, sometimes giggling. When I interrupted they threw me a ball, and we played football, or they made a Frisbee from a flap of cardboard, and they launched that for me to catch. These games always ended too quickly, because Mike and Rab had to carry boxes upstairs. In the shop, under the baleful, Viking eye of Bob Cruickshank, they communicated in winks and whispers and secret, passing taps on the shoulder.

After a couple of weeks, I grew bored of putting out the sugar, pricing cans and reading comics in the creepy basement. Instead, I went out to explore.

I took my 10p to the newsagent. I bought a Texan bar. I liked the adverts. When I got back to St Cuthbert's, there was a queue at the till. Mum was ringing up the prices, taking the money, counting change into outstretched hands. She didn't see me come in, so I went back out. I went for a long walk. I went to the museum and I wandered round the echoing display of stuffed animals. They were creepy. Then I walked back to the shop.

The next day, I walked to Princes Street and caught the bus back to St Cuthbert's. I enjoyed being on the bus alone. It was like being on the aeroplane, except I had the responsibility of pushing the bell at the right time.

Every day, I walked a bit further. I walked to the old town. I walked up the Royal Mile, to the castle, and in the opposite direction to Holyrood House. I walked across the gardens to Princes Street.

Once, I got back to find that Mum was on her tea-break. She was angry. She asked me where I'd been. I told her that I'd spent most of the day in the basement.

Rab perjured himself on my behalf. He told Mum that he'd seen me not half an hour ago, in the basement, reading my comics. She didn't believe him, but she was satisfied. She was pleased that he liked me enough to lie for me.

The next day I went out again. Edinburgh sent taproots into my brain.

*

In the pantry there lived a mouse with the habit of poking its pointy little head under the door and surveying the room, to see if all was well. When Derek clapped his hands, the mouse whipped its head back under the door.

But there is never just one mouse, especially not in a block that old, with a communal garden so overgrown and stuffed with junk – fridges, TVs, old bike frames, sofas, mattresses – it was not possible to take a single step into it.

Eventually, the pantry mouse, or one of its descendants, grew bolder and took to skittering along the skirting boards, towards the kitchenette. At first, when Derek clapped his hand it would spin in terror, expanding and contracting like an accordion, then return to the pantry with the haphazard rush of a house-fly.

For a while, that was good sport. When the mouse popped its head under the pantry door, we sat still and silent, allowing it to think itself unobserved. Then, as it grew close to the kitchenette, we made a single loud noise – *boo* – and it nearly died of shock. Its terror was comical.

But the mouse, or its descendant, grew still less afraid: eventually, it learned to expect the loud noises, then to ignore them. Eventually, frustrated, Derek followed it to the kitchen. He slammed down a metal tea-tray, cutting the mouse in half. He stood back, the tray in his hand.

Mum scooped the quivery halves into a carrier-bag with the edge of a newspaper. She rinsed the edge of the tea-tray under running water. Her face was grim.

Then one evening, as I lay on the floor with my chin cupped in my palms, a mouse leapt over me and into the duct behind the gas fire. We laughed because it was an impressive leap. But, as I sat up and turned round, laughing, another mouse streaked over my lap. Then a third. One mouse jumping over you might be cute. But three made me squirm.

I sat on the sofa with Mum. Derek was in his deckchair.

That night I imagined that, while I slept, my bedroom was carpeted by a shifting knot of mousy grey, and that pink anemones of baby mice pullulated behind the skirting boards. When a trickle of sleep-sweat woke me, I believed it was the scuttering paws of a night-mouse. And that when I stirred, the fidgety bedroom paused: the darkness, watchfully silent.

On Saturday morning, we bought a cat. The pet shop stank of sawdust and shit, but the grey kitten just smelled of sawdust. I cupped her in my hands and sniffed her, soft as a paintbrush, a sharp little undercurrent of urine, not unpleasant.

Perhaps because the cat been housed next to a wire cage of puppies, it was an eccentric creature. It followed me round the flat, hogging my heel. I threw a ball for it, underarm. It followed the ball's arc of progress with laser eyes, then pounced on it. It killed the ball and returned it to me with a tilt of puppyish pride to its chin. It nuzzled the palm of my hand, impatient to play. It would have killed the ball all afternoon, if I let it.

In the morning I got out of bed, impatient to see the cat, and I ran barefoot in my pyjamas to the living room. The light was pearly with sunrise.

I opened the door and went in. I put my foot down on the cold, wet corpse of a mouse. Its fur was in black spikes and its teeth were comically bucked. It was flat, as if it had been pressed in a book like a flower. I leapt back, into the hallway. I shouted.

Mum came rushing from her bedroom, belting her dressing gown.

I said, 'She got one.'

Mum knotted the dressing gown.

'Where?'

I pointed. 'Down there.'

But I wasn't pointing at the same mouse. This one's teeth were also bucked, and its fur was similarly spiked. But it lay on its back, not on its side, with its tiny pink paws in the air. It lay several inches from the mouse I'd stepped on. And there was another dead mouse next to it, and another next to that. Mice were distributed all over the room: all over the floor and chairs and sofa and kitchenette. The room was carpeted in dead mice, as if somebody had run around shaking out a large bag of them.

I hopped to the bathroom and sat on the edge of the bath and soaped my foot. Then I went to my bedroom. I didn't want my feet to touch the floor. The carpet made them feel funny. In my room, I put my trainers on.

Mum and Derek spent a long time wearing one yellow Marigold glove each, picking up dead mice by the tips of their tails and dropping them into a St Cuthbert's carrier bag. After a few minutes, they stopped counting them.

I sat on my bed, hugging my knees. The cat ambled in. Sinewy as a gunslinger, it leapt on to the bed and wormed its way into my lap. It was purring, tired. It had been up all night. It nuzzled my chin, and its breath smelled of raw mice.

It clawed me for comfort. Its eyes were in blissful slits.

I couldn't throw it away, not for being a cat and doing what we'd bought it to do. So it fell asleep on me while Mum and Derek cleaned up the aftermath of its slaughter.

After that, I knew the mice were still there. They watched from the corners; in the cracks and the shadows were innumerable frightened eyes. The cat killed several a week, and we lay out traps and caught them that way, too. They liked chocolate, not cheese. They were still there, but none of them felt confident about running over your feet.

Late at night, the cat joined me in bed. I'd hear no movement: just sense the tiny displacement of air as it tensed and leapt. Touching down, it began to purr. It worked its way into the bedclothes and lay on my chest. It pulsed its claws into my sternum. It hurt, but the cat was mine. And it kept away all those little ghosts, those resentful little eyes in the dark corners.

That September, I started in Miss Dick's class: Primary Three. Miss Dick was a thin, pale woman in A-line skirts and dark blonde hair, worn in a long pageboy. She had a pointy nose.

In her classroom, which was on the first floor, the desks and chairs were arranged in the shape of a U. I sat at one corner of the U, my back to the great sash windows that let in all the daylight. Miss Dick had to stand on tiptoe to open them, even when using the hooked pole she kept propped in one corner. I sat next to Nicola Barton.

By now, I knew all my classmates' names. Nobody in class bothered to ask if I was a Fenian or an American, or if I was an English cunt. Nobody asked me to say something because

I spoke strangely. Nobody fell expectantly silent whenever Miss Dick asked me a question.

But lunchtimes weren't so easy. At lunchtime, someone was always angry. Because I was small and not well-liked, and because nobody's parents knew mine, an angry boy and his friends would often hassle me into a corner, push me, call me names ('wee fucken bastart'). The angry boy would punch me. He grabbed a handful of hair and pulled down on it, so I was forced to my knees. He kicked me.

While it was happening, I always smiled.

Looking scared made things worse. So did speaking: if I opened my mouth, the angry boy chose a word and made me say it again and again, slapping me each time I said it. He looked over his shoulder so his friends would laugh. Then, although I spoke with a West Country accent, he put on a Little Lord Fauntleroy voice and asked if it was 'awfully nice'. And he kneed me in the guts or in the testicles.

The worst effects of being kneed in the testicles could be offset by pressing your thighs together and bending away from the blow. It looked girlish, but it was effective. Looking girlish was better than being kicked in the balls. Being kicked in the balls really hurt. Sometimes it made you puke.

When it was over, I waited until the angry boy and his friends had gone. Then I returned to class and sat next to Nicola Barton. If my clothes were damaged, I was anxious and unable to concentrate, because Mum would be angry when I got home. Sometimes, the sight of my torn clothes threw her into panic, like a bird in a living room. Her hands shook so badly she couldn't hold anything.

She said, 'Why can't you be more careful?'

I was getting through two pairs of trousers a week, she said, although it wasn't true. How was she supposed to cope? Where did I think the money came from, to keep me in bloody clothes?

We were silent until Derek got home.

When Mum was really unhappy, it filled the flat like smoke. Derek could smell it when he opened the door. He kissed her hello and she followed him to the bedroom. I heard her sobbing.

Later, she sewed a patch on the trousers or repaired the shirt collar, and returned the clothes to me and said, 'There.'

Some days, Mum came to meet me at the school gates. In my class, only Peter Macdonald and I were met by our mothers. But I didn't mind because the walk home, although short, was perilous: often, there were Big Kids in the concrete park opposite 30 Duff Sreet. If I walked home alone, my arrival was routinely delayed.

Sometimes, there was just a bit of name calling, or a bit of shoving or a few stones lobbed at my head. Once, a kid stepped out in front of me and threw a piece of roofing slate like a Frisbee. It arced in the air and sliced through my upper lip.

The kid hadn't wanted it to happen. I could tell by the way he stood there with his mouth open. It had been a lucky throw; it had caught an updraught or something. I felt stupid, with my lip cut in two, and I pressed my hands to my mouth and walked past him with blood percolating through my fingers. I took a few days off school, until it healed.

Other days, the children in the park ignored me. But there was no way to predict that, and there was no way to get home without passing the park; it was directly opposite the entrance to 30 Duff Street. So I was happy when Mum came to meet me, even though it was embarrassing.

But one day, she was late. When she arrived at the school gates, she saw a flexing scrum in the playground. It pulsated like a jellyfish.

That afternoon, as I waited at the gate, a boy had started to shove me and call me names. I nodded and smiled and said, 'Yeah, yeah'. He reached up and grabbed the hood of my parka. He tugged it over my head. Then he pulled down on it, so I was bent double. He kept me bent while his friends and a lot of onlookers made a circle around me. It was a tight circle. They kicked me in the ribs and in the guts and in the arse. He tried for my face, but it was difficult, the way my hood was bunched. It was claustrophobic inside the coat. I couldn't see anything except afternoon sunlight filtering through the blue nylon, and I was being pulled and kicked in a continuous, jerky circle. I couldn't see where the next kick was coming from.

Mum saw this and ran towards the chanting group. In the process, she spilled a bag of mint imperials. She had just been to Bessie's corner shop to buy them. The mint imperials rolled away in all directions, like marbles, and for a second she hesitated, as if to chase them down and pick them up. Then she walked into the crowd of children. It parted, but didn't disperse. It just broke into individuals who stood there, staring at their feet, catching each other's eyes and grinning. Mum pulled me free by the elbow. She took the boy by his collar.

She said: 'Right, you little sod.'

She went as if to drag him to the headmaster's office. But I stood in front of her and begged her not to. So she let him go. He was flushed and breathing heavily, a fat kid in a dirty argyle sweater.

By the time we got home, Mum was laughing about the mint imperials. Sometimes, the oddest things struck her as funny. Whenever she told the story, the mint imperials were the point of it. She thought it was hilarious, the way they'd spilled all over the playground. She would say, 'Do you remember the time I spilled my mint imperials?' and laugh.

What I remembered was the claustrophobia inside that hood, the sound of my own breathing, my clothes bunched up around my chest, the air on my back, the chanting. I didn't think of mint imperials.

The next day, the fat kid and I shook hands. Boys thought shaking hands made them men. This time it seemed to mean something, because nothing like that happened again, not between that boy and me.

9

Something in Derek stirred and grew restless. At first, he tried to keep it from us, but he failed. I knew him too well. Sometimes, when we were watching TV, I could tell he wasn't really watching. He was just pointing his eyes at the light.

It alarmed me when he went blank like that. I didn't look at him, but I was aware of his empty presence – as if, while he sat, his soul had departed the room.

Around that time, he decided that Sunday was to be a day for attending church. I was bewildered. Derek's knowledge of the world had always seemed to bring him peace, a kind of wisdom. I could not imagine what he needed God for. But there was no peace inside Derek: there was a raggedy hole. He crammed it with soiled rags, but they grew blood-wet and sopping and fell loose; the wound remained. He went to church like a thirsty man to a dirty ditch.

We never discussed it. Had I argued, he'd have said I was to do as I was bloody told. Had I enquired after his motive, he'd have said: 'Yours is not to reason why.'

So on Sunday, we got dressed up and went to the local Catholic church, the smell of incense and moist stone. A pale Jesus hung writhing and bloody on a high cross. His thighs were pressed together, as if he was trying to avoid being kicked in the testicles. There were flower-heads of blood on his palms and feet. Fat drops of it ran from a second set of lips, under his ribcage.

At great length, a man in a white dress and Ronnie Barker glasses addressed a smattering of old women in hats. There was listless singing. We sat looking at him. I was bored beyond description. We went home.

All afternoon, Derek was quiet and irritable.

I asked if we were going back next week.

He said, 'No.'

Instead, we went to the more austere Church of Scotland.

As we were preparing to go – we were bathing and dressing, knotting our ties – Derek became tense and unforthcoming. The thought of church made him grim. I couldn't understand why he so wanted to go.

But to the Church of Scotland we went. Inside were more old ladies with hats. Derek Cross smiled for them and said 'good morning, good morning', as we squeezed down the old wooden pews. But it was his St Cuthbert's smile – affected courtesy and therefore not quite real.

It was because he was nervous. He sat rigidly through the sermon, as if expecting the minister at some point to announce his name and the congregation to turn and admire him, like somebody who'd won the bingo. But nothing happened. Derek awaited a revelation that didn't come.

The next week, we went somewhere else. A week later, somewhere else again. We never went anywhere more than twice. Then it was nearly Christmas and Derek gave up. He seemed to rally himself: to fill up whatever was breached, to concentrate on other things.

The day before Christmas Eve, he called me to one side. He was sitting in his deckchair.

He said, 'Why don't you sit down for a moment?'

I sat down. He half-stood in the deckchair and repositioned it so he was facing me. Our knees were nearly touching.

He said, 'Now. I've been thinking.'

I said, 'Yes?'

'How would you feel about calling me Dad?'

Derek never had another name for me. There was no equivalent of Nipper, or Nip, or Sonner. I considered it to be an unspoken function of respect.

And he never got angry; not if I did as I was told, which was always. He was never too tired to read me a chapter of *Kidnapped* or *Treasure Island* or *Tom Sawyer*.

If there was something I didn't understand, he found a way to help me understand it. He never said 'I don't know' and opened the newspaper. If he couldn't help, he explained why not – and then, if I was still interested, he talked to me about how we could find the answer together. We went to the museum together, the zoo, the cinema. He never made me feel that it would be better, was I not there.

And now he was asking me to be his son. Even Gary and Wayne only called my father Alan. I felt like a hero.

I said, 'Okay.'

And he said, 'Good. Jolly good. Right, then.'

At first, I was self-conscious about it and so was he. I hesitated before addressing him, because the word caught in my throat. I could feel him sensing my hesitation and ignoring it. But soon, calling him Dad began to feel natural. It was calling him Derek that felt wrong.

On Christmas eve, he drank some beer and told me the truth about Christmas. As it turned out, the Star of Bethlehem wasn't a star at all: it was probably an alien spaceship. Jesus was most likely some kind of alien.

I found this very interesting. It hadn't occurred to me that Jesus might be an alien, but now I thought about it, it made sense. Derek could see my excitement and went on to tell me that UFOs appeared throughout the Bible. There were hundreds of them, if you knew where to look. And there were aliens, too.

He went to the bedroom and came back with the black book, gold stamped on the cover, and he read to me from Ezekiel[1]

And I looked, and behold, a whirlwind came out of the north, a great cloud, and a fire unfolding itself, and a brightness was about it, and out of the midst thereof as the colour of amber, out of the midst of the fire. Also out of the midst thereof came the likeness of four living creatures. And this was their appearance; they had the likeness of a man. And every one had four faces, and every one had four wings.

Then he lay the Bible in his lap, face down. He put on his baddie voice. Sometimes it sounded German, sometimes Japanese – sometimes it sounded both in the same sentence.

'You see?' he said, narrowing his eyes. 'It is velly intellesting. Velly, velly intellesting.'

Back in Bristol, Dad threw a party for New Year's Eve. My sisters and brother were there, with their partners and their children. Gary and Wayne's uncle was there, too, and so was their grandmother. She hunched like a cockroach and wore a knitted cardigan. She smoked so heavily the leading coil of her grey hair was stained yellow.

Everyone called me Nipper. It sounded wrong, but nobody knew how to stop. To call me by another name would admit that I had become someone else: an imperfect, shoddy copy of a lost boy.

We put the Rolf Harris LP on the record player. Dad was red-faced and jolly. His sleeves were rolled, his collar was open and his white vest showed beneath it. My nephews, my nieces, my stepbrothers, my real brother, my sisters, Margaret and I all marched and danced in a line behind him. The younger ones were over-excited. We sang 'Six White Boomers' and 'The Wild Colonial Boy'. Then Dad put on Showaddywaddy and we danced to 'Three Steps to Heaven' and 'Under the Moon of Love'. Dad waltzed with Margaret. He whirled her round the floor. She screamed and laughed. She said he was bloody mad, that man, your dad: he was a bloody lunatic.

10

The people in the flat upstairs had a German shepherd called Sheba. She was big and shaggy; her coat sashayed flirtatiously when she walked. Across the road lived another German shepherd, Sabre. We didn't see him around much, because his owners couldn't control him. He attacked other dogs, straining at the leash in his craving to eviscerate them. So they tried to keep him indoors.

But somehow, Sabre and Sheba mated. I noticed her, shambling and newly bulbous, up the stone steps to the top floor. She lived next door to the genteel Blackwoods.

Derek decided that a boy needed a dog, and I agreed. So one evening in 1977 we went upstairs.

Spring rain beat against the high glass ceiling, with its Meccano of metal struts. The staircase was like a salt-cellar, vast and discarded, and we were like Borrowers living inside it.

The floor plan of the upstairs flat resembled our own. In the living room, Sheba lay on a sheet of pulpy newspapers. Her tongue flopped. She was panting. As we entered, she raised her head in greeting, then dropped it again, disappointed.

She began to strain and tremble, like she was forcing out a turd. I watched it ease out of her. But the turd was grey, sheathed in a veined, stretchy membrane. And from it unfolded a tiny puppy, black and wet and blind. A rich smell came from it, earthy and autumnal. The owner passed the puppy to Sheba; she whined, so high you could hardly hear it, and began hungrily to lick the puppy.

We watched six or seven being born. When it seemed like Sheba had finished, I was asked to select one of her brood. I looked at them, a shiny knot wriggling at the dog's pink dugs, like baby's toes. They were soaking the newspaper with their birth juices and they made me think of the dead mice we found downstairs, and of the mice that sneaked in their unseen thousands throughout the buildings.

I looked at Derek.

I said, 'Which one?'

He pointed. He said, 'I think we'll have that one.'

Six weeks later, I came home from school, and we had a dog. I didn't know if it was the dog Derek had selected. How could they tell? She looked so different; she had become a skinny Alsatian, black and tan, with big paws and a lazy ear that hung in a bunny flop.

When I came through the door, she hurried to the corner of the room and cowered there, to assess me in safety. She knitted her eyebrows. She had brown eyes, the colour of treacle toffee.

I knew you couldn't oblige an animal to like you, especially dogs. Dogs could smell your fear. So I showed her how the cat and I played fetch. I balled up a page of newspaper and threw it, underarm. The cat gambolled on weirdly stiff legs, batted the ball with her assassin's claws, then returned it to me.

The dog watched. Then she pranced on her paws to show the cat how it should be done. She flattened the ball with her great, flat feet, shook it until it was stunned, then returned it to me.

For a moment, the cat seemed impressed. But then she grew competitive. I watched the dog and the cat race each other, skidding, bumping into furniture, for the privilege of returning the ball to my hand.

Finally, the cat grew impatient and batted the dog's face, open-handed. Her claws caught in the dog's upper lip and stuck there, like fish-hooks. The dog shrieked. Then leapt back, still shrieking. The cat was trapped. Evidently astonished, she was dragged along by the yelping dog. Her back legs clawed the carpet for grip. The dog howled. The cat looked scared.

Mum separated them. It took a while; she had to catch them first. Then she had to unhook the cat's claws, one by one. It was like undoing a duffle coat.

When they were freed, each animal sulked in a different corner. The dog kept touching her upper lip with the pads of her paw, and trying to lick it. Her tongue wasn't long enough. She made a comical snuffling sound and tied herself in knots. The cat observed her gymnastics with arctic contempt.

Mum put out food. The cat cautioned the dog with a malevolent glare. The dog didn't touch the cat's food. And later, they slept curled up round each other. We laughed at them as we watched TV.

Derek decided the dog's name was Tara. It didn't sound like a dog's name – especially not this dog. I didn't like it.

The dog was locked in the front room overnight. In the morning, we discovered a curl of her shit on the kitchen linoleum. The newspaper Mum had laid out for her was pulpy and urine-soaked, so she had the idea; she'd tried.

But Derek believed in firm discipline for animals. He grabbed the dog's loose scruff and rubbed her face in the shit. She made panic noises and tried to back away. She struggled and squealed and scrabbled and finally twisted from his grip. So Derek punched her in the neck. She was stunned. She looked at him. He slapped her in the mouth, open-handed.

He stood there, florid, breathing heavy in his sweater with epaulettes on the shoulders and patches on the elbows. A lock of hair had fallen across his brow.

He said 'Pig dog' and strode from the room.

I looked at Mum.

I said, '"Pig dog"?'

She hushed me, and that made me want to laugh. I stood there, trying not to. But it was difficult. Then Mum started to laugh too. She turned her back so she wouldn't have to look at me. She pretended to do the washing up. Watching Mum pretending to do the washing up to hide her laughter made me want to laugh some more.

Then the door opened and Derek came in. He was white. His hair was black. He was breathing through his nose. I stopped laughing, and so did Mum. She kept washing up.

Derek pointed at me. He said, 'Don't you dare bloody laugh at me. I'm warning you.'

I said, 'I wasn't laughing at you. I was laughing because you said "pig dog".'

He stood there, staring at us. He looked short in his anger; a breathless, angry little man. It was as if there was someone else living inside him: someone wrathful and malignant, glaring out through his eyes.

One morning in August, Derek came into my room and sat heavily on the bed. His face was blank with shock.

He said, 'I have some bad news.'

He told me to get up and get dressed. I did as I was told. I was in a half-panic.

I ran to the front room. Derek was waiting for me. He put his hands on my shoulders. He said my name.

I said, 'What?'

He said, 'Elvis Presley has died.'

He was about to cry. The gravity of that terrible thought was enough to start me off, too. I sobbed for Elvis, and for Derek's bereavement: but mostly I sobbed with relief that nothing worse had happened.

Derek hugged me and drew strength from my sorrow and he did not weep. He hugged me and let me sob into his shoulder for the loss of dear, dead Elvis.

A bit later, I saw my first punk rocker. He wore tartan drainpipe trousers, with zips and a bum flap. He had spiky orange hair and National Health spectacles. I hesitated as he passed, and made eye contact with strangers, and we laughed because he looked a bit stupid.

Then Derek's mother came to visit.

I waited in the hallway outside the flat as she levered herself upstairs. Derek was behind her, carrying her luggage. On the landing, she paused to catch her breath, then minced imperially through the front door. She squeezed through the hallway like a ship in a canal.

She was an immense sugar mouse, swathed in layered gauze. Her skin was soft, like chamois leather, and it hung loose from dimpled jowls. Her face was cherubic, talcumed and white as the full moon. Her mouth was a scarlet rosebud, too dainty for her face. She wore it in a permanently pursed kiss, which she placed on my mother's cheek. Then she held out her arms. Empty bags of flesh swayed on them. She enveloped me in a embrace. She kissed my cheek.

'So this is Neil.' She spoke with a deliberate lisp, like a little girl playing kings and queens.

'This is Neil,' said Mum.

'Then come here, darling, and give your gran another kiss.'

I gave her another kiss. It was like surrendering to a mattress. I feared her. Her teeth might have been needles, clogged with skin and snotty blood.

She let me go. She looked at Mum.

She said, 'So. This is home!'

Mum smiled for her.

'Yes,' she said, 'it's not much.'

She sounded proud that it wasn't much, or perhaps it was defiance.

Gran's husband followed. He was Derek's stepfather, just as Derek was mine. But Derek didn't call him Dad; he called him John.

John looked like a comedy husband. He was thin and wore a pasted combover haircut. His spectacles were thick and made his eyes washy and unspecific. But the husbands in comedies were defeated, gently rebellious souls, and John was not that. He looked at me through watery-crooked eyes and I could read his thoughts.

At least Derek's mother was mysterious: at least she had the grace to smell like I had always imagined witches might, of good things like talcum and icing sugar and roses. And she affected that baby-doll voice, which any child would recognize as an ensign of malevolence. John was just sour inside, like a half-sucked sweet.

They sat on the sofa. She vast, he made of liver spots and sinew. Sparse hair greased to his freckled pate.

Gran said, 'Give them their present, John.'

He pretended to have forgotten. He was trying to annoy her. Perhaps they'd argued in the car, and now he was exacting his revenge. Then he leaned over the side of the sofa and picked up a brown-papered square, the size of a bathroom window. He handed it to Gran, who handed it to Mum, who began to unwrap it.

Gran said, 'I hope you love it.'

Mum finished unwrapping it. It was a painting, a still life; irises and daisies in a vase.

'Oh, Helen,' said Mum, 'it's lovely.'

She held it to the light, to see it better.

I said, 'Did you do it yourself, Gran?'

Derek had suggested that I call her Gran. She'd like it.

She simpered. Her face folded in on itself. She squirmed. She said, 'Yes, I did.'

I said, 'What, the colouring and everything?'

'Of course, darling.'

It looked just like a real painting.

Mum put it down, leaning it against the chair.

I said, 'Did it take ages?'

'Quite a long time, yes.'

'So,' said Derek, 'how was the drive?'

'Bloody awful,' said John. Then he said, 'Is it always brass bloody monkeys up here in Haggis Land?'

Derek giggled. I'd never seen him giggle. He did it behind his hand. He looked at me.

I said, 'What does "brass monkeys" mean?'

'Never mind,' said Derek.

He never said that. I asked him again.

He met John's eyes. Amused exasperation passed between them. But it was false. Derek was only pretending to be exasperated and John was only pretending to be amused.

Derek said, 'It means it's very cold outside.'

'But what's that got to do with brass monkeys?'

John fixed me on the line of his gaze. Something hard beneath the water, like jagged boulders in a summer stream.

He said, 'It means, it's cold enough to freeze the bollocks off a brass monkey.'

Mum looked at him. There was a brief silence, like when someone's name is called in a waiting-room. But I wasn't embarrassed.

I said, 'Why should a brass monkey's bollocks fall off?'

'Good question,' said Derek, and narrowed his eyes. 'Velly intellesting. Velly intellesting.'

*

Mum made a cup of tea and put out some Mr Kipling's
Madeira cake. Derek and John had a couple of lagers. Then,
while Mum rinsed the cups and plates, Derek, Uncle John and
Gran sat around talking about South Africa.

Uncle John wasn't South African. He was from London.
He used different funny words from Gran and Derek. Their
funniest word was 'kaffir'. John's funniest words were 'coon',
'nig-nog' and 'jungle bunny'.

I wasn't sure what a kaffir was. I said, 'What's a kaffir?'

'A kaffir,' said Gran, 'is a black person.'

'Like you get in Africa.'

'That's right.'

'You know,' said John. 'Nig-nogs.'

Mum was washing up behind us.

I said, 'Why do you call them kaffirs?'

Gran said, 'Because it's the Afrikaans word for them.'

'What does it mean?'

'Jungle bunny,' said Derek, and John laughed.

I said, 'Does it?'

I thought a jungle bunny sounded like quite a nice thing.

Derek said, 'Actually, it's not Afrikaans. It's from Arabic. It's
just a word we use for black people.'

'For natives?'

'I am an African native,' Gran said, 'and I am not black.' She
said, *Blik*. 'And Egyptians are Africans,' said Gran, 'and they're
not black either. They're Arabs.'

'So really it just means nig-nogs,' said John. 'Wogs.'

'John,' said Derek.

(He told me later that a wog was something else entirely).

'It's just different words for the same thing,' said Derek.

'Then why not just call them Africans?'

'Because there are all sorts of African,' said Derek. 'They're divided up into tribes –'

'Like red Indians.'

'A bit, yes,' he said. 'But a bit different too.'

Everyone laughed at that, except Mum, who still had her back turned.

Derek's eyes flicked to mine as he chuckled at himself, but he wasn't laughing really. There was an apology in there somewhere, I didn't know for what.

I began to ignore their conversation, sitting cross-legged in front of the TV with my back to them. The volume was down low, so I had to lean forward to hear what the people on screen were saying.

Later, Derek read to me in bed, but not as much as usual.

I said, 'Gran's a good painter isn't she?' and he laughed. It was a big smile, a proper smile.

He said, 'It's called "painting by numbers".'

Someone else had done the drawing. All the grown-up had to do was the colouring-in. Even this was made even easier by colour coding: a number 1 printed on the petal of a flower meant, for example, Paint This Bit Red.

I said, 'That's cheating.'

He said, 'I know,' and kissed my forehead. Before he left, he said, 'But don't tell her I told you.'

They stayed up late, laughing. Every time I drifted off to sleep I snapped awake. Sometimes, I heard Mum join in, but her laughter was shrill and not true.

John had a raspy, insidious chuckle, like the tongue of a cat. And Gran laughed like a little girl. It didn't make a happy sound, all this hilarity – it wasn't like the sound of adults forgetting to be quiet on Christmas Eve, which was oddly soporific; it made you feel safe. This was the opposite of that, the opposite of Christmas Eve.

When the lights were out and everyone was in bed, the house felt wrong.

They stayed for a week. I felt Gran's voice on my skin. It had something dark and rich at its centre, like shit concealed in honey. Whenever she complimented Mum or me or the flat or Derek, I could taste it.

John watched as I sat in the corner, playing. His eyes were yellow behind the spectacles. I could feel him looking, even when he laughed or accepted a cup of tea, or a biscuit and a slice of cake.

We took them to the castle, the Royal Botanical Gardens, Arthur's Seat, Holyrood House. They were contemptuous, Gran with her rosebud mouth and John with his sour combover.

When they left, Gran smothered me in her flesh, kissing me with her sugar mouth. She told Mum how lovely it had been, and she told Derek that we really must go to stay with them. John said something about brass monkeys and laughed and stalked off down the stairs behind her, walking in italics. Derek followed, carrying the bags, and they left.

But their essence hung in the air. It was if they had altered something in the walls, the way exposure to light will alter film.

At night, I sensed that somebody was in the living room, asleep. It was a Siamese twin. John and Gran had fused into a single creature, with fat legs and thin legs, and four eyes open in the dark. The creature looked through the walls, at the room where I slept. It was hungry. And it never blinked.

During his mother's visit, Derek had, as usual, filmed everything. He directed the camera upon us as we strolled the castle grounds, self-conscious with the lens on our backs, or ate ice-creams on a park bench. He filmed the squirrel that scrambled up my body and perched on my shoulder, eating peanuts. Its quick little claws nipped my skin. Watching the film, we laughed to see the horrified look on my face.

At first, I was captivated by the novelty of seeing myself up there. I was laughing, running across the grass, cringing in terror from the nibbling squirrel. So it was only after watching the film two or three times that something at long last occurred to me – in our flat, there were no photographs.

In the flickery darkness, I glanced round. I wondered if familiarity had simply rendered them invisible, like the tick of a clock. But no.

I turned again to watch the film and thought about it.

It made sense that Mum had no mementoes: the day she left Bristol, she left everything. And anyway; she didn't take photographs, she featured in them.

But for Derek, it was different. He had a need to record and to watch that I recognized but didn't understand. Watching the films, he was bearing witness. They comforted him. And yet he owned none that pre-dated his move to Edinburgh.

He'd been married all those times (four times, or five, I couldn't quite remember, and sometimes it seemed that neither could he). It didn't seem possible that he had failed in some way to document those who came before us. But there were no old cine-films, no old photographs. There was nothing of his childhood. Nothing of his father and mother. Nothing of his former wives. Nothing of his son. There was nothing of him.

I had no doubt that earlier films, earlier photographs, had existed. If nothing else, there must have been pictures of all those wedding days: snapshots of Richard's first birthday, his first Christmas, his first ride on a bicycle.

I realized that Derek had gathered up those images, all those pointless memories, and he had destroyed them. When he walked out on a marriage, he snuffed out an entire reality. That is why he'd spoken of his former wives and his biological child with such neutrality. They no longer existed for him, any more than he existed as the man he'd been, when he was with them. I thought of a snake, sloughing its skin, leaving behind a brittle hollow of itself. The cast of a serpent, translucent and empty.

I looked at Derek, watching us on film. I watched the cone of dusty yellow light that joined the projector to the screen, a radiant umbilicus. However we twisted and turned, however those unsteady images fell off the edge of the frame, the lens always jumped back to us.

As long as he wanted to watch us, we were trapped up there, in the projected light.

11

The dog had a lot of energy; she was still a puppy. But we lived in a flat; there was nowhere nearby to exercise her properly, and Derek and Mum were out most of the day, working. So she began to chew up the flat.

Mum came home to find she'd ripped apart the sofa, or chewed up Derek's record collection. Debris was scattered all over the floor: bits of book, shoes, bits of the *Radio Times*, fragments of sofa, of carpet, of kitchen lino.

The dog cowered on her pale belly, ashamed. Then she dragged herself towards Mum, her tail thumping slow time on the floor.

Mum didn't punish her. She'd be punished enough when Derek got home, unless we could hide the evidence. We never could. When I got back from school, Mum would be on her hands and knees, her lips compressed, brushing detritus into a dustpan.

The dog would bound to me. She'd put her paws on my shoulder and lick my neck and face.

I took her out to shit, round the corner by the railway lines. Once, as she squatted, a loop of audio tape popped out of her. It wasn't shitty; it was just audio tape, shiny grey-brown. When it had emerged to the length of several feet, I stamped my foot down on it. The sudden increase in tension shocked the dog and she ran away. I kept my foot on the tape, and as the dog ran it unspooled from inside her.

I was laughing so hard that she took it for approval and began to frolic, skipping and running in excited circles. More tape came out. It was very long. There were metres and metres of it. When the breeze caught it, it rose and fell in waves. I didn't want to touch it; it had come out of a dog's arse. So I watched as the wind whipped at it, wrapping it round cars and lampposts. When it had all come out, I stood for a while, watching it making waves and half-circles in the breeze. Then I took the dog inside and in the morning the audio tape had disappeared.

But I didn't take the dog for proper walks, because I was too scared. Not of other children; not even I got beaten up when I had an Alsatian with me. But, a year before, I'd been attacked by two mongrels called Laddie and Lassie. They'd bitten my calf and thigh when, stiff-legged, I tried to hurry past them. Derek and Mum had taken me to hospital. There were adverts on TV about rabies. But the bites weren't too bad.

Laddie and Lassie still skittered unaccompanied around the cobbled backstreets. Usually, they ignored me, having forgotten our earlier acquaintance. Once or twice they trotted over to sniff my crotch and I went rigid with terror and smiled like a monkey and went clammy-handed until they trotted off.

I was scared of being bitten again, and I was scared of a dog-fight; that my loyal dog would see Laddie and Lassie for villains and set about them. Dog-fights were vicious, and I didn't want my dog to be hurt.

Mum didn't walk the dog either. It was not the kind of area, she told me, where a woman could walk unaccompanied, not unless they were interested in men. She told me this because one sunny day I went out to play in the park across the road. It was the summer holidays. Mum had been urging me to venture outside, just for five minutes, to get some fresh air. She promised to watch out, to make sure I was safe. I scuttled out when the park was empty, and I started clambering over the climbing frames. Climbing frames were safe from dogs.

Because Mum was in the window, watching, I wasn't too bothered when Tam Higgins's big brother came sauntering down the street. Tam Higgins's big brother lived in the ground-floor flat. He was fifteen or sixteen, the eldest boy of the family who owned Suzie the neurotic dog. His brother Tam was in my class.

Tam's big brother saw me. I was sitting on the climbing frame, pretending not to have noticed him. He had a cigarette in his hand. He snorted and walked up to me. He stopped. He puffed on his cigarette. Then he slapped me in the face. He told me I was a fukken wee radge.

Tingles danced on my skin like bubbles. I didn't respond. I knew Mum was watching. Soon she'd shout something, or come rushing downstairs to help me. But Tam Higgins's brother kept his face jammed into mine, like a lid about to be screwed on to a jar. He was so close he was spitting on me.

When I glanced over, I saw that Mum wasn't watching over me. A car had pulled to the kerb beneath the window, and she was busy having a conversation with the driver.

I couldn't call out. The humiliation of that would be far worse, and far longer lasting, than a kicking. So I did what I always did: I laughed. So he did what they always did: he got angry because I was laughing. He hit me again, harder. I laughed again. He got angrier. We were trapped.

I glanced at home. The car wasn't there any more, but Mum was gone from the window.

Tam Higgins's brother pressed me into the climbing frame. Its cold rungs dug into my back and my ribs. He grabbed a handful of hair and tugged it until I was looking at him. He puffed on the cigarette a couple of times, to get the coal good and red. Then he began to move the cigarette towards my eye. He told me to fukken laugh at this. The coal was red and black.

It was an old woman who stopped it, a passer-by. She wore a powder-blue mac, buttoned to the throat, and a headscarf. She carried two string shopping-bags.

She stopped, halfway across the road. She called out, 'You. What do you think you're doing?'

Tam Higgins's brother stopped moving the cigarette. He kept it hanging there, in front of my eye. He said nothing. The old woman told him to leave the laddie alone.

He swore and spat, then walked off, swaggering, bandy-legged, puffing the cigarette. From behind the fence, the old woman asked if I was okay, if she should get my mum. The bags were still in her rooty hands.

I said, 'I only live over there,' and I pointed.

She told me I'd best away home then, and I ran across the concrete playground, scattered with half-bricks and broken glass and through the door to the stairs. I ran, because Tam Higgin's brother lived in the downstairs flat and I was scared he'd be waiting for me in the piss-stinking shadows. But he wasn't.

The man I'd seen talking to Mum had stopped his car to ask if she was open for business. She told me this, thin-lipped. She told the man to bugger off, then came inside to calm down.

I asked what he'd meant.

'Some men,' she said, 'like to buy sex.'

That was interesting. I said, 'Why?'

'For relief.'

'Relief from what?'

She said, 'You'll understand when you're older.'

I didn't want to wait until I was older. But I could see that Mum wasn't going to tell me any more, so I waited until Derek got home. I asked him what it meant, asking Mum if she was open for business. He raised an eyebrow at Mum.

He said, 'And where does this come from?'

Mum told him about the man in the car, and he laughed.

He told me the same things Mum had.

I said, 'But why do some men want to buy sex?'

'Because some men are lonely. They live alone, or their wives are sick, and part of being a man is needing sex. Men need sex like you need water or food or sleep.'

'But why do they have to buy it?'

'Because when somebody needs something, someone else

will sell it to them. No matter what it is. And some women get their money by selling sex to men who need it. They're called prostitutes.'

'And that man thought Mum was a prostitute?'

Derek said yes without saying anything. I was angry at the strange man. I wanted to throw something at his stupid car.

I didn't tell Mum or Derek that Tam Higgins's big brother had tried to stub out a cigarette on my eye. And later, when Tam Higgins and I became friends and I spent weekends with him, his brother was older and married. He'd surprise us with bags of chips or pirate videos.

He was nice by then, even when he had the opportunity not to be, when he and I were alone in the front room. I wondered if he had forgotten trying to blind me, or if he had confused me with somebody else, another boy. Or if he remembered very well and, like me, was too embarrassed to think about it.

12

In the Autumn of 1977, I was eight years old and in Miss Galloway's class.

Derek had given up looking for a church and, once again we spent our Sundays in the hills, walking. Mum stayed at home – she enjoyed the time to herself – so it was just Derek and me. We put a picnic in our rucksacks and caught a bus to the foot of the Pentlands. Sometimes we left on Saturday and spent the night on the hillside. We slept in sleeping-bags in a two-man tent that Derek carried rolled-up beneath the frame of his rucksack.

When it rained we put on kagouls and waterproof trousers and I liked that. I liked the hissy concussion on the nylon hood. I liked the misty-prickle on my exposed cheeks and forehead. We trudged in near-silence up stony paths. Even when it was raining, I liked to drink from burns. When it was hot, the water was refreshing. When it was cold, it made me feel hardy and self-sufficient.

We rested and talked about the end of the world. It would be soon. The Americans and the Russians had hundreds of nuclear weapons pointed at each other –

'Because they're madmen,' said Derek. 'All madmen.'

– and sooner or later, something would happen. Most likely it would be a mistake. A big meteor would hit somewhere. Thousands of them hit the earth every second, but they were tiny, the size of dust particles; it was only a matter of time before a larger one came along. All it would take was a piece of rock the size of a small car, a Mini perhaps, but travelling at such speed that its impact would be like a nuclear bomb. Something like that had already happened: in Siberia in 1908, the blast from a large meteorite flattened trees and killed wildlife over an area of 800 square miles. That night, the London skies were bright enough to stand outside reading a newspaper.

If it happened today, one president, or perhaps both of them, would mistake it for a deliberate nuclear attack. From there, the escalation to doomsday was inevitable.

I asked when it would be. Derek shrugged, stoical. He said, 'Soon, I expect.'

I enjoyed the rushing, terrified thrill. I knew what a nuclear bomb would do. Cities would be destroyed like toys. Billions of people would die. Those few who remained would have to start again. I liked the idea of starting again. It would probably involve something like this, being in the hills with a rucksack on my back, in a kagoul and walking boots.

Derek said, 'We'd need a gun.'

'Where can you get a gun?'

'I can get us a gun.'

'Where from?'

He tapped the side of his nose with a rigid index finger. We were sitting beneath a wind-leant tree, looking over Edinburgh in the grey rain.

I said, 'Can you shoot a gun?'

He chewed his answer like a toffee. 'I'm rather a good shot, actually.'

I knew he would be.

'My Dad's got a gun,' I said. 'Alan. He's got a gun. A flare gun. He keeps it on top of the wardrobe.'

Derek assessed this intelligence.

'A flare gun might be useful. But you can only use it once. What you'd need is a decent rifle. And a couple of handguns.'

'Can you fire one of them? A rifle.'

'When I was your age, I spent all my time in the bush, practising. Target practice. A bit of hunting.'

'What did you hunt?'

An enigmatic smile. A pause.

'This and that.'

'Lions and that?'

'Not lions, no. Different animals.'

I assessed this. I mirrored his posture.

I said, 'If it's going to happen soon, we should get a gun soon.'

'It's not quite time to get a gun,' he said. 'The time for guns is later.'

I enjoyed getting home that afternoon. I'd gone a long way. I'd been given a glimpse of the future: an empty city.

Desolation, the low boiling sky. And being alive and self-sufficient and free.

After that, whenever military jets roared low overhead, I looked up with a tingle of elation and thought, Here it comes. I scanned the horizon, expecting to glimpse a flash: a regal, silently unfolding mushroom cloud. Light travelled faster than sound. So I'd sneak a glimpse – just to say I'd seen it – and then I'd throw myself under the desk, or into a doorway or a handy basement. All around me the city would be ripped asunder, torn like paper. A vast conflagration would whip around my head, a bedlam of orange and red and blue. Everything would be consumed, and when it was all over I'd emerge from my hiding place. My clothes would be torn, black-crisped at the edges. My hair would be awry and my face would be smudged. Blood would trail from one nostril. I'd scramble over the still-hot rubble, the fallen blocks of ancient houses, the higgledy-piggledy wreckage of cars and buses.

I'd make my way beneath still-furious skies, from which rained damned aircraft. And I'd find Derek. Nobody else. Just Derek. We'd gather our rucksacks, full of tinned food and bottled water, and we'd make our epic way to the safety of the hills. We'd fight past the near-dead and the undead, the blind and the burning, and we'd sit under a blasted tree that stood on the burned hillside, and we'd watch the city blaze, and we'd turn to the west and see the horizon bright with the death of Glasgow. We wouldn't speak. We'd grimace, a way to admit to our aches and pains, our injuries. I'd reach into my rucksack and withdraw a bottle of water. I'd take a grim sip, then wipe my lips and pass the bottle into Derek's sooty hand.

And that would be the first day of the end of the world.

One afternoon, the council tested Edinburgh's air-raid sirens. I was on the street when the wailing began. It was a newsreel sound, the sound of the Blitz. I swelled with exultation, because it was here. I orientated myself to Leith, because that would be where the bomb fell; the place from which the mushroom cloud would unfold into the sky, from where the awesome concussion would rumble and spread.

I waited. I fingered the black-handled lock-knife I carried in my pocket. It secured me to the purity of the moment. After the blast came, I'd need it for jemmying open doors and windows, and opening cans of food, and stabbing people.

The siren slowed to a lament, then stopped.

The end of the world didn't come, and I went back to school and sat in Miss Galloway's class, next to Nicola Barton and Judith Collins. The disappointment was a mortal pain, a kind of grief.

I thought of a family story, one of the few I knew. One Christmas before I was born, Dad gave Caroline a sack of broken toys. It was full of bald and eyeless dolls' heads and naked, limbless bodies.

Caroline was bereft. She could not be consoled, even when her real presents were given to her, properly gift-wrapped.

At school, the morning and afternoon breaks were fifteen minutes long, which made them easier to handle than lunch-breaks. During break, pupils weren't permitted in the school building – not even kids who wanted to hit you. It was a deep, structural rule they obeyed without deliberation.

But I'd learned to penetrate the school's defences. The hall-ways were patrolled by teachers on dinner duty, but not diligently. It was easy enough to nip through the empty school and out through another exit, or onto the street, where I could use parked cars for cover. If I was desperate, I could nip into Bessie's sweet shop across the way and pretend to be choosing sweets until the bell was rung.

Sometimes, it was possible to take such evasive action over the course of a dinner hour: but not every dinner hour, five days a week. Sometimes, it was easier just to accept whatever was dished out, whenever it came. But it was even easier to sit safely in the classroom, and for a year I'd taken a packed lunch and eaten it alone, munching on fishpaste sandwiches and reading *Iron Man*.

But that autumn, it became fashionable to have lunch in a café. It was called the Junction because it stood where Dalry met Gorgie Road. Eight or nine of my classmates started going there together and, one day, Colin Fairgreaves invited me along.

I hectored Mum until she agreed to give me dinner money instead of a packed lunch. By the time she said yes, the fashion for eating at the Junction Café had flared and abated. Only two or three kids still went. I went with Colin Fairgreaves and Brian Hunt.

Brian Hunt was called Babs. He was the only kid I knew who had a proper nickname. Everyone called him Babs, even the older kids. He was sandy-haired and freckly and over-weight and under very slightly different circumstances, his experience of school might not have been so congenial. But the nickname marked him out as okay. It was like a magic talis-man, a name that had been earned.

Colin Fairgreaves was a skinny kid with a German-helmet haircut and a Rod Stewart nose. Other kids teased him about it, sometimes.

I didn't know why they invited me along. I felt privileged and blundering.

They'd seen *Star Wars*, and they had liked it: but that had been ages ago and their attention had long since moved on. It did me no good that I'd read the tie-in novel six times and could quote passages from it. (Han Solo walked with the 'loose-limbed gait of the experienced space-traveller'. I wanted to walk like that too.)

So I kept my counsel and I listened to them discuss Hearts, who were the local football team, and their big brothers and sisters and their mums and dads, and what they watched on TV. I listened to them mutter dirty jokes that none of us really understood, and I laughed when they did.

I ordered what they ordered: beans and chips and an ice-cream float. That was a sundae glass of cola topped with slowly dissolving vanilla ice-cream.

Our food was brought to us by a middle-aged woman who was not much taller than me. She wore big spectacles. When we left the café, she waved her hand and said, 'Bye, lads.'

That felt good. It was how things were supposed to be. My clumsiness evaporated. I was watching myself behaving like a normal kid.

Babs and Colin Fairgreaves eventually tired of the Junction Café. They missed the lunchtime kickarounds. Soon, I was the only person going.

The moment I stepped off school grounds, I stepped into a

drama, a *Play for Today*; the kind that opens with an Everyday Kid walking down a familiar street, passing familiar faces, walking into a familiar café – a place where he is a regular.

The woman always greeted me with a smile and said, 'Hiya, son.'

Soon, I was such a regular, she didn't need to ask what I wanted. That was even better: as soon as I opened the door, she looked up and said, 'Beans and chips and an ice-cream drink?' and I said 'Aye' in my mongrel accent and sat down.

I ate my meal, looking out of the window. The bean juice soaked into the chips, and the ice-cream melted into the cola.

I went to the till to pay. The woman took my money and put it in the drawer. Then she closed the till and gave me my change. Into my palm, she secretly pressed a little bit more money than I'd just spent. I always left the Junction Café five or ten pence richer than when I entered. It wasn't the money that I loved about it. It was the knowing and lovely look in her eye.

One afternoon, I forgot to pay. I just stood up and got my jacket and walked out the door and went back to school. I remembered in class, with a start and a drowning gasp. I stood up. My chair scraped on the floor. I explained to Miss Galloway, who excused me from class, and I ran the length of Dalry Road, weaving between pedestrians.

I arrived at the Junction Café breathless and sweating. I was scared the woman might think I'd taken her secret kindness for granted. But she didn't think that. She greeted me by saying, 'Here he is!'

At the till, she said she knew I'd be back, the minute she saw how quickly I'd gone through the door.

She said, 'Laddies your age are always in a hurry to be somewhere.'

When I paid my 50p, she put it in the drawer. Then she palmed two more 50p pieces and pressed them into my hand, a pound, and she closed my fingers round them and she smiled. I walked back to school, holding the money.

One lunchtime, before the end of term, I found the Junction Café's windows blinded with loops of whitewash. The sign on the door had been reversed to read *Closed*.

I never saw the woman again. But I still dream about her sometimes.

13

In the morning, Derek's first duty was to beat the dog.

Once, she gouged a long, powdery scar in the wall, just above the skirting board, as if she'd been trying to tunnel free. When Derek entered the room, she whimpered and pressed back her ears and squirmed as far into the corner as her bones would allow.

Derek was pale. He said, 'What has this pig dog done *now*?'

Mum said, 'It looks much worse than it is.'

Derek kicked the dog in the belly, just under the ribs. Then he slapped her, open-handed, in the face. She trembled and cowered further into the corner. But she took it, even though she was a big dog by now.

Once, it got too much and she twisted at the spine and bared her teeth. Derek went to the bedroom and returned with a yellow golf umbrella. He grabbed it with two hands, like a club, and smashed it down across the dog until it snapped. Then he kicked her. The kick was weak, half-hearted. He was tired. He went back to the bedroom, taking the fractured umbrella with him.

He began once again to talk about God. His desire to find the right church hadn't been the passing fancy it had appeared: it was Derek's fundamental requirement. He never specifically articulated or gave shape to the true nature of this longing, but it squatted inside him like a cane toad.

His need for God often manifested as a fascination with the enigmatic: the Bermuda Triangle, the Pyramids at Giza, the *Marie Celeste*. He told me about rains of frogs and fishes, the yeti, big foot.

He kept a number of paperbacks on the paranormal. When I turned nine, he let me borrow from this secret library books by Erich Von Daniken and Charles Berlitz – *Chariots of the Gods?* and *The Bermuda Triangle*.

Their emphatic, declarative covers unnerved me, and their pages had a fearful solemnity, so at night I made sure they were stacked under the bed: I didn't want to glimpse them in the darkness. I didn't want to think about aliens experimenting on abducted human beings, or about secret continents, or Nazi black magic, or about midnight visits from the Men in Black.

One tale in particular tormented me; the story of a Tennessee farmer called David Lang. In 1880, Lang was working in the fields. His wife watched from the porch of the house and his two children played in the front yard. In full view of them all, David Lang vanished.

With the help of some friends, Lang's wife and children searched the area of his abrupt disappearance. The land was quite firm. There were no old mine works under the farm, no subsidence. But David Lang was never found. The only marker of his vanishing was a strange circle that appeared on the ground where he'd last stood. Nothing ever grew there. Animals would not enter into it. Not even insects. David Lang's terrible disappearance became famous because his daughter, Sarah, later wrote an article about it. It was called 'How Lost Was My Father?'.

Derek needed these books because, while he prepared for Armageddon, he was also suturing together the severed, patch-work past. Human history, which was about to end, had begun with the intervention of space-men. Lost, ancient civilizations had possessed their extra-terrestrial technology. Disorder and decay were exemplified by bestial Negroes and malicious Jews. Nothing was meaningless and nothing was random.

It gave shape to his world, but the shape was never quite right. He kept looking, kept reading. He kept trying to believe something: that everything had a cause, and that behind the cause was a reason.

This was true even of the fact that trainloads of people had been taken to a frigid place and starved and shaved and stripped and gassed. Derek told me that, because they had scrambled over each other in their brutal death-fear, they had formed tangled, naked pyramids of corpses. He wondered at the significance of the pyramid shape.

He said, 'The Jew is selfish. It isn't his fault. He's made like that. And Hitler wasn't a good man. He was a very bad man, in some ways. But he was also very clever: he was a genius. What he did to the Jews wasn't good, even though in some ways they asked for it. But Hitler also did great, great things for his country.'

He looked me in the eye.

'They bulldozed them into graves,' he said. 'Thousands of them, tens of thousands. They fell into the holes. They were piled on top of each other. Men and women and babies. Like sticks.'

'Derek,' said Mum.

He stopped. Thinking about it always made him grim.

(And later, when I angrily announced in class that 'Hitler was a genius,' there was another acute, peculiar silence.

Miss Galloway looked at me with her eyebrows raised, as if a punchline was about to follow. The class looked at me as though I'd announced my intention to fart.

Miss Galloway said, 'Well, Neil, a lot of people certainly thought so', and moved us dextrously on.)

Derek had been born with something missing, and he knew it. But he couldn't fathom the discontinuity inside him. It was an unbroken code, an apparent clutter of letters and shapes that somehow contained meaning, like the jumble of spots in a colour-blindness chart.

He delved for answers in strange corners and sometimes found treasure. But whatever pearl he unearthed changed shape as he examined it. All flowers wilted in Derek Cross's hands. Everything went rotten.

And he rocked on the balls of his feet and put his hands in his pockets and grinned. And on Saturday night he'd have a few beers, and get a bit tipsy and tell me about Little Richard and Chuck Berry, and he'd play me 'Lucille' or 'Route 66', and later he'd tell me stories about distrustful niggers, who were as close to animals as they were to men.

I wondered what went on behind his eyelids when he lay down at night, or when he went in the storeroom at the supermarket in Corstorphine to cut up boxes with a carpet knife. Catch him unawares while he was doing that and he had a dead look in his eye, like the look in the eye of a great white shark. He was pale and there was a raven sheen to his hair. It was the face he wore when he beat the dog. He felt angry because he feared there was nothing. He carried it around like a tumour, like something voracious munching at him from the inside, from the middle of his brain. He cut at it when he cut the boxes. He kicked at it when he kicked the dog. His soul was rotten and full of gaps, like an old curtain.

And then the American boys came to the door, smiling.

14

The knock came early in 1978. We knew it must be important, because we never had visitors. The only person who had ever visited the flat was Derek's assistant, who was also called Derek, but he never came any more.

By now, the dog was fully grown and fully insane. At the sound of the knocking, she exploded into a mass of teeth and saliva. Derek grabbed a fistful of scruff, but she squirmed free and ran. She stood on hindlegs, snarling and gnawing sideways at the door, trying to chew through it.

Mum dragged her into my bedroom. The dog howled with bloodlust as we gathered, curious, in the narrow hallway. Derek straightened his cardigan and opened the door.

It was the Men in Black: two young men in dark suits, white shirts, sober ties, CIA haircuts. Each of them carried a leather briefcase. Each of them smiled a Cadillac smile.

They stood there, smiling, apparently unconcerned by the maniacal wolf baying in my bedroom. After we said hello, their smiles only widened. They were from the Church of Jesus Christ of Latter-Day Saints.

There was a moment. We were looking at them. They were looking at us. The dog was barking. Then Derek invited them in.

They hesitated; shared a glance; stepped over the threshold. Derek shut the door behind them and led them to the front room. Mum had gone first and was already in the kitchen, waiting to offer them tea or coffee. They declined, with thanks, and asked if they might have a glass of water instead.

('Wadder,' said Mum, mimicking their accent, delighted: 'I'd like a glass of wadder if I may.')

They didn't sit until Derek suggested they might like to. Then, having first placed their bulky briefcases on the floor, they sat straight, like boardroom members in a film. Derek sat in his deckchair.

They introduced themselves as Elder Baxter and Elder Follett and reminded us they were from the Church of Jesus Christ of Latter Day Saints, which we might know better as the Mormons.

Mum had no idea who or what the Mormons might be. I could tell by her earnest, wordless affirmative, from the kitchenette. But Derek seemed familiar with them. He made a cheeky moon face. He said, 'You're the ones with all the wives.'

They'd heard that one before. You could tell. Certain members of the early Church had believed in polygamy, they said. But it was an Article of Faith that Mormons should adhere to the law of the land. That law prohibited polygamy and accordingly, they didn't practise it. Granted, there were small offshoot groups in the Utah desert who did, but they were not accepted by the church.

They sipped water.

I asked what polygamy was.

'Having lots of wives,' said Derek.

Elder Baxter opened his big briefcase and took out three books. One of them was a Bible; you could tell, because it was black, with gold writing stamped on the spine and the pages were edged in gold. The other books were cloth-bound in deep, navy blue. He also produced a small, leather-look portfolio, which he flipped open to show us.

This was the First Discussion, in which we talked of many things.

Joseph Smith was born in Vermont in 1805, the son of an impoverished farmer. He was a gifted but unschooled young man who lived in a time of great spiritual tribulation. During the emotional turmoil of his fifteenth year, Joseph despaired ever to know which of the many churches was true. Contemplating this most terrible question, he read from James 1:5: *If any of you lack wisdom, let him ask of God.*

Taking the Bible at its word, on a beautiful, clear day early in the spring of 1820, he went to a grove of trees not far from his home. He fell to his knees and prayed to be granted wisdom. A great light descended upon him, brighter than the American sun. It revealed 'two Personages whose brightness and glory defy all description, standing above me in the air.'[1]

Here, Elder Follett interrupted. He said, 'Now, Neil. Okay. Tell me. What do you think God looks like?'

It was a trick question. He wanted me to say that God was an old man with a long white beard. I knew that was the wrong answer. But I hadn't spent much time thinking about God.

I said, 'I don't know.'

'Well,' said Elder Follett, 'at this point, you're probably picturing an old man with a long, white beard . . .'

I said, 'No.'

'Well,' he said, 'if you *had* been, you'd have been absolutely right.'

He swivelled the portfolio and showed me a picture. It was rendered in the hyper-real style of a *Marvel* Summer Special. It showed a young Joseph Smith, on his knees in a grove. He was looking upon two glowing, robed, bearded men. Each of them was barefoot, and they hovered several feet in the air.

God spoke to Joseph Smith. He said, 'This is My Beloved Son. Hear Him.'[2]

And, to answer Joseph's question, Jesus revealed that none of the existing churches were true. Even worse than that: '. . . all their creeds were an abomination'.[3]

This was called the First Vision, and it marked the beginning of the restoration of the true church of Jesus Christ to the planet earth.

Later, God sent an angel called Moroni who disclosed to Joseph the existence of a long-lost treasure: a holy book, inscribed on plates of pure gold. This book accounted for the former inhabitants of the American continent, and the 'source from which they sprang'.[4] It also contained the 'fullness' of the biblical gospels. One thousand, four hundred years ago, it had been hidden beneath a rock on a nearby hillside.

Nineteen witnesses testified to seeing the golden plates. They were about 'six inches wide and eight inches long and not quite as thick as common tin. They were filled with engravings in Egyptian characters and bound together in a volume, as the leaves of a book with three rings running through the whole.'[5]

Joseph completed the translation in June, 1829. Nine years after meeting God in an American copse, he finally revealed the fullness of the gospels. It was called *The Book of Mormon*.

It was a good story. It had the ring of adventure. Joseph Smith reminded me of David Balfour, the gauche, faulted hero of *Kidnapped*.

The Book of Mormon was 'the most correct of any book on earth, ever written'.[6] But it was also the first blockbuster. Opening in Jerusalem, around 600 BC, it tells the story of a Hebrew tribe lead by the virtuous Lehi, who is instructed by God to relocate his tribe from Jerusalem to America. Having successfully completed this voyage of several thousand miles, the tribe splits into quarrelsome factions: the Nephites are descended from Lehi's youngest son, who was favoured for his grace and obedience. The Lamanites are descended from Nephi's older, jealous brothers.

The Lamanites are 'an idle people, full of mischief and sub-tlety', for which God smites them with a 'skin of blackness'. More favoured, the Nephites remained 'exceedingly fair and delightsome'.[7]

For many years, the tribes wage war on one another. Peace is

only established in AD 33, when the recently crucified and res-
urrected Jesus Christ makes a surprise cameo appearance. Jesus
urges the Nephites and the Lamanites to live in peace which,
following his departure, they manage for several hundred
years. But eventually, the false-hearted, ominously dark-
skinned Lamanites descend once again into base idolatry,
which leads to another war. During this final conflict, the
superb leader of the fair-skinned and Godly Nephites is called
Mormon.

Despite Mormon's piety and tactical excellence, the Nephites
are defeated in a final, titanic battle, after which the victorious
Lamanites graduate into genocide. They put every last breathing Nephite to the sword.

All but one of them. The last of the Nephites is Mormon's
son, Moroni. Moroni lives just long enough to preserve the tale
of his routed, Godly people. He does so on the pages of a golden
book, which he later buries on the slopes of a hill called
Cumorah.

It was the same Moroni who returned in glory fourteen hun-
dred years later, restoring the lost and true church of Jesus
Christ to the face of the earth. During this time, the pernicious
Lamanites had continued to inhabit the land that became
America. They were the peoples Joseph Smith knew as 'Red
Indians'.

The Holy Spirit was in the room with us, that night.
Everyone could feel it. If you could feel it, it was there.

The story of ancient Hebrew tribes piloting boats to America
sounded no more implausible than many of the Old Testament
stories with which Derek had already familiarized me. And it

seemed less fantastic that the Risen Christ should visit America than that he should rise in the first place. It even made a kind of sense that Satan was Jesus's evil brother, especially if you'd read enough comics and seen enough movies.

But it was the missionaries, not their story, who made me want to go to their church. I wanted to be near them, to make them approve of me. They seemed unearthly, outsized, made of different materials, possessed of strange glamour. I wanted them to be my friends.

Mum was lonely. That was all it took for her: loneliness and a knock on a door that never knocked.

But Derek saw something else. In Joseph Smith, he had at last discovered his soul-mate. Derek saw himself mirrored in Joseph's eye.

Joseph Smith looked Derek Cross in the eye, across all those years, and told him how it was. Here was the shape of things, at last. Here was the piece that was missing.

And Derek saw, and it was good.

15

One Saturday morning, wandering down Nicholson Street, I noticed a bright yellow shop which stood alone, halfway down a side street. It was opposite the sunny side: a yellow shop in violet shadow. It was called the Science Fiction Bookshop.

I'd passed that side street many times. I'd have noticed a yellow shop, had one been there before. It seemed to have materialized like Dr Who's Tardis. It was impossible to see inside the shop: the windows were full of posters of big-breasted women in scanty armour and men in elaborate space-suits, carrying lasers. So I went in.

Because it was on a side street, and because it had so many posters on the windows, it was a pleasant shade of twilight inside. It smelled nice, of books and comics and new T-shirts. Several young men were in there. Behind the counter stood a short man in a frayed blue sweater and glasses. He had long, frizzy hair and a scanty beard. As I entered the shop and stood there, taking it in, he smiled and said, 'Hiya'.

I said, 'Hiya'.

It was a novelty to be spoken to, in a bookshop. Bobby – if that was even the name of the silent man who occupied Bobby's Bookshop – had never yet acknowledged my presence, let alone bidding me an immediate and cheerful hello.

There were no spy books in the Science Fiction Bookshop and there were no Westerns or books about German punishment battalions on the Russian front. The shelves were full of books whose covers showed spaceships and astronauts and muscled barbarians. They were called *The Mote in God's Eye*; *Soldier, Ask Not*; *In Our Hands the Stars*. Next to the counter stood a wire spinner, on which were displayed novels based on *Marvel* comic superheroes. One of them featured Spider Man.

The man at the counter looked at me, looking.

He said, 'Those are American imports.'

I nodded, looking at the Avengers in *The Man Who Stole Tomorrow*.

I fingered the glossy blue spine.

I said, 'Have you just opened?'

He said, 'Oh, no. We've been here for ages.'

'But I've never seen you.'

He smiled. 'Everyone says that.'

Originally, he said, and for a long time, the outside of the shop had been painted black. But the shop didn't have enough customers, so they tried to sell it. Because nobody wanted to buy a black shop, they painted the outside. The yellow was supposed to be an undercoat, something to cover up the black before they painted it a proper colour. But as soon as the undercoat went down, customers started to come through the doors.

So they painted the outside an even brighter yellow and even more customers appeared. Now they weren't selling the shop any more.

I said, 'That's great,' and I meant it. It would have been terrible to discover and lose such a place at almost the same time.

I picked up *Mayhem in Manhattan* with awe and reverence. I was loath to put it back on the wire spinner. But I had no money.

I spent the rest of the afternoon in the shop. When I got back to St Cuthbert's, Mum was wearing her coat and ready to go. She'd been worried; she asked where I'd been. I told her. But she didn't believe that a nine-year-old boy could spend so long in a bookshop without buying something. The shopkeepers would mind.

But they didn't mind. There were two of them, both short. One was hairy, the other was square and clean-shaven. Both wore frayed sweaters and jeans and old trainers. They showed me everything. They kept finding new things to show me, authors whose names I didn't know and to whom they seemed excited to introduce me: Harry Harrison, Gordon R. Dickson, EE 'Doc' Smith. They offered to let me take home a second-hand copy of a book called *The Stainless Steel Rat*. I could bring in the money next week, if I liked.

'Trust me,' they said. 'You'll love it.'

It was a handsome book, creased and yellowing a little with age, with a vast, half-built space-vessel depicted on the cover. I had to say no, because I knew Derek would be angry if they gave me something for free, even if I went back and paid for it later.

That night, I told him about the Science Fiction Bookshop. He thought the story about the paint was funny. I asked him to take me there. I had to wait until it was his day off work, but he did.

He entered the shop with an air of amused sufferance. He stood behind me, rolling on the balls of his feet. I moved from shelf to shelf, trying to remember what I'd decided to buy, if I got the chance.

The hairy assistant came in from the back. He had a mug of coffee. He said, 'Hello again. Neil, is it?'

I said, 'Hello. This is my Dad.'

Derek arched an eyebrow in misjudged complicity. The hairy assistant looked through him like a window. I wanted to say something, to let the hairy assistant know that it wasn't fair not to like Derek, that he always bought me books. That all the books on my shelf were there because of him.

And the fact that he was here, now – in a shop that sold the kind of books he didn't really like – was an affirmation of that. But I didn't say anything. I just blushed.

The first books I bought with my own money, were *The Stainless Steel Rat* and *Han Solo at Stars End*, in which Han Solo owned a 'droid whose name was Bollux. That was the funniest thing I'd ever read.

In subsequent, British editions, the 'droid had another name: they changed it to Zollux. But I had the American import. So it was always Bollux to me.

The Church of Jesus Christ of Latter-Day Saints building in Edinburgh was clean-lined in brick, with a sloping roof and a spire. Inside, it was like a modern school: a main corridor with a squeaky floor, doors leading off it. The meeting hall was at the far end, behind double doors that opened inwards. It was a bright room, full of blonde wood pews. The service was led by Bishop Steele. He was a pale, thin, ginger man of milky infirmity.

After an introductory prayer and a hymn, Bishop Steele introduced us: Brother and Sister Cross, and Neil. We stood. The congregation turned its head. A shine of smiles passed mouth to mouth, line to line.

When the service was over, we herded with the rest of the congregation into the corridor. We were swamped in handshakes and more smiles. Everyone was delighted to see us. Grown men called me Brother Cross, and welcomed me. I said thank you. Mum was engulfed in kisses and joyful hugs. Derek grinned. He shook hands. He turned in a circle, shaking hands. He said how happy he was to be here, at last.

After all that time, after all those places and all those people, after all those ideas and all those books, after all those years in the arid wilderness, Derek Cross had found a place to be.

Mum and Derek hadn't told the missionaries they were living in sin. But, before they could be baptized, they had to get legally married. So they did it in secret.

I accompanied them to the Register Office. Bob Cruickshank went along, too, to act as a witness. So did Derek, the deputy-manager of Derek's shop. He was a tall, stooped, raw-boned man with curly hair to his collar. There were no flowers or rice or confetti. There was just five of us in a little room. Nobody dressed up. When the wedding was over, Mum and Derek thanked the witnesses and we caught the bus home and had our tea.

We were baptized on 5 May 1978. The baptismal room was small, white-tiled and humid. There was a small congregation. We were dressed in white, and we were barefoot and, one by one, we were led into the pool. It was waist-height, warm as a bath. Elder Follett held me round the waist and raised his right arm, bent at the elbow. He said, 'Being commissioned by Jesus Christ, I baptize you in the name of the Father, and of the Son, and of the Holy Spirit,' and he dunked me under the water.

There was a moment of full immersion. Bubbling water closed over my upturned face, my screwed-up eyes. Then I was up again, it ran in rivulets from my eyebrows. The assembled faces were smiling. I stepped out of the pool, the white shirt and trousers clinging to me, instantly cold: you could see the outline of my vest. Someone wrapped me in a big towel and I stood there, shivering, as Elder Follett baptized Mum and Derek, too.

They wrote to Elder Baxter, who by then had been shifted to another ward:

The church is a very wonderful thing. When we go there we feel we could just stay for ever. We are indeed very grateful to you for knocking on our door, that evening just a few weeks ago and for the wonderful friendship that Elder Bolz, Elder Follett and yourself have shown to us. We will treasure it for ever as we progress in our knowledge of this true religion. We knew from the very beginning it held

*something special for us if only we would reach out and hold
on tight to it.*

The letter is in my mother's handwriting, and it is signed by
her. I own a photocopy of it. But it's in Derek's voice. I can see
him, standing with his hands in his pockets and rocking on
the balls of his feet, as he dictates to her.

Very quickly, the church came to dominate even our weekday
lives. The first of these obligations, family home evening, was
held every Monday. It was given over to prayer, scriptural read-
ings, refreshments and spiritual discussion then rounded off
with games and sometimes food.

As new members, for several months we attended them at
other people's houses. I was a bad guest: nervous, too polite,
uneasy about other people's way of doing things.

At the house of a big family called the Aitkens (the father
wore sandals), a big, steaming bowl of spaghetti Bolognese was
passed along the dining table. I choked back tears of anxiety. I
fretted that I'd take too much, or too little, or that I'd spill
tomato sauce on the tablecloth.

Even worse, the food had cheese in it. I was still powerfully
revolted by cheese: I could detect it in minute quantities, the
way baying dogs could smell escaped convicts. If I entered a
room where it had recently been cooked, I vomited. But neither
Mum nor Derek noticed the cheese in the spaghetti. They were
too busy talking across the table. And I was too polite and
scared to do anything but eat.

Belonging to the church had changed Mum and Derek's

spoken language. Sometimes it made me feel weird to hear it. Mum saying, 'Thank you, Sister Aitken', or Derek making casual, smiling reference to 'Our Heavenly Father'.

Eventually, we began to hold our own family home evenings. But we felt self-conscious, trying to apply a formal structure to what until recently had been quite normal: spending an evening in each other's company. So we cheated. Derek asked me to say an opening prayer, then he read from *The Book of Mormon* or *The Pearl of Great Price* – not much, a verse or two. When he closed the book, he asked mum to say a closing prayer. Then we turned on the TV and relaxed.

Also, during the week, Mum had 'sisterhood meetings' and Weekday Relief Society, where the women prayed and discussed home-making. I had youth club and Weekday Primary. Derek had priesthood meetings. And there were many informal social evenings: Mormons loved to spend time in each other's houses, praying and discussing Heavenly Father.

Saturday evening was free, but only because, as the song had it: 'Saturday is a special day: It's the day we get ready for Sunday.' Nevertheless, on that evening, we almost reverted to former patterns of behaviour. Derek sat there with his ukulele, playing three chords and singing country and western songs. My new favourite was *'You Picked a Fine Time to Leave Me, Lucille'*. I sang it, word for word – a long, maudlin ballad about the errant wife of a good man – and at the end Mum and Derek clapped.

But now, Derek drank water, not lager. And, when the singing was done, he said a prayer of thanks. He thanked Heavenly Father for this special time and for the special love that we shared. And he said these things in the name of Jesus Christ. Mum-joined him in saying *Amen*.

On Sunday, there was more Relief Society and another priesthood meeting. And there was more Primary for me, a kind of Sunday School. Its purpose was to help children learn and live by gospel principles; to remember and keep their baptismal covenants. It was to teach us to build strong, enduring testimonies.

After Sunday's auxiliary gatherings came the sacrament meeting. It was taken by the bishop. The bishopric sat on an elevated platform behind him, facing the congregation. We sang an opening hymn; my favourite was number 196, 'We Thank Thee, O God, for a Prophet'. It had a stirring tune, not unlike *The Dam Busters*.

When the hymn was finished, a member of the congregation approached the front to say an opening prayer. After that, testimonies were given. The speakers had been assigned this duty the previous week: as you were leaving, the bishop pressed a folded square of paper into your hand. You spent all week dreading it; but it got easier with time. Mormons were expected to become confident public speakers, in order to better proclaim their faith. The testimonies were about two minutes long and in essence identical. They were about being lonely and unhappy, then being filled with joy and love. They were about knowing this to be the true church and knowing that Joseph Smith was a true prophet of God.

After the testimonies, a prayer was given to bless the sacrament: small chunks of bread and plastic cups of water symbolizing the savage, blood atonement of Jesus Christ. This was passed round in metal trays. The young men who performed this duty were called deacons: they were boys who, from the age of twelve, had entered into the Aaronic priesthood. This was the first ministry of God and – unlike the Melchizidek priesthood, which was conferred upon all worthy males aged eighteen and above – it was open to black men.

This was a gracious concession on the church's part, because being black was a badge of divine execration. To be born black was to be punished for sins committed in the pre-existence, and so constituted much more than a life sentence: it was a demonstration of God's timeless wrath. Not even the crucifixion could save a black man from his blackness. In case any Mormon be left uncertain, Joseph Smith's successor, Brigham Young, proclaimed that: 'No person having the least particle of Negro blood can hold the Priesthood.'

This doctrine helped persuade Derek of the church's eternal truth and its fearless integrity. But he was irked by its too-compassionate decision to allow black members more latitude than, theologically speaking, they merited. This indulgence was perhaps best articulated by Elder Mark E. Peterson of the Council of Twelve Apostles who said in 1954 that:

> . . . we are generous with the Negro. We are willing that the Negro have the highest education. I would be willing to let every Negro drive a Cadillac if they could afford it. I would be willing that they have all the advantages they can get out of life in the world. But let them enjoy these things among themselves.

I think the Lord segregated the Negro. And who is man to change that segregation?

It reminds me of the scripture on marriage, 'What God hath joined together, let not man put asunder.' Only here we have the reverse of the thing – what God hath separated, let not man bring together again.

Think of the Negro, cursed as to the priesthood . . . This Negro, who, in the pre-existence, lived the type of life which justified the Lord in sending him to the earth in their lineage of Cain; with a black skin and possibly being born in darkest Africa – if that Negro is willing when he hears the Gospel to accept it, he may have many of the blessings of the Gospel. In spite of all he did in the pre-existent life, the Lord is willing, if the Negro accepts the gospel with real, sincere faith, and is really converted, to give him the blessings of baptism and the gift of the Holy Ghost. If that Negro is faithful all his days, he can and will enter the Celestial Kingdom. He will go there as a servant, but he will get Celestial Glory.

Then, on 9 June 1978 – shortly after we joined – the church issued a press release that gave notice of a radical doctrinal change: the most radical, in fact, since the policy on polygamy was rescinded, a century earlier. The Prophet Spencer W. Kimball announced that the 'long promised day' had arrived, from which non-whites would be permitted to enter into the priesthood.

It was a pragmatic acquiescence. The church was becoming ever more popular in both South America and Africa, countries where many Mormons could be found who had more than the least particle of Negro about them. Such was the rapidity of the church's expansion, it had become unworkable to keep shipping in white priests from Europe and America. The church, after all, was a lay organization.

Although still a new member, Derek was saddened. It was self-evident to him that coons should not be permitted to enter into the priesthood of God: it made him shudder to think of their impudence, even to imagine that Christ's blood had been shed in their name.

Nevertheless, he recognized the sagacity of the new revelation. And besides, he had become accustomed to the fact that kaffirs always got something for nothing. It was no surprise that even their salvation could, in the end, be ascribed to the toil and charity of righteous, hard-working white men.

Derek entered the Melchizidek priesthood on 25 May 1978. The first black men were ordained into it less than two weeks later. But not in our branch.

The sacrament meeting ended with another communal hymn and a closing prayer. Then there was some happy milling around in the corridor, after which a couple of missionaries came back home with us, to have lunch.

The missionaries lived in a large, stone building that sat in grounds next to the church. It might once have been a Victorian private school, and the regime they tolerated there wasn't so different. They weren't allowed a social life: they prayed, slept, ate and studied there; they walked the streets looking for converts. They went to church. They were never alone, not least because solitude promoted masturbation. They were even encouraged to keep the door open while showering or engaging in other 'toilet activities'. They weren't allowed to do anything except be missionaries. Most of them were about nineteen.

So on Sunday, Mum and Derek invited them to our flat, two by two. Here they became louder; they laughed and gossiped. Much of the gossip took the form of candid anecdotes about the misery of being a missionary; of spending two precious years being laughed at and spat on and having doors slammed in your face.

These stories were always told about some other missionary, in a different city, a friend of a friend, and they were designed to make you laugh. But at the heart of each was a queasy core of unhappiness and homesickness.

Mum laid their plates before them. There weren't enough little tables, so I balanced my dinner on my lap and so did Derek, in his deckchair. While the food was passed out, the missionaries grew solemn, because a prayer was coming up.

Whoever was elected to say grace dutifully folded his arms and tucked in his chin and closed his eyes. He thanked our Heavenly Father for what we were about to receive. And when *Amen* was said, he became nineteen again. He picked up his fork and began to eat and tell stories and laugh.

While they ate, Derek listened, smiling. He topped up their glasses of Schloer sparkling grape juice. When their plates were clean, they rubbed their bellies and frankly praised the meal and offered to wash up. Mum never let them. So, while she did the dishes, the missionaries secured a length of string across the room, using Blu-Tac. And they removed their dark jackets

and plain ties and rolled up their white shirtsleeves and we
played feather volleyball.

You kept your arms clasped behind your back and blew up
on the feather to keep it aloft, or blew down on it to slam it to
the carpet on your opponents' side. The missionaries howled
and laughed. When I scored a point they clapped my shoulder
and roared.

They made great use of audio cassettes. They used them to
record letters home – it wasn't so easy to admit how homesick
you were, talking out loud into a microphone. And they gave us
tapes of the Prophet Spencer W. Kimball talking in the temple
in Salt Lake City. They were tapes of tapes of tapes, hissing and
warbling and faintly sinister, with the Prophet shakily expos-
tulating behind a storm of white noise.

This inspired Derek. He began secretly to record the Sunday
lunches. It was better than filming them. When the missionaries had gone, he produced the mono cassette recorder and
immediately rewound the tape. We sat still and mostly silent
when he played it.

I looked at the spools going round and round. Sometimes,
Mum cooed and laughed at something a missionary had said –
Pass the wadder, she always liked that – and Derek sat there
with a grin on his face, reliving and revelling in what had just
ended; confirming it. The burst of life and noise and happiness
and spirit in that quiet little flat.

One night, two new Elders knocked at the door. Both had
recently been transferred to Edinburgh. One had curly ginger
hair, clipped close at the back and sides, unruly on top like an
unsprung cartoon mattress. In his hand he clasped a roll of

Super-8 film. He'd been told that Derek owned a projector. His family had sent him a film. He wondered if we'd mind.

I was ill that night. I had a fever. I lay in bed listening as the ginger Elder yelped with surprise and joy as his sister smiled jerkily for the camera and waved, projected on the warped screen.

The noise kept me awake and the shouting worsened my headache. When the film was finished, the missionary came quietly into my room, followed by Mum and Derek. He lay his hands on my forehead and spoke to me, softly. It was like being touched by a doctor. He said a prayer to Our Heavenly Father that I be healed. When he said *Amen*, I began to feel better. I turned on my side. The elder, Mum and Derek left the room.

Behind them, they left Jesus. He stood at the edge of my bed in his white robes and his long, clean hair and his auburn beard, a bit forked, and those smiling, infinitely indulgent eyes.

My grandfather Claude was there too. I'd never met him, because his allegiance to a religion called Christian Science had caused him to die, preventably, shortly before I was born. But now he stood to the right of Jesus, and just behind him.

I didn't actually see them. My eyes were closed. But I could feel them there: Jesus softly glowing, like a nightlight; Claude in shadow, looking down on me, until I slept.

16

I tried to keep the church a secret.

The worst thing about it was getting there. It was important not to be seen by anybody who knew me; anybody who might guess where I was headed in my shirt and tie, with my mum and dad.

Collington Road wasn't far, less than a mile, and relative safety was closer than that. We walked along Dalry Road for a bit, then turned up a steeply rising, high-walled alleyway that edged the vast, fearful Dalry graveyard. The crumbling wall was topped with broken glass, contrived to keep children from scrambling over. It didn't work: occasionally, my classmates would speak of their adventures in there. I thought them insane. The graveyard was full of aged gravestones, leaning and collapsed. They were Edinburgh grey, and green with moss and lichen. All of this was subsumed by a twisting mantle of grass and dandelions and overhanging trees.

In dreams, I often found myself in there, trapped in the word-less and spreading dark. The sun was setting and the glass on the high walls shone malicious in the fading light: white and bottle green. I ran through the twisting undergrowth, towards the great gates. But they were obstructed by a huge black pyramid. It was veined and knotted with vines and creepers. I never learned what it stood in monument to, because I always woke up when I saw it.

After the alley, we turned on to Collington Road and I began to relax because from that point, nobody was likely to see me.

For a couple of weeks, I got away with it. But soon, the news got round that I was attending the weird church, the one with all the Americans. Not only that: I went there using another name. There was the whiff of insurgency to that, the aroma of something not-right. And there was the coincidence of the sur-names. That I was attending a bizarre church was peculiar enough, but that I went there calling myself Cross – of all things, Cross – was too alluring.

I began to discover crosses everywhere. Little Christian runes were scrawled over every page of my exercise books. Plasticine crosses were left in my desk drawer. Crosses were chalked on the blackboard when I walked into class after lunch. They were the insignia of universal suspicion and their power was ampli-fied by anonymity. I never knew who was responsible, and it didn't matter, because everyone found it funny. Crosses turned up in my bag, in my coat pockets, in the pages of the science-fic-tion books I kept in my drawer. It went on for months.

One morning, I noticed that some new graffiti had appeared on the wall of the park. You could see it from the window of the flat. Whoever wrote it probably knew that. They'd used white paint and a paint brush and made the letters two feet high. The words said:

NEIL GO HOME

Every morning, I vomited before leaving the house. In the classroom I ground my teeth until my jaw ached. Sometimes, the ache squirmed up behind one eye and cramped there. Back home, I lay in bed, perfectly still, until the migraine had passed. I waited for sleep, the opalescent Jesus at my bedside in the throbbing darkness, my grandfather beside him.

That year, I'd been in several scuffles with a boy from my class. He was new, and he was a fighter. But I wasn't really scared of him, because he had no friends.

Then, one afternoon, he waited for me at the school gates. There was a crowd with him. Some of them were big kids. Some of them were unfamiliar. They were the friends I thought he didn't have.

He walked up to me. He put his hands on my chest and pushed me into the high gate. This is how fights always began.

I held up my hands and said, 'I don't want any trouble.'

He punched me in the face. There was a detonation, but no pain. The crowd pressed in, like a held breath.

He grabbed my hair and pulled back my head. Behind me, somebody reached through the gate to grab my wrists. They tugged and twisted until my arms went through the bars. Then they bent my arms up, behind my back. I bucked and writhed.

Someone else gave my hair a sharp tug. There was a crack, and a slow, wet spreading, like when someone pretended to break an egg on your head.

I couldn't stop laughing. I was laughing and laughing.

When it was finished, I walked home. My coat was ripped;

white stuffing was coming out of it. There was blood on my knees and in my hair, and on my face and elbows. My bag was torn at the strap.

I walked past Susie the nervous dog, who showed me her teeth and her trembling lips. I walked through the smother of chip fat and piss and went upstairs. I knocked on the door and waited, looking at the nameplate that read *Cross*, white on navy blue, until Mum answered the door.

At first, I saw the usual exasperation: I'd torn my clothes again. Then the expression slipped off her face, leaving nothing behind it.

Sobs backed up in my throat and jammed there. I stood in the doorway. I spoke in canine yelps. I remembered what Derek had told me about speaking in tongues: sometimes, when people were possessed by the spirit of God, they thrashed and contorted and uttered forth in a strange language, the pure tongue of Heaven. I stood there, in the doorway, with blood on my head and clothes, and I spoke it.

Even in his rage Derek first established that I didn't need to go to hospital. Then he went to the phone box and called David Chapple. David Chapple was a friend from church. But he was a policeman, too.

He came round that night, still in uniform. He was a very tall man, a Londoner. He sat down and took off his hat and asked me to sit next to him. He ruffled my hair. He asked what had happened.

I told him. I was moved by the gentleness of his concern. And I was ashamed that I hadn't defended myself. I began to cry.

The next day, David Chapple spoke to my headmaster. The

headmaster spoke to my teacher, Miss Galloway. She cried because she hadn't noticed what was going on. I supposed she'd erased all those post-lunch crosses from the blackboard without ever really seeing them. *Neil is a very lively and cheerful member of the class*, she had written in my autumn report.

It was nearly the end of summer term, but I took a fortnight off school anyway. On my way to Bobby's Bookshop on Saturday, I saw Babs and Colin Fairgreaves. They affected a very adult concern. It made them feel grown up, to knit their brows and ask how I was. They agreed that I was looking pale. I heard them talking about me as they walked away, about how pale I was.

The next week, after the children had gone home, I went in to see Miss Galloway. We all thought her pretty. She wore Scholl sandals. She sat with her hands clasped between her knees and told me if anything like that happened again – anything – then I should tell her immediately. I nodded, ashamed because it hadn't really been that bad. It had just been more visible because I cried when I got home. Now I just felt stupid.

On my first day back in class, a beam of light shone down upon me. The joke with the crosses stopped.

I'd seen other new kids come and go. One of them was also from Bristol. His name was Seamus Neagle, and one day his mum sent him to school in tight grey shorts, long socks and sandals. Nobody wore shorts, long socks and sandals. Seamus Neagle got laughed at, and he never wore the shorts again. But that was it. He stayed for about two terms. And there was Debbie, a quiet blonde girl, from South Africa, who also stayed a term or two, then evaporated.

The children in my school were just kids. And on that first

day back, I felt their embarrassment on my behalf, for my inex-
plicable and self-renewing oddness. I ached for their small acts
of kindness – passing the coloured pencils, the glue.

I'd learned that it all happened not because of them, but
because of me: because of something about me that rendered
me broken and askew. I didn't know what it was, or how to fix
it, and I was ashamed.

For most of my summer visit, Dad was very jolly. We spent a
week in a caravan at Great Yarmouth: cricket on the beach, fish
and chips and lager shandy in pub gardens. It was followed by
a week in Bristol, much of which involved sitting next to a
bowling green, picking apart cigarette butts.

Then, on my last evening in 92 Bifield Road, Margaret
took Gary and Wayne to the pictures. The house was empty.
In the big, square living room, there was just the table and the
storage heater and the sofa and the swirly carpet. And there
were the windows that overlooked the long garden: twilight,
going dark. And there was me and Dad, and all the space
around us.

He said, 'Sit down, Nipper.'

I sat at the table and so did he. He had a tumbler of whisky
and water. He was in shirtsleeves.

He said, 'I want to talk to you.'

I said, 'Okay.'

'What's all this about a church?'

Mum must have told Caroline or Lin about it, in one of her
letters.

I shrugged. 'It's just a church.'

'What do you do there?'

'You know.'

'Do you pray?'

'I suppose.'

'And sing hymns?'

'Yeah.'

'And what else?'

'The sacrament is passed round—'

'And what's that?'

'Bread and water.'

'And what else?'

'Don't know.'

'I've heard about them. The Mormons.'

'Its proper name is the Church of Jesus Christ of Latter Day Saints.'

'But people call them the Mormons.'

'Yeah.'

He sipped whisky. He leaned his elbow on the table and massaged between his eyebrows with two fingers and thumb. The whisky had made him pink under his white hair.

I didn't know what to say. I knew he wouldn't understand. And down there, in Bristol, neither did I. Bristol was a different colour. The sunlight came at a different angle.

In Bristol, I didn't fear that Jesus was judging my every move. I feared being elbowed in the face by Gary or Wayne, when nobody was watching; or being half-suffocated by them under the bedclothes. I feared one of Margaret's rages, when she came rushing in, moving quickly for a big woman, and beat Gary or Wayne with a beanpole or a slipper. When that happened, Gary and Wayne wailed biblically. It didn't matter which of them was bent beneath the butcher-armed onslaught, raising an arm to protect himself. Margaret's shrieks echoed round the room.

When that happened, Dad carried on reading the *Western Daily Press*, or watching the sports results or the weather. He never hit any of us, never even threatened to.

These were the things I feared in Bristol. Most of all, I feared the cryptic frigidity of Margaret's contempt.

He said, 'And how did you get involved? Derek was it?'

'It was these missionaries. They came round.'

'The blokes who come round, knocking on people's doors.'

I nodded. I was embarrassed on the missionaries' behalf, and I was embarrassed by them and I was ashamed of my embarrassment.

'So, these Mormons come round and you go to church with them and what?'

'You know.'

'Well, not really, Nipper, no.'

'It's just a church.'

'And do you have to do things? They don't drink tea or coffee or anything like that, do they?'

'No.'

'You've drunk tea since you been here.'

I shrugged. I wasn't supposed to drink Coca-Cola either, because it had caffeine in it. I wondered if I should mention that, just so he knew.

There was a long silence. Dad was thinking about something. We sat at the table, thinking.

He said; 'And Derek?'

'Yeah?'

'What do you call him?'

'What do you mean?'

'I mean, what do you call him? Do you call him Derek? Or do you call him Dad?'

I kept my body still. 'I call him Derek.'

'That's what you call him.'

'Yes.'

'Are you sure?'

'Yes.'

He looked at me. 'And what about your surname? What are you called at school?'

'Neil Gadd.'

'And at church?'

'Neil Gadd.'

'And you're sure about that?'

'Yes.'

He sipped the whisky.

He said, 'All right then, Nip.'

Soon, Margaret, Gary and Wayne came home. It was my last night and there was all the packing to be done. Dad and Margaret came to the bedroom to do it with me. They dry-mocked Derek's prissy note: 1 × kagoul, 5 × sox, 2 × sweaters.

Then I lay in bed, lit yellow by the streetlight. I was all wrong inside.

The next day, I flew back to Edinburgh, back to the older light. Mum and Derek met me at the airport.

I said, 'Hello, Mum. Hello, Dad.'

At home in Duff Street, Derek said, 'And while you were away did you keep your promise? Did you obey the Word of Wisdom?'

I didn't hesitate. 'Yes,' I said.

'No tea, no coffee?'

'Nope.'

'No Coke?'

'Nope.'

'Honestly?'

'Honestly.'

'Good chap.'

He ruffled my hair. And that night, I slept under Jesus's gaze.

Unpleasant knowledge passed between Jesus and me like heavy traffic. But Jesus understood. Jesus always did.

A few weeks later, Bishop Steele approached me after the sacrament meeting. He lay a frail hand on my shoulder and said, 'Brother Cross.'

I turned. Bishop Steele offered his hand. I shook it. It was like damp twigs wrapped in tissue paper. He used the gesture to press upon me a folded square of paper. I crushed it without looking. I knew it was an assignment to give my testimony at next week's service.

That afternoon, I was so quiet that Derek asked if something was wrong. When I told him, he laughed and clapped my shoulder. It was a big moment: my first testimony.

I said, 'But I don't know what to say.'

'Just listen to that still, small voice,' said Mum.

'And say your prayers,' said Derek. 'Ask our Heavenly Father.'

I asked Heavenly Father. And I listened for the still, small voice. But when I thought about giving the testimony, my heart beat so loud in my chest, it drowned out their response.

On Saturday, I sat down with a pad of paper. It was the pad I wrote stories on. I stuck the tip of my tongue through the corner of my mouth and I began to work.

When it was done, I gathered up the paper; thick with my heavily smudged, blunt-edged, left-handed graffiti: the writing that all my teachers said I must work hard to improve and which never did. I ran to Derek.

I said, 'Done it.'

He said, 'Come here.'

He gave me a hug. He said, 'You see. Trust in your Heavenly Father.'

On Sunday I was fidgety, unable to concentrate on the sacrament meeting. I didn't hear what the other speakers were saying. I jolted when the room proclaimed its communal *Amen*.

Then bishop Steele announced my name. I stood and edged down the pew. Members intercepted me as I passed them, in order to take my hand and squeeze it. They smiled and nodded encouragement.

I walked to the front. There were so many faces, all of them smiling: even the missionaries who stood at the rear, guarding the double doors.

I took the paper from my pocket and unfolded it.

I said: 'Good morning, brothers and sisters. It's a privilege to be up here bearing my testimony to you this Sabbath morning.

'I'd just like to say that I know this is the true Church of Jesus Christ on the Earth today, that Spencer W. Kimball is a true prophet of God. I'm grateful to the missionaries that knocked on our door that night, Elder Follett and Elder Baxter and for the words they spoke to us.

'I'm grateful for the Church in our lives and the difference it has made to it, for the Word of Wisdom and especially for the scriptures. I can't say I read them as often as I should, but it is a great comfort just knowing they are there when we really need them.

'Joseph Smith was truly a prophet of latter days. The Book of Mormon is God's word.

'I'm grateful to my family for the very special love we share. I'm thankful for our knowledge of the church and the scriptures, for the teachings of the church – which are just, plain common sense: we believe in God the eternal father and in his son Jesus Christ and in the Holy Ghost. We don't drink or smoke or take any habit-forming substances. We don't steal or commit adultery. We believe in the family unit. We believe in being honest and true, chaste, benevolent and in doing good to all men.'

I paused: a beat before the big finish.

'Where is the weirdness in that?' I said.

17

In fact, I never read the scriptures. There was no need. I had memorized the twelve Articles of Faith, which summarized Mormon doctrine to an extent I found more than adequate.

Sometimes, Derek surprised me with a test. He stood up and turned down the TV. He said: 'Neil, what is article 10?'

I scrolled through them in my mind. Then I said: '"We believe in the literal gathering of Israel and in the restoration of the Ten Tribes; that Zion (the New Jerusalem) will be built upon the American continent; that Christ will reign personally upon the earth; and that the earth will be renewed and receive its paradisaical glory."'

'Very good,' said Derek, and turned up the TV again.

Nevertheless, I lacked any perception that God was present in my life. He was too remote, too judicial. Being unable to imagine his personality, I found his motives inscrutable. God was difficult to love. Instead, I was intensely attuned to the living presence of Jesus Christ.

In sunlight, Christ walked always beside me. He was relaxed when I was relaxed. He hurt when I hurt. When I was afraid, his infinite and gentle affection enveloped me. Sometimes the thought of him made me want to weep, because he was so perfect and because he loved me so much.

But even in his tenderness and mercy, Jesus was untouchable: he smiled upon me from a distance. It wasn't like that with the Devil. The Devil wasn't distant. The Devil dogged my footsteps. He flickered in the shadows beside me. In darkness, he slipped into my skin. He grinned behind my eyes. The Devil knew me as utterly as Jesus knew me. But the Devil was closer.

Our best Mormon friends were David Chapple, the policeman, and his wife Pat.

Pat worked in a lunatic asylum. She told Mum about secret rooms in the basement; rooms she had never visited herself, but whose existence was an open secret. They contained grotesque malformations, half-human monsters. Most were the issue of men who looked on with pleasure while their wives were pleasured by rutting dogs and squealing pigs. And later, driven mad by the sight of their terrible offspring, these debased fathers became inmates of the asylum. They were silent in the rooms above, moving their chairs to follow the fall of sunlight while their monster children howled and wept in the darkness below.

The Chapples had three children. Richard was autistic. His hair was neat and he wore tank-tops and National Health spectacles. Everyone ignored him. And there were two teenage girls who were identical twins. They wore dark pageboy haircuts and the same clothes. Pat and David Chapple could tell them apart without hesitation. Either that, or the girls didn't bother to correct them.

David Chapple often called round to Duff Street. He came on Christmas Day, in his uniform, to rest his big, copper's feet.

He tried out my toys. A big policeman, still in his hat under the tinsel, bent over my presents, asking about them with real curiosity. Then he sat on the sofa and crossed his long legs at the ankle. He drank his Barley Cup, had a mince pie and wished us all a 'Merry Christmas', then went back on the beat.

For my tenth birthday, Derek gave me a book called *Phenomena*. It was a hardback, white, with a medieval lithograph on the cover. It was about rains of fishes, stigmata, ghosts, UFOs, spontaneous human combustion. I was tormented by it.

When I showed the book to David Chapple, he flicked through without pausing – not even to double-take on the horrible photograph of the nun. She was looking to heaven in a state of joyous ecstasy. Black blood seeped from her eyes in rivulets. Nor was David bothered by the remains of Dr John Irving Bentley. The photograph showed a walking-frame that had toppled onto a white porcelain lavatory. On the floor was a single human leg, burned off just above the knee. The foot was still obscenely clad in an old man's soft shoe. The rest of Dr Bentley had gone. The floor beneath him had burned through, but the rest of the room was left undamaged by the fierce heat of his weird combustion. The exact circumstances of Dr Bentley's death still required explanation.

David closed the book, satisfied. He said, 'So. Are you interested in this stuff?'

I said, 'Aye.'

He looked at me for a long time. He made a decision. He reached into his pocket and produced his wallet. From the wallet he withdrew a photograph. He kept its face turned away from me.

He leaned forward. He was very tall.

He said, 'Now I don't want to show you this if it's going to scare you. Because I'm telling you, it's pretty creepy.'

The atmosphere in the room contracted, like flesh pricked with a pin.

I didn't want to see it.

I said, 'Can I see it?'

He gave me a twinkling look and turned the photograph.

It showed an old churchyard; tree-bordered, well tended. The gravestones were crumbling and spotted with lichen. Above the nearest of them floated an old man. He was a shepherd. He carried a long crozier. His hair was white, blunt and clumpy, as if he'd cut it himself. His face was lined and weathered. Below the knee, his legs faded away. He looked directly at the camera.

I looked at the photo.

I said, 'How did you get this?'

David said, 'I took it.'

I looked at him. 'Really,' I said.

'Really,' he said, 'I took it.'

'Where?'

'Corstorphine.'

I passed the photograph back to him, and he smiled at me and tucked it back into his wallet. Although it would be many years before I learned what was meant by double exposure,

I knew the photograph was a fake: it was too good. But sometimes, you just can't help believing.

On Tuesday afternoons, the church held a youth club. I went
there to cheat at volleyball and squeeze people until they passed
out. Mum walked me up there. She took the dog, who stretched
out like a pointer, her ears pressed close to her auburn head. She
whined and strained at the leash. Mum fought to drag her to
heel, yanking back on the choke-chain. But the dog was strong.
She pulled and yelped. Saliva oozed from her tongue and gathered in a froth at her lips. Behind her, Mum half-jogged in her
shoes, like someone being dragged by a kite. She had pain in her
elbow for years, the nagging ghost of my dog.

The youth club didn't involve prayers or any other form of
observance. It was just Mormon children playing games while
their mothers met to discuss successful home-making.

I enjoyed playing volleyball. I was the youngest player on
court and the missionaries let me serve by lobbing the ball over-
arm.

Outside, when it was sunny, the children played another
game. It involved a kind of resurrection. You took twenty deep
breaths, deep as you could make them. You held the twentieth
breath, as if you were about to duck your head under water.
Then someone came up behind you, wrapped you in a bear hug
and squeezed, as hard as they could.

When they squeezed, the world went quiet. Then everything faded out like a Polaroid developing in reverse. You woke
on the grass, looking up at a ring of grinning Mormon faces.
You stood up, shaky, laughing, a bit scared. Then it was your

turn to squeeze someone else. You counted out their twenty breaths then embraced them, hard. Their face went purple. They went limp in your arms.

It was hard to believe they weren't joking. Their eyes rolled back, showing white. They became semi-liquid and twice as heavy. You stumbled to catch your balance and half dumped, half-lay them in the grass. You looked at them. Their eyes were closed.

We gathered in a circle, sniggering. We were scared that whoever lay on the grass was dead. When their eyes opened, I was one of the grinning Mormon faces they saw. I was grinning because I was pleased to see them alive. I was pleased because I was relieved. I was relieved because I didn't want to be in trouble. It was a popular game.

Then, under the dappled shade of a tree that overhung the church's perimeter, a girl lay unconscious for much too long. She just lay there, like an uncurled fern. Somebody poked her with their toe. She didn't move.

A younger girl kneeled and reached out. She touched the silent girl's hair. Abruptly, the girl sat upright. She looked around. She did it like a robot. Then she began to scream.

The circle around her widened as we backed away. Our smiles flickered like old lightbulbs and died.

The girl sat there, in the lilac shadows on the summer grass, screaming. Then she scrambled to her feet and ran away. We followed. The girl looked over her shoulder and saw us, following. She screamed even more and ran even faster.

So we kept chasing her. But not too fast: nobody wanted to actually catch her. We drove her round the perimeter of the church. It was like the closing scene from Benny Hill. When an Elder came out to investigate the screaming, its pitch shifting like a siren as the girl ran round the church, he found her in a state of berserk hysteria.

It took three or four missionaries to calm her down. She shrieked and struggled in their gentle grip. She scratched at their faces and pulled at their shirts and ties. She kicked and spat.

It was hard for the rest of us to look innocent, but we tried.

An ambulance took the girl away. She had stopped screaming by then. The ambulance men wrapped her in a grey blanket and guided her into the ambulance.

She had run because she feared for her soul: when she woke on the grass, she'd seen the blue sky and a circle of demons, grinning maliciously down on her. When she ran, the demons followed, capering at her heels. They chased her round and round the church.

That was the last time we played the game.

But it was not necessary to play it in order to see demons. Demons were everywhere. The Devil squatted in the corners and the cracks, keeping counsel with the scuttling mice in their million hordes. He owned the air and the waters – Mormons, whose spiritual heartland was a desert, did not like to swim – and he dogged my footsteps. I sensed him leering in the shadows behind me.

On my way home from school, I found an interesting scrap of jewellery. It was gold paste, set with red and blue gems. It looked like a piece of Tutankhamen's headpiece. It was lying in the gutter. I picked it up and put it in my pocket, and when I got home I showed it to Mum.

She frowned. She took it from me and examined it under the window. She twisted it this way and that. The light shattered into lozenges of gold and red and green that shimmered on the wall. Her brow knit even deeper. Her mouth pursed and twisted.

She said, 'I don't like it. Get rid of it.'

I said, 'No way.'

But Mum had sensed a powerful evil radiating from it. She threw it out the window. I watched it spinning through the air, catching the light, then falling from sight.

On my way to school the next day, I looked for it. It couldn't have fallen far from the window. But, if the Devil had put the golden paste fragment in my path, he also saw fit to remove it.

But it wasn't the Devil: I knew the Devil. I knew him because Derek had acquainted us. Derek told me about the terrible things people did to each other. He told me about brutality and venality and rape and mutilation. He made me watch the news when it was bad, just so I would understand what an evil place the world could be.

To be in the dominion of the Devil was to be subjugated by terror and humiliation. It was to have stripped from you everything that was yours: your house, your family, your body, your mind.

Evil was intelligent, but not wise. It was inventive, but not clever. It could not construct; it could only desolate. Evil was shit and blood and torn limbs and eyes rent from sockets. It was starving children suckling at the breasts of raped and murdered mothers. Evil was cannibalism and it was zombies raised from cold graves by dark gods. It was a thrashing sacrament of chicken blood and menstrual fluid. Evil was the loss of all control, all wit, all humanity. Evil was a beast.

Evil could manifest as the Devil, who in turn could manifest as a gentleman. One day, I might even meet him, disguised as such. But, beneath his good smell and his smile there would be a faint stink, like perishing fruit and human shit. And when Satan knew you'd smelled him, he'd reveal himself; he'd show you all his boiling rage and his furious hate and his aching lust, the leaking pus and the flies and the creeping maggots of his face. His compulsion to annihilate, disfigure, putrefy.

I knew the Devil, and I understood him, and one day on the radio I heard his voice. It was on a radio programme.

Between August 1977 and September 1978, Peggy Harper and her four children, who lived in a council house in Enfield, were afflicted by every poltergeist phenomena ever recorded. There were unexplained sounds. Strange objects materialized. There was knocking on walls. Something unseen wrenched Peggy Harper's daughters from their beds. It threw them across the room. Pressed them to the ceiling.

Peggy Harper called in the Society for Psychical Research, which in turn contacted an investigator called Maurice Grosse. Soon the newspapers learned of the story. The other media were close behind.

Maurice Grosse had made recordings of a harsh, male voice that emanated from the throat of a girl called Janet. Janet was twelve years old, the same age as the girl in *The Exorcist*. It claimed several identities. It discoursed in obscenities. One of its personalities claimed to be called Bill. Bill said he'd died in the house, an old man. It was this I heard on the radio, during a programme about the Enfield Poltergeist.

A BBC journalist was interviewing Janet, who was in a trance. He asked to whom he was speaking. An abominable, guttural voice replied: 'Bill.'

It was the voice of an evil, unsexed, malicious old man. It was the kind of voice that belonged to men who hung around stinking public lavatories, waiting for boys my age to wander inside. The kind of man who might slit my belly with a fish knife and wolf on my insides.

That was enough. I turned off the radio. I didn't even want to touch it, as if it might in some way be contaminated; as if Bill might leap into the wires and travel at the speed of light, through my fingertips and into my body. I imagined his terrible, cracked voice emerging from my throat.

At night, I tried to concentrate on Jesus, on his white robes and his soft beard and his smiling eyes. I thought about the white-teethed missionaries who let me cheat at volleyball, clapping whenever I scored an unearned point. But my mind always returned to the stinking, shivering darkness where Bill and *The Exorcist* lurked, like cold currents just beneath the surface of a sun-warmed river.

I couldn't discuss my fear of the devil, my terror of possession. I feared even to give voice to it, because to give it words would make it real. Even to think of it sent me into panic. It swelled inside me like a balloon. It swelled and I readied myself. If it should burst I'd go mad. But it always deflated and left me exhausted, like someone shipwrecked and washed up on a dirty shore. It happened at home, at school, in the street: a mushroom cloud of madness, growing inside me. Then receding. The blast wave sucking backwards.

Alone in the darkness, I tallied it. Our block of flats was, say, 150 years old. There were four floors. One flat on the ground floor, three flats on each of the others. So, how many people had died in this building since it was built? How many had died in this flat? How many had died in my *bedroom*? And how many of their shades gathered to scrutinize me while I slept, crowding the square window that overlooked the hallway?

I thought of them, purblind, wandering the cold stone floors. Jesus was barely with me then. His glow faded like a torch whose batteries are old. And I feared to pray, because to pray would admit my helplessness. The ghosts – perhaps just one of them, the most ravenous, the one with teeth and hate and a screech – would latch onto it like a radar signal and would race through the walls and into my body and it would throw me and shake me and it would milk obscenities from my mouth like turds, and Mum and Derek would find me, jammed against the ceiling, white-eyed and growling.

There was an exorcism rite. It was one of the secrets imparted to Derek during a priesthood meeting. He told me about it. Any Mormon who sensed an evil presence should raise his right arm, bent square at the elbow, just as Elder Follett had held his arm, the evening he baptized me. He should then demand in the name of Jesus Christ that Lucifer be gone from the room.

But the thought of Derek rushing in, throwing the door aside, and seeing me being whipped this way and that by a nameless malevolence only served to acknowledge the possibility of it.

Still awake, I chewed on mathematics. I was ten years old. I could expect to live until I was seventy. That meant I'd already lived *more than ten per cent of my entire life*. I was at least ten per cent of the way to becoming a white-eyed revenant.

At the thought of the numbers, I lurched with vertigo, as if the bed tumbled beneath me.

Eventually, I confided to Derek that I was scared of dying. That I lay in bed, unable to sleep for thinking about it.

He looked tender and ruminative.

He said, 'Perhaps Bishop Steele will guide you.'

He took tremendous pride in this counsel. I could see it in his face. He beamed with satisfaction. But neither I nor my anxiety was the point of it. I was incidental: I had simply provided him with an opportunity to prove himself a first-rate family man, a fine Mormon, a virtuous patriarch. I saw it in his changing face. His new faith had given him another shape to adopt. And here he was, contorting himself into it. Beneath his skin, bones were easing from their joints, making new connections, new configurations.

I didn't go to see Bishop Steele, because I didn't want his counsel. I wanted Derek's. And when Mrs Elmsley in the flat below died, she became another of the ghosts who wandered the corridor outside my room, tarrying until the day came when they could return to warm child flesh.

In bed, I read comics. The words, familiar and memorized, were like a mantra, a protective rune. By then, Mum and Derek were asleep. I could feel the darkness all around, full of hate, inhabited.

18

Mum became friends with a young woman called Sister Dixon. She wore a blonde pageboy, wedged at the back; men's shirts, jumbo cords. She was from Glasgow, but she was working in Edinburgh as a school secretary.

Mum invited her to Sunday lunch, then to Family Home Evening. Sister Dixon was lonely. Her family and friends were in Glasgow. There was some tension with her mother, some unhappiness.

Soon, she was coming round several times a week. She brought her guitar, a six-string acoustic, resting it on her knees in the bus. She played 'The Old Rugged Cross'.

She was always cold. She wore big, woolly sweaters, scarves, bobble hats. She got chillblains on her thin, blue hands and feet. She wrote comical poems, one of which ended: 'Why do I wear six pairs of socks?/ It's freezin', that's the reason.'

As she and Mum grew close, it felt awkward to keep calling her Sister Dixon. So we just called her Yvonne.

She was a fan of *Star Wars*. Her favourite character was Princess Leia, but she liked Han Solo too. (I didn't believe that people whose favourite character was Luke Skywalker really liked *Star Wars*.) We went to see *Close Encounters of the Third Kind*.

For *Grease*, we queued for hours, eating sweets and talking. That weekend, she bought me the *Grease* photonovel: a paperback book of film stills, captioned like a comic. And she lent me her copy of the *Grease* double album.

I played it on Derek's record player. I pretended that my favourite song was 'Greased Lightnin'', but really it was 'Sandy', especially the bit when Danny Zuko wonders what they will say, on Monday at school.

One morning, we found tatters of the album cover – Danny Zuko's eye and quiff, the black, capped-sleeve of his T-shirt, Sandy's virginal smile – distributed like confetti all over the room. The records were scratched and bitten and chewed. Even to me, it looked like an act of calculated malice, or perhaps suicidal self-hatred. But I still wept when Derek beat the dog for it.

She showed her teeth. He slapped her in the snout, open-handed, for her insolence. Her head whipped to the side and he slapped it back straight, so she was looking at him while he hit her. The dog had caused him to be embarrassed: had destroyed someone else's property, forcing him to apologize. More than anything, Derek hated to be embarrassed. It made the power go out of him.

Yvonne took me to the Science Fiction Bookshop. She bought me a book called *Doc Savage: Man of Bronze*. We went to see *Airplane!*, and *The Empire Strikes Back*. At some point, the half-joke about being my sister stopped being a joke at all.

She began to call my mother 'Ma'. Although Mum had not been with her own at their weddings or the birth of their children, she accepted Yvonne as a daughter.

And so we became a bigger, wholly fictitious family. I had a sister who was not my sister, and a dad who was not my dad. My sister was in no way related to the woman she called Ma, and she called the man I knew as Dad by his first name.

We had been pulled by that strange attractor, the compulsion to forge from what we are given and the places we find ourselves, something ordinary, something normal, something to which to belong.

19

In September 1980, I moved into Primary 7: the oldest class: There were no more big kids to avoid. They'd moved on, to become small kids at a bigger school. I was eleven. But, over the course of the summer holiday, I'd mutated. My voice had broken. There was hair on my upper lip, on my legs, on my genitals. And I'd grown. Suddenly, Tam Higgins and I were the tallest in our class.

Our teacher was called Mrs Simmons. She was a sometimes cantankerous woman, curly-headed and greying. She wore tweed skirts and clumpy shoes. Once, vexed by the incessant braying of her surname – *Mrs Simmons! Mrs Simmons!* – she slapped the desk and shouted, 'For God's sake my name is *Margaret*.'

Nobody ever called her Margaret.

In the top, right-hand drawer of her desk, she kept *the belt*: a fearsome creature, a thick strip of brown leather, fringed at one end. When the class grew rowdy, she removed it from the drawer and laid it on the table. She never used it. But once or twice she hit the desk with it, and that was enough.

Quietly, Mrs Simmons often gave me books. *Red Planet* by Robert Heinlein, *The Flying Saucer Conspiracy* by Donald E. Keyhoe, *2001* by Arthur C. Clarke.

She created the Top Group, a little island of six children who sat on a square of tables at the head of the class. It consisted of Brian Hunt, who was still called Babs, Judith Collins, Nicola Barton, Paul Stewart and me. Paul Stewart was new. He was tanned, with blonde hair.

Then Tam Higgins was moved up. Tam my neighbour: he lived in the ground-floor flat. Suzie was his dog. His brother had once tried to stub out a cigarette on my eye. Tam was a pale, lanky kid, messy-haired. His fringe fell over his eyes. He wore scruffy jeans and old trainers. He liked Madness.

I liked Madness too. They were a band from North London. I liked their exaggerated Englishness. I saved up to buy their album. They were pictured on the sleeve, doing something like a conga line. They wore good suits and narrow ties, pork pie hats and Dr Marten boots. I played the album again and again, on my little mono Dansette record player, a gift from Brother Burton.

Brother Burton was a nervous, liver-spotted and softly spoken old man. He smelled of whisky and cigarettes, but nobody ever mentioned it. One Sunday, on the way to sacrament meeting, he stopped me and placed a gift-wrapped box in my hands: the record player.

He said, 'Here you are, son, from Brother Burton.'

He moved shyly on before I'd even registered receipt of it, let alone that it was a gift. I hurried through the milling congregation to find him and thank him. But it felt somehow ungrateful to ask why he'd decided to give it to me, and I never found out.

In my bedroom, I practised the appropriate dance moves, a kind of staccato stomp, as pictured by Chas Smash on the back of the sleeve. Because the bedroom was small, I could smell the plastic of the album and see the stylus riding the warp of the vinyl.

Derek didn't like Madness. They weren't Mormon enough. But Mum was reassured by their suits and their crew-cuts and she pronounced them 'clean-cut young men'. I itched to correct her mistake, because Madness belonged to me. But I knew a tactical miscalculation when I saw one, and clean-cut young men Madness remained, notwithstanding their songs about razor-blade alleys and underwear thieves and dirty old men who still lived with their mothers.

Paul Stewart gave me posters of Madness from the centre pages of *Smash Hits* magazine. I sellotaped them to my bedroom wall. I dreamed of Camden Town, which was the place they lived and sang about. I'd never seen Camden Town, but it sounded to me like the most English place in the world.

20

Derek left the supermarket in Corstorphine. I didn't know the circumstances. He wouldn't talk about it. But he seemed to leave with a lot of money – enough to lease and stock a corner shop on the far side of town. He called the shop Romco. He thought it was a good name for the retail empire it would someday become.

It was one of those small stores that tried to sell everything: milk, bread, beans, chocolate, toilet paper, lightbulbs. It had that small-shop smell. Derek stood behind the counter in a brown overall. When a customer entered, he gave them a big welcoming grin and his eyes followed them as they browsed.

I no longer had to spend time in the basement of St Cuthbert's, but the back room of Romco had the same cardboard boxes, the same damp smell: the smell of the secret room behind all shops. I felt at home there, reading and drawing while Derek stood at the counter, bagging J-Cloths and scouring pads and Fairy Liquid.

Once, while a customer waited, he popped out the back to get something, some carrier-bags or a length of string or some Sellotape. He told the customer he'd be just a moment and he smiled, then turned and stepped through the fringed plastic curtain. The grin dropped from his face. It didn't fade, like a polite smile at an unfunny joke: it fell as if weighted at the corners, and it took his eyes with it. For a moment, while he thought nobody could see him, Derek's face was utterly vacant.

I looked away, because it was like seeing someone naked. But naked people looked human and silly and tender: you felt sorry for them. Derek's naked face belonged to something ancient, something unspeakably resentful.

It made me sad, and later that evening, I hugged him and kissed his cheek and I told him I loved him.

He peeled my hands away to look at me. He laughed. He said, 'What's all this in aid of?'

I said, 'Nothing,' and he laughed some more, because he didn't believe me. He thought I wanted something. But I wasn't laughing, and when I looked at Mum she wasn't laughing either. She had the dishcloth in her hand, and she was looking at us, and I could feel things changing.

He bought a van, a big, green Commer, very old and battered. He used it to transport stock for Romco's shelves. My classmates called it the Armoured Tank.

There was something normal and unmalicious about their mockery, so I didn't mind – besides, everyone wanted to ride in the back of the Armoured Tank. One afternoon, Derek obliged. He drove some kids home: Babs and Colin Fairgreaves and Paul Stewart. We jostled in the back, like paratroopers waiting for the drop.

The next day, everyone took the piss again, mocking Derek's posh voice, but only because they were embarrassed to have been so excited, just to be bumping around in the back of his old van.

After school and at weekends, Tam Higgins and I began to hang around together. We walked all over Edinburgh. We talked about Madness and *Star Wars* and sex: about how much we wanted to do it, and who we wanted to do it to. I wanted to do it to everyone.

We walked into town and wandered round the shops. I took him to the Science Fiction Bookshop. We went to John Menzies on Princes Street. It was a big shop, on two or three floors. It sold toys and books, newspapers and magazines, singles and albums. It was a good shop.

We went to the magazine section. We looked at the top shelf, at *Club* and *Men Only* and *Playboy*. The women on the covers were smiling: their hands or their forearms covered their breasts, squashing them a bit. Or they were sitting, covering themselves with a crossed leg.

My eyes alighted, flicked away, alighted. I'd spotted a magazine called *Club: Celebrity Edition*. In it were naked pictures of famous women. On the cover was Victoria Principal, who played Pam Ewing in *Dallas*. It became a matter of immediate and absolute importance that I see Victoria Principal without her clothes on.

Tam and I were tall for our age. We had scrubby moustaches. But nobody would believe we were eighteen. So we couldn't buy the magazine, even if we'd had the courage to try.

Tam nudged me in the ribs. He said, 'Knock it.'

We stood together, gazing up at Victoria Principal. She looked younger than she did in *Dallas*. She had a heavy fringe. Inside, she was naked.

I said, 'You do it.'

He said, 'You.'

We spent some time doing that.

I said, 'All right, then.'

I had no choice. My breathing was loud in my ears.

The adult magazines were shelved over more sedate periodicals, some of which were given over to model aircraft. I selected one of these and took it from the shelf. I flicked through and made interested noises, looking at the skilfully painted Stukas and Hurricanes and Lancasters.

I mimed to whoever might be watching that I was seriously considering buying the magazine. Then I communicated that, although the magazine was very interesting, I'd probably buy it another day. I went to replace it on the shelf. But, distracted by some other interesting journal, I unintentionally placed it one shelf too high, with the soft pornography.

But my hands were shaking and, when I tried to slip *Airfix Modeller* next to *Club: Celebrity Edition*, half a dozen magazines fell from the shelf and tumbled in noisy, flapping slow motion to the floor.

There was a long moment. Then I stooped and picked up the *Men Only*s and the *Playboy*s and the *Club*s and the *Airfix Modeller*, and I replaced them all on the shelf, in their proper places. I stood back and pretended none of it had happened.

Tam called me a radge. I felt like a radge. I didn't know what a radge was.

But I needed to see Victoria Principal naked. I waited for as long as I could stand it, until everybody who'd looked at us was looking away. Then, still blushing, I stood on tiptoes and, from the top shelf, took down a *Club: Celebrity Edition*, shoving it immediately up and inside my jacket. Then Tam and I about-turned like well-square-bashed squaddies and strode across John Menzies, to the back door. A check-out assistant followed our progress with some compassion.

At the back door, I tried not to run. Then I pressed the magazine to my side with my elbow and ran. I was weightless. I was a good runner. I was very fast. Tam was at my heels.

We rounded the corner and turned onto Princes Street. It was crowded. We slowed. Then we began to run again. We hopped on a maroon and cream bus and stamped up to the top deck. We sat in the front seat. We still hadn't looked at each other.

We got off the bus outside Dalry School and headed for the no-man's-land between Dalry and the West Approach Road, behind the petrol station. We went to a bushy, shaded area and sat down. We looked around, in case a security guard had followed us and was waiting in ambush. You could just hear the traffic.

Then I took the magazine from under my jacket. In my haste and terror, I'd stolen two copies. I hid my surprise and passed one to Tam like a benediction. Then I opened the magazine and flicked through it. I ignored the flash of celebrity breasts and celebrity thighs until I found Victoria Principal.

She wasn't naked. She was topless, in faded blue jeans. She was smiling. The photo was old. She looked different. But there she was.

Eventually, Tam and I stashed the *Club: Celebrity Edition*s in a scavenged carrier-bag and placed it in a soil hollow beneath a lump of concrete. I thought about Moroni and the golden plates.

If you knew where to look – under bushes, by railway lines, holes in walls – kids' places abounded with pornography that had been stolen, ogled and discarded. Tam and I began to collect it. It was much easier than stealing from shops. We went on porno hunts. We usually found something. We assessed it, discussed it, usually kept it. In the carrier-bag beneath the lump of concrete, our collection grew thick-paged and damp. Pages would rip when you tried to turn them. When they dried, they dried into a mass.

One day, we found a curious magazine. It was in black and white and badly reproduced. The women inside weren't pretty and they weren't smiling: they weren't even naked. They were dressed as schoolgirls. They posed, bent over old-fashioned school desks, the kind with lids, with pleated skirts lifted above their arses. Men stood with canes rested against the women's exposed buttocks or posed, mostly out of shot, while the women in uniform bent over and sucked them off, their eyes looking at the camera. Or the women sat on the desks with their legs spread and their shirts open and one breast exposed. They looked angry. Tam and I looked through this book, mystified and unexcited, then agreed to put it back where we found it, under a bush at the graveyard end of the wasteland.

Several times a week, Mum, Derek and I passed that scrubby no-man's-land on the way to church. It made me feel good to know they were there, those grinning, naked women; those precious books, buried in the earth.

I didn't worry about God. How could he disapprove, when he'd sired his own son in lust, like a stud-bull?

The Mormon God was not just a physical being, an old man with a white beard; before becoming God, he'd been a mortal, an ordinary man – albeit an ordinary man on a distant planet. He was conceived through sexual intercourse and nurtured in the womb. He suckled at the breast.

His human name had been Elohim. He ascended to Godhood by obeying the will of his own God, who himself had once been mortal man, on yet another planet. There were infinite Gods, infinite planets.

Being a physical being, God naturally had a functioning penis. It became erect in the presence of Mary, the mother of Jesus. Into Mary, God inserted himself. Inside her, he worked himself to orgasm. Presumably, he was a skilled lover, leaving Mary satisfied as well as fertilized. But, whatever his dexterity, it remained that Mary was a married woman: God fucked Joseph's young wife and got her pregnant.

I thought about it a lot. He was God, so he could do what he liked. But more importantly, he was a man. And Derek had several times gravely instructed me in the ferocious nature of male sexual desire.

To a second-rate mind, this might have looked like cuckoldry. But of course, it wasn't. God, by his very nature, cannot commit sin, and nothing that he commands can be sinful.

So I wondered what else God got up to, driven by that sinless appetite. Derek had often hinted at 'secret things' that took place inside the temple, rituals that he and Mum would undergo one day, about which they'd never be able to tell me. I wondered if Mormon women went to the temple to have sex with God. It made sense. I looked at some of the younger women in church on Sunday, and the thought filled me with queasy excitement.

Then, shortly after Derek was made a Melchizidek priest, he and Mum took a special coach to London. In the temple, their marriage was sealed to time and all eternity.

They returned tired and joyless. Neither would tell me about the marriage ceremony, or about anything else. Once again, Derek hinted darkly of an oath to silence, taken under pain of punishment, which convinced me the temple ceremony had something to do with sex. Only sex was ever kept that secret.

Eventually, worn down by my nagging interrogation, Mum surrendered a detail: now that she'd been sealed to Derek for time and all eternity, she was required to wear sacred undergarments.

I asked her to tell me what they were like.

The idea of sacred pants struck us both as hilarious. Mum got a set and held them up to the light, and my ribs hurt for the laughing. They were white long-johns, marked on the breast with compass and square.

I said, 'Do you *wear* these?'

She was laughing. She couldn't believe it. She said, 'Yes!'

'Are you wearing them now?'

'Yes!'

The saintly long-johns were contrived to deflate the appetite of any man who sought to gaze upon the disrobing wife of a good Mormon patriarch. Only the patriarch himself – and his patriarch, God – was permitted to be aroused by a Mormon woman, or to know her full beauty.

We shouldn't have laughed about the holy pants in front of Derek. But there was nothing funnier than being told 'please be serious' by a man demanding that due reverence be extended to his knee-length undergarments. He grew white-lipped and red faced and sent us from the room.

Undaunted, I nagged Mum to tell me something about what she'd seen in the temple. Anything. There were rumours of *proof*. That people who went there and made the appropriate, terrible vows, were shown something – something that rendered their faith beyond question.

I said, 'You must be able to tell me one thing. Just one little thing. A teensie-weensie thing. Tiny tiny tiny.'

She said, 'I can't.'

So my imagination grew rich with Byzantine ceremonies, with robes and chanting and smoke and mystic chants. And I wasn't far wrong.

The ceremony[1] began with washing and anointing of the initiate. For this Mum and Derek were naked but for a cotton poncho. Their heads were oiled. Each limb and member was touched and a blessing pronounced upon it. The celebrant reached under the poncho to touch their 'shoulders, back, breasts, bowels and loins'. Then each of them had another name, a secret name, whispered into their ear.

Derek was told Mum's secret name: he'd need it if he wished to summon her to heaven. But his new name was none of Mum's concern. It was between Derek and God.

Then Mum was dressed in white, with a veil. Derek's outfit, also white, was accessorized with a soft white cap and a green apron in the shape of a fig leaf. They joined many others, also jauntily attired, in a large auditorium. Women on the left, men on the right, separated by an aisle.

The endowment ceremony took the form of a dramatic, filmed presentation that addressed the 'terrible questions': the eternal nature of God and Jesus Christ, the pre-existence and eternal nature of man, the sanctity and eternal nature of the family. The reality of Satan.

The hero of the film was Elohim, which was God's other name. Lucifer, naturally, was the villain. Jesus and Adam also appeared, using the names Jehovah and Michael.

Elohim said, 'Jehovah, Michael, see yonder is matter unorganized. Go ye down and organize it into a world like unto the worlds that we have heretofore formed. Call your labours the First Day and bring me word.'

And off Jesus went, to create the world on God's behalf.

There were hours of this.

And later, Peter, James and John appeared. They instructed the initiates in the secret handshakes and passwords that would be required for them to gain entry to Heaven.[2]

Only after all that did Mum and Derek take part in their second secret marriage ceremony, so different from the first. The symbolism of it was never explained to them, or to anyone else. When the ceremony was finished, they just bought some holy underwear and came home on the coach.

Mum hadn't joined the church to reflect on theological allegory, and she found the endowment ceremony disturbing. She put it to the back of her mind and laughed at the silly under-garments that God from that day forth required her to wear.

But Derek understood. That afternoon in the temple, he promised never to reveal its secrets, on pain of his throat being cut from ear to ear and his tongue torn out by the roots. And he never did.

Derek understood secrets. He understood why they must be kept. And he knew there was more to come, because secrets beget secrets. That was the way of things.

21

Romco didn't last. Locals came out of curiosity, bought some odds and ends, then left and didn't come back. Soon Derek was spending all day at the counter, waiting for business that never arrived.

When he closed the doors, ending another dream of empire, he blamed the customers and walked immediately into another job. He always did. He took the position of deputy-manager at an immense cash and carry, a warehouse that supplied shops and businesses. I was proud when I saw him in this sweeping hangar, to think him in charge of it. He was proud, too.

He sold the Armoured Tank, replacing it with a green Skoda. I said, 'Why did you sell it?'

He twirled the jangling car-keys round his index finger. 'Because we're going to need a car.'

'Why?'

He grinned. 'Because we're about to move house.'

Long before, the Duff Street tenements had been scheduled

for demolition. Nobody else wanted to live there, which is how Mum and Derek moved so quickly to the top of the council waiting list. After spending a year together in a bed and breakfast, the flat at 30 Duff Street hadn't looked too bad and they were pleased to accept a tenancy. But now it was time for the building to be demolished.

I said, 'What about school?'

Derek said, 'You'll be staying at Dalry for the time being.'

I relaxed.

I said, 'Where's the new flat?'

'House,' he said. 'We're moving to a house.'

'Where?'

I was excited.

He smiled. 'Wait and see.'

So we went downstairs and got in the green Skoda, and he drove us there.

Even on a large-scale map, Tarbrax was a tiny village, little more than a cluster of mouse droppings. It was about 20 miles west of Edinburgh. We got there by driving along the A17 which, Derek told me, was known as the *lang wang*. (It meant long bootlace, not long penis.) Then we turned off the A17 and onto a wandering, rose-pink road that ran between fields of sheep and cattle. After a mile or two, we turned right.

Tarbrax was white, terraced cottages assembled round a village green. It had no shop; just a pub called the Lazy Y, where plaid-shirted truckers and farmers went on Saturday night, to hear people singing songs recorded by Gentleman Jim Reeves and Tammy Wynette. The nearest shop was seven miles away, in West Calder.

Our new house was a whitewashed cottage on the corner of
Crosswood Terrace. The front door opened onto a gravel track.
Stepping across it, you entered a small, fenced garden which
gave onto a wild pitch of long, wet grass, from which poked the
crooks of an old shed and the curves of an even older caravan.

'A quarter-acre,' said Derek, surveying it. 'I thought we'd get
some chickens. Fresh eggs in the morning.'

I ignored him. I hoped he'd forget about the chickens.

I scanned the horizon and pointed. I said, 'What's that?'

From the earth at the edge of the village, a great bite had
been taken. Behind this ragged scoop receded a mountain-sized
wedge. It was the highest thing for many miles, a monolith.
The area of desolation dwarfed Tarbrax.

'That's the bing,' said Derek. 'This used to be a mining area.
The bing is all the stuff they dug up.'

Oil shale had been mined and heated to extract paraffin oil.
The spent shale, red from the burning, was swept into just
such bings. They were larger than those that attended coal
mines. Vegetation did not grow on them.

I said, 'Am I allowed to play on it?'

'I expect so.'

'Can I walk the dog there?'

'The dog will love it here.'

He said it like it really mattered to him, like he wanted the
dog to be happy, and in that moment it was true.

After exploring the house, we walked through the wet quarter-acre, soaking our trousers to the knees. Then the sun began
to set and we drove back to Edinburgh. It took a while. The
lang wang undulated through commercial pine forests. We

drove for miles in tree-lined darkness. An oncoming car was a blue glow on the crest of an approaching hill, then a white rush of headlights. Then there was darkness again, the trees to the side, the night sky above.

We moved house that weekend. People from the church came to help us load the hired van. David Chapple drove it for us.

Mum, Derek and I went in the Skoda. The dog sat in the back with me. We didn't take the cat: a few days before, Derek had kicked her out for shitting in the hallway. He picked her up and kicked her through the door like a rugby ball. I saw her on the street once – I thought it was her – and tried to lure her home. But she ignored me and walked regally by.

I looked at the graffiti that said *Neil Go Home*, and then we drove past it: Mum, Derek, me and the dog.

The cottage on Crosswood Terrace was small and it smelled of gas, undercut with coal and mildew. I slept on a camp-bed in Mum and Derek's bedroom. There was no bath. A shower room had been added in the 1960s, a small extension off the kitchen. It was cold getting in and even colder getting out, especially when there was snow outside.

Mum couldn't drive a car and didn't want to learn. But there were no buses to Tarbrax, so in the morning she went into Edinburgh with Derek and me. She got to work several hours before her shift officially began – so, because she had nowhere else to go, she began to work full-time hours for part-time pay. She said she had no choice, but didn't look for another job. She was just accustomed to working at St Cuthbert's.

In the morning, we drove through the pine forests, twenty

miles east, into Edinburgh and the sunrise. Our route took us right past Dalry School, but much too early. Nobody was there yet, not even the teachers, so I stayed in the car until we got to St Cuthbert's. Mum and I sat in the basement while everyone had their early morning cup of tea. Then it was time to catch the bus to school. It took another half-hour.

After school, I bussed it back to St Cuthbert's and waited in the basement until Mum finished work. Then we caught another bus, this time to the cash and carry. We sat in Derek's car, waiting until all the customers had gone and he appeared in his camel coat and his string-backed driving gloves. He got in and said hello, then drove us twenty miles back home again.

Sometimes on a Wednesday afternoon, Mum and I went to visit Rhona, who'd left St Cuthbert's when her husband bought into a funeral director's. Now they lived in a very floral flat, directly above it.

She told me about the bodies. She liked having them there; they felt like friends.

She said, 'It's my job to make them feel at home while they're with us.'

Sometimes, when she went downstairs, she might find one of them sitting up in an open coffin. It had been quite upsetting at first, she said, and she'd dreaded going down there in the morning.

('Dreaded it,' she said, with a delighted grin.)

But there was nothing to be scared of. Nowadays she chatted to them all quite happily, sitting up or not. They were only bodies.

I thought of them, downstairs, dead, as I ate my cake.

We began attending church in Livingstone. It was the nearest city, a gaunt concrete new town, built in the 1960s to ease Edinburgh's overcrowding.

The first time Derek drove us there, he got lost. Between his teeth, he hissed, 'The bloody road signs are all wrong. They don't make sense.'

I saw landmarks – pubs, shops, parks – pass us for the second, third and fourth time.

He said, 'It's a joke. It's a bloody joke.'

Mum and I sat, rigid-faced and avoiding eye-contact, trying not to laugh.

Eventually we found the place. Because the Livingstone branch didn't have a building of its own, they held their services in a hired school hall. The school was empty because it was Sunday.

Derek parked the car and we hurried inside. It was strange, walking through the school. The same smell of floor polish and faded body odour, but nobody in it.

Perhaps forty people were gathered in the echoing room, listening to the bishop. As we entered, very late, he interrupted himself. He said, 'Ah, Brother and Sister Cross.'

The congregated heads turned and cast the Mormon smile, a welcome touched with ruefulness, feeling for our embarrassment.

Derek returned his most sincere beam. In it I could see all the horror for being an object of their pity.

When the meeting ended we drove home in silence.

22

Our terrace of cottages backed onto another, which faced the village green. The cottage that opposed ours, a mirror image, was vacant. So, to solve the problem with the number of bedrooms, Derek rented it.

The other cottage was decorated in faded browns and oranges, like a box of chocolates left too long in a newsagent's window. It smelled of cold paint and damp. In the corner of the living room was a narrow walk-in cupboard. Derek knocked through the wall of it with a lump-hammer – so you stepped into a cupboard in one house and emerged in another. There was some magic to that.

Yvonne moved in with us. She had her own room in the other cottage, what would have been the bedroom. There were sheepskin rugs, a sofa, a portable TV on a low table. Her guitars were propped against the wall, next to her Abba and John Denver albums. She didn't mind me going in there to watch *Top of the Pops* and *Dallas*. (I preferred to watch *Dallas* alone.)

We shared the living room as a bedroom. I slept in a single bed in one corner, the wall covered in posters. She had a double bed in the other corner. She wore stripy cotton pyjamas and several layers of thick socks. When it was really cold, she wore a bobble hat.

At first, she motored to work on a 50cc motorcycle. Mum, Derek and I left first, but sometimes Yvonne caught up with us on the outskirts of Edinburgh, and it was good to watch her buzz through the traffic on the straining bike. But, following a near-collision on an icy junction, she sold it and bought a car. It was another Skoda, the colour of Caramac.

Because she was a school secretary, she started work later and finished earlier than Derek, so – now she had a car – Mum and I went with her in the mornings instead. In the afternoon, we waited in her car until she walked up, in her work clothes, and said hello. She and Mum were always pleased to see each other. Yvonne made Mum laugh. Sometimes they laughed all the way home.

In February 1981, shortly after I turned twelve, I was ordained into the Aaronic priesthood. My duties were to demonstrate obedience and to provide practical assistance in all matters pertaining to the running of the church. It was also my role to pass the sacrament. My companions in this task were two boys called Michael and Adi.

But I had become bored by the church. Getting up early on Sunday and putting on my smart clothes and driving to Livingstone, then listening to all those identical testimonies had become passionless and routine.

During the week, we no longer attended church activities; we got home too late. Our family prayers, intoned dutifully every evening, had lost their initial intensity, the wonder and fervour of speaking directly to God. Being a Mormon had become something I did on Sundays, out of habit.

Nominating me to pray, Derek said: 'Now, Neil. This is not a criticism. But I was wondering if tonight you might vary what you say, just a little?'

I was angry. Everyone – including Derek – said the same prayer every time they were nominated. There was only so much you could say: Thank you for this, thank you for that, thank you for a loving family, thank you for the revelation of Joseph Smith and the sacrifice of your Beloved Son, we pray for a safe night's sleep. (Mum always hoped aloud that we might sleep fitfully. I never had the heart to tell her what it meant.)

I said, 'No. I'm not doing it.'

'Fine,' said Derek.

He said it with grim forbearance, as if he'd been expecting as much. He asked Yvonne instead. She glanced at me, then bowed her head and began to pray.

Neither Derek nor Mum had noticed what had become plain to at least one member of Livingstone's bishopric. In my bedroom, not particularly hidden, was the letter he'd written me:

Dear Neil
  I saw you in church today, before any of the meetings started, and I saw you were extremely unhappy . . . Times can get hard within the church Neil, but you must hold on

*to the iron rod because that is just Satan trying you and
Satan is a real person, as real as you and I, and his power is
strong enough to lower even the most holy and humble
person to the ground. To fight back at Satan you must be
more than humble, more than spiritual; you, Neil, must be
superhumble, superspiritual and superprayerful.*

*You are 12 years old, Neil, a deacon. You are maturing
and growing into a man. Many people mature before others
on the road to maturity. Your attitude to others will change
dramatically. Your voice breaks, a moustache and facial hair
grows. This is natural but it does affect your attitude
because you are at the age of questioning, wondering, and
sometimes you become unsure of things.*

God bless you, Neil, I am proud of you.

In one way, the letter was right; the age of questioning was
upon me. But in most ways, it was wrong. As it turned out,
what I had come ever more strongly to suspect about the value
of Mormon worship was accurate.

Although it claimed to be the direct, revealed word of God,
The Book of Mormon contained a number of similarities to a
novel called *View of the Hebrews*,[1] whose successful publication
preceded it by some years. And – perhaps even more surprisingly – it contained a number of errors. In *The Book of Mormon*,
the reader will find the Nephites and the Lamanites familiar
not only with horses, but with elephants, cattle, sheep, wheat,
barley, steel, wheeled vehicles, shipbuilding, sails and coins.
None of these things existed in early America. Not even the
Spanish thought to take elephants along with them.

The massacred Nephites and the genocidal Lamanites left nothing behind them: no evidence of their extensive agriculture, not a single brick of their once-great cities. There were no human remains left on the murderous field of Cumorah, where so many millions were violently slain. All there was, was a golden book. And soon enough, even that was taken into the custody of an angel.

Joseph Smith was a fraud, and not even a very good one.

Years before he dreamed up the golden plates, his mother recalled that young Joe took innocent delight in describing 'the ancient inhabitants of this continent, their dress, mode of travelling, and their animals upon which they rode; their cities, their buildings, with every particular; their mode of warfare; and also their religious worship. This he would do with as much ease, seemingly as if he had spend his whole life with them.'[2]

As a young man, Joe employed himself as a hunter-for-hire of lost Indian gold. Although this adventure has the wholesome ring of Tom Sawyer about it, such money-digging was illegal and Joe was convicted in court in Bainbridge, New York, of being 'a disorderly person and an impostor.' He was convicted in 1826: that's fully eight years after he later claimed to have met God and Jesus in the secluded copse. But the vividness of Joe's exploits would never be dulled by consistency. Even his accounts of the First Vision beam with cheerful incongruity.

Sometimes, he was fourteen when he met God, sometimes sixteen. Sometimes he was seventeen. And sometimes, it wasn't even God that he met.[3]

Only one First Vision account survives in Joe's own handwriting. There are six pages of it, dated to about 1830. Known as 'Joseph's Strange Account', it was never finished, and it was kept from public examination for more than a hundred years.[4] In the 'Strange Account', having arrived at the grim conclusion that 'there was no society or denomination that built upon the Gospel of Jesus Christ as recorded in the New Testament'[5], Joe goes for a walk in the woods where, to his surprise, he meets Jesus Christ. If God was there too, Joe neglects to mention it. It was only later, in 1842, that he thought to add the detail of Elohim's presence, floating several feet above the ground in a pillar of light. Later still, and perhaps not incidentally, Joe remembered that God had blue eyes.

One afternoon, on my way to St Cuthbert's, I saw Derek. His car had broken down on the corner of Nicholson Street. It was the beginning of the rush hour and other cars had backed up behind it. They beeped their horns and tried to creep round, into the oncoming traffic. There was a bad-tempered knot of them. Derek stalked around the Skoda as if about to kick it.

I wondered what he was doing there. He was supposed to be at work.

I didn't offer to help, because he didn't like to be patronized. So I hurried to St Cuthbert's. Mum was on the check-out, but the shop was empty of customers. Rab and Mike were stacking shelves, pausing to furtively chuck bits of packaging at one another.

Bob Cruickshank took Mum's place. She put on her coat and followed me. But when we got to the corner, Derek had gone. The traffic was flowing freely again. Mum looked at the place where his car had been. Then she looked at me.

Later, Yvonne drove us home and Mum made the tea. Derek came home to eat, which was becoming unusual. He couldn't always be home in the evening, especially if he had to supervise the cashing up.

He charged Yvonne with saying grace – she was best at it – then we ate our tea. We were watching TV.

I said, 'How's the car?'

He was chewing. He chewed five or six times, then he swallowed. He took a sip of water. He said, 'The car's fine. Why?'

'Because I saw you.'

'Saw me where?'

'Broken down, on the corner.'

'What corner?'

'The corner by Mum's work.'

He smiled. 'I'm afraid you didn't.'

'Yes, I did.'

He said, 'What nonsense is this?'

It's what he said when he saw me reading a new comic book or a science fiction novel. He'd pick it up and examine it and say it. It was a kind of joke between us.

'I saw you,' I said. 'You were broken down. You were walking round the car. I thought you were going to kick it. I went and got Mum, but by the time we got there you'd gone.'

'I'm afraid you're mistaken.'

'No I'm not.'

He looked at me. I wasn't looking at him. I was watching TV. But I could feel his eyes.

He said, 'Don't contradict me.'

'I'm not contradicting you.'

'Good.'

He went back to eating.

'But I saw you.'

He lay down the knife. He said, 'I'm warning you. Don't defy me.'

'I'm not defying you. But you were there.'

I watched TV. My heart was beating.

Mum said, 'You must've seen someone else, love.'

'I didn't see someone else.'

'Well,' said Derek. 'You certainly didn't see me.'

'Fine,' I said. 'But I saw you.'

He stood.

I stayed sitting. My eyes were on the screen.

He stood there. He was a shape in the corner of my eye.

He said, 'Go to your room.'

I wanted to leap to my feet, because I was angry. But I made myself stand slowly.

He said, 'When you're ready to apologize, you can come back in.'

'I can't apologize. I saw you.'

'Then get out of my sight.'

I entered the other cottage through the hole in the cupboard. I closed the door behind me and lay on the bed, my hands laced behind my head. I listened to them talking about me. Derek's voice was soft and full of compassion.

I heard him say, 'You can see why they're not allowed to testify in court, can't you?'

In the morning everything was normal. My hallucination was not mentioned again. It was just one of those things.

Mum had many reasons to believe Derek. At least one of them was simple: he couldn't be lying, because recently he'd been made Bishop of the Livingstone branch, and Mormon bishops didn't lie.

Now he was Bishop, Derek oversaw the running of the branch. It took up a lot of his time. He conducted the meetings. He made assignments. He presided over all pastoral and financial matters. Most of being a bishop involved being away from his family. Even on Sunday we rarely got to see him, except from a distance. He listened to everyone's problems with concern and authority.

We watched him.

It was now his responsibility to raise a tithe from his congregation. It was equal to ten per cent of their gross earnings. A tithe was used, in part, to pay for a building's upkeep, or in this case rental of the school. It was also used to fund young missionary programmes, to print free copies of *The Book of Mormon* and, at the bishop's unofficial discretion, to make welfare payments to Mormon families in need.

It was Derek's stated ambition to move the Livingstone branch out of the school assembly hall and into a building of its own. For that, he needed more members. The church required a minimum number of worshippers before it would commit expenditure to land acquisition and church building. Derek was sure he could do it: raise enough cash to build a church of his own. And under his steerage, attendance – and the tithe received – continued slowly to grow.

*

During my Easter visit to Bristol that year, I scarcely saw Dad. He was at work. I was alone in the house with Gary, Wayne and Margaret.

I seemed to gather silence and trail it behind me. When I entered a room, it hushed. Margaret exchanged looks with Gary. When I left – I'd go to my bedroom and lie on the bed, reading – exhalations and sibilance of distaste tracked me up the stairs. The walls of the house grew tense around me, like flexed muscles.

Dad remained doggedly oblivious. He came home from work, said, 'Hello, Nipper,' and hello to his family. He watched the early evening news, the sports results, the weather, and then we had tea.

I sat at the table, grinding my teeth. Pretending to be exhausted, I went to bed at eight. The release of leaving them was like a cool breeze. I lay on the bed. I couldn't make sense of the page until some of the tautness had left my legs and neck. In the morning, I woke with a headache and a sore jaw; I'd been grinding my teeth as I slept.

It was at its worst just before tea-time. We sat in the living room, waiting for Dad to come home. It looked odd if I wasn't there. So I slunk down, taking my book with me.

On Thursday, as I sat there, Margaret, who'd been quiet since that morning, suddenly stood up and strode from the room. She stomped right past me. Gary followed her to the kitchen. Wayne was watching *Grange Hill*.

For a while, I couldn't hear anything. Then I became aware of low voices, growing steadily louder. Margaret was confiding something. Gary muttered something back. Margaret began to shout.

She said, 'I can't stand it.'

Her voice came through the wall.

She said, 'Alan's so different when he's here. It's not like it's my home. I don't want him here any more, Gary. I don't want him in our home.'

She was crying. Gary tried to comfort her. I couldn't hear what he was saying.

I wanted to go and hide. But I couldn't leave the room because it would mean passing the kitchen door. So I pretended to read. My teeth hurt. Wayne didn't look up from *Grange Hill*.

Margaret cried for a long time, but eventually she went upstairs. Gary came into the living room and sat before the TV. When I looked, I saw that he was crying, too. I didn't want to be in the living room any more. I didn't want to be in the house. I sat without moving. So did Wayne. My jaw hurt for the clenching.

When Margaret came downstairs, she was smiling and normal. She got on with making the tea. Then Dad got home from work, in his suit and tie and we ate together, round the table.

For the rest of the week Margaret was smiling and friendly, a knife behind it.

In Edinburgh, I worried about telling Mum and Derek the things Margaret had said. But in the end I had to; they knew something was wrong. So I told them and that night I listened to Derek and Mum, conspiring quietly over the sound of the TV.

We went to meet their solicitor. I sat in the office, between Mum and Derek, looking at a wooden desk. The solicitor wore a dark suit. I looked at his tight face and he looked at me while Derek recounted all the things that Margaret had said.

When the meeting was nearly over, the solicitor read the letter out loud, to make sure I agreed with it. *Neil feels that his stepmother, Margaret, resents him* . . .

Mum listened. She looked pinched. Her handbag was on her lap. Derek wore a face of businesslike triumph. It was his shopkeeper's face.

Within a day or two of it being posted, I knew Dad would read the solicitor's letter, which was called an affidavit. It would make him cry. His face would collapse, slowly at first, like a demolished tower-block, because that's how he looked when he cried. But it was either make him cry or keep going back. So I agreed without hesitation that the letter should be sent.

23

Derek's prediction about the dog had been correct. She was happy in Tarbrax.

We lived close to the Post Office, which was run by Mrs Lamb. She was elderly and slight, in green Wellingtons and a sleeveless anorak. But she was Presbyterian, courteous, in brisk health. Within a week of our arrival, Mum had entrusted her with a set of house keys.

Mrs Lamb kept a venerable, radically untrimmed husky dog, a globe of white fluff called Sindie. Every morning and every afternoon Mrs Lamb and Sindie came to collect our dog and, together, they went for a long walk around the village. Mrs Lamb liked our dog. I suspected that she kept her all day.

Now, when we got home in the evening, there was no neurotic, joyful barking, nor any terrified cringing. There were just welcoming barks and paws on the shoulder and a beating tail.

The dog ignored Derek, and Derek ignored her. He no

longer had any excuse to beat her. Sometimes, if she was in his way, he threatened her with a rolled-up newspaper. She looked at him with nobility and sadness and slinked away, not quickly, not slow.

If the evening was fine and I was in the mood, I took the dog for a walk over the bing. We passed through the still overgrown (and still chickenless) quarter-acre, then crossed the main road into the village. It was surfaced with rose-coloured tarmac. Then we walked down a wide, muddy path and passed an old No Entry sign, pocked and warped by decades of airgun pellets.

We went through the collapsed gates and into perfect, postapocalyptic isolation. The little bing was like a city destroyed by a nuclear firestorm. There were boulevards of shale and ash, mounds as tall as broken houses and hollowed churches. All of them were easy to climb and easy to explore.

At first, the dog trotted at my heels, sniffing the blighted ground. Then she pressed her ears flat and sprinted off, hunting for rabbits. There were thousands of them. The dog's heedless charge startled them from the long grass on the bing's perimeter. Rabbits scattered in all directions, like fat on a skillet.

The dog's acceleration and persistence were astonishing. She never caught a rabbit, but she never grew tired of trying. Eventually, I decided to test the limits of her endurance.

She and I walked to the big bing; that colossal wedge, a pinkish doorstop the size of a mountain. A kind of path ran up the centre of it. The dog followed me to the top. It was a long, lonely walk.

I sat down on the upper lip of the wedge and looked down at the surrounding farmland. It was cut into patches. The dog sat with me, panting.

I picked up a piece of shale. It fit my palm. It was the shape of a hip-bone and the weight of pumice. I showed it to the dog. She stood. Her hind legs trembled. She made little yelps under her breath. I pulled back my hand and threw.

The dog launched herself in pursuit. She raced down the yielding, near-vertical incline. Her feet caused little avalanches.

At the foot of the bing, she sniffed round for a while. Then she *woofed* and looked up at me. She scooped something in her mouth and laboured up the shifting slope. It was hard going, even for her.

At the top, she approached me at a pleased saunter. She dropped the shale into my lap. It was the same bone-shape, now dark-spotted with dog slobber.

She barked, asking me to do it again.

She had not tired of the game even when the sun began to set and I grew anxious to be gone. Darkness could come quickly, and it was a good walk back to the village.

On the way home, the dog trotted at my heel, content but not exhausted. At the base of the big bing, she set off after a rabbit. I sensed it as a sudden alertness, then a frantic rustle in the long grass.

I walked the rest of the way alone, the shadows growing longer and deeper in that shattered, imaginary city. When I reached the gate, several minutes later, the dog was waiting.

I thought of all that energy, confounded in a tiny flat on Duff Street. I hugged her. She was a good dog. She sat erect and allowed herself to be hugged. When I disengaged, she lay a muddy paw in my lap. I took it and shook it, and we walked home together.

The bing had a supernatural quality. I loved the isolation and desolation of it. I liked to frighten myself, timing myself home against the fall of night.

Sometimes, as the sun faded to orange and I grew pleasantly anxious to be gone, I became aware of a low, persistent hum. It seemed to emanate from whichever direction I turned. Its was pitched like plainchant, like cloistered monks singing a single, unwavering note.

I made some effort to identify its source and found nothing. There were no power lines until you reached the village, half a mile away. And power lines couldn't explain why the hum rose from the landscape only when the sun set, or why it grew louder as the darkness quickened.

The first time, I made myself walk home at a deliberate pace. I was not pursued by the hum, but enveloped within it. It seemed to rise in pitch with the beat of my heart. When I stepped onto the road, I realized it had gone.

The next time, fear got the best of me and I ran through the violent sunset, the dog romping at my heels.

When Tam came to stay for the weekend, we stood on the lip of the big bing, waiting for the sun to go down. As the light faltered, the hum rose like mist from the ground. Tam heard it too.

At first, we stood there, discussing it with self-conscious seriousness. Then, as our shadows grew long, we began to scare each other.

A couple of years before, there had been a peculiar incident on the A17 just outside Livingstone. That was our route home. On 9 November 1979, Bob Taylor – a forestry worker for the Livingstone Development Corporation – was making a check in those eerie, endless pine forests. In a clearing, he noticed a metallic object shaped like the planet Saturn. It was fading in and out. As he watched, it launched two metallic balls, each emitting spikes of light. They rolled over the ground. They smelled bad, and they made the inside of Bob Taylor's head burn.

He passed out. When he awoke, the object had gone. His clothes were ripped and his skin was scratched. He was shocked and drained and disorientated. He had to crawl to his truck. But he was too dazed to drive. He went into a ditch.

Eventually, he called the police. Where Bob Taylor had seen the UFO, they photographed a 4.5-metre ring of 'spiked holes', 10 centimetres deep and 9 centimetres wide. Nobody knew what they were, and nobody ever found out. Eventually, the council erected a plaque to mark the location of the encounter, which became known as the Livingstone Incident.

On the bing in that deepening evening, Tam was quick to identify the hum with the malevolent UFOs that had nearly taken Bob Taylor. Perhaps they used the bing as a base. It was a good place to hide: desolate, miles from anywhere. Right then, malevolent UFOs frightened me more than anything else.

At first we giggled, because we were scared and we didn't want to show it. Then we broke and ran like hell. We ran all the way to the village, on through the quarter-acre, the small fenced garden and through the door of Crosswood Terrace.

Later, we slept top and tail, our feet jammed in each other's faces.

Derek was working late, supervising the cashing-up, when four armed robbers entered the cash and carry. They wore ski-masks and carried sawn-off shotguns. They forced Derek and some other staff into a locked room. They put a gun to Derek's head and ordered him to open the safe. They stole all the money.

When they'd gone, Derek broke free of the room in which they'd all been locked and called the police.

He got home very late that night, unspeakably weary. He didn't want to talk about it. A lot of money had gone. It was just his luck, that he was in charge when it happened.

In the morning, his picture was on the front page of the newspaper. The story described the events of the previous evening as *an ordeal*. In the photograph, Derek looked desperately drawn.

He drove me to West Calder and idled at the kerb while I went into the newsagent and bought half a dozen copies. In the shop, tucking them under my arm like a swagger-stick, I pointed to the photograph.

I said, 'This is my Dad.'

The shopkeeper didn't seem interested. Perhaps he didn't believe me.

Even at home, the robbery was not much spoken of. Mum didn't like to think about it – it had been a bad night for us all. And talk of it made Derek shifting and uncomfortable.

To recreate the events of that evening, my only resources were the newspaper reports and my imagination. And so I imagined that Derek was involved with the robbery. His escape to alert the police seemed too easy. If I'd been one of the raiders, I'd have tied him up a great deal more competently than they had. Yet otherwise, the hold-up was perfectly executed. They arrived when the maximum amount of cash was on site, along with the fewest members of staff. It was almost as if Derek was supposed to escape, in order to call the police – that way, nobody would suspect it of being an inside job.

The thieves were never caught. Nobody was ever charged with anything, least of all Derek, and the money was never found.

Several weeks after the robbery, Derek came home in a temper. He took off his driving gloves but forgot about his dripping coat.

Yvonne slipped to her room. She paused in the cupboard to look at me. She jerked her eyes sideways. But I didn't want to go with her. I pretended to watch TV while Derek and Mum talked. I caught fragments. Derek was recounting an argument with his boss. He and his boss hadn't been getting on for some time.

He muttered, 'So I told him where to stick it.'

He sat there, calming down, still in his wet coat.

I thought of him, livid, driving along the A70, that lonely road, through the pine forests, the starry skies above him. Past the turn-offs for West Calder, the signposts for Edinburgh and Glasgow. The slowing of tyres on gravel outside Crosswood Terrace. On the way, he had been rehearsing the conversation he'd just repeated for Mum's benefit. It consisted of things he wished he'd said, but hadn't.

I thought of another morning, not long before. As we were entering Edinburgh, a car cut us up. A young man was at the wheel, his mate in the seat next to him.

Derek gave them the finger and mouthed the words, 'You prick.'

The car braked with a shriek. It paused in the road, then described a smooth U-turn.

Mum said, 'Oh God, Derek.'

Derek fumbled with the wheel. Then he forced the Skoda into a blind right turn. The other car followed.

Derek turned right again, into an amber light. He turned again. He was breathing oddly. His feet were jerky on the pedals.

Eventually, the other driver overtook the Skoda and braked just in front of us, hard. Derek stamped on his own brake. We jerked in our seatbelts. The Skoda came to a noisy halt, just behind the other car. We waited.

The other driver turned in his seat. He smiled. He gave Derek the finger. He unfolded it slowly.

He enunciated the words 'Fucking wanker' then pulled away.

When he'd gone, Derek swept the shiny lock of hair from his forehead. His eyes flicked into the rear-view mirror. They narrowed.

He said, 'If he'd have taken one step out of that car, I'd have killed him. I'd have bloody killed him.'

I said, 'I know.'

He looked comical in that moment: imperious and absurd.

And he looked just as silly now, sitting there in his wet coat with his driving gloves still clasped in one fist, repeating fictional ultimata he'd delivered to his boss, pretending to have walked out when he'd been cast. Derek had been sacked. His boss had told him to go and not come back. And on the way home, he'd turned this effrontery into a triumph of dignity. He had walked. He had bloody walked.

Mum believed him, because she had to. Otherwise, what was she doing here, in a village in the middle of Scotland, far from her family, far from everything: far even from the far place to which she'd run away. She barely saw her daughters or her daughters' children. Her eldest son, her first born child, had not seen or spoken to her in nearly a decade. She had never seen his children. Her own mother, approaching her eighties, was living alone in a sheltered flat with a Yorkshire terrier and a crucifix on the wall.

It was not possible to have done all this for a man who proved to be a liar. And when they spoke of it at church, this run of bad luck, they would say it was the devil's doing. It was the devil, tempting them from the true church, away from God. It was the devil, who sometimes was a gentleman.

And Derek soon landed a new job. He told us about it one Sunday afternoon, on the way home from church. His new job was selling vacuum cleaners. They were called Kirbys. They were magnificent machines. They would sell themselves. He was going to make a fortune. He was very excited.

He ran through what we'd do with the money. We'd get a big house. I'd have proper pocket money. Kirby was the best possible turn of events. It was a gift from Heavenly Father. It was good luck. It was *velly intellesting*.

My final day at Dalry Primary School ended at lunchtime.

Just before the bell went, Mrs Simmons took five minutes to address the agitated class. She thanked us for being lovely boys and girls and wished us good luck for the future. She hoped we'd go back and see her one day, to tell her how we were getting on. Then the bell went. Everyone scrambled to be gone. Mrs Simmons stood there, laughing, watching the children leave without a look cast backwards.

For my classmates, leaving Dalry Primary School was a small ending. They all lived nearby. The summer holidays lay ahead. They'd see each other and play together, and they'd see each other as first years at Tynecastle Comprehensive. But I'd never see them again. My final weeks had hurt with nostalgia. I had wanted to stop time moving, but I couldn't. I reviewed the five years I had spent there with gratification and shame. After all this time, I belonged with them. I had earned my place.

I waited at the gate until everyone had gone. I wanted to bid each of them goodbye. I was cataloguing, trying to set each of their faces in memory, each of their names. When they had all gone, I walked round the empty school grounds, remembering it, the layout of it, the smell, the exact fall of light and shadow.

I walked to Duff Street and stood outside the old house. It was empty and boarded-up but not yet demolished. I looked at the graffiti on the wall: *Neil Go Home*.

It made me sad, for a child that I wasn't.

Yesterday, I came into possession of my final class photograph. I saw those children for the first time in twenty-five years. The faces were familiar, but almost all their names had gone.

24

Derek's job, selling Kirby Heritage vacuum cleaners, often kept him away, sometimes overnight. But when he was at home, we watched TV together in the evenings. One of the films we enjoyed was called *The Wild Geese*. It was about a group of British mercenaries sent to Africa by Stewart Granger; their mission was to release an imprisoned African opposition leader, thereby establishing democracy in his country. Stewart Granger turned out to be a villain. The other stars – Richard Burton, Richard Harris, Roger Moore – were too old for all the running around, but they seemed to be enjoying themselves. Another of the team was played by Hardy Kruger, an actor whom Derek admired.

The film began on an aeroplane, with a murder. A man was stabbed in the back, through his seat.

Sunday was a hot day. After church, I went outside with Michael and Adi, the other deacons. We walked across the car-park and sat on a low wall, kicking our heels. We talked about *The Wild Geese*. Michael and Adi had watched it, too.

I enjoyed discussing films. Who shot who, who blew up what, who died.

I said, 'And did you see that bloke getting stabbed on the plane? The one guarding the nigger.'

I made a face, to show how much it must have hurt, and how cool it was.

Nobody said anything. I wondered if they had heard me.

I said, 'There's this nigger on a plane . . .'

They weren't looking at me. They were looking at the sky.

I felt something hot rise from the small of my back. I felt it rise up my neck and my cheeks. It rose into my scalp. I had forgotten that Adi was a nigger.

I wanted to apologize. But I couldn't, not until he or Michael acknowledged what I'd said. Neither of them did.

We sat on the low wall and kicked our legs to beat out the passing silence, and I didn't look at them. After a while we began to discuss *The Wild Geese* again. My hands were shaking. A bit later still, we went inside.

Now Derek was Bishop, we were usually the last to leave, so it was several hours before we got home. We sat in Derek's car: me, Mum and Yvonne. Derek at the wheel, pleased with how things had gone that week.

At home, we turned on the TV. Mum was in the kitchen, making roast leg of lamb. Roast leg of lamb was my favourite. We watched TV until dinner was ready. Then Yvonne and I laid the small tables, putting down a knife and fork and a glass of water on each; a glass of orange squash on mine. Mum brought in the dinner, two plates at a time. I turned down the TV while Yvonne said grace. Then I turned it up again and we began to eat.

I cut up my lamb and put some in my mouth. I chewed.

I said, 'Dad?'

He said, 'Yes?'

'I'm not going to church any more.'

He looked at me: the smooth, chubby face, the broad forehead, the shining, nearly black hair. He raised an eyebrow. He plucked them. He said that good grooming was a very masculine trait.

He said, 'And what makes you say that?'

'I don't believe in it.'

Mum sucked in her breath. She said, 'Oh, Neil.'

I looked at Yvonne. Her eyes were guarded, but she was okay. She nodded, so small you could hardly see it.

Derek said, 'And when did you reach this conclusion?'

'Ages ago. A long time.'

I looked at my food. I cut up a roast potato. Shovelled gravy on it with my knife. Watched the gravy running off again.

I said, 'I just don't want to go any more.'

Mum said, 'It was you who got us involved in the first place. You used to love it.'

I said, 'I was nine, Mum.'

She went to speak. She was angry. But Derek silenced her by half-raising his knife. He was looking at me. There was no rebuke in his eyes. He had dignity and in that moment I could have wept for loving him.

He said, 'I'd like you to come to church. But I know that if I force you it will only drive you away in the long run. So, if you don't want to come, don't come. But the minute you want to come back, you'll be very welcome.'

He kept his eyes on mine. They were the eyes that I remembered. I had not seen them for a long time. I could see that he believed it all. He believed it so much, he was willing to let me stray from the true path. That way I could discover it again, all on my own. That, after all, was the way he himself had found it.

After dinner, I took the dog for a walk. It was summer and it was still daylight, but I wore a jacket because the evening was paling.

Every time I thought about Adi, I had the compulsion to curl into a ball on the floor, in the shadow of the bing's weird contortions. It made me want to moan out loud, just to let it out, and sometimes I had to stand still and press my fist into my mouth and bite down, to stop it coming.

I thought about Derek, telling me never to let a nigger through his door. And I thought of him, proud before his congregation while Adi passed round the sacrament, those silly chunks of Mother's Pride and little plastic cups of tap water which represented the agonized blood sacrifice of Jesus Christ. Adi, not knowing that his own grinning bishop hated him. I wondered at the scale of that betrayal. And I thought of the way Derek had looked at me over dinner, with those soft eyes, and I began to run.

But the dinner lay heavy in my belly, and before I'd run very far I had to stop or risk being sick and I sat in that false desert, that scrap of barren wilderness, and watched the dog as she fossicked for prey.

At the end of June, I flew back to Bristol. On the plane, the cabin crew no longer gave me special attention. I looked older than I was. At Birmingham airport, I was met as usual by Dad and Margaret. Gary and Wayne stayed at home.

I smiled. I could feel it on my face.

They smiled too. They said, 'Hello, Nipper.'

We waited at the carousel, to get my suitcase.

Dad plucked at my lapel.

He said, 'What's all this business?'

Mum had bought me a fake Crombie, a knee-length overcoat, black. And I wore Dr Martens. My trousers were taken up a bit short, to show off the boots and their yellow laces.

We went to the car-park and found Dad's Lada. The Yellow-Wheeled Speed was long gone. I got in the back seat and watched the motorway lights pulse overhead, like a squadron of invading UFOs.

I walked into 92 Bifield Road, into the familiar smell and, all week, I waited for someone to mention the solicitor's letter, but nobody did.

On Wednesday, I was alone in the car with Dad. He parked. We were on the other side of Bristol. He gave me the car keys.

He said, 'I won't be long, Nip.'

He gave me money, 'for a book or something,' and told me to wait. Then he hurried into a bowls club. It was not a bowls club that I'd seen before. Someone had been taken ill and Dad was taking their place in an important game. Or it was something like that.

I got out of the car and went for a walk. I found a W.H. Smith. I browsed the books, then bought one and took it back to the car. It was called *The Fellowship of the Ring*. When Dad got back, I was halfway through it.

On Saturday morning, I asked him to let me know when it was five o'clock.

He said, 'Why? Do you have to say a prayer or something?'

I said, 'No, Suggs is being interviewed on Radio 1.'

Suggs was the singer with Madness.

I dreamed that the letter had been lost in the post. I prayed to a God in whom I did not believe. I petitioned his imaginary son, Jesus. I fell to my knees at the side of the bed. I prayed in the shower and over breakfast. I prayed while I pretended to watch TV. And as the days passed – the same Saturday evening football results, the same Sunday dinner, with Jimmy Savile on the radio, followed by Dad taking the same forty winks on the sofa, sleeping with the newspaper open, face down on his belly – I lost the resolve to deny the possibility of it.

Then, on the last night of my visit, Margaret took Gary and Wayne to the cinema again. Just like before, it was just Dad and me. He turned off the TV and sat at the table. He was wearing his work trousers and a white shirt. You could see his white vest, beneath it. He had a glass of Bell's whisky in front of him. He clutched it in his hand.

He said, 'Sit down, Nipper.'

I sat down. As I sat, it telescoped in my mind. A discon-nected part of me began to narrate the scene.

Dad took a sip of whisky.

He took a sip of whisky, I thought.

I gripped the edge of the table. I wasn't wearing my boots. Without them, I felt half-dressed and weak. I crossed my ankles behind me. Put my feet flat on the floor. Crossed them again.

Dad said, 'So, what's all this business with the solicitor's letter?'

Inside, I felt a swirl of pity for Margaret. She had sobbed in the kitchen because I was spoiling her home.

I said, 'Well, it's true.'

Dad said, 'Oh baloney.'

That was the closest he ever came to swearing. He took a sip of whisky. He looked at the wall. There was silence between us.

He said, 'I've spent thousands of pounds on you. Flying you down here.'

He didn't pay maintenance, though, because Derek wouldn't accept another man's money. I wanted to say that, because I wanted to say something malicious. But I didn't have the courage.

I wished I had my boots on. My feet felt peculiar.

I said, 'Margaret doesn't like having me here.'

He said 'Baloney' again, more angrily. Then he said, 'Is this your mother's doing? Or Derek's?'

'It was Derek's idea to go to the solicitor,' I said. 'But only after I told him what Margaret said.'

He was still looking at the clock. It didn't appear to be moving. The light in the room was slow and old.

He said, 'Look at what I do for you, Nipper. And all you do is turn round and stab me in the back.'

The words went through my chest and out between my shoulders.

He said, 'All you do is betray us.'

Most of the year, Dad lived with Gary and Wayne, who loved him and respected him and obeyed him and were good sons. They were well-behaved at school and they played football for local teams. When they scored, their names were in the local paper, in small print on the sports pages. Dad watched them from the sidelines.

And every few months, I turned up: a strange boy who in some minor ways resembled a child he'd lost, five years before. I was taller, dressed differently, or I'd joined a strange American church of which he knew nothing. I began to change the day I left Bristol in the hired Morris Marina. The change consolidated and accelerated, like a malignant tumour. It wasn't stopping. It would have been better for Dad to have said goodbye when I was seven. Then he could have mourned me, the way you mourn any death. And by now he'd have recovered, the way people always did, eventually.

He loved me because he couldn't help it: he loved me because of who I'd been. But he didn't like me. There was no reason why he should; he barely knew me. I wanted to point that out to him, but I didn't know how to say it. I was narrating it in my head and all the words were wrong.

The conversation wound in a descending spiral and wore itself out. It never concluded.

He said, 'Do you ever want to come and see me again?'

I said, 'Yes, of course.'

Then we drifted into an exhausted silence. For a long time, neither of us moved from the table. Then I stood and went upstairs. I left Dad with his whisky in the quiet room with the tired light.

On my bedroom door was a small plaque. It had been there for years. It showed a vintage car, a Model T Ford. Beneath the car it read: Neil's Room. There was a similar plaque on Gary's door, and one on Wayne's.

In the bedroom, I saw that Margaret had washed and folded my clothes and left them out on the bed. I packed, leaving out something to wear in the morning. I picked up *The Fellowship of the Ring* and got into bed and began to read.

Later, Margaret, Gary and Wayne came home from the cinema. Gary and Wayne came up to bed. I heard them on the stairs. I heard them peeing and cleaning their teeth. Dad and Margaret came to bed, too.

It sounded ordinary, and it nearly was, but for my presence. Dad had said what was to be said, and they were all relieved it was over. I was like a ghost, haunting their life from a silent corner. When I left, things would return to normal. And that's all anyone ever wanted. Just to be normal. Nobody wanted a ghost in their house.

The next day, Dad drove me to the airport. We said goodbye at the gate. He smiled and waved and I smiled and waved.

He said, 'Cheerio, Sonner.'

I said, 'Bye, Dad.'

He said, 'Look after yourself.'

I went through the gate, carrying my suitcase.

He stood there in his soft shoes. He didn't know what to do with his hands. He put them in his pockets. It was pointless, both of us standing there, waving.

25

I spent the summer alone in Tarbrax.

In the morning, Mum, Derek and Yvonne left before I was awake. I got up late and read *Doc Savage: Man of Bronze* or *Conan of the Isles*. When I was bored of reading, I wrote my book. It was the story of an ordinary man, a bit of a coward, who unexpectedly slipped into a parallel universe, where a war was being fought between the forces of good and evil.

In the book's early chapters, the hero was incarcerated in a POW camp on a vast, desert planet. With the aid of a mysterious, elderly prisoner known only by his number, 73172, the hero effected an uprising and a mass escape. They hijacked a supply ship and escaped to join the rebellion. The rebels were a various bunch, most of them characters borrowed from films and books and comics, but given other names. Making up names was the worst bit. That's why I called the old man 73172.

The end of the book was sad: the rebels lost and everyone was killed. Every time I finished it, I read it back, discovered it was rubbish and started all over again. The book was called *Another Kind of Warrior*, and I had been writing and rewriting it for four years.

Yvonne had typed two early versions for me during her lunch hours, but she knew I'd just keep starting again, and stopped doing it. She told me she'd type it again when I was absolutely sure I'd finished. I began to consider asking for a typewriter for Christmas.

After writing, I practised dance moves to songs by Madness, The Specials and The Beat. I taped the songs off *Top of the Pops*, onto a mono cassette recorder: the one Derek had used to tape the missionaries over Sunday lunch. We lived too far away for any of that now; nobody came to lunch any more. As I danced, I watched myself in the mirror to see if I got it right, and never did.

I spent hours attempting to transcribe lyrics: pausing the songs, rewinding, playing back verses. There was something in the songs, something underneath them, that I wanted to get to. And I thought, if I knew the words, I could get to it.

I made lunch, then took the dog for a walk. I spent Saturdays with Tam at his new house in Edinburgh. Sometimes I stayed overnight, sleeping top and tail, his feet jammed in my face and mine in his.

We went to see Madness. They were touring to promote an album.

Outside the concert, the National Front were handing out leaflets. Madness had denounced the National Front several times very publicly.

The National Front had stolen its uniform of jeans, Dr Martens, Fred Perry's and shaved heads from the skinhead movement of the late 1960s and early 1970s, which had been a white, working-class celebration of Jamaican music. So the National Front was a parody of the class it claimed to glorify.

But sometimes it was difficult to tell the two kinds of skinhead apart. Sometimes, you could only tell by looking at the badges they wore on the lapels of their Crombie or tartan-lined Harrington.

Inside, the concert hall was crammed with thousands of skinheads. When Madness appeared on the stage, the venue bubbled into a single, violently tidal mass of them. But each time Tam or I stumbled, a sweating skinhead would stoop to pick us up. He'd make sure we were okay, then start dancing again, his braces round his waist.

We walked home that night, along Princess Street. We were too sweaty and exhilarated to wait for a late bus. There were sirens and drunks. It was dark. It was good.

Early in September 1981, I put on my new school uniform for the first time. Then I left the cottage and walked to the corner by the Post Office, opposite the village green. Three other kids were already waiting there. They were older than me, wearing the same uniform. I hadn't met them, or even seen them hanging round Tarbrax. I supposed they had jobs during the summer.

I clutched my new Adidas bag. Everyone had an Adidas bag. Adidas bags were the bags to have.

The kids ignored me, except the gaunt and lanky girl. She looked down at me. She was tall and angular, with short, greasy hair. She said, 'Nice laces,' and laughed.

I had yellow laces in my Dr Martens. Everyone had yellow laces in their Dr Martens. Yellow laces were the laces to have. I grinned, because I didn't know what was wrong with them.

When the school coach arrived, it was almost three-quarters full and very noisy. Older kids sat near the back. I took the wrong seat. I was told to move, and moved.

The coach stopped off at a number of villages. At each one, it picked up two or three children. Some of them were nervous first years, like me.

Eventually, we drove into Biggar. It was a small town in South Lanarkshire. The coach turned into the school car-park. It was already full of other coaches. The first day of school looked like a big event, like a concert.

The first years were herded into the sports hall, lined up and assigned to classes. I looked at the strange faces. Most of them had lived in local villages all their life. I lugged around a pain in my lower stomach, a peculiar nostalgia for Dalry Primary School.

After school, everyone gathered in the car-park again, waiting for the coaches. Next to me stood a tall prefect. He had highlights in his hair. You could tell he was a prefect because the lapels of his blazer were piped in light blue. I had already learned that this thin, blue piping acted like a policeman's uniform. It invested the prefects with authority. It meant he was sixteen or seventeen.

He looked at me. He said, 'The fuck do you think you're looking at?'

I smiled. I said, 'Nothing. Sorry.'

He grabbed my Adidas bag. He moved very quickly. He

wrestled it from my grip and tried to throw it away. He wanted to strike like a mantis, but it turned into a clumsy scuffle. I intercepted the throw. I reached out and slapped the bag and it landed at my feet. I picked it up.

He shoved my shoulder. I ignored him. He shoved me again. I said, 'Fuck off.'

He punched me in the mouth. It was a full punch. It took him by surprise, because he expected me to duck. But I hadn't expected him to punch me. The punch split the inside of my lower lip. But it hurt the prefect more. I could tell by the way he laughed and shook his hand, loose at the end of his wrist, like it didn't hurt at all.

Everyone was looking. I felt clumsy and goofy and conspicuous.

The prefect said, 'Spastic.'

I grinned at him, to show him I could.

The coach doors opened. The prefect shoved me between the shoulder blades. I stumbled a few steps, then got on the coach. But nobody was impressed by him. Everyone just wanted to get on the coach and go home.

I sat in the seat behind the driver because I thought it would be safe. And as the coach jerked and growled from village to village, it grew quieter. By the time we reached Tarbrax, it had become almost silent. Everyone was looking out of the windows.

By the time Mum and Yvonne got home, I'd changed my clothes and eaten a big peanut-butter sandwich. I'd watched TV and played with the dog. My lower lip was still swollen, but not much.

Mum said, 'How was your day?'

I said, 'Fine.'

But I was bored with it. I knew that tomorrow, there would be the same wait on the same corner. There would be the same coach trip and the same jeering from the same idiot prefect.

I traipsed from class to class, dragging my Adidas bag.

Physical education was taught by a stunted, crew-cut man called Mr Boyd. He squinted when he talked. Rumour had it, he'd been in the SAS. Even if it wasn't true, you could see why everyone believed it. Mr Boyd leered and squinted when he warned of his happy facility with corporal punishment. He produced the familiar strap of leather and draped it over his forearm while he spoke to us. It hung there like a half-erect penis.

He stood there with his silver crew cut and his tight shorts, his rugby top stretched taut across his chest. He planted his feet heroically far apart. He was about five foot six. He let us know under what circumstances he would belt us. There were many such circumstances. Mr. Boyd thought it comical to call nervous, twelve-year-old boys 'four eyes' and 'Dumbo' and 'fattie'. He thought it a fine idea to send them onto the sports field to play rugby, having first made them physically afraid of him. And, on the pitch, he mocked them for fumbling the ball or being hesitant into a tackle.

I was big for my age, I was an exceptionally fast runner, and I quickly discovered it was possible to play rugby while lacking any particular dexterity or skill with a ball. I had only to knock an opposing player off his feet, then pass the ball to someone who knew what to do with it.

Mr Boyd saw this. He sidled up to me on the field and sneered something through the corner of his mouth. It was supposed to be a confidence. I hated him. It was a strange feeling, almost sexual in its immediacy and its privacy.

That was in the morning. In the afternoon, we had music. The teacher was a tall man in a loose cardigan, bald too young: he wore a combover that aged him. He stood at the back of the class while we copied something from the board: notes on a stave. It was dull. I talked to the kid next to me. He was a very fat boy, with big square spectacles. On his bag, he had carefully painted the words: *Ant Music for Sex People*, because he liked Adam and the Ants. I thought it was cool that such a fat boy was happy to declare himself a sex person.

The teacher sneaked up behind me and slapped me hard across the back of the head. There was shock, and a loud, dull noise.

He roared. The words were: 'Work in *silence*, boy.'

Although he'd slapped me so hard my forehead nearly struck the desk, there was almost no pain. I turned to the teacher.

I said, 'Keep your hair on.'

The class laughed, although the joke was obvious and not that funny. The teacher locked eyes with me.

During afternoon break, I was discussing music with the fat boy. I didn't like Adam and the Ants, but they were better than Iron Maiden and Black Sabbath, which were the bands most of the other boys seemed to like.

The fat boy and I were outside.

I said, 'So, what's your favourite song?'

He said, '"Prince Charming".'

I'd readied my next question: why? But now I knew, there was no need of it. 'Prince Charming' had been a number 1 for weeks and weeks. During the chorus, Adam Ant sang: 'ridicule is nothing to be scared of', and when Adam Ant sang it, you believed him.

I thought it was cool that Adam Ant thought ridicule was nothing to be scared of, but I thought it cooler that he'd made the fat boy believe it. I realized that 'Prince Charming' had been number 1 for so long because so many fat boys and fat girls, and spotty boys and spotty girls, and thin boys and thin girls, and short boys and tall girls, tens of thousands of strange children played that record in the sanctuary of their bedrooms, and whenever they heard it they felt brave and better.

And there were far more of them than there were prefects whose blue piping lent them temporary licence; more of them than there were people like Mr Boyd and his comical squint. I realized that pop music was a strong thing and a good thing. And that is what had been beneath the words of the songs I had worked so long and hard to transcribe.

On Friday, I didn't take in my PE kit because I'd decided never to do PE again; at least as long as Mr Boyd was teaching it. Everyone hurried to get changed. I sat on the bench with my Adidas bag on my lap. Mr Boyd came to inspect us. He looked down the rank of boys, in their sports kit, and me in my uniform.

He squinted at me and said, 'Have you got a note, boy?'

I said, 'No.'

'Then why aren't you changed?'

I wanted to say, Because you are a prick.

I said, 'I forgot my kit.'

'You forgot your kit.'

'Aye.'

He knew I was calling him a prick anyway.

He made me stand. I held out my hands, palm up. The boys watched, ranked on benches beneath coat hooks. They wore shorts and football boots and rugby tops.

Mr Boyd took a couple of practice swipes, then slammed the belt across my hand. He did it twice. It hurt, but not too much: not as much as I thought it would. And it was worth it, because it was all he could do. After it was done, Mr Boyd stared at me through his squint and I blew on my hands and that was it.

Most mornings, the prefect greeted me with a slap to the face or a knee to the testicles and in the afternoon we went through it all again. But it was just a ritual. He wasn't even trying to hurt me. He was a prick. The school was full of pricks.

When the coach got back to Tarbrax in the afternoon, I was weary and grubby, needing a shower. The autumn light, the early-setting sun, made me feel closed-in.

I didn't like Biggar High School, and it was easy to stop going. In the morning, Mum and Yvonne and Derek all left for work. I said goodbye to them. I even put on my school uniform. I put my bag in order; my sandwiches, my can of Coke, some Penguin biscuits. I laced my boots. Then I went and lay on the bed until the school bus had stopped, exhaled, opened its doors, closed them again and was gone.

Then everything drained away. I took off my tie and blazer and put on some jeans. I wore the shirt, to make it authentically smelly, and I stayed away from the windows. When Mrs Lamb came to pick up the dog, I hid in the bedroom. She always stood in the doorway without coming in. She whistled and the dog ran to her without a backward glance. I'd been right: Mrs Lamb did keep her all day, returning her ten minutes before the school coach came back. By then, the autumn light had grown yellow and treacly.

When it was dark, I lit the coal fire. When Mum and Yvonne came home, the fire was going well, crackling and popping. They bustled in, cold and wet, complaining about the weather.

Mum asked how my day had gone and I said, 'Fine', and that was it. We settled down to a normal evening. These days, normal evenings were just the three of us: me, Mum and Yvonne watching TV.

At the weekend, Derek came back from a trip with a present for me. It was a large poster of a Kirby vacuum cleaner. I didn't really want a picture of a vacuum cleaner on my bedroom wall: it would cover my posters of *Star Wars* and *Raiders of the Lost Ark* and Madness and The Specials. But Derek seemed pleased when he gave me the poster, as if he'd been looking forward to this moment. I was embarrassed by my ingratitude. So I pinned it to the wall, in pride of place.

That term, although I usually went to school only twice a week, I was belted more often than any other pupil. Mrs Skelsie said I had probably broken some kind of record.

But the belt was a feeble sanction. Its use was attended by a kind of bewildered respect from my classmates. Even the prefect began to leave me alone. Everyone on the coach knew I wasn't scared of the belt: so they knew I wasn't scared of him either. He just looked silly, trying to kick me in the balls with his pointy knees and getting laughed at.

Mrs Skelsie was my English teacher. She liked the short stories I wrote. Most of them were violent – they involved decapitations and mutilations – but she read them to the class anyway. She peered over her spectacles during the gory bits, like someone reading a Hallowe'en story, and she seemed to relish her pupils' cheery disgust as eyes popped and kneecaps shattered.

The girls in my class treated me with openly curious mystification and I liked it. They affected concern for my wellbeing, for my attendance, and I liked that too. They sat next to me and asked me why I wasn't coming to school, why I was always in trouble, and I liked that even better.

I was a charlatan. I was the English boy who was dragged round the playground of Dalry school by his hair, the kid who didn't swear and went to the weird church. But I was prepared to live with being a charlatan, because of the girls' mystification. When I turned up to class, they said, 'So, you decided to put in an appearance then,' and rolled their eyes and smiled, and that made me feel good. I told a girl called Anne that I hated God and she put her hands over her mouth and slapped my arm, and that made me feel good too.

I got away with truanting for a couple of months – October and November – but eventually I was caught. One morning,

I didn't bother to put on my uniform. Mum found my clean shirt hanging where she'd left it, with the stripy tie draped over the hanger.

There was no point lying, but I did. I said that it was just so cold that morning. I got out of bed and looked outside and there was so much snow. I felt shivery. Too ill to go in.

Mum knew I was lying, even though the snow still lay deep outside, reflecting the light of the moon. It covered the bing. It made it look like a collapsed cake. But she seemed too tired to care. In those days, she always seemed tired.

In the morning, Yvonne arranged to go in late to work. She and Mum waited while I put on my uniform then went outside and got on the coach. Once you'd done that, you had no choice but to go to school. The town of Biggar was far too small to wander aimlessly round. And anyway, it was freezing outside.

Then Yvonne phoned the school and spoke to Mrs Skelsie about my attendance. That didn't seem odd. I'd never have expected Mum to do it. Her nerves were too bad. And Derek was away a lot.

So I returned to school, full-time. I talked to Mrs Skelsie and promised not to truant again, which was a lie, and I went to class.

At lunchtime on Friday, I was outside. Kids milled around: the sensible girls and the boys with *Iron Maiden* written on their bags. A boy called McEndrick stepped through the crowd. He was a big, ruddy farmer's boy with curly hair. He was older than me; fourteen. He had his head lowered.

He walked up to me.

He said, 'Hey, cunt.'

He pushed me. I was scared of him.

I said, 'Oh, McEndrick, just fuck off.'

He pushed me again.

He said, 'Come on then, cunt.'

I said, 'Just fuck off.'

He kicked me in the balls. I wasn't prepared for it. I lay on the ground. I curled up. I gagged.

A crowd began to gather and, as it grew, it became hungry.

I stood up. I was inside the crowd. I was sweating. My balls hurt and so did my lower back. I felt sick. I began to shove my way through the kids. They were jammed, shoulder-to-shoulder, smiling. No eye-contact. McEndrick stomped behind me on big, flat feet. He was shoving my shoulder.

He said, 'Come on then, cunt.'

I was used to it. You ignored it until it withered and fell away. You told yourself it was braver to walk away, even though it wasn't. But now there was nowhere to walk. The crowd moved with us like a weather system. As it did, its eye narrowed and its body grew and condensed. It became impossible to move. McEndrick was shoving my shoulder. My balls hurt.

I turned around. The crowd made a noise. I jumped up. I grabbed McEndrick's hair in both hands and pulled down on it. I bent him double. I kept my arms straight and backed away from his flailing arms. I stepped forward and kicked him in the face. I kicked him in the face for a long time. Then I pushed him over and kicked him in the head. I couldn't get a proper kick because the spectators were packed so tight. I was still trying to kick him properly when a number of prefects ran, shoving, through the suddenly silent crowd.

I kicked McEndrick until the prefects grabbed my arms and my collar and my legs and yanked me away. They manhandled me, still kicking, through the doors and down the empty corridor. I called them cunts. It echoed off the walls and ceiling. I told them I was going to fucking kill them. McEndrick followed, wiping his nose, led by the elbow.

By the time we arrived at Big Dave's office, I'd stopped fighting. My shirt was untucked and my tie had been pulled into a knot so tiny I'd need to buy a new one.

The prefects told us to wait and stood there like policemen. McEndrick and I put our hands in our pockets. We looked at each other. Looked away. We were dishevelled, untucked, scraped, bruised. I felt good. I offered McEndrick my hand. He refused. I offered again.

I said, 'Come on,' because that's what you did.

Finally, not happily, he gave up and we shook. Then Big Dave came from his office to shout at us. Big Dave was the head teacher. He was big, and his name was Dave. He had one ear. Where the missing ear should be was a rude hole. I didn't want to look at the hole as he yelled at me, but I couldn't help it. When he'd finished shouting, he whipped his belt from its legendary housing, over his left shoulder, under his sports coat.

He delivered four stripes across my palms, two on each. Then McEndrick's. He made it hurt far worse than Mr Boyd. He was much taller and his arms were longer. His technique was better, too. But still it wasn't too bad.

Then he told us to tuck in our shirts. He watched as we did it. He told us to straighten our ties and we tried. Then he sent us away, past the silent prefects, down the empty lunchtime corridors. And after that, everything at Biggar High School was all right.

Soon it was the Christmas holidays. Everyone said goodbye to each other and wished each other Merry Christmas and it was good to feel part of it. As the coach pulled from the playground, away from the school, I felt pretty good. There was deep snow on the ground. Christmas was coming.

On the first few days of the holiday, I dressed up warm, put on a woolly hat and gloves and I walked the dog on the snowy bing. She loved the snow. She rolled and skipped in it, like surf, and she scooped it into her mouth and tamped it down, and she left complex trails, paw-print mandalas. I trudged in her wake with my hands in my pockets.

At home, I played Christmas songs on the record player: Bing Crosby, Nat King Cole. I read the Christmas edition of the *Radio Times* and the *TV Times*, and I planned what I was going to watch.

A few days before Christmas, Mum and Yvonne came home early. Mum looked ill. She had been losing weight for a while. But now, as Yvonne led her inside, I thought she looked haggard and gaunt, even confused.

She sat down in the front room. She kept her coat on. So did Yvonne. I sat down too. The dog couldn't tell that something was wrong. She went from chair to chair, wagging her tail, burrowing her cold nose in our hands, waiting to be patted and told she was a good girl. Eventually she gave up and sat in the corner, watching us.

I said, 'What's wrong?'

Mum said, 'Oh, God.'

She tugged the skin on her throat with a thumb and fore-finger. Her eyes were raw. She had been crying.

I said, 'What?'

She couldn't tell me. She couldn't speak. You could see it. There was a mess inside her head: a bank of screens turned to different channels. That schoolgirl serving behind the counter at The Sweet Basket. That woman who stood at the side of the road, thinking *Just one step*. The woman who lived for a year in an Edinburgh bed and breakfast. The Bishop's happy wife, laughing when the American boys said *wadder*. She couldn't make sense of it. There was no sense to make. So it was left to Yvonne to tell me that Derek had left us.

There'd been gossip for quite a while; months, in fact. Church members in Edinburgh had seen Derek with another woman. They looked intimate, happy. They looked like people in love. The woman was not a member of the church.

Yvonne spoke to friends in Livingstone. They were shocked to lose their bishop so suddenly. You might have expected them to take some pleasure in the circumstances of it, in our humiliation, but not one of them did.

Yvonne also spoke to old friends from Edinburgh. Many of them had known about Derek and his lover. Eventually, she called David Chapple, who had liked Derek and been his friend. So it was through David Chapple we learned that Derek, patriarch and racist, had fallen in love and left us for a black woman.

26

I knew Derek. I'd known him since that moment in Romco, his failed shop, when I saw the false smile drop from his face as if weighted at the corners. And ever since he once, with shocking bitterness, incorrectly advised me that Yvonne was a lesbian, I'd long suspected him of trying to seduce her. He wanted to make her his spiritual wife. Having two or more sexually available women under one roof appealed to him.

Nevertheless I wondered if that failed seduction clarified Derek's purpose for moving us to Tarbrax. Mormon polygamists in Utah lived in what were always described as *isolated communities*. We didn't live in Utah, but he'd done the best he could. And so his sense of profound fellowship with the Prophet continued to deepen.

Joe Smith enjoyed success, celebrity, notoriety, gratifying tribulations and a large, mostly devoted following. At one point, he even decided to run for President of the United States. But he also enjoyed a great deal of sex.

In the summer of 1831, he was unlucky enough to sleep with Miranda Johnson, the fifteen-year-old daughter of his land-lords, an adventure for which he nearly paid with his pearls of great price. A scandalized mob numbering forty or fifty – some of them energetically disappointed Mormons – dragged the prophet from his bed by the hair, carried him down the street, stretched him on a board, mocked him in 'the most insulting and brutal manner', stripped him naked and requested of one Dr Denniston that he perform a public emasculation. Denniston demurred when he took pity on the prophet 'stripped and stretched on the plank'.[1] Instead, the mob satis-fied itself by giving Joe a beating, covering him in tar, rolling him in feathers and dumping him in the woods.

But Joe kept his pecker up. And soon, God was revealing unto to him the expediently sacred nature of polygamy. Joe took his first 'plural wife' as early as 1833, two years after his near-castra-tion. Between 1840 and 1844, he took about forty more of them.[2]

Emma, Joe's first and only legal wife, was so repulsed by this incontinence that God was forced to make a revelation which threatened her by name, if she didn't behave herself and let Joe do as God commanded. She explicitly didn't believe a word of it. But that didn't stop Joe; he just stopped seeking Emma's blessing.[3]

Some of his plural wives, like Mary Kimball, were as young as fourteen. In addition, a number of them were at the same time married to other men, with whom they continued to live. Joe simply had divinely mandated sexual access to them.

So everyone was happy, not least Joe, who cheerfully lied through his teeth about the subject whenever necessary, which was often. 'What a thing it is for a man to be accused of committing adultery,' he wailed in 1844 when he was committing it with at least thirty-nine women.[4]

By the time he received the divine commandment expressing the sacred nature of plural marriage (and the amendment, expressing the cussed nature of Emma), Joe had been trying for many years to keep his complicated sex life a secret. And even with God's written authority, a secret it remained until eight years after Joe's perhaps inevitably violent death.

But finally, in 1852, Joe's disciples concluded that, if plural marriage was good enough for the prophet, it was good enough for the men who followed him. And for the women, too. For a time, the sacred institution of polygamy was adopted as official Mormon practice. But it caused grave difficulties, not least of them with the government of the United States. In October 1890, with some regret, it was dropped again.

The missionaries hadn't told us any of that, probably because they didn't know: the church was wary of its own history. It spent a great deal of money buying up problematic documents and locking them away from scholarly investigation.

But that didn't matter. To Derek, there were always deeper doctrines, always layers of truth, always secret histories. And it was all there in the theology, if you made the connection. Like Joe Smith, he had never chanced upon a single church or a single woman that met his particular needs: that answered his questions, that explained to him the intolerable mysteries of the universe. He and Joe had found them all wanting. He and Joe always wanted more. Perhaps failure to establish a polygamous household had pushed him into the open legs of a lover.

He'd told me often enough that sex was different for men. It was like a hunger for fresh food. So I wasn't surprised by his infidelity. But I had never expected that he would leave us.

There was a funny feeling in my chest, under the ribs.

I said, 'That fucking cocksucker.'

I said it because I wanted to shock them and because I imagined it to be an adult response. But neither Yvonne nor Mum noticed and I felt diminished and childish and powerless.

We talked about it all evening, even though we knew nothing, except that he'd gone. We said the same things, again and again. We used the same words.

I wanted to do something. I wanted to go running, but it was dark and cold and treacherous outside. I went to my bedroom and threw darts at the Kirby poster. I tore it down. Mum helped me rip it to pieces. But it was a paltry reaction. Nobody's heart was in it, except mine. I wanted to break everything in the house.

Already, Mum looked like a face on the news, like the survivor of a train crash or a hijacking. In the days that followed, the skin sucked onto her bones like a special-effect. She was addled. She couldn't hold a conversation. She sat in confounded silence. When I spoke to her, she looked at me with fuddled eyes, as if I'd spoken in a different language.

Friends from the church were benevolent and unembarrassed. We were visited by a cheerful man who called himself Norman the Mormon. He had big Michael Caine spectacles and hair to his collar. He drove a long way to see us, over icy roads, to make sure we were okay. He invited us to stay over Christmas.

He said, 'Just for a couple of days. Or maybe just for Christmas. Just come for dinner, if you like.'

But Mum couldn't leave the house. When she stood, her limbs trembled. She looked thirty years older.

Nobody knew where Derek had gone. Nobody had heard from him – not even the people at Kirby, for whom he hadn't worked for some time. He hadn't been a very good vacuum-cleaner salesman. In fact, he was no longer working for them when he gave me the poster. It had been a kind of merciless joke. He just wanted to see if he could make me do it – cover my posters with a picture of a vacuum cleaner. He must have thought of it, hanging there, and chuckled to himself.

Around the time he went missing, so did the money from the Livingstone Ward's Bishop's fund – the money that his congregation had given in tithing, 10 per cent of their gross earnings, accumulated over many months. They had entrusted this money to their Bishop, who of all people they could trust. Derek had frequently expressed his desire to build a church with it – a building of their own, a place to belong, of which they could be proud for the rest of their lives. Nobody suggested that he had stolen the money. Nobody could bear to.

But Derek hadn't just run away. It was nothing so simple as an abandonment. The hatred that boiled inside him had secretly bubbled for us too, like a tar pool, as it bubbled for all the people who loved and respected him, because they did not love and respect him enough.

It had been revenge. He'd fantasized about it, and seeded his fantasy with details, little time-bombs, such as giving me the poster. He'd wanted to trip us up and kick us in the kidneys and run away, laughing,

On Christmas day, I opened my presents. Mum had been saving all year, at Mr Strachan's Xmas club. My present was a music centre, something a bit better to play my records on. Yvonne had bought me some records to play on it.

Mum and Yvonne cooked the dinner. It was roast chicken and veg. Mum couldn't eat. She prodded her plate with the tines of her fork and she smiled down at her lap. The rest of the day she sobbed in her bedroom.

I played The Specials at top volume and, in the late afternoon, I took the dog for a walk on the snow-blanketed bing. The landscape was fresh, halogen blue, edged with pink as the sun began to set. I sang 'Walking in a Winter Wonderland' and the dog nosed at the snow and followed scent trails that ran over paw prints, and that was good.

The days that followed were strained and desolate and silent. Mum shrivelled up on herself. I thought of those burning ants, long ago.

Norman the Mormon came round to help us pack. We packed the boot and the back seats of his car. He said he'd bring our things to us as soon as he could, and he drove away.

We stuffed our clothes into a couple of suitcases. I put my records in a carrier-bag. Everything else, we left behind: the furniture, the TV, the stuff in the kitchen, the beds, the toys I had not quite grown out of. Most of my books.

Mrs Lamb agreed to look after the dog for a fortnight, until Yvonne was able to bring her to us. I said goodbye to the dog.

I hugged her neck. She knew something was wrong. She looked at me with brown eyes. Her tan brows knit in the middle. We said goodbye to Mrs Lamb and we left Tarbrax, the bing shrinking in the window behind us until it was a smudge on the horizon; the pine forests snow-covered, like a Christmas card.

Yvonne drove us to Waverley Station. I remembered everything. We passed Dalry school. We drove past John Menzies on Princes Street. I thought of the *Club: Celebrity Edition* with Victoria Principal in it, and I wondered if it had mouldered to nothing in that plastic bag beneath a lump of concrete on the waste ground, or if it might one day be discovered by a foraging young boy.

It felt like everything had been ending for longer than it really had: everything had been ending since it started. It felt like Biggar High School had already slipped into another life – Mr Boyd and the prefect and attendant girls and the fat boy who was a sex person. And Dalry Primary School had happened to someone else altogether, a little boy it made me sad to think of.

Yvonne parked and we got out of the car. She carried Mum's suitcase. Mum was too weak. I wore a donkey jacket and my Dr Martens. I had a newly shaved head. I was taller than Mum and Yvonne. I hardly recognized myself in the shop windows. I carried a suitcase in one hand, my records in the other.

The train stood on the bitter platform. We said goodbye to Yvonne. Mum was too stupefied to be upset, even when Yvonne hugged her tight and said, 'Goodbye, Ma.'

Yvonne hugged me too. I said goodbye. Then Mum and I

took our seats on the train. Yvonne stood outside, at the window. She had on a woolly hat and mittens.

When the train pulled away, slowly at first, we looked out the window. Yvonne waved, then slipped away. Mum was saying goodbye to Edinburgh. I could see it in her face. Her reflection looked very old.

The heating on the train was broken. We huddled in our clothes. Yvonne had given Mum some food for the journey, but I couldn't eat. My teeth hurt. I couldn't close my mouth, they hurt so much.

Eight hours later, we arrived at Bristol Temple Meads. There was a light powdering of snow on the ground, and Bristol had been brought to a near-standstill by it. Mum and I laughed. We felt superior. We told everyone how deep the snow had been in Scotland, but it hadn't stopped anything. Nobody in Scotland was bothered by a little bit of snow.

27

We moved in with my sister, Caroline.

She was twenty-two, divorced, a mother of two young boys called Marc and Nathan. She lived in a council house in Stockwood. It was a short walk from Dad's house; five minutes from Stockwood Primary School; the place where Clive Petrie and I had once been friends, clambering over the apparatus.

The house had three bedrooms. Marc and Nathan shared one of them. The big one was Caroline's. The third, which had been spare, was now mine. Caroline put in an old sofa bed.

Downstairs was a living room and a small back room, off the kitchen. Mum used the back room as a kind of bed-sitter – a place to go and sit and be alone, which is all she wanted to do.

She furnished the room with things Norman the Mormon drove down. He turned up early in the New Year. Norman the Mormon, from Livingstone, stood at my sister's door in Stockwood, south-east Bristol. He helped us to unload our things from the back of his car, then bid us a merry goodbye and drove straight back to Scotland. Norman the Mormon was a fetch, a ghost of the living, a thing that flitted between worlds.

Mum spent most of her time alone in the back room. She had stopped eating. She was permanently confused. She forgot what you said to her, even as you were saying it. The end of a sentence was not connected to its beginning.

On Friday nights, Caroline and I watched horror films, the kind starring Joan Collins or an overweight Elizabeth Taylor. We sat in the blue, flickering dark. Marc and Nathan slept upstairs. Mum sat silent and still in the back room, looking at the walls.

A week or two after Norman's visit, Yvonne delivered the dog. The dog was delighted to see me. She skipped and yelped and put her paws on my chest and licked my face. But when Mum stepped forward to greet her, her tail stopped wagging and she turned pointedly away. She greeted my sister instead, and the children, and immediately became theirs.

Yvonne didn't linger. There was tension between her and Caroline. Caroline thought it sinister that Yvonne called our mother 'Ma'. Yvonne must have sensed it, because she addressed her as Edna, instead. It sounded false. She'd never been Edna: she'd been Sister Cross, then Ma.

Yvonne bid us another goodbye, but it was hesitant and awkward. We'd said our goodbye on the freezing platform at Waverley Station. She had stopped being my pretend sister the moment I boarded the train. The family she belonged to had never existed.

For a while, she and Mum exchanged letters. They were always addressed 'Dear Ma'. But over the years, the letters diminished in frequency. They dwindled to birthday cards and a wedding invitation, then just faded away and became silence.

Because Mum was confined to the back room, it was Caroline who registered me at Brislington Comprehensive. She'd been a pupil at the same school, in the days when she wore stripy socks, and liked to dress me up as a little girl then threaten me with Daleks. Now Gary and Wayne, my stepbrothers, were pupils there.

I no longer required any surname but Gadd. The man whose name I had sometimes taken was long gone. But it was only then, when its use was an insult to myself and to everyone around me, that I decided Cross would be my name.

On Sunday, I walked to Dad's house and ate lunch with him and his family. Margaret was pleasant and relaxed, serving up roast beef and potatoes and peas. Perhaps it was safer, now I was just a visitor from down the road – and now my mother was no longer a fabled, absconded first wife, spoken of in whispers if at all, but a shrivelled wreck confined to the back room of a house that belonged to a daughter she had once abandoned.

As for Dad, he'd always known that my mother would one day come home in fragments. Perhaps in the early days, he'd consoled himself with the thought of it. But by now he didn't much care. That was his revenge.

Over lunch, Gary and Wayne were keen to tell me about Brislington Comprehensive. They spent a long time detailing who was *brick*, which meant good at fighting.

We went to the Fruit Market, which is where everyone

bought their clothes. Dad bought me a green flying jacket, the kind that Madness wore, and some new jeans.

Late in the afternoon, Dad offered to drive me home to Caroline's. But it was a short and easy walk, downhill mostly. And if I walked, he wouldn't have to risk glimpsing the remnants of his ex-wife through his daughter's living-room window. So I walked.

There was a short-cut to Brislington School, across the fields, but I didn't want to take it: it would mean walking with hundreds of other kids who knew me for a stranger. And there was a school bus, but I didn't want to take that either; I'd had enough of being a new kid on school buses. So I walked the long way, and on my first morning I was late.

It was a big school – the biggest in the county of Avon – and by the time I got there it was silent. Even the stragglers had made it to registration. So I walked through the main doors. It smelled like all schools did.

There were no surprises. I was big for my age and, unfashionably by early 1982, I was still a skinhead. So I attracted some of the usual new-kid attention, but not much. For a short while, I acquired the nickname Hamish. But it didn't last. There was nothing Scottish about me.

I was scared of Chrissy Thomas. He was an inordinately large, heroically stupid boy of whom even the teachers were wary. Several times, he cornered me and told me what a fucking prick I was. But he never did anything about it, and soon it became obvious that he never would.

My form tutor, Mr Ashcroft, went to some effort to ensure

I was settling in. He was the nicest teacher I ever met, and Brislington School was easy, Brislington School was a piece of piss. But I stopped going anyway.

I sat on walls in car-parks and read books, or beneath a tree in the cold fields. Or I walked to Broadmead, the ugly shopping centre, and back again, just for something to do. I walked around, looking in shop windows, then walked home. I didn't know Bristol well enough to do anything else.

But one morning, I found inspiration. Above the front door of Caroline's house projected a functional, concrete lintel. My bedroom window opened onto it.

In the morning, I paused in the hallway and called out, 'Bye.' I closed the door behind me, then turned and jumped: I grabbed the edge of the lintel and hauled myself up onto it. Then I crawled through the open window and into my bedroom. I removed my tie, blazer and boots and got into bed.

In the afternoon, I wriggled back onto the lintel and lowered myself to the ground. Then I walked round the side of the house and went in through the kitchen door, as usual.

It lasted until the day I decided to re-read *Eat Them Alive!*. It was a book about giant preying mantises who ate human beings; they particularly liked to snip off and snack on women's breasts. The word *succulent* was used a lot. Halfway through *Eat Them Alive!* I fell asleep.

At first, it appeared to everyone downstairs that I was late back from school. Then it grew dark and Mum lurched from hazy indifference to frenetic torment. She assumed that another terrible thing had happened to her: that I had been raped and murdered.

She and Caroline searched the house. They even looked in my bedroom. The room was dark and they didn't see me asleep in it. They saw that the bed was disordered, but the bed was always disordered. My head was beneath the covers. I'd left only a small breathing hole to poke my nose through.

I woke late and, blearily, slapped out into the hallway. I went downstairs, where Mum wept to see me alive and inviolate. She used the wailing, melodramatic language of suffering she had learned at church.

She said, 'Where have you been? Oh, where have you been?'

She kept saying it. She looked mad. It was frightening.

'I've been in my bedroom.'

'Tell me where you've been.'

'Upstairs.'

'We've been to your room. You weren't there.'

'I was there.'

'Why won't you tell me where you've been?'

'Look,' I said.

I took Caroline by the shoulder and led her out the front door. I told her to wait. She stood there, crossing her arms and jiggling on the spot because it was cold, while I demonstrated how I jumped onto the lintel, then wriggled through my bedroom window.

I came downstairs.

I said, 'See?'

Caroline came in and closed the door.

'I've been upstairs,' I said. 'I didn't go to school. I do it all the time. I spend most of my week up there.'

Mum pulled at the hair on her nape.

She said, 'Why can't you just tell me where you've been?'

It was the end of a good place. But its time had been ending anyway: the school had written home about my attendance.

Mum couldn't face the shame of meeting my teachers. So she stayed in her room, looking at the wall and Caroline went instead.

She came home brisk and angry. She said, 'Is someone bullying you?'

Nobody had ever asked me that question.

I said, 'No.'

'Because if they bloody are . . .' said Caroline, and let the sentence hang. Her eyes were fierce.

The school put me on report. It was a little book. I had to get it signed by every teacher at the end of every lesson. At the bottom of each page was a section marked 'comments', where the teacher was to summarize my behaviour.

There was frequent use of the word 'disruptive', but I didn't think myself disruptive, I just wanted to be left alone. If they didn't hector me about homework we both knew I wasn't going to do, or about getting to class on time; if they just let me sit quietly at the back and read a book, then we'd all have been a lot happier. That was their favourite sentence. *If you would just do as you're told, we'd all be a lot happier*. But it wasn't true.

Because corporal punishment was illegal in England, putting me on report was one of the school's sternest sanctions. But it didn't do any good. After being on report, the next level of discipline was punitive suspension – they punished me for not going to school by not letting me go to school any more. I was awed by the logic of that.

Mr Ashcroft asked to see me after school. He was slight,

curly haired, greying a bit at the sides. His five o'clock shadow
was heavy and he wore his shirtsleeves rolled. He was gentle
and funny. I liked him, and I wished he'd leave me alone. He
was a French teacher, and we sat on desks in the language lab.

He said, 'Mr Cross, Mr Cross. What are we going to do?'

'I don't know.'

'You're never here.'

'I know.'

'And when you *are* here, you spend half your time in the corridor because you've been thrown out of class.'

'I know.'

'But you're a clever lad. Anyone can see that. And you seem
happy enough. You're always smiling.'

I showed him my helpless palms.

'So why do you hate school so much?'

'I don't hate it,' I said. I didn't want to hurt his feelings. And
I didn't hate it. I just didn't want to go.

'Then why not give it a go,' he said. 'Just give it one proper
go. See how you get on. You've only been here five minutes.'

The school was quiet because everyone had gone.

He said, 'You're going to get in real trouble if you carry on
like this. You do know that.'

Then he said, 'What I don't understand is, you always seem
so cheerful.'

I realized then: it was because I took after my Dad.

The thought made me want to laugh. But I didn't say
anything to Mr Ashcroft, because it would have taken far too
long to explain.

*

Most afternoons, I walked home the long way. Usually, there weren't many other kids around because I'd been in detention. The school couldn't keep me for more than half an hour without prior notification, so I sat and did nothing until they were obliged to let me go. There was nothing else they could do. They could suspend me, but I'd welcome it. They could expel me: I'd have welcomed that, too. I'd be sent to another school, but all schools were the same. I wouldn't be there long.

All they could do was give me detentions, after which I wandered home, content to be alone. I walked round the back of Caroline's house and let myself in through the kitchen door. I called out 'hello'. The house was quiet. No TV. I hung my blazer on the banister and walked into the front room, to turn it on.

In the front room sat Derek Cross. He was wearing fawn trousers and an army-style sweater. It had epaulettes on the shoulders and patches on the elbows.

28

He said, 'Hello, Neil.'

I said, 'All right?'

I was bigger than him. But he made me feel little. I thought of him sitting at my bedside, reading *Kidnapped*:

> . . . coming down from the top of the hill, I saw all the
> country fall away before me down to the sea; and in the
> midst of this descent, the city of Edinburgh smoking
> like a kiln

I wanted to hit him.

Mum was in the room, too. She was sitting next to him. But she was washed-out like a watercolour. She seemed less present than Derek.

I looked out the window. Then back at them. There were Mum and Derek, sitting next to each other, in Caroline's living room. The room seemed very small. All the perspectives were wrong.

I said, 'Where's Caroline?'

Mum said, 'She's upstairs.'

I thought, *This is Caroline's house.*

Derek said, 'Why don't you sit down.'

I wanted to tell him that I'd fucking well stand up if I wanted to. But my legs felt funny and I sat down.

I said, 'What are you doing here?'

'I've come here to see you and your mother. I made a terrible, terrible mistake, Neil. An awful mistake.'

He was more sorry than he could ever tell me. He looked at me to show me how sorry he was. He had his hands in his lap and he looked at them. He had very dainty feet.

He said, 'But I've come to take you home. If you'll have me.'

I said, 'All right.'

I began to cry.

Derek reached out to squeeze Mum's hand. For months, she had looked like something desiccated; like something you needed to add water to, to bring it magically to life. And now here he was. I thought of animals beneath the parched desert, scrabbling to the surface when the rains begin.

The way the light fell, it made a lens of Derek's eyes. I could see the room, reflected on their convex surface.

I began to sob. I tried to stop it. But it was like there was a motor in my chest. It hurt, and I felt stupid, but I couldn't stop.

A bit later, I asked what the plan was. Derek always had a plan.

He said, 'Well. It'll take a few days to organize things.

But I expect we'll be back in Edinburgh by next week.'

I said, 'Edinburgh?'

'Yes.'

'Not Tarbrax.'

'Not Tarbrax,' he said. 'No.'

I thought about Tam. I thought about hanging round the dark stone streets with him, scraping our knuckles on rough walls, to make ourselves look hard.

There was something grim in Mum's relief to have Derek back, something hard and determined, like the exhalation that follows the first cigarette of the morning. And in the days that followed, I saw little of them. They took my room and spent their time in there, alone, with the door closed. Sometimes I heard them giggling. They were hatching plans. They were arranging the future. Erasing the past.

I didn't know if Derek was still Bishop, or even if he was still attending church. I thought probably not. I hoped not. I detested the idea that he might parade Mum and me before his betrayed congregation, a token of his power to repent. But it didn't matter. I had nowhere else to go. If Derek wanted to drag me round the church, and if he wanted me to call him 'Dad' like a well-trained dog, then I'd do it.

My teeth hurt. Even touching their surface with the tip of a finger was tormenting. I couldn't eat. I drank cups of luke-warm tea.

In the morning, I vomited. I had vomited almost every morning since I was seven years old. At first, it used to worry people. It was loud, because my belly was empty, and it sounded painful. But everyone soon got used to it. My guts squeezed up green bile and indeterminate, foamy liquid. I coughed until it was over. Then I went to clean my teeth.

On the morning of the third day, Derek and I walked to the local shops. It was a ten minute walk: along Dutton Road then down onto Sturminster Road. It was a windy day. I wore a black woolly hat.

We walked in silence for a bit. Then Derek said, 'I can't believe how much you've grown.'

I grunted.

'And in such a short time.'

It didn't feel like a short time. But I was content for him to acknowledge that I'd changed. There was silence again. We walked on.

He said, 'You're a big lad, now. I'll teach you how to shave properly.'

'Okay.'

'We'll get you a decent shaving brush. Proper badger hair.'

'Okay.'

'And we'll get you to a massage parlour,' he said. 'To sort out some of that tension.'

He glanced at me. There was a squint of miscalculation at the corner of his eye.

But I said, 'All right, then,' and I meant it.

Even if we were still living together in Tarbrax, I knew he'd have made the same proposal. It would have been a secret between the bishop and his son. He'd have given me his lecture about the nature of female desire, about what women wanted and how they wanted it. And he'd tell me again about what men needed.

I'd have gone with him, and I'd have been proud; more proud than ashamed. I'd have let him choose the woman for me, and when it was over I'd have discussed it with him. I'd have told him what I did to her and what she did to me. He'd tell me how to do it better next time.

But we weren't living in Tarbrax, and he wasn't the bishop. He was just Derek Cross, offering me a hooker. I hated him for suggesting it and for knowing I'd say yes – just the way he'd known I'd hang the Kirby poster on my bedroom wall.

We walked to the shops and bought some milk, some bread and a newspaper. And on the way back, he told me about the new job he was about to start, about all the money he'd be making. That meant pocket money for me, a nice house to live in.

I nodded.

It should have been spring, but it was still winter. The days were drawing out but there was ice on the edge of the air. I huddled in my coat and my feet, in the boots, were cold.

Mum had some money in a building society. It had been left to her the year before, in a will. It wasn't much. But it was everything she had.

Nevertheless, we had to get ourselves and our things back to Scotland, and Derek didn't want to travel back in shame. No more hired cars. Our return should have some dignity about it. It was a fresh start.

The green Skoda had long gone. Derek had sold it. So he borrowed Mum's money, to buy a new car. She went into town with him. She withdrew the money in cash and together they visited some showrooms. They chose a car together. And they drove home in the car, proud of it because it was red. I admired it, parked on the street outside my sister's house. It was much better than the Skoda. It was a proper car.

Derek took the car keys. He walked out, twirling them on his finger, whistling. He took the car and drove away, and I never set eyes on him again.

29

As soon as he asked for the money, Mum knew. But she wouldn't acknowledge it, because he had begged her forgiveness. He had sobbed. He had shared her bed, had embraced her as they giggled together, projecting the bright future like a cine film onto the bedroom ceiling.

That's what she'd desired with the blind, heedless mania of the true addict. It's what she had dreamed about, while sitting in the back room. It's what she had conjured from her derangement and wretchedness. She had prayed for him to come: she had demanded it of God. And he had come, as unlikely as Christ on American shores. And he'd taken what little she had left, and he'd stolen it.

Caroline said, 'The fucking bastard. The fucking bastard.'

But they weren't the right words. I could feel the right words in my stomach and in my arms, and I can feel them now, but I don't know what words they were. So I said nothing. And

Mum shrivelled on this final impalement. She withered like a vampire. It was a kind of murder.

We soon found out where he was. That night, I laced my boots and I put on my donkey-jacket. Caroline went down the road, to her boyfriend's house. His name was Garry. He had blonde highlights in his hair and he wore baggy jeans. He drove a white Ford Capri, rusty round the rims.

He drove us to Cottham, where Derek's mother lived. It was the hilly part of central Bristol, the old part. It was late. The streets of Cottham were quiet. We soon found the red car. It was parked outside Helen Cross's flat; Derek had run to his mother. His lover was staying there too. Derek hadn't ended their relationship. He'd just suspended it for a few days. While he was with us, his lover had been a few miles away, enjoying the hospitality of a sweet-scented, obese old woman who thought it uppity of blacks to learn to read.

I rang the buzzer. I thought about that sweetly powdered, fat woman, that creaking oar of a husband. The unimagined woman with them.

I rang and rang.

No answer.

I stood back. I yelled at the window. I said, 'Fucking come down here.'

Caroline yelled too. She stood next to me and shouted. Mum wandered up and down on the pavement, shaking her head and muttering like someone on medication.

Garry waited at the wheel of the white Capri. He was embarrassed and nervous. It wasn't his family drama. He'd only come because Caroline asked him to.

Nobody answered the buzzer. Nobody came to the window. I thought of him in there, Derek Cross, exchanging supercilious, nervous glances with his mother and her husband and his lover. All of them pretending we weren't there: hoping we'd just go away.

I wanted to shout to his lover that he thought her a nigger, that he was fucking her because he hated her. And sooner or later that hatred would manifest itself in more than a grunted orgasm. He'd be gone while it still glistened wet inside her thighs.

I stood there and shouted and pressed my finger to the bell. But the windows stayed lighted and blank, like an autistic face.

Mum stopped wandering. She took off her shoe and, with the heel of it, smashed the headlights of the red car. She found a jagged quarter-brick and started on the windows, but couldn't smash them. She scraped at the paintwork. She tore off the wing mirrors and the windscreen wipers. She was silent. Her mouth was set. In one hand, she held on to her handbag.

I was about to join her; to take the brick from her hand and do some proper damage. But Garry got out of the Capri, put his hand on Mum's shoulder and ushered her away from the red car. She went with him. She was confused and compliant. She got into the Capri, with Caroline.

I stood there. I wanted to obliterate Derek's car. I wanted to take off the petrol cap and drop in a match. I wanted the concussion to shatter the windows of Helen Cross's flat, to send shrapnel whirling into the furniture, the doors: into their heads and bodies. But Caroline was calling me, so I went to the Capri and got in. The engine was running. Garry pulled away before the door was closed.

He was laughing. He said: 'Bloody hell, Ed.'

We drove back to Caroline's house. In the front room, I lit one of Garry's cigarettes, an Embassy Regal. Nobody said much. Eventually, Garry went home. He only lived down the road. He lived with his mum and dad. They all had a drink together, Garry's family, Sunday afternoon down the Antelope.

The next day, the police phoned. Mum panicked and didn't listen. She just heard the word 'police', and that was enough. She put down the phone with a quivering hand and said, 'They're coming to arrest us.'

She sat on the sofa in a state of nervous terror. Her hands were in her lap. I went upstairs and put on my boots. I didn't want to be arrested in bare feet.

There were two officers, one with a big copper's moustache. They crowded the doorway, monumentally. They seemed too big. They stood in their dark uniforms, their white shirts and black ties, and I thought of the missionaries, smiling in the doorway at 30 Duff Street. The same dog went similarly crazy behind a different door. She howled and gnashed and clawed at the wood. The police, like the Mormons, were unmoved.

They asked if they could come in. They took off their hats and wiped their feet. They went through to the living room. They sat on the sofa. Mum sat on the chair. Caroline and I sat on the floor with our backs to the gas fire. Caroline was wearing pin-striped jeans. They were fashionable. She turned down the TV, but left it on. I was aware of it, flickering silently in the corner of my eye, like somebody trying not to laugh.

The officers introduced themselves.

The officer with the moustache said, 'And this is Neil, is it?'

He looked at Mum, not me. Her foot was tapping. Her fingers fiddled with loose skin at her throat.

I said, 'Yes.'

He looked at me.

He said, 'What's so funny?'

'You leave him alone,' said Caroline. 'He's nervous.'

He looked at his little notebook. 'So he should be, by the look of it.'

The second officer said, 'Neil has been reported for criminal damage.'

I said, 'What?'

'Your gran saw you, mate. Smashing up the car. She watched you from the window. You weren't very clever about it, were you?'

There was quiet.

I looked at Mum.

She tapped her foot. Tugged at the skin on her neck.

I said, 'I didn't do it.'

'Well, your gran made a statement that says you did.'

I waited for Mum to speak. She didn't look at me.

I said, 'It's not even their car.'

The second officer said, 'You'd better wipe that smirk off your face, mate.'

'Don't you dare speak to him like that,' said Caroline.

They ignored her. They were glaring at me.

She said it again: 'Don't you dare.'

Mum was looking into space with her head weirdly cocked, as if none of us were there. She sat there, tapping her foot and playing with the skin on her throat, rolling it between thumb and forefinger.

The officers read it as shame on my behalf; shame that her son was a vandal. They took some notes. They weren't arresting me, but they'd be back. They got their hats. They'd be in touch.

Their presence faded slowly from the room, like the memory of an argument or an afterimage of the sun.

It wasn't late, but my teeth hurt and I went to bed. Caroline brought me a packet of cigarettes and an ashtray. I sat on the bed, smoking, tipping ash out the window.

Because it was essentially a domestic incident, because I had just turned thirteen and because it was a first offence, I was given a caution.

Caroline came to Broadmead police station with me. Mum stayed home. She didn't want to risk people seeing her walk into a police station. Caroline sat on the bus with me, not saying much. At the station, she waited while I was taken into a room. A bored police officer in shirtsleeves talked to me for a long time like I was a cretin. He told me that I was on the wrong path, a bad road, and this was my only chance to put things right. And it was no good to sit there smirking because this was deadly serious. It was only a caution, but it would be held on record until I was eighteen. If he or any of his officers had cause to speak to me again, he would personally come down on me like a ton of fucking bricks, and we'd see who was smiling then, mate. Did I understand?

I nodded and agreed. When it was over I went out of the room and my sister gave me a cuddle. And, as we walked out the doors, she linked her arm through mine, like she was proud that I was her brother and wanted everyone to know it. She kept her arm in mine at the bus-stop, and when the bus came she gave my arm a squeeze and let go. And we caught the bus home, the number 54 back to Stockwood.

30

Every Wednesday, Reeves Nightclub at Arnos Vale held a divorced, separated and singles night. Pernod was 50p a glass, and it was free entry for ladies. Caroline had split up with Garry, amiably enough. So she and Mum decided to give Reeves a go.

Mostly, the women went to have a laugh, to have a cheap drink and a giggle. For most of the evening, they danced to Abba and the Dooleys and Chic while the men lounged round the edges of the dance floor, watching and sipping pints of lager. Later, when the men were drunk enough, they nodded to their friends and strolled onto the dance floor. When that happened, most of the women left.

Mum met Brian Stone on her first visit, her first Wednesday night. A couple of nights later, she went out with him again. On Sunday, she brought him round to meet me.

He was fifty, divorced, particular. He liked cricket. He wore a neat parting. He was ursine and very hairy, but there was something womanly about his broad hips and big thighs. When he wanted to make a point, he tucked his chin into his neck and peered over his bifocals. Looking at him made my skin feel unpleasant. His voice made my scalp tighten.

He took us on holiday: me, Mum, Caroline and her boys. It was early in May. He chose the cheapest holiday he could book, cramming us into a little caravan in a deserted holiday camp.

In the holiday photographs, my mother sits in the grey-brown sea. She is splashing and smiling. She is very thin. She is all alone in the water. In the same set of photographs I am on the beach in a sweatshirt and a coat, and I still look cold. I have let my hair grow.

Mum's desperate, skeletal jollity made it impossible to relax. I went to the camp shop. It was too early in the season for it to have developed the intoxicating, English smell of half-molten beach balls. From the spinner by the checkout, I took a copy of *Salem's Lot* by Stephen King. It was big and I had time, and it looked frightening.

I began to read it that night, babysitting the boys while Mum and Brian and Caroline went to the empty clubhouse. It rained, and as the young vampire Danny Glick tippity-tapped on Mark Petrie's window, asking to be let in, the rain drummed hard on the thin metal ceiling and I huddled in a blanket, too scared to stop reading.

After the holiday, Mum said we were moving in with Brian. We'd been in Bristol less than six months. His house was on the other side of town, on the edge of a vast council estate called Hartcliffe. It was a starter home on a neat private estate called

'The Ridings'. His lawn was demarcated by a tiny white fence. His neighbours were young, married couples. He was like an old maid living among them, this hairy, prissy man who hurried to fluff the cushions the moment you stood up to go to the bathroom.

The living room was narrow, and Brian kept it swelteringly overheated. Upstairs was a small double bedroom with a mirrored wardrobe, and a single bedroom the size of a death cell. The walls were painted magnolia. The house was pale and sterile. It had no smell, other than dust burning on the radiators.

I said, 'But what about school?'

'There's a lovely school close by,' said Mum.

I had learned that 'there's a lovely school close by' meant simply, 'there is a local school'. I didn't want to change schools again.

I said, 'Can I live with Caroline?'

'Caroline won't have you living there.'

'That's not true. If you asked her, she'd let me.'

Caroline wouldn't let anybody criticize me. It didn't matter who it was. Nobody dared, not while she was in the room. She watched horror films with me. And having Marc and Nathan was like having two little brothers. I drew pictures for them and carried them on my shoulders.

I said, 'Have you asked her?'

Mum wore that pursed, disgusted look. It looked worse, bitter, now she'd lost so much weight.

She said, 'You can't go and live with Caroline. I'm not having it.'

I said, 'I don't want to live here.'

'Then perhaps you should go and live with your father.'

I said, 'Okay, then.'

I went to Dad's house that weekend. I told him about Brian: that he lived in a creepy little hutch, that he fluffed the pillows behind you when you stood up, that the wheedling sound of his voice made me want to scream. I told him I didn't want to change schools again. I told him I was sick of always moving.

I said, 'Can I come and live with you?'

He didn't hesitate. I might have been asking for bus-fare.

He said, 'Of course you can, my Sonner.'

I supposed they'd been considering this possibility since I got back to Bristol. Margaret was breezy and generous. She talked about how we could redecorate my old room. I'd grown out of it, the way it was.

She said, 'And we'll have to see about getting you some new bloody clothes.'

There were no undercurrents to her generosity. There were no lies in it. There was just Margaret, offering me a home. Whatever had been wrong before, it wasn't wrong now.

Dad drove me to The Ridings – Brian liked to give the full address as 'Lower Dundry', which the Post Office didn't recognize – and dropped me off. I said goodbye. Then I walked to Brian's house and knocked on the door. Mum opened it.

She said, 'Well?'

I said, 'I'm moving in tomorrow.'

She stepped back and let me in. I went upstairs, to the tiny bedroom that overlooked the two-tier, patio garden. Some of my clothes were there. Mum followed me. She sat on the edge of the bed. It smelled of washing powder. All the fabric in the house smelled of washing powder.

She said, 'And Margaret was all right about it, was she?'

'Actually,' I said, 'Margaret was amazing. She said we could decorate my room. And I could get new clothes and stuff. She was really good.'

Mum nodded. She said, 'Well. I hope you're very happy, living there with her.'

She began to cry. I watched her for a while. I wished she'd stop.

I said, 'Mum. I can't stay here. It's miles away. I don't like Brian and he doesn't like me. He doesn't want me here.'

'Yes, he does.'

'You know he doesn't. He won't even speak to me. I say something to him and he pretends I'm not there. He acts like I'm not in the room.'

She was nodding. She said, 'What am I going to do?'

She was fifty-three. She had nothing.

I looked at my clothes. It would take me five minutes to stuff them into a bag and be out of there. Five minutes; less, if I hurried. And no time at all if I forgot about the clothes and just left. It was a question of strength.

She sat on the edge of the bed, sobbing.

The next day, I caught two buses to Dad's house. Brian didn't want to drive me. He was too tired. He sat on the sofa reading the *Bristol Evening Post*. He read with his head tilted back and his bifocals slipped down the bridge of his nose and his mouth agape. You could hear him breathing through it.

I walked from the Stockwood terminus to 92 Bifield Road. I

walked up to Dad's door and knocked on it. Margaret answered. She said, 'Come in, Nipper.'

I went inside.

In the front room, I sat on the sofa, next to Dad. I took his offer of a home and I threw it back in his face.

He wasn't surprised. He just said, 'Well, you've got a home here any time you need one, Nipper.' And that was the last time he or anyone else ever called me by that name.

I spent most of the summer at Caroline's house. She'd met a man, too. His name was Steve. He was an ex-copper and in those days he still wore a copper's moustache.

Steve didn't like the same music as me, but he liked music and he played me things I'd never heard of. He wrote poems; he had a bin-bag full of them. It poured out of him. Sometimes he read them to me and we discussed them. On Saturdays, he drove us to Schwartz Bros, on Gloucester Road, to buy us hamburgers. There was still a shop on Gloucester Road called The Sweet Basket.

That fine summer was at its best when Caroline's neighbour went on holiday. Scared of being robbed, she lent us her new VCR. So Caroline, Steve and I spent two weeks driving to the big video rental shop in Whitchurch and renting six or eight films at a time. We watched them, one after the other, sitting in a darkened room in the mid-summer sun, and on through the evening and into the early hours of the morning. Steve didn't like horror films, but Caroline and I watched *I Spit on Your Grave*, *Driller Killer*, *The Evil Dead*. Eventually, we watched *The Exorcist*.

Just holding the case frightened me. It had gravity. It showed the silhouette of a tall man in a Homburg hat. He was staring up at an ominous house, from one window of which beamed down a sinister light. The box seemed to radiate corruption, and when I slotted the cassette home, ferns of evil unfolded in the corners of the room.

The girl's first use of the demon's voice – that old, genderless croak spitting horrible obscenities – pinned me to the sofa like a fist.

Caroline thought my terror hilarious. I'd never seen anyone laugh so much, or felt so bewildered by someone's amusement. *The Exorcist* was a scary film, she said, but not *that* bloody scary.

It was a long time before she felt able to make me a cup of tea or let me smoke a cigarette without first croaking 'Fuck me, Jesus, fuck me' in her best *Exorcist* voice.

Because of that, *The Exorcist* lost its grip. And gradually it, too, faded away.

31

When we lived in Edinburgh, what other people thought hadn't seemed important to Mum — not when she bought her clothes from the Spastic's Shop, or invited the smart young missionaries to eat Sunday lunch at the vermin-ridden flat on Duff Street. It hadn't been important then, because she believed herself loved. But it was important now.

So, once it had been publicly established that I lived with her and Brian in the funny little magnolia house at 38 The Ridings, Lower Dundry, and not with my father and his wife, it wasn't necessary that I actually spend much time there.

I didn't. Brian's dislike for me permeated even the closed door of my little bedroom, like the stink of toilet bleach. I couldn't relax. I sat alone in my bedroom and ground my teeth until the muscles cramped in my jaw.

I'd agreed to move in on the condition that I didn't change schools. But Brislington was a long bus-ride away, so I left early in the morning. (And was still late every day.) I went home after school, but only to change my clothes and be on the next bus back to hang around with my friends. I caught the midnight bus home. It emptied as it went, and I walked alone to The Ridings from the local terminus. It was night-time silent and the streets were patrolled by skinny, skittering dogs and I was scared.

When I got home, Mum and Brian were asleep. I let myself in, crept upstairs and went to bed. Days passed and I hardly saw them.

For a year or two I was close to my stepbrother Wayne. He was big, beefy, excellent at sports, well-liked. He still had the cowlick; it made him look innocent and good, despite his size. His good nature was belied by a local reputation for having a dangerous temper. The reputation meant it was irrelevant if the temper actually existed.

When I had just turned fifteen, a young man called Gary Ball beat the living shit out of me, head butting me while still wearing a motorcycle helmet, then punching and kicking me up and down Ladman Grove. It was only Wayne's tearful intercession that gave Gary Ball pause.

'I know you've got a temper on you, Wayner,' said Gary Ball, and walked away, leaving me to bleed in someone's front garden.

Wayne suggested that I spend more time at Dad's house.

I began to alternate a week at Dad's with a week at Brian's. But there was something wrong with me.

Dad disliked the way I looked: my hair and my clothes. And he disliked the friends I made. They were different from

Wayne's friends. They didn't play football. Although Wayne
didn't much like them either, he defended my friends on my
behalf. But even that did no good.

Dad never shouted at me. Occasionally, he showed his frustration and disappointment by joking about my clothes or what
I'd done at school that day – what had I done at school that
day? Had I done anything?

Margaret tried, too. She bought me clothes that I never wore.
She cooked for me and cleaned for me. They tried. They tried
much harder than I did. But, by degrees, I stopped staying with
them. In the end, and although they never showed it, it must
have come as a relief.

I spent hundreds of teenage evenings in Victory Park, drinking
from a plastic gallon-container filled with a mix of sweet and
dry scrumpy. I wore my hair dyed black and backcombed.
I wore make-up and boots and rips in the knees of my jeans.

Kids met in Victory Park to sit round and drink. There were
always people there. Sometimes twenty of us, sometimes half a
dozen. Being drunk in Victory Park was the happiest I had
ever been and the friends I made there felt like the best I would
ever make. I loved it in winter, when it was so cold you spent
half your night pissing into the frosty darkness. And I loved it
in summer, when you sat on the creaking swings with the
gallon warming in your lap, just talking.

Sometimes when I was drunk and on the way home,
I smashed things: I threw bricks through shop windows,
through house windows. If I found an unbroken line of cars,
parked down the street, I ran along their roofs. I never fell off.

Sometimes I just walked along the street, snapping off wing-mirrors and aerials as I went, tossing them into the gutter.

One night, I was walking with a boy called Andy Smith. He was tall and blonde. As we walked, Andy Smith happened to nudge the shoulder of a fat, middle-aged man who was on his way home from the pub.

Andy and I went on down the street. We were laughing at something else, something that someone we knew had said or done. Then we turned, because we heard running footsteps. The fat man was lumbering towards us, because he thought we were laughing at him. He punched Andy in the face. The back of Andy's head hit the wall and he fell over.

The fat man ignored me. He was too focused on beating up Andy Smith. I grabbed his punching arm by the elbow.

I said: 'Leave it out, mate.'

He turned to me, because my voice was deep.

He looked at my hair and my make-up. I was no longer tall for my age, but when he looked at my build, he realized his mistake.

He said, 'I thought you were a fucking girl,' and he kicked me in the balls so hard I landed on the bonnet of a car.

I was beaten up many times. I was beaten up on the street and in nightclubs and in Victory Park. I was chased by carloads of young men who wanted to hit me with sticks. I was glassed. I was kicked and punched and head-butted. But that was the last time anyone ever got me in the balls.

If it was too late to go home, or if it was Saturday night, I walked to Caroline's house and banged on the door. Steve opened the bedroom window, still mostly asleep, and dropped down the keys. Caroline and Steve never turned me away; not even when I turned up filthy with blood or my own shit.

When I slept at Caroline's, the dog wandered up to say hello. She nudged my palm with her cold nose and I told her she was a good girl, even when I was very drunk and very tired and just wanted to sleep. The dog and I always took care to acknowledge the fine friends we once had been, walking on the snowy bing. Then she wandered downstairs again, to sleep in her corner.

Eventually, Steve took her to the vet to be killed. Her back had been bad for many months. In the end, she couldn't walk. It was all the beatings she took as a puppy.

Caroline cried when she told me about it. She said that Steve hugged the dog while the vet administered the injection; that he cuddled her and told her she was good, and at the end she had not been afraid.

She said, 'Good old Tarbar. She was a lovely dog, really.' Tarbar is what Caroline had called her. It was a good name, a name with love in it.

Often, I slept at a friend's house. A night here, a night there. It was surprising, how long I could go, without going home.

When I was fifteen, a boy I knew very slightly was killed in a motorcycle accident. He was racing along Stockwood road when somebody opened a van door. He went straight into it.

It was a dramatic day at school. Everybody who had exchanged two words with the dead boy were transported by their lamentations.

After a sombre evening in Victory Park, I passed the house

of a boy called Brian Jones. He noticed me walking by. I was looking up at his window because I knew he lived there. He tapped on the window and invited me inside.

I sat in his bedroom and we talked about the boy; not because we knew him well, because we didn't, but because it was possible for him to be dead. We related his death to ourselves. It seemed profound.

Brian Jones's mother knew what had happened and she made us long glasses of vodka and orange. She was a kind woman, hard-faced, with old tattoos on her forearms, gone blue. Although I was already drunk, I had three glasses. Then I lit a cigarette. I puffed on it until it was good and hot, then I rolled up my sleeve and pushed the coal slowly into my upper arm.

Brian Jones watched with drunken concentration.

I took the cigarette away. Curls of smoke came from the skin.

Brian Jones said, 'Fucking hell, mate.'

I didn't reply. I was too studious. I lit another cigarette, puffed until it was hot, and stubbed that out on my arm as well.

'I think you'd better stop now,' said Brian Jones.

But I did it a third time, more slowly still. I moved the coal in little circles, to make the burn bigger.

I don't know how I got back to The Ridings that night. I know I stood in my stepfather's little front garden and pissed on the spindly thing that grew in the middle of it. And when I woke up, my arm was gummed to the white sheet. Mum came into my room, to get something from the airing cupboard. She noticed the burns. They were weeping, full of yellow pus that had dried like egg yolk to the bedding.

She nodded at the burns. 'And who did that to you?'

I said, 'I did.'

'I'm not having that rubbish,' she said. 'Somebody's done this to you.'

She gave me a look. Then she got some towels from the airing cupboard and walked out in disgust. The towels smelled summer-fresh.

In June 1984, Mum and Brian married at Bristol Register Office. Mum wept during the vows. She couldn't sign the register because she kept crying.

After the wedding, she put her leg on the spoiler of a car and raised her skirt to show a garter, and she wore the rictal smile she'd worn, the day she sat alone in the cold sea and splashed and said it was lovely, that we should all get in.

On Saturday nights, they went out dancing. Brian, who thought it repulsive that I wore eye-liner, carefully dabbed foundation on the purple discoloration on his left cheek, blending it in with circular movement of his fingertips. Then he splashed with Aramis. You could smell him coming downstairs. The smell of too much aftershave made me think of a toilet that someone has just shit in, then tried to deodorize.

They'd been married for a couple of months when Caroline came round with a letter from Derek Cross. You could tell, just by looking at the handwriting; his ostentatious loops and curls. Derek was proud of his penmanship.

He'd addressed the letter to Caroline's house because he

didn't know where Mum and I lived. Caroline sat on the sofa with her handbag on her lap and Mum sat in the chair and opened the letter. She was very composed. She smoothed down her skirt a couple of times, and coughed into her fist before she began to read it. But that was all.

In the letter, Derek asked us to come back. He said he was sorry. He said he couldn't live without us. I believed that he meant every word, that he'd wept as he'd written it. He had failed and was lonely and naturally blaming someone else: this time it was us, for not being there. Our coming back would make it all better.

Had I said I was willing, Mum would have packed her bags and gone to him that afternoon. But I said, 'That wanker,' and Mum set her mouth and tore the letter to confetti.

Long before, Brian had made her destroy her photographs. We had no pictures of Derek, no images. I wouldn't have trusted them anyway. He'd have become transparent, like the snapshot of a ghost, a double exposure. That torn begging letter was almost the last of him. Derek Cross, in shreds.

But not quite the last. Now and again, I heard something, caught a glimpse of his after-image. Before the end of the 1980s, he married at least twice more; neither time to the woman for whom he left us. He even tried going back to church, the Edinburgh branch. But he didn't stay for long. He turned up, humbled and diminished, and soon dwindled away.

Gradually, Mum fell out of contact with her remaining friends in Scotland, with all those loyal Mormons who remembered her as Sister Cross, and who were not acquainted with a different woman whose name was Mrs Stone of 38 The Ridings, Lower Dundry, Bristol.

When a member stopped attending church, the Mormons called it going inactive. And that's what happened to Derek Cross, in the end. He went inactive. He tied himself in a knot and vanished inside it, just like the American farmer with whose disappearance he had once, a very long time ago, so terrified me.

There's no point wondering what became of him. He preened himself in the mirror and saw nothing looking back. If he's alive, he's still doing it. But he probably isn't alive. He probably never was.

In 1985, just before my sixteenth birthday, I was finally arrested for vandalism. There was blood on my knuckles and on my hands and down my arms and on my clothes. I'd left a long spoor of smashed windows and vandalized cars. The police had followed it until they found me. They shoved me around and handcuffed me, and I spent that night in a cell.

I was given another caution. Another sergeant shouted at me. Told me I was on the wrong path. And I had to discuss my feelings with a psychologist. But I didn't have any feelings, except when I cut myself on the arms or burned myself. And I wasn't going to speak to a psychologist about that.

When she learned of my arrest, Mum wept with shame and panic.

She said, 'There's no excuse. No excuse.'

And, 'What will people think?'

I thought it was funny, her saying that. But she didn't think it was funny. She was ashamed to be seen with me, just walking down the street, because of my clothes and my hair and my make-up.

One Saturday afternoon, I saw her in the town centre. She met my eyes and made a jerky, panicked movement with her hands. She flashed me a warning expression that said that I was not to acknowledge her. She didn't want people to think she knew me.

She hoiked her handbag on her shoulder and walked on by, a bit more quickly. I remembered how I had pictured her, when I was little, the day she left us. I had imagined her, clutching her bag exactly like that, clutching her bag and running and running and running.

Later that spring, somebody set fire to the headmaster's office. It wasn't me, but I was questioned about it by the police and by the school. And not long after that, I was expelled on a pretext.

After everything they'd punished me for over the years, the pretext was a haircut. Ian Hand had given me a mohican by shaving the sides of my head in his back yard. We were listening to Joy Division through his bedroom window.

I spent the summer letting school go out of me like a long exhalation. It was good to be gone before it ended. Already, friends were drifting away. You could sense them, pausing, the way you do before diving into a pool, then stepping on, into other lives: to jobs and cars. My stepbrother, Wayne followed my dad into the Post Office, and Dad was proud.

I moved from friend's house to friend's house, and spent much of my time at Caroline's. Playing with a candle, I set light to the sofa and nearly burnt the place down. But even that Caroline forgave.

I was walking down Sturminster Road, on my way to Brislington. The sun was low in the sky and blinding. The hot concrete smelled good; it smelled like being young.

Dad's car pulled up in front of me and stopped at the kerb. The same Lada. He leaned over to open the passenger door.

'Hop in.'

I got in and said hello. I put on my seatbelt.

He said, 'Where are you going?'

'Briz.'

He pulled away from the kerb. He was looking at the road.

He said, 'Look at the state of you.'

On top, my hair was still long and backcombed and dyed black, but at the back and sides it had been shaved: the mohican had been a bit lopsided. I wore boots and ripped jeans and a leather jacket and eye-liner. But I didn't think he was talking about my clothes or my hair.

We drove to Brislington. It was a short drive and the evening traffic was light. Dad stopped the car outside the White Hart, just opposite the Kentucky Fried Chicken. It was close to Victory Park.

He leaned over to open the passenger door.

I took off my seatbelt.

He said, 'I'm glad you changed your name. I don't want you to have my name. You're not my son.'

I looked at him. He was trying not to cry. I had the metal end of the seatbelt in my hand.

I said 'Okay' and went to go. I opened the door.

He said, 'Wait.'

He dug into his back pocket and took out his wallet. In his fist, he crunched up a five-pound note. He passed it into my hand as if it were a secret.

He said, 'Keep hold of this. Wherever you go, you should always have a fiver in your pocket. In case you should ever need it.'

I said, 'Cheers, Dad.'

After what he'd said, I hesitated to call him that. But there was nothing else to call him. To me, Dad was the only name he ever had.

I got out of the car.

He said, 'You look after yourself, mind.'

And I said, 'Okay.'

And that was that.

I closed the door and he drove away. I stood there, shrinking in his rear-view mirror.

Sometimes I slept in the park. It was an adventure, but even in summer it grew very cold at night. I always woke up feeling ill; the cold had oozed from the ground and into my bones. I was sick with cider and cigarettes. Sometimes I puked and shat in the bushes.

My friends and I had never spent much time in local pubs; the way some of us looked made us unwelcome. But, late in the summer, we discovered that a new nightclub had opened in Bristol town centre. It was called the Whip. It was held in the anteroom of a larger nightclub, the Studio; years before, it had been called the Locarno.

The people who went to the Whip seemed unutterably elegant: skinny boys and girls with long, backcombed hair, dyed black or bleached white. There were meaty psychobillies with sleeveless T-shirts and enormous, lurid quiffs. It looked like a better place to be. Much better than sitting on a park bench, drinking cider.

The Whip was held every Friday night. The DJ played songs I already loved and songs I came to love: a song called 'In Shreds', a song called 'Heartland'. The dance floor was violent and amicable. The girls wore basques and painted nails. I never wanted to leave.

I began to stay with people I met there – at their bed-sitters and their squats and their squalid, shared houses. I stayed all over Bristol, and believed myself cosmopolitan. In the morning, I woke up, lit a cigarette, put on a record, made coffee; instant, black. I much preferred a cup of tea, but coffee seemed more suitable. The bed-sitters and squats smelled of patchouli and incense and garlic. There were posters on the wall, records on the floor.

But, wherever I slept, I still sometimes returned to Brian's house. I was sixteen. It was supposed to be where I lived. The last time I went to Lower Dundry, it was a Wednesday. Mum was at my grandmother's. She went there three days a week, to cook and clean and to walk Tiny, the Yorkshire terrier. She was a good and attentive daughter.

I let myself in and went upstairs to my bedroom. I lay down. I was tired, needing a bath. I put on an album. I played it on the music centre: it was four years old by then, and sometimes it played records at the wrong speed. But it was okay. I played an album called *Pornography*. It was by The Cure. I was obsessed by The Cure. I lay on the bed and listened to the record.

Brian came upstairs and to my bedroom door. He was wearing blue jeans and a white vest, tucked in nice and tight. His shoulders and arms were snarly, hairy, auburn, grey. The hair on his head was neatly parted. He had hair like a Tory MP. His bifocals ran low on his nose; he was sweating because he'd been doing something in the little patio garden. He'd heard me playing The Cure.

He stood in the doorway. He had a little trowel in his hand. He said, 'Turn that rubbish down.'

I sat up. I turned it down.

He said, 'You should be out looking for a bloody job. Paying your own way.'

I said, 'Give me a chance.'

He said, 'I wish I'd known your mother had a little bastard like you, the day I met her. I'd never have bothered.'

His voice was girlish with indignation. He stood there, trembling. I thought of the times I'd seen him jogging naked to the bathroom, his shrivelled little cock cupped in a hairy paw.

For some reason, Brian had always hated that I had sex with girls. When a girl telephoned me, he sat behind the *Bristol Evening Post*, pretending to read but humming with anger and hatred, like an electricity substation. I spoke to the girls in a code I knew Brian would understand, and it enraged him: the thought of it. When I put down the phone he gave me a dead-eyed look, over his bifocals, and I knew what he was thinking.

Eventually, he'd banned me from using the phone. I'd never been permitted to make outgoing calls. Now, people weren't allowed to call me. Especially girls. He thought them filthy; filthy little girls. He was full of hate.

He stood there, in my bedroom doorway, trembling with rage.

He said, 'Turn off that muck –'

I'd already turned it down. And it wasn't muck, even though it was called *Pornography*. There wasn't even any swearing on it. It was an album about paralysed rage. Perhaps Brian had simply seen the word on the cover, and it was enough to make him quiver with excited disgust.

He said, 'Get out of my house and don't bother coming back.'

He was still shaking. I thought he might hit me. I hoped he would, because then I could hit him back. But he didn't hit me. He just stood there, in his vest, glaring over his bifocals.

I laughed at him, because it was the best thing to do, laughing at people who hated you. I had learned that, when I was a child.

I smiled. I said, 'Calm down, Brian.'

I went downstairs – he stood there and made me shove past him, past his hairy shoulders and his womanly hips in his Primark jeans – and I went to the neat little kitchen with the novelty clock that was A Round Tuit and I took some carrier-bags from the drawer. I took the carrier-bags upstairs and began to stuff them with my things; my clothes and my records.

On a shelf above the bed was a bag of comics that had come from Scotland; I'd packed them myself, with great care, in the back seat of Norman the Mormon's car. Some of them might have become valuable, if they'd been in better condition. But their condition was poor because, when I was little, I read them over and over again to ward off my fear of the dark. I didn't care how much they might have been worth. I loved them. They still smelled of Bobby's Bookshop; of comics and yellowing spy novels and Sven Hassel and Louis L'Amour. They were all I had of those days. But I couldn't take them with me, because I didn't yet know where I'd go. They were fragile and precious.

So I took a carrier-bag of clothes and a carrier-bag of records. I went down the narrow stairs and through the UPVC door, a bag in each hand. I felt Brian, in his vest, watching me from the bedroom window, behind the net curtains. And I went down the little garden path with its peculiar little fence, and I boarded the number 36 bus at the terminus and sat at the back, alone, until the driver folded away his newspaper and started the engine.

A couple of days later, Mum and Brian were clearing out my bedroom, removing the traces of me from it. Mum found the comics, still in the bag on the shelf, dog-eared and musty and old. She took the bag down from the shelf and threw it in the dustbin.

The day I left, I went to Simon Hall's house. I knew him as Hally. Hally and I had been through more than seemed possible, at sixteen. Now I told him I'd become officially homeless. I wasn't worried about finding somewhere to stay: there would always be somewhere. But I felt we should do something, to mark the day.

Hally said, 'What do you want to do?'

I said, 'I don't know.'

He'd just bought his first car – an old Ford Anglia. And the late summer sun was setting over Bristol, so we went for a drive. We drove until it was dark. And, very late at night, when the streets were silent, we parked. We walked onto Clifton suspension bridge. We stood in the middle of it.

We looked at all the lights of Bristol. The spectacle of a city on a summer night, from a high place, erases everything.

32

It is more difficult by far to recapture lost belief than lost love. For lost love, we forgive ourselves. We were different people then. We didn't know so much; we learned by it. But about lost beliefs, we are sheepish, evasive. Nobody is proud once to have been a fool.

The disappearing farmer, David Lang, never existed. The tale was a hoax cooked up by a travelling salesman called Joseph Mulholland: he borrowed it from a story called *The Difficulty of Crossing a Field*, by Ambrose Bierce. The nun with the bleeding eyes, like most stigmatics, almost certainly suffered from something similar to Münchhausen's syndrome; she inflicted the wounds on herself, in secret. Dr John Irving Bentley, who burned so horribly and so mysteriously, was ninety years old and in the habit of dropping burning matches and hot ashes from his pipe. He also kept a box of matches in each pocket of his day robe. The evidence suggests that Dr Bentley woke to find himself on fire and made his way to the bathroom, using his walking frame, where he tried to extinguish the flames. But in his efforts to do so, he fell down, igniting the linoleum. Beneath it was a wooden floor. Cool air was drawn from the basement, to intensify and localize the heat of his combustion. It's called the chimney effect.

I'm not sure that I ever believed in God, at least not God as Joe Smith would have him. I did believe in Jesus, though. For many years, he crept back into my mind. I missed him. Sometimes I missed him so much it was a physical pain, a knot in my belly. I hungered to believe in him; I yearned to. But I never quite could. And now he too is gone, and I do not expect or desire his return.

I don't believe in those things any more. But I do believe in ghosts. I am compelled to, because one day I saw one.

In the days when Mum and I lived with her, Caroline's boyfriend Garry came round two or three evenings a week. He'd have a beer, watch some TV. Then I'd go upstairs to my room, to leave them alone.

When it was dark and quiet, Caroline would creep silently upstairs. She'd sit outside my bedroom door, singing. It was never a song I recognized; I could never quite catch the tune, because she hummed it very quietly. It was barely a melody at all. I ignored it for as long as I could. But the half-tune insinuated into my consciousness, and it was a bit creepy: this singing from behind my bedroom door.

I always cracked. I put down my book and went to the door and opened it. But Caroline had heard my approach and hurried silently downstairs in the dark. I followed her. I knocked on the living-room door and walked in before she and Garry had the chance to tell me to go away or to properly rearrange their clothing.

I stood in the doorway. I said, 'Stop it.'

'Stop what?'

'The singing.'

'What singing?'

'Don't wind me up. It's really creepy.'

'I'm not singing.'

'Yes, you are.'

'I'm not doing anything!'

'Just stop it,' I said, and slammed the door and stomped upstairs.

Usually, when everything was quiet, the singing came back. Caroline stood outside my bedroom door and hummed beneath her breath. Eventually I fell asleep and the singing stopped. I didn't know which came first.

It was years later that Caroline saw the ghost that had always shared her house. She woke alone in the night. A woman stood at the foot of her bed, furiously nodding.

In the morning, Caroline phoned me. She was still distressed. I went round and we had cups of tea and cigarettes. We talked. After some time, she'd convinced herself that the nodding woman had been a dream.

Caroline's children, Marc and Nathan, had been spending the night at their father's. Having calmed down, Caroline insisted that, whatever she had or hadn't seen, nobody must ever mention it to them. They were still very young.

But, that Christmas, Marc and Nathan saw her, too. The nodding woman stood in the centre of their shared bedroom. They screamed. By the time Caroline rushed in, the nodding woman was gone.

Nobody ever saw her again, and nobody heard her singing.

The nodding woman is not the ghost I saw.

A couple of years before I turned thirty, my boss and I flew to Edinburgh. We were to attend a formal dinner marking the retirement of a well-loved man. My boss was called Chris. He was my friend, too. The dinner ran late, there was dancing, and Chris and I drank a lot of wine. Eventually, we stepped into the early hours of a winter morning. It was freezing.

It was my first return to Edinburgh. I hadn't really thought about it. Our working day had been busy. Meetings overran, because they always did. The taxi-ride to the airport had been slow and fraught. Our flight had arrived late; there was a rush at the airport to get to the party on time.

Besides which, I never thought about Edinburgh. A lot had happened since then, and my life was very different. I felt no connection to the child who had lived there. I was embarrassed by him. I had no wish to admit he had ever existed.

But as we stood there, huddled in our overcoats, I realized that we were only a short walk from Dalry Road. It was 2 a.m., and we were a little drunk. I told Chris that I'd gone to school, very nearby. It was his idea to go and take a look. So we buried our hands in our pockets, and in our suits and good coats and shoes, we walked through the night.

At the Haymarket end of Dalry Road lingered an assortment of mostly teenage prostitutes. They wore skimpy vest-tops and short skirts and no tights. They looked very cold. We walked past them.

We walked down Dalry Road. And as we came closer to the

school, I ran out of things to say. Chris knew, and understood my silence.

Then we reached the school. I stood by the gates and looked at it. It had not changed. It was close to a hundred and twenty-five years old. It had seen many generations of children pass through its doors: it had seen them leave, grow up, grow old and die. It was not wholly impervious to my presence; it knew I was there. I just didn't mean a great deal to it.

I looked at its blank windows. Inside the classrooms, children's paintings were pinned to the walls. You could see them as paler smudges in the darkness.

I felt something pass through me. It was the ghost of the boy I had been. For a few moments, I allowed him to possess me. I saw the school through his eyes and my eyes, simultaneously. And I saw that the boy and I were somehow the same person.

Chris put his big hand on my shoulder because I was crying a little bit. Then we turned and left and went back to our hotel. We ordered more drinks, and in the morning we flew back to London.

But that is not the ghost I saw.

When I was twelve years old, living in the village called Tarbrax, I had a dream from which I awoke in stark terror. The dream took place in the bedroom I shared with Yvonne. In the dream, I sat up in bed. At the foot of it stood a blond child. He wore red shorts and a red- and yellow-striped T-shirt. He stood divided by light and shadow, so that only half of him was visible. He looked at me solemnly, his face bifurcated by darkness.

I didn't understand exactly what about the dream had been so frightening. But it always haunted me.

More than twenty years later, I caught a glimpse of my first child as the sunlight streaked down on him through a Velux window. It was set into the sloping ceiling of an attic flat in Finsbury Park, North London. I saw that my son was the child in the dream. He wore red shorts and a red- and yellow-striped T-shirt. He had blond hair. The way the light fell on him, he stood half in light, half in shadow. He looked at me with the absolute gravity of his love.

End Notes

chapter 9

1   Ezekiel 1:4 through 1:24.

chapter 14

1   *The Pearl of Great Price*, Joseph Smith – History, 1:17.
2   Ibid., 1:17.
3   Ibid., 1:19.
4   Ibid., 1:34.
5   Joseph Smith, *Times and Seasons* (Periodical of the Mormon), 1 March 1842.
6   Joseph Smith, *History of the Church of Jesus Christ of Latter Day Saints*, vol. 4, p. 461.
7   Nephi, Book 2, 5:21.

chapter 20

1   From *Temple Mormonism: Its Evolution and Meaning*, W. M. Pagden (New York, 1930). Quoted from on-line sources.
2   Ibid.

chapter 22

1   The full text can be viewed at www.2think.org/hundredsheep/
    voh/voh_main.shtml
2   *History of Joseph Smith* by his mother, p. 83, 1954.
3   For an extensive discussion of Joe's First Vision disparities see
    Mormonism, Shadow or Reality?, Jerald and Sandra Tanner, Utah
    Lighthouse Ministry, 1987, chapter 8.
4   It was eventually published as 'New Light on the Historical
    Setting of the First Vision', in *BYU Studies*, vol 9, spring 1969,
    p. 278ff. Also included in *The Personal Writings of Joseph Smith*,
    Dean C. Jessee. How the 'Strange Account' came to be published
    is documented in *Mormonism: Shadow or Reality?* (as above).
5   *Personal Writings of Joseph Smith*, p. 5.

chapter 26

1   Deseret News, 19 May 1858, quoted from *Under the Banner of
    Heaven*, John Krakauer, Macmillan 2003, p. 118.
2   Main source is *Under the Banner of Heaven*, John Krakauer,
    chapter 11, 'The Principle', pp. 15–33.
3   *Under the Banner of Heaven*, p. 125.
4   In a speech given to the citizens of Nauvoo, ibid, p. 122.

Underneath
the
Christmas
Tree

Wynter's Trees is the home of Christmas. For the people of Wynmouth it's where they get their family Christmas tree, and where Christmas truly comes to life.

But for Liza Wynter, it's a millstone around her neck. It was her father's pride and joy but now he's gone, she can't have anything to do with it. Until her father's business partner decides to retire and she must go back to handle the transition to his son Ned.

When Liza arrives, she discovers a much-loved business that's flourishing under Ned's stewardship. And she's happy to stay and help for the Christmas season, but then she has other plans. But will the place where she grew up make her change her mind? And can it weave its Christmas cheer around her heart . . . ?

AVAILABLE IN PAPERBACK AND EBOOK NOW

A Christmas Celebration

When Paige turns up unannounced at Wynthorpe Hall, she discovers the place she knew when she was growing up has changed beyond all recognition.

One night while driving home after delivering library books and shopping to residents she stumbles across an isolated cottage and meets Albert, its elderly and rather grumpy owner. She quickly realises there's more to Albert than meets the eye and the same can be said for the other man she can't seem to help running into, handsome but brooding Brodie.

Each of them has a secret and a desire to hide away from the world, but with Christmas on the horizon, is that really the best way to celebrate the season?

AVAILABLE IN PAPERBACK AND EBOOK NOW

The Summer Fair

Beth loves her job working in a care home, looking
after its elderly residents, but she doesn't love
the cramped and dirty houseshare she currently
lives in. So, when she gets the opportunity to
move to Nightingale Square, sharing a house
with the lovely Eli, she jumps at the chance.

The community at Nightingale Square welcomes
Beth with open arms, and when she needs help
to organise a fundraiser for the care home they
rally round. Then she discovers The Arches,
a local creative arts centre, has closed and the
venture to replace it needs their help too – but
this opens old wounds and past secrets for Beth.

Music was always an important part of her life, but now
she has closed the door on all that. Will her friends at
the care home and the people of Nightingale Square
help her find a way to learn to love it once more ...?

AVAILABLE IN PAPERBACK AND EBOOK NOW

About the Author

Heidi Swain lives in Norfolk. She is passionate about gardening and the countryside, and collects vintage paraphernalia. *The Book-Lovers' Retreat* is her sixteenth novel. You can follow Heidi on Twitter @Heidi_Swain or visit her website: heidiswain.co.uk

for their seamless running of the Heidi Swain and Friends Facebook Book Club and to the many, many club members who make the space such a wonderful place to be. Thanks also to the numerous bloggers, librarians and newsletter subscribers who are still waving a banner with my name on and have found me many, many more readers over the past few months. As you know, I love to connect with you all and my social channels are always buzzing with pics and posts.

Thanks also to my mum, who I have seen more over the past few months than I have in many years. She has been a total rock and we've spent hours laughing as well as setting the world to rights, which is always time well spent.

Congratulations to Catriona Merryweather who has been waiting to see her name in one of my books since December 2021! I hope you like the part you have played, my lovely, and thank you for your patience. Such is the schedule attached to writing two titles a year, I know you've had an extraordinarily long wait but, that said, it really does feel like this one was the right fit for you.

And last but by no means least, I reserve a huge thank you for you, dear reader, for picking this book up. I hope to see you again in October for a book that's going to be packed full of festive frolics! In the meantime, may your bookshelves – be they virtual or real – always be filled with fabulous fiction.

With love,
H x

Acknowledgements

Having already embraced a whole raft of life changes at the beginning of 2022, I felt more than ready for the professional challenge my wonderful editor, Clare Hey, offered me after I had submitted *A Christmas Celebration*. My first standalone read was what she had in mind and a perfectly timed Netflix binge with my daughter ensured inspiration almost instantly struck and here we are, not all that many months on, spending summer in the Lake District on *The Book-Lovers' Retreat*. Thank you so much for picking it up. I hope you have enjoyed reading it as much as I enjoyed writing it, because I had a total blast!

As always, there are numerous people to thank for making the process a pleasure. Along with Clare and the rest of the Books and The City team, my fabulous agent, Amanda Preston, has been just a phone call away whenever I've needed her. Thank you, my darling. You really do go above and beyond!

Thanks also to my Famous Five, to whom this book is dedicated. I'm not going to reveal their identities but they know who they are. Thank you, my loves, for both your friendship and support, especially over the past twelve transformative months.

Huge thanks too (as always) to Sue Baker and Fiona Jenkins

Praise for

Heidi Swain

'Sweet and lovely. I guarantee you will fall in love
with Heidi's wonderful world' **Milly Johnson**

'An absolute joy' *Heat*

'So full of sunshine you almost feel the rays'
Woman's Weekly

'Sparkling and romantic' *My Weekly*

'The queen of feel-good' ***Woman & Home***

'A summer delight!' **Sarah Morgan**

'The most delicious slice of festive fiction: a true comfort read
and the perfect treat to alleviate all the stress!' **Veronica Henry**

'Sprinkled with Christmas sparkle' **Trisha Ashley**

'A story that captures your heart' **Chrissie Barlow**

'A delightfully sunny read with added
intrigue and secrets' **Bella Osborne**

Heidi Swain

The Book-Lovers' Retreat

**SIMON &
SCHUSTER**

London · New York · Sydney · Toronto · New Delhi

First published in Great Britain by Simon & Schuster UK Ltd, 2023

1 3 5 7 9 10 8 6 4 2

Simon & Schuster UK Ltd
1st Floor
222 Gray's Inn Road
London WC1X 8HB

Simon & Schuster Australia, Sydney
Simon & Schuster India, New Delhi

www.simonandschuster.co.uk
www.simonandschuster.com.au
www.simonandschuster.co.in

A CIP catalogue record for this book is available from the British Library

Paperback ISBN: 978-1-3985-1951-0
eBook ISBN: 978-1-3985-1952-7
Audio ISBN: 978-1-3985-1953-4

Typeset in the UK by M Rules
Printed and Bound in the UK using 100% Renewable Electricity at
CPI Group (UK) Ltd

To my Famous Five
You know who you are!

Prologue

It was utterly impossible for the three of us to get our heads around the fact that we'd been living in the cottage by the lake for three whole months now or to believe that in just a few hours we'd be handing back the keys and setting off for opposite ends of the country.

We had been serendipitously thrown together, three strangers leaving reality behind for one whole summer but now we'd got our lives working exactly how we wanted them to and we were ready to face the future, armed with our fresh starts. The three of us had become a unit, a solid one. Our shared trauma and soul-searching had pulled us together during our three-month journey and consequently we had formed a bond which we all knew would last for life.

'Unshakeable and unbreakable,' carefree Rose had said the night before as we sipped chilled champagne by the campfire next to the lake.

When she'd arrived, Rose had maintained she was just 'along for the ride' but between us we had scratched off the surface of the veneer she had coated her life in and discovered someone sweet, vulnerable and lost, floundering beneath. Now she had

a life goal and a plan as to how she would achieve it. She was still the most outgoing and laidback one out of all of us, but she no longer used her up-for-anything attitude as a smokescreen.

'Unshakeable and unbreakable, for life!' Laurie had beamed, slurring the toast slightly and then snorting with laughter because she still couldn't drink more than one glass of anything without getting the giggles.

Even though she had been reluctant to admit it, Laurie had been the one out of all of us who had been properly running away. In the early days, when we were first getting to know each other, she had insisted that she was looking forward to her fast-approaching trip down the aisle with her Mr Right (Mr Not So Right as it turned out), but it took until our visit to Hope Falls for her to crack.

We'd each of us made a secret wish at the waterfall. Rose and I had been happy with ours, but Laurie had burst into tears and confessed between sobs that she had wished for something to happen which would enable her to break off her engagement without upsetting anyone.

It had been a big ask, but between the three of us we had managed it and Laurie had promised she'd never run away from a situation again and would stop trying to be a people pleaser, which was the thing that generally made her want to run away.

And what about me? Well, I'd arrived with my head in every bit as much of a muddle as the other two, but I was sorted now. Feeling brave and set to follow my heart, I had let go of the ifs, buts and maybes. I had decided that I should stop dithering and blindly following the path already set out for me in the family business and embrace my creativity while the spark was still

ignited and I had allowed myself to fall in love again, too. It turns out you couldn't – and really shouldn't – tar all relationships with the same brush . . .

'Heather!' Laurie screeched, pulling my thoughts away from the new man in my life. 'Please, hurry up!'

'Are you chickening out?' pouted Rose, standing naked as the day she was born and with a hand on one hip as she looked me up and down.

Laurie by contrast was mostly covered by the huge hoodie she'd just pulled over her head. I was sure she'd chosen to wear it with the purpose of covering her modesty until the last possible moment.

'No!' I shouted back, unzipping my jeans and wriggling out of them. 'Of course not. I'm coming now.'

Laurie peeped over the edge of the jetty and into the dark water beneath.

'I can't believe you've talked me into this,' she muttered to Rose as I quickly stripped and joined them.

'It will properly seal our bond,' Rose insistently said.

'Skinny dipping in the lake and developing pneumonia will seal our friendship?' Laurie frowned.

'Either that or the shock of the cold will kill us,' I shot back, grabbing both their hands which made Laurie drop her hoodie. 'Think of the headlines!'

Rose threw back her head and laughed and Laurie joined in too.

'Come on then,' she said, pulling us further back so we could have a decent run up. 'We'll do it on three.'

We looked at each other again and I felt a lump begin to form in my throat. No matter where our lives took us next, I would

never forget the summer I'd spent beside the lake with these two incredible women.

'Let's go then!' Rose smiled, her eyes full of tears as Laurie sniffed.

We squeezed hands and ran.

'One, two, three!' we shouted together, not caring who could hear as our voices reached a crescendo and we jumped with complete abandon as far and as high as we could into the lake beneath us.

Chapter 1

Friday night drinks with my two best friends, Rachel and Tori, had been a solid tradition for almost a decade. Nothing was supposed to get in the way of our end of the week regular night out, but Rachel's increasingly clingy boyfriend, Jeremy, Tori's Thursday night hangover and my, at times, obsessive work ethic, had meant the ritual had taken a bit of a hit of late.

Not that my work ethic was much in demand now that I'd been made redundant from what I had once assumed was a data analyst job for life with a defined career path, but you get the idea. Friday night drinks had always been a big deal, even when cashflow was tight – for me and Rachel at least – at the end of the month. The trip out had been a priority since our student days so why Tori hadn't showed up after she'd picked The Flamingo, of all places, as the venue for our extremely important get together on that first Friday in July, was a mystery.

'She said this place was beyond tacky when I chose it three months ago,' Rachel reminded me as we made our way to a table as far away from the marabou bedecked bar as it was possible to get. 'And not in a *good way*,' she added, putting down her glass

and embellishing her comment with air quotes. 'I am remembering that right, aren't I?' She frowned.

'You are,' I confirmed, twirling my glass to shift the paper umbrella and flamingo topped twizzler before taking a sip of the over-sweetened cocktail. 'But,' I added, wincing at the syrupy taste as I took another look around, 'I don't care about any of that. Not tonight.' I felt my insides fizz again and with more than the alcoholic hit. 'Nothing can spoil tonight.'

Rachel shook her head but didn't crack a smile as I had hoped she would. She'd been preoccupied all week, but then given the high school she worked in, trying to coax and coerce students into digesting and dissecting an English literature curriculum which they had no interest in, along with books that bore no resemblance to their lives, it was no surprise that she was looking stony-faced.

I opened my mouth to remind her that it was almost the end of term but then snapped it shut when I realised that reminding her of *that* would remind her that she still had three gruelling weeks to go until the summer break and our long-anticipated dream come true.

'Here,' she then said, and her face did finally break into a smile as she held out a long paper straw for me to take. 'I pinched this from the bar. We'll need it later, won't we?'

I took it from her and danced about on the spot, almost spilling my drink. 'You are excited then?' I ventured, once I'd done a few twirls.

'Of course, I'm excited,' she giggled as she watched me. 'I'm not going to let the prospect of end of term burn-out ruin anything.'

I was relieved to hear it.

'We should have gone to Glitter to have a celebratory bop,' she beamed, naming a popular local nightclub as I carried on jiggling about completely out of time with the music.

'Or we could have gone to Raunch, for ...'

'I don't need to go to Raunch,' she cut in with a laugh. 'Not now I've got Jeremy.'

I didn't respond to that but mentally crossed my fingers in the hope that he wouldn't somehow miraculously turn up and spoil our fun. Again. His Friday night gatecrashing was becoming a horrible habit.

'We're not going to be able to hear ourselves think in here,' Rachel pointed out when I didn't say anything. 'Let alone final-ise details.'

'I still can't believe it's happening,' I grinned, pitching my voice above the noise of the DJ who had just turned the volume up further. 'We really are doing it, aren't we?'

'We are,' she shouted back, tapping her glass against mine before we downed the contents in one. 'Well, we will be if Tori shows up and we can firm up the final details.'

The three of us had The Best (caps totally justified) summer break on the horizon and, as the countdown on my phone and the circled date on the kitchen calendar reminded me, we now had only twenty days to get through until it would finally be happening.

'Six whole weeks,' I dreamily sighed, mentally recalling the images on the website I must have visited at least a million times. 'Six whole weeks in that cottage.'

I wondered what my grandad would say if he knew we were going to be staying in the very lakeside property which had been used as the main setting for the film adaptation of *Hope Falls*, the

most wonderful of all the books he had introduced me to when I was growing up.

The book had helped us through my annual summer stay in the Lakes after Nanna had died and I loved it all the more for that. Not a day went by that year when Grandad didn't read from it and by the end of August, I could have recited great chunks of it almost by heart.

To begin with, it was the descriptions of the dramatic landscape which captured my young imagination, but as I was transformed from a gawky tween to a moody teen, it was the love story and the friendship of the three very different main characters, strangers thrown together in a bid to escape their individual problems and tragedies, that I had fallen for. I still wished Grandad had been around to see the film and I knew that if he'd met my friends, he would definitely have wanted to make the trip with us!

The getaway had been years in the planning and I still couldn't really get my head around the fact that it was so close to happening. I had the book and film obsessed friends I had always dreamed of and we really were moving into *the* cottage next to the lake for almost the entire summer!

'We won't be spending the whole time inside,' Rachel keenly reminded me. 'Not with all the locations to check out.'

'And lakeside picnics to re-enact,' I nodded, getting into the familiar but still thrilling swing of it. 'And the skinny-dipping.'

'Not forgetting the trips to the pub.'

'Absolutely not forgetting those,' I squealed, feeling like I was going to combust.

'I wonder who will get Heather's room?' Rachel asked, nodding at the straw which we would use to finally settle the argument.

'Me, I hope,' I quickly said. 'I'm more Heather than you and Tori put together.'

'Hm,' she said, pulling at one of the many threads we had always good naturedly tussled over. 'We'll see about that.'

Rachel and I had initially bonded over our obsessive love of the book when we spotted it in each other's packing boxes the day we moved into the same flat in university halls and then, having decided to spend a freshers evening giving our respective livers some respite from the endless shots which were still the favoured rite of passage used to initiate eighteen-year-olds into student life, the deal was sealed when we watched the film and sobbed and laughed in all the same places.

I had then wasted no time in recruiting fellow enthusiast Tori, who was on the same course as me, to take up the role of third superfan. I had easily picked her out on the first day of lectures because she was wearing a *Hope Falls* T-shirt.

Unbelievably, the three of us had added our names to the cottage waiting list and stumped up the deposit to stay at the idyllic location almost three years ago, such was the demand of *Hope Falls* obsessives and we'd been saving to have enough in our bank accounts by the time we reached the top of it and had to pay off the balance ever since. Well, Rachel and I had been saving, Tori just had to ask her super wealthy dad to sign a cheque when the time came. Which was going to be very soon!

We had plans to re-read the book, re-watch the film and visit all the locations featured in and around the village of Lakeside. We were going to literally be living the book-lovers' dream and, unbeknown to my friends, I had another hope for the trip too.

I was going to use it to work out what I was going to do with

the rest of my life now I had been made redundant, in exactly the same way that Heather had done. Granted, it was an ambitious ask to transfer something so monumental from the pages of a novel into real life, but one I felt the time spent living in the cottage would be equal to.

'I'm going to message Tori,' I said, pulling out my phone as another kaleidoscope of butterflies began to flutter in my tummy. 'I don't want anything screwing up tonight.'

'No need.' Rachel grinned, lightly touching my arm. 'She's here.'

As ever, it took a while for Tori to reach us. Her profusion of dark curly hair, porcelain skin and commanding presence always drew attention and coupled with the sequined cami romper and Suola So Kate Louboutin heels, both of which pulled admirers in like a moth to a flame, it took even longer.

'Oh my,' said Rachel, when Tori eventually arrived at our table.

'I agree,' I joined in, my relief that she'd finally turned up chasing the butterflies away. 'No wonder you're late. You must have been fighting them off ever since you left your flat. You look stunning.'

'She didn't leave her flat,' Rachel said meaningfully with a nudge, as Tori took the empty seat opposite ours and crossed her long legs. 'She was wearing this outfit last night.'

Tori had the grace to blush as I threw her a faux shocked expression. Faux because, in truth, nothing Tori did shocked me anymore.

'Oh my,' I added myself as Rachel showed me the pre-drinks photos Tori had posted online as she had got ready to head out the night before.

'It's not how it looks,' was Tori's opening line, and not for the first time since we'd become friends.

'No?' laughed Rachel, arching an eyebrow.

'No,' said Tori, her usual sparkle and shine looking a little faded in spite of the dazzling outfit. 'But I'm here now, so . . .'

Looking back, I probably should have spotted something was amiss, but in the moment, I was too giddy and excited about our up-and-coming adventure to pick up anything other than another cocktail.

'So,' said Rachel, in a teacherly tone. 'Let's get down to business, shall we? First things first, let's find out once and for all who gets to sleep in Heather's room.'

'Me, me, me!' I giggled and Rachel rolled her eyes.

Having torn the straw into three pieces, two short and one longer, she flagged down a stubble enhanced server, who was wearing a pink feathered sheath dress and carrying a tray of garishly coloured drinks, to help.

'Make it quick then,' they said, putting down the tray and taking hold of the lengths of straw, once Rachel had succinctly explained the purpose. 'And good luck,' they added, lining them up in their grasp so they all looked the same length.

I held my breath as Tori took her turn first. She didn't react when she showed us how short her piece was, but my heart thumped. Unlike the others, I didn't just want the room because it was the prettiest. I wanted it because it was where Heather had decided about her future and that was exactly the purpose I had in mind for it. It was going to be my sanctuary and my safe place to explore all of the life-changing possibilities ahead of me.

'You go next, Em,' Rachel said generously.

'Sure?'

'Come on, girls,' said the server. 'I need to deliver these drinks.'

I swallowed hard and pulled at one of the pieces of the straw. It was longer than the one Tori had picked, but I didn't want to count my chickens. Rachel took the third and I finally realised I had been victorious. I had bagged the room!

'I can't believe it,' I said breathlessly, kissing a less than enthusiastic looking Tori on the cheek as I brandished my piece of the straw in her face and the server sashayed away. 'I can't believe it!'

I hoped everything else was going to fall as neatly into place.

'I bloody can,' said Rachel, but with no rancour. 'Looks like we'll be sharing the twin room after all, Tori.'

'Actually,' she croaked, folding her straw in half before dropping it on the table as she cleared her throat. 'We won't.'

Her porcelain skin had turned pale under her custom blend foundation and Rachel and I exchanged a look.

'What do you mean?' I asked, slipping my straw stub into my pocket as a memento.

'I'm really sorry,' sniffed Tori, her eyes suddenly filling with tears, 'but I'm not going.'

My mouth opened and closed, but no sound came out.

'What do you mean, Tori?' Rachel gasped. 'I don't understand.'

'You have to come,' I said, trying to jolly her along. 'We're the three musketeers, remember?'

Tori shook her head. 'I'm not coming,' she said again, her thickly mascara-lashed eyes flicking from one of us to the other. She looked mortified. 'Because I can't.'

'What do you mean, you can't?' I gasped, the conviction behind her words finally sinking in and the desire to carry on dancing deserting me.

I had wondered before if Tori was really as invested in the fandom to the same degree as Rachel and me, but I'd never for one second thought she'd bail on the summer of a lifetime. Not when we'd been planning it for so long and especially when she knew how much it meant to us. She might have been spoilt to a ridiculous degree by her father and the most like how Rose had started out in the book among us, but she wasn't mean.

'I can't,' she then said, shuddering. 'Because Dad's cut me off.'

As the youngest of four and the only daughter, Tori's dad had always given her anything and everything she wanted. Rachel and I thought it was his misguided way of trying to compensate for the death of Tori's mum when she was just a toddler, but obviously we'd never said as much.

'But you're still paying your share, right?' Rachel then blurted out. 'You're still going to pay your third of the cottage rental, aren't you? Sorry,' she then immediately apologised. 'I didn't mean it to come out like that . . .'

She sounded desperate, as well she might. Without Tori's share of the money, the trip couldn't happen for any of us.

'I'm so sorry,' sobbed Tori, swiping away a tear. 'I can't do that either. Dad turned up at my flat after I'd posted those photos last night and said my spending has to stop. He's cut up all of my cards and frozen my allowance,' she further blubbed, as more tears fell. 'And as if that's not bad enough, he's refused to renew the lease on my place and made me move back home. He says it'll be for the best in the long run and it's what Mum would have wanted.'

It might well be, but his timing was appalling and it was a harsh lesson for Tori given he'd previously been so indulgent. More of a shock tactic really.

'Well,' said Rachel, trying to sound calm, 'perhaps it will be, but you have commitments, Tori, and your father's a reasonable man. I'm sure if you explained . . .'

'I've tried,' she cut in. 'That's why I was so late. He said no. He said that if you two bore the brunt of my irresponsibility then the repercussions of how I've been living and how I behave, might hit home. And that even if we somehow raised the money to pay my share, he still doesn't want me to go.'

'But you're a grown woman,' Rachel pointed out. 'He can't do that. We're supposed to be doing this together. We need to do this together.'

Tori shrugged, looking far more resigned to the situation than I would have been in her position, but then our lives were nothing alike.

'Well, what about savings?' I suggested, grasping at the last spark of hope but knowing it would be instantly snuffed out. 'Could you perhaps pay for your share of the balance out of any money you might have set aside and therefore prove to your dad that you really are entitled to come?'

Rachel threw me a look.

'You know I've never saved a penny in my life,' Tori whimpered.

'Of course, you haven't,' I sighed.

Why would she when the bank of Dad had funded everything she'd ever wanted and at the drop of a hat? This mess wasn't really Tori's fault at all. Had her father not been so willing to pander to her all her life, then she would never have had this harsh lesson to learn.

'I'm so sorry,' she said, sounding wretched. 'I've tried to reason with him but he says he'll listen to me when I've decided what

I'm going to do with my life. But how am I supposed to work that out when I've got no funds to have a go at anything?'

That was part of the problem. Tori was Mr Toad in extremely pretty packaging. She'd spent half her life flitting from one thing to another with no thought for the expense when she dropped whatever happened to be the latest craze or the hobby she hadn't been able to get the hang of. Sticking at anything had never been her strong point. She'd dropped out of university the moment we got down to some real hard work and hadn't committed to a single thing for more than three weeks at a time since.

It was ironic that the cottage in Lakeside might just have been the place where she would have been able to successfully fathom a few things out and now she wasn't going to get the chance to go there.

'Here,' she sniffed, opening her Tom Ford clutch and shaking its contents on to the table. 'This is all I've got. I'm hoping it might at least cover your train fare now I can't drive you.'

'Train fare?' Rachel frowned, as Tori smoothed the few crumpled notes out. 'I appreciate that you can't drive us, Tori, but couldn't we borrow your car?'

Tori shook her head.

'He hasn't confiscated your Range Rover!' I gasped. 'We could have borrowed that!'

'It's locked in one of the garages,' Tori wailed. 'He said you can't borrow it and I can take the bus everywhere from now on.'

The thought of Tori on public transport was very sobering indeed.

'Well, that's as maybe,' said Rachel, 'but if we do somehow find the money for your share of the cottage, we can't go to the

Lakes on the train because it won't take us anywhere near as far as we need to go and a taxi from the station would cost a fortune and then leave us completely isolated.'

'And besides, I can't take my sewing machine on a train,' I added. 'We need a car.'

'Your sewing machine?' Tori frowned, momentarily distracted. 'Why are you taking that on holiday?'

'Because I have some commissions to complete,' I told her, trying not to sound too proud in the face of her crisis. 'I'll need to finish them and send them off while we're away.'

'I thought that patchwork stuff was just a hobby,' said Tori, wrinkling her nose.

'An increasingly lucrative one,' said Rachel, flashing me a smile in spite of our predicament. 'Especially now Em's creating more than just the memory pictures.'

'She is?'

'Yes,' Rachel said, sounding exasperated because we'd previously spent hours discussing it. 'She's adding the patterned patchwork panels to the skirts and dresses she designs and makes now, too, remember?'

'Of course.' Tori nodded, but I wasn't convinced she did.

'You're sounding keen all of a sudden,' I said to Rachel, her enthusiasm further diverting my thoughts from the catastrophe Tori had just landed us with. 'I thought you said patchwork was for grandmas.'

'I thought the stuff you started out doing was,' she admitted. 'All that measuring and precise matching up. It was as rigid as the graphs and spreadsheets you produce for your work. Zero creativity required.'

'The spreadsheets I *used* to produce,' I corrected, ignoring

her slur on the much-loved traditional craft. 'And the panels still have to be precise.'

'But they're in a different league now,' she praised. 'And the framed pictures, utilising fabrics with special meanings, are free-style and extremely creative.'

'So, you approve?' I laughed, raising my eyebrows and feeling flattered as a cheer erupted because a stag party had arrived and was making its presence felt.

I didn't need her validation, but it did feel good to have it and knowing how much value she placed on the security of a regular pay cheque, her attitude towards my designs would be a huge help when the time came to tell her that I was considering making them my only source of income.

My secret plan for my time at the cottage was to finally decide if I was going to launch my own business or commit to the job I'd been offered earlier that week as a data analyst for a far less appealing company than the one I had previously worked for.

I knew my parents would be all for me taking the safe option and, until recently, I would have been too, but this change in patchwork direction had sparked something of a change in me. Not that that would matter, I suddenly remembered, if the holiday didn't end up happening and I was denied the perfect opportunity to think it all through.

'Absolutely,' Rachel then said, squeezing my arm as the DJ turned the volume up another notch. 'It's a great little hobby.'

Her words rather deflated my sails, but I quickly regrouped.

'Truth be told,' I bellowed above the din, before turning back to Tori, 'I've been dreaming of finishing my current commissions at the cottage in Lakeside, so we need to work

out how we're still going to make that happen, don't we? And
how to convince your dad to let you come, too.'

At that exact moment, a dazzling bearded drag artist took
to the stage and draped a fuchsia dyed feather boa around the
embarrassed looking groom to be, much to the delight of the
rest of his stag and Tori grabbed my arm.

'Fuck,' she muttered under her breath and I followed her line
of sight towards the bar.

'Rach,' I said testily. 'What's he doing here?'

Pushing his way through the crowd towards us and looking
like a fish out of water was her partner, Jeremy.

'Did you tell him we were coming here?' I frowned.

On a previous occasion when he'd legitimately joined us on
a night out, he'd almost decked a poor guy who was asking
Rachel where the loos were and since then, he'd managed to
track us down with one excuse or another on a regular Friday
night basis.

'No,' she insisted, sounding flustered. 'I didn't. I said we
might try that new bistro as we had stuff to sort out, but I never
mentioned here.'

'Well, whatever his excuse for turning up,' I brusquely
said, 'can we not discuss the holiday hiatus in front of him?' I
truly hoped it was just a momentary pause in our plans. 'He'll
only gloat.'

Rachel didn't contradict me.

'So, what will it be tonight?' Tori tutted, reeling off a few of
Jeremy's former pretexts for turning up without an invitation.
'Place your bets, folks. Will it be the lost wallet and no funds to
get home combo?'

'Or the misplaced keys to our flat?' I joined in.

'Or a double-booked meal with his parents?' Tori finished up, adding in a low voice, 'Who Rach was nowhere near ready to meet.'

'Hey,' he said, bending to kiss Rachel's cheek, when he finally reached us.

'Hey,' Tori and I said dully back.

'It looks like rain out there,' he said, waving a handbag umbrella about. 'And you left this at the flat.'

'Pathetic,' Tori mouthed at me, her own woes momentarily forgotten.

'Thanks,' said Rachel, taking it from him and shoving it under the table.

Under normal circumstances and had I not still been in a state of panic about coming up with Tori's share of the cottage rental and convincing her dad to let her come with us, along with planning new transport arrangements of course, I would have been tempted to make something of Jeremy's flimsy excuse for turning up again. But only tempted. Rachel seemed to have a blind spot where he was concerned so it really wouldn't have been worth it in the long run.

'I went to the bistro first,' he said, when none of us spoke. 'I thought you said you were meeting there tonight, Rach.'

'I did,' she said. 'But we changed our minds.'

'So, what made you come in here instead then?' I couldn't resist asking. 'It's a far cry from the bistro.'

Given that he knew we had holiday details to finalise, it would have made more sense for him to check out quieter venues. The Flamingo was the noisiest bar in town by far.

'He's probably got one of those tracker app things rigged up to Rach's phone,' Tori quipped.

I shot her a look and then looked at Jeremy who I could see had turned red, even under the neon lights of the bar.

'I think you might be right,' I muttered back.

It was yet another red flag, but I knew I wouldn't get anywhere by waving it in front of Rachel. For some reason she was convinced that Jeremy's behaviour was proof that he cared, as opposed to proof that he was borderline dangerous, and the last thing I wanted was for us to fall out over him.

'He's crazy about me,' she had said when justifying his former lashing out.

Crazy was one way of putting it. As I looked at the mismatched couple, I felt determined to get Rachel away from him and to the Lakes for the summer, and if at all possible, I still wanted to take Tori along with us too.

Chapter 2

Having finally parted company with Jeremy, dropped a tearful Tori at her family home in an Uber that Rachel and I footed the bill for, and with her designer clutch still carrying the money she'd tried to give us, Rachel and I headed back to the flat we shared and spent a fractious weekend trying to come up with a rescue plan.

By the end of Sunday, not only did we not have one, but Tori's father had refused to change his mind about her coming even if we did somehow raise her share of the money. He had gone as far as to cite disinheritance if we made more of an issue of it and that soon dampened Tori's determination to still join us. Nothing, apparently, was worth risking that.

And as if that wasn't all bad enough, I had also foolishly mollified my parents by telling them about the interview I'd recently attended. Having both grown up in households where money was less than plentiful, my parents were all for structured careers, annual pension contributions and regular savings.

It was what made them feel secure and consequently, they had always assumed it would make me feel safe too. It had for a while, but with the exciting prospect of launching my own business

to now consider, I was wondering if it really was 'the only way to go,' as my father always endorsed. If I did now decide to go ahead, I was going to have even more explaining to do.

Thankfully, however, I had taken on my parents' regular savings advice which could make my change of career a more palatable option. Added to my redundancy money I still also had the modest financial gift kindly left to me in Grandad's will, so I had enough tucked away to live off, albeit frugally, for a year should I decide to screw my courage to the sticking place and put my patchwork plans into full-time practice. The only problem was, I had set my heart on making up my mind about it all at Lakeside and now it looked quite likely that I wouldn't be going.

Our landlord had been happy to know that Rachel's mum was going to pop in every other weekend to keep an eye on the flat while we were away but vetoed our proposition to sub-let for a month. Our last remaining hope was to pick the winning lotto numbers and that wasn't likely to happen, no matter how much effort we put into manifesting them.

'I could use some of my savings to pay Tori's share,' I suggested to Rachel who was still crunching numbers at the kitchen table late Sunday evening. 'And between us we could replace them a bit at a time in the same way we've been saving up to book the cottage.'

It wouldn't be ideal but if I didn't get to Lakeside to make my decision, I wouldn't need the funds immediately because I would most likely forget the business idea and take on the job I'd just been offered.

'Absolutely not, Em,' Rachel said firmly, frowning at the calculator and jabbing at the keys with the end of a pencil. 'You know how long it's taken us to save for this in the first place. We're not touching a penny of your nest egg. That's ring-fenced

and I won't hear another word about it. Lending money to friends never ends well, in my experience.'

I daresay she had a point, so let it drop.

'I had no idea car rental was so expensive,' she then groaned, as she winced at the numbers on the display and puffed out her cheeks.

'Well, maybe you could ask Jeremy if he wants to come?' I suggested as I twisted the tea towel around my hands. 'He's got a car, hasn't he?'

That obscene proposal was proof of how utterly desperate I was feeling.

'I'm going to pretend you didn't just say that,' Rachel tutted as she dropped the pencil on the table and drained her cut price Pinot Grigio Blush in one huge gulp. 'You don't even like him.'

I screwed up my nose, unwilling to tell another lie. I had tried my best not to make my dislike quite so obvious since she'd dismissed mine and Tori's concerns after loo-gate. The last thing I needed was to give Jeremy enough ammunition to brand me the bitchy best mate, but perhaps I already had.

'Bloody hell,' I huffed, throwing the tea towel at the sink and sharing the last of the wine between our glasses. 'This is all Tori's dad's fault. I blame him entirely for this mess.'

'What?' Rachel spluttered. 'I can't believe you're saying that when only last week you were the one saying that he needed to curb her spending!'

'Oh, I know,' I conceded. 'But I didn't expect him to do it right before our holiday and,' I added, so I didn't sound quite so self-centred, 'before Tori had experienced something which might actually have turned out to be of benefit to her.'

'Be that as it may,' sighed Rachel, pulling back the sleeve of

her Sunday sweater and stroking the entwined hearts tattoo on the inside of her wrist, 'it's happened and we need to find a way around it.'

I put down my glass and looked at my own tattoo. It was identical to the ones the girls in the book had had done to show their solidarity just a few weeks into their time at the cottage. Rachel and I had also had ours done together, paid for by some of our first student loan cheque. Tori had been supposed to get one too, but she'd missed the appointment and then never booked another. A classic carefree Rose trait.

'You know,' I said, unusually voicing my opinion, 'I'm not entirely convinced that Tori has ever been invested in *Hope Falls* in quite the same way as we are.'

'The only thing Tori has been truly invested in up until now,' Rachel smiled ruefully, 'is having a good time. But we love her anyway.'

'That we do,' I agreed. 'God, I wish she was coming with us.'

'At least you're saying it like it's still happening.' Rachel smiled.

'It is,' I insisted. 'It must. And it won't be right with just the two of us.'

Rachel's phone rang then. It was Jeremy, still sulking that Rachel hadn't seen him since the umbrella drop-off in the bar and keen to let her know that he felt particularly affronted about that because he wasn't going to see her over the summer break either. Personally, looking at my friend's dark circles and furrowed brow, I couldn't help thinking that if we could still find a way to pull it off, that might be no bad thing.

The following Friday was my last day working for Visionary and it was also the day of the self-imposed deadline Rachel and I had

set to either come up with the money or find someone to take Tori's place. We'd both drawn blanks and Tori, bless her heart, had been making the most random and off the wall suggestions to raise the funds which would enable us to still go.

'This is nice,' said Rachel, looking around the bistro when she joined Tori and me for Friday night drinks. 'Far better than The Flamingo.'

We were only there because I had spotted a voucher in the local paper which made the cost of a meal out almost justifiable. I wondered how long it would be before Jeremy showed up, but didn't say the words out loud.

'Oh, I don't know,' I said instead, taking in Rachel's dishevelled appearance and smudged eyeliner. 'You look as if you could do with a bit of a pick-me-up. Maybe we could go on to there after we've eaten here. What do you think, Tori?'

Tori had already been at the bistro when I arrived, which had never once happened before. She was *always* late, even if only by a couple of minutes. It was Rachel who was unfailingly on time.

'Best not,' Tori said, with a small smile. 'My curfew is eleven, so . . .'

'You have a curfew?' Rachel frowned. 'Should we be worried?'

'No, no,' said Tori, sounding surprisingly accepting of her current predicament. 'It's fine. I don't like traveling late on the bus anyway and Dad's not some sort of controlling ogre. I know deep down that he's doing this for my own good.'

It really was a strange position for a thirty-something to find themselves in, but I admired her for accepting it, though I didn't say as much for fear of coming across as patronising. I didn't comment either on the fact that Rachel was concerned about Tori's

curfew but completely unaware that Jeremy was every bit as controlling of her.

'So,' Tori said. 'Have you found anyone to take my place?'

'Afraid not,' Rachel sighed.

'And, therefore, I'm guessing that means you're still getting on for five thousand short of what you need, right?' she asked, sounding slightly perkier, though goodness knows why.

'It's nearer ten actually,' said Rachel, biting her lip.

'Ten!' Tori gasped, her cheeks suddenly flushed. 'How do you work that one out?'

'It's the car rental,' I explained. 'We could probably buy a car for what it would cost to rent one for six weeks.'

'Hey,' said Rachel, clicking her fingers. 'If we do win the lottery, that might not be a bad idea.'

'If you did win the lottery,' Tori tutted, 'I hoped you'd spend more than a few grand on a car.'

'Well,' I reminded them both. 'We haven't won the lottery, we aren't likely to win the lottery and as a result, we don't have the funds to buy a car. We don't even have Tori's share of the cottage balance and we're out of time now.'

I squeezed my eyes shut and swallowed down the lump in my throat which sprang up every time I thought about giving the dream up.

'It's not going to happen, is it?' I then burst out, feeling light-headed.

At the start of the week, I'd been full of fight, but it was leaching out of me now faster than a puddle evaporating in a heatwave.

'I'm not giving up yet,' Rachel said determinedly.

'Me neither,' added Tori. 'Although I'm not as convinced that you're still going now as I was five minutes ago.'

'Why not?' Rachel asked, handing me a tissue to dry my burgeoning tears.

'Because the money I've raised is nowhere near enough,' she sighed.

'You've raised some money?' I asked, having wiped my eyes. 'How have you managed that?'

'I've got a good chunk towards my share of the rental now, but . . .'

'How?' Rachel asked again.

Tori waved her hands around trying to make light of what she'd done. 'I sold some stuff,' she said airily. 'A few pairs of shoes, a Valentino dress and that Tom Ford clutch.'

'What?' Rachel screeched. 'You loved that bag.'

'Not as much as I love you two.' Tori swallowed. 'I couldn't get anywhere near what I paid, I mean, Dad paid, for any of it, but I have four grand sitting in my bank waiting to be transferred to whoever needs it.'

'I can't believe you've done that,' I said, reaching for her hand.

'Well,' she confided, 'I would have done more but Dad cottoned on to what I was up to when the courier came to collect the parcels and put a stop to it. I told him I had to honour the sales I'd already made and he agreed to that but said no more because it was cheating.'

'Oh, Tori.'

'He wanted me to hand the money over too, but when I told him it was for you two, he relented.'

I didn't know what to say. Tori parting with even one thing from her precious walk-in Carrie Bradshaw style dressing room was a huge deal, but shoes, a dress *and* her beloved clutch was a truly selfless act, especially as she was handing the proceeds over.

'Thank you, Tori,' I said, releasing her hand and raising my glass to toast her generosity.

'My pleasure,' she said, clinking her glass against mine and Rachel's. 'I only wish it was enough to get you out of the dilemma I've landed you in. Four grand isn't going to make any difference at all, is it?'

I opened my mouth to reassure her that her efforts were hugely appreciated, but was pulled up short by the smile lighting up Rachel's face. I sent up a silent prayer hoping that she hadn't invited Jeremy along after all. That said, he wasn't known to be free and easy with his spending, so surely, he wouldn't have signed up to take on Tori's shortfall, would he?

'It might make all the difference, actually,' Rachel said mysteriously.

'How so?' Tori asked, sounding intrigued.

'Yes,' I added. 'How so, Rach?'

'Well,' she said. 'And please don't be mad about this, Em.'

'What have you done?' I croaked.

It was Jeremy. It had to be. I was going to end up being the third wheel on my once-in-a-lifetime book-based dream getaway.

'I know we said we wouldn't contact Catriona Carson until a couple of days before the balance was due,' Rachel began.

'That's the name of the cottage owner, isn't it?' Tori cut in.

'Yes,' I confirmed. I had felt bad about agreeing to not letting her know what had happened until the last minute but I was desperate to cling on to the dream until the very last gasp.

'But then I remembered the waiting list,' Rachel carried on.

'The waiting list?' Tori echoed.

'Catriona had previously told me that she has this long list

of people waiting to jump in and stay at the cottage at short notice if, for any reason, a party had to drop out.'

'Oh god.' I panicked. 'You haven't given up our booking, have you?'

'Of course, I haven't,' Rachel tutted. 'Do you really think I'd do something like that without talking to you first, Em?'

'No,' I said, feeling chastened. 'Sorry. Of course not.'

'So,' said Tori, sounding frustrated. 'What have you done?'

'Nothing yet,' Rachel said, 'because I wanted to discuss it with you first, Em.'

'Go on.'

'Well, I called Catriona and explained our predicament.'

'And?'

'She was really sympathetic.' Rachel smiled. 'She knows how much it means to the fans of *Hope Falls* to stay at the property.'

'And how much it costs,' Tori added with an eye roll.

Just a few days ago that wouldn't have been a consideration for her at all, so perhaps her father's plan wasn't as cruel as I had first thought.

'And,' Rachel continued, 'she has offered, but only if you're completely onboard with the idea, Em, to contact some of the other people on the waiting list and find someone who could step in and take Tori's spot.'

I sat for a moment and let the reality of that sink in. Was I onboard with that idea? It certainly sounded as though Rachel was.

'Are you annoyed with me?' Rachel asked, when I didn't say anything.

'No,' I reassured her. 'Not at all. It really was only fair that you

let her know that there was a problem with our booking because we were cutting it fine for her.'

'Good,' said Rachel. 'Great. I did worry that you'd think I'd overstepped the mark, but . . .'

'Honestly,' I smiled, 'it's fine.'

'So, you'd be staying with a stranger?' Tori grimaced.

'Um,' Rachel mumbled. 'Well, yes, but . . .'

'But a stranger who loves the book and film as much as we do,' I said, the idea growing on me and my smile spreading further. 'And given where we're going and what we're going to be doing, that's the most important thing to have in common, isn't it?'

'Exactly,' said Rachel, sounding even keener.

'But are there single travellers on the waiting list?' I asked, trying not to get too swept along. 'I've always kind of assumed that this was the sort of trip you made with friends or maybe a partner.'

The perfect number was three, though, because that was how many stayed at the cottage in the book.

'Well,' said Rachel. 'According to Catriona, there are lone names on the list and all she has to do is match us up with some-one who can join us at such short notice for the full six weeks. She said we could email each other before we go, just to make sure there's the right sort of vibe between us and we don't end up being stuck with someone we can't gel with.'

I mulled the idea over a bit more. In theory it sounded like the perfect solution. Had this just been a random two week holiday somewhere I wouldn't have even considered it, but with the pas-sion for the book prompting the entire trip, then surely, we were bound to gel with whoever Catriona had on her list, weren't we? And of course, added to that there was the knowledge that the

entire book was about three strangers, so in a way, the idea of staying with someone we didn't know made the adventure even more authentic.

'But what about the bedrooms?' Tori asked, sounding to my ears at least, a little put out and suddenly not quite so willing to accept her situation. 'You've drawn straws now. What if this interloper . . .'

'They won't be an interloper,' Rachel said seriously. 'They'll have paid just as much as we have to be there and have exactly the same rights to the place as we will. If we go into this thinking that the other person has crashed our party, then it's never going to work.'

'All right,' Tori relented. 'I get that, but what will you do if this other person wants that double room?'

'Well, that's non-negotiable,' said Rachel. 'I'll share the twin with whoever signs up and Em will still have the double.'

'Unless Catriona signs up a couple?' Tori added mischievously. 'The place is advertised with space to accommodate four.'

'No,' said Rachel, sounding exasperated. 'That's not going to happen. Catriona was happy to tick just one name off her list and keep our group limited to three. It'll be one person and one person only. You probably won't get your deposit back, Tori, but this could be a solution to our problem. The only solution and one that kind of fits in with what happens in the book. What do you think, Em?' she asked, turning her dark, doe eyes on me.

'I think our hope has been restored.' I nodded. 'I'm still truly sorry that you can't come with us, Tori, but I think we should go for it, Rach.'

'Yes,' Tori then relented, with a sigh and a kind smile. 'So do I.'

Chapter 3

Right at the beginning of the following week, Rachel and I exchanged emails with Catriona to discuss exactly how the new arrangement might work. She had the names of three people who could potentially join us, and, having shared the details those people were happy for her to pass on, we opted to contact – and hopefully spend our summer with – Alex, a self-employed graphic designer who lived in Manchester.

In an ideal world, given our proximity, we would have met up – Leeds to Manchester was only about an hour away on the train – but it wasn't meant to be. Alex was working flat out tying up a big design project and Rachel was at school every day and spending most of her evenings either with Jeremy or, thanks to Tori's fundraising efforts, looking for a car.

As I wasn't heading out to work, I'd offered to take on the vehicle search, but my car knowledge turned out to be – to directly quote my friend – utterly useless. Apparently, my colour matching skills were of no relevance in this instance, it was the mpg we needed to be mindful of and I didn't even know what that meant.

Zoom calls hadn't worked for getting Rachel, Alex and I

together either. Even though I was available when I wasn't working on my commissions, the other two had full diaries which never tallied. However, as the emails flew backwards and forwards between us, and mine and Rachel's excitement reached fever pitch again, none of us thought it was an issue because we had instantly bonded over our shared love of the book and film and were satisfied to leave it at that until the day we arrived at the cottage.

Alex was the epitome of a *Hope Falls* enthusiast with far more knowledge of both the book and the film than Tori (not that we told her that when we shared the details about our new holiday-mate) and, like me, also had a penchant for perfect packing.

This became the source of much amusement when I revealed that my luggage was already good to go days before the off, but Rachel, by contrast, hadn't even started thinking about hers because she was the consummate, chuck it all in a bag the night before type. Alex and I both agreed that just the thought of that brought us out in hives. There was no way we weren't going to get along and the subsequent shared laughs, in-jokes and mild ribbing of Rachel started to secure our bond, days before we'd met.

'I'm still sad Tori's not coming,' I told Rachel as I waved her off for her last day at school at an even earlier time than usual, 'but I'm really looking forward to meeting Alex.'

'Me too,' she said, buzzing Jeremy – who had offered to drive her to pick up the ancient, but hopefully reliable Volkswagen she'd found for us in a local garage – into the building. 'Especially after her reaction to the skinny-dipping email. She sounds like she's going to be great fun!'

'She really does,' I agreed happily.

Of all the scenes Tori, Rachel and I had been planning to re-enact while staying at the cottage, I had assumed it would be the skinny-dipping in the lake which would have to be set aside in the presence of a stranger. However, if Alex's up-for-it attitude stretched beyond her email response then perhaps not.

'All set?' asked Jeremy who, as always, was dressed impeccably in a navy suit, crisp white shirt and navy tie. 'The traffic's starting to build, so we'd best head off.'

'Yep,' said Rachel, handing him the huge box of cupcakes she'd been icing for her form until way past her bedtime. 'Let's go.'

Standing side by side, Jeremy's clothes pristine and Rachel's already creased, the pair were not an obvious match. What was it, I wondered, that had drawn them to each other? Whatever it was, I wished it had missed. I'd only had two semi-serious relationships in my life so far, but neither had been a case of opposites attracting and both had ended without too much weeping and wailing. I couldn't imagine, should Rachel decide to call it a day, that the same would be said of her and Jeremy's parting of the ways.

'I won't be late,' said Rachel, kissing my cheek which was warm as a result of my uncharitable thoughts. 'I still need to pack.'

Jeremy shook his head and rolled his eyes and I felt my dislike of him bristle further. When I rebuked Rachel for not packing it was in good humour, but when he did it, without even uttering a word, it felt critical and on a completely different level.

'What?' she flushed, noticing his reaction. 'I haven't had time. It'll be fine.'

'It might well be.' He then brightly said, 'Because at this rate, you won't be organised enough to go off on this prolonged girls' getaway and that would suit me fine.'

Rachel looked at me and beamed, his unspoken criticism dismissed in less time than it took her heart to beat or before the implication of what he was saying had opportunity to register.

'I love that you're going to miss me that much,' she said, squeezing his arm. 'Isn't that sweet, Em?'

'Yeah,' I said, feeling my stomach roll. 'Ever so.'

'I'll message you before I set off from school tonight,' she told me, as she headed out the door. 'Then you can come down to see the car.'

'Okay,' I squeaked, feeling my excitement stirring again and surpassing the negativity Jeremy's presence always evoked.

Our neighbour was kindly letting us park in the space he paid for but wasn't currently using and the headmistress at Rachel's school had agreed to accommodate the car there until we sold it if the space was unavailable when we got back at the beginning of September. Ideally, I hoped the car would be quickly off our hands and we could return some of the money she'd selflessly raised to pay for it to Tori.

Once Rachel and Jeremy had gone, I sat down at the kitchen table, fired up my laptop and sent off a 'hedging my bets' email which I knew was long overdue. The company which had offered me the new job were aware that I was heading off for the summer and had proposed scheduling my start for September when I could join the team as they began working on a brand-new portfolio.

I felt rather guilty about agreeing to their generous offer, but knew that in order to make a well-balanced decision about my future, it was necessary to share my eggs amongst more than just the one basket.

Having done that, I rechecked I'd packed everything I was going to need for my heavenly holiday then waited for my

over-excited and racing heart to settle. Anything to do with the holiday triggered the biggest adrenaline rush, so it was some time before I could settle to planning out the details of a secret commission Rachel's mum had asked me to undertake.

Thankfully, Rachel was used to me asking her to act as a model to size the flowing white cotton dresses I then embellished with patchwork panels and hadn't given my recent request to measure her again a second thought.

I was beyond excited when Rachel eventually arrived back with the car, which was plenty big enough for ferrying everything we needed to take on our extended vacation. As I walked around, ostensibly inspecting it, I experienced another rush of happy hormones. After the stress of the last few days, it was a huge relief to know the trip really was happening. Even though it wasn't in quite the way we had originally planned it, the way it now fitted more neatly into the plot of the book gave it a more thrilling edge. Sorry, Tori . . .

I grinned at Rachel, thinking that not only was I finally heading back to my beloved Lake District, I was also taking with me all those happy memories of summer holidays spent there with Nanna and Grandad while my parents carried on working, as well as their treasured book.

'I think it'll be all right,' Rachel said, scrutinising the car and also smiling from ear to ear. 'Although,' she added, her smile faltering, 'there was a bit of a rattle when I went around a few corners.'

She bit her lip as I opened the passenger door and peered inside. 'Did it sound like a metal water bottle rolling about by any chance?' I asked.

Rachel frowned as I retrieved the offending article bearing the name of Jeremy's gym from behind the driver's seat.

'Oh yes,' she beamed. 'He must have left it in there when he was having a look while I paid.'

I knew the sabotage was pure gaslighting, but didn't point it out and helped her carry the multiple boxes and bags she'd filled the car with, and which signified the end of another school year, up to the flat.

'Is Jeremy still feeling fed up about you going away for so long?' I asked, as I later sat cross-legged on her bed and watched her random packing.

We had decided not to open a bottle of fizz, as was the usual custom on the last day of term, because Rachel would be driving the next day and we were both already completely wired. However, I couldn't drink my tea either because I was forcing myself to sit on my hands to stop myself reaching out to fold her crumpled clothes.

For someone who was so conscientiously organised in her professional life, certain aspects of Rachel's personal life were surprisingly messy. But then everyone needed an outlet, didn't they? Even meticulous Monica in *Friends* had that secret chaotic cupboard. As with most things in life, it was all about balance.

'It's linen,' Rachel grinned when she saw me struggling to keep my hands to myself. 'It's supposed to be creased and yes, he is. Well, not fed up exactly,' she loyally corrected. 'And I do get where he's coming from. Six weeks without seeing each other is a really long time, especially when . . .'

'Especially when what?' I asked, when she didn't carry on.

'Oh, it doesn't matter,' she said, her change of tone letting me know that she had no intention of finishing whatever she'd unguardedly started to say.

I knew better than to try and push her for an answer, but she was right, six weeks was a long time. Secretly, I was hoping it was going to be long enough to turn her off him completely.

'Tori briefly dropped by earlier,' I said, to move the moment on. 'She wanted to wish us both the best time.'

'That was kind of her,' said Rachel, sounding relaxed again. 'If it was just you and her going, and not me, I don't think I could have done that.'

'Me neither,' I agreed.

'Was she okay?'

'I think so.' I shrugged. 'Happier than when the threat of disinheritance had been hanging over her but still a bit flat. That's only to be expected though, given that she'd had to bus it here which is totally not Tori's style, is it?'

'Definitely not,' said Rachel, sitting on the lid of her crammed suitcase. 'I still can't believe she's going along with her dad's wishes, but saying it's what her mum would have wanted was a masterstroke on his part. I really do hope she gets some benefit out of the situation and finds something meaningful she wants to commit to.'

'Me too,' I agreed, tugging on the suitcase zip. 'It would be a total travesty if she went through all those trips on public transport and there was no pay-off at the end of it.'

We were a bit behind our time from the off the following morning because Jeremy kept Rachel talking on the phone for so long and then we had trouble closing the car boot. It took multiple attempts to secure it and we only managed it then because Rachel's mum, who had travelled up to collect the flat keys, added her strength to the endeavour.

It wasn't because we'd over-packed the space, the catch was obviously faulty or knackered. Or possibly, given the age of the car, both. Not that we cared as long as it got us to all of the places we were so looking forward to seeing and exploring.

'I hope it won't spring open en route,' I nonetheless panicked, thinking of my perfectly packed bags of patchwork and my precious, not to mention, expensive Janome sewing machine. 'I don't relish the thought of looking in the wing mirror and seeing my fabrics strewn all along the road behind us.'

'It'll be fine,' said Rachel, waving my concerns away with another yawn as she dropped a bag on the backseat.

I hoped she was going to be okay to drive. She was always worn out at the start of the summer holidays but this year she seemed wearier than ever and given the conversation we hadn't finished the night before, I had the feeling she had more on her mind than just recovering from the end of another hectic term.

'Have you got that special bag of fabrics?' Rachel's mum asked me with emphasis and in a clandestine whisper while her daughter was distracted. 'I hope they were all right?'

'They're perfect,' I told her with a smile. 'I've already started matching them up and because they're all cotton, they'll work together a treat. That said, I haven't cut them out yet. Are you completely sure it's okay for me to do that?'

'Absolutely.' She nodded, giving my hand a squeeze. 'They were only sitting in the back of my wardrobe. At least this way we'll be able to enjoy them again.'

'What are you two whispering about?' Rachel demanded, before I could say anything else.

'I was just saying to Em that if I know my daughter,' her mum blagged, 'and the state of her packing, then her clothes might

benefit from a trip along the road if that boot does spring open. The breeze might help blow out some of the creases!'

'Ha, ha,' said Rachel, pulling her mum in for a hug.

'Grandma would be thrilled to know you're doing this,' her mum then said tearfully.

'I know,' Rachel sniffed.

I hadn't been the only one to benefit from a grandparent loving the book. Rachel had introduced her grandma to the story and together they had read it multiple times and also watched the film before the old lady's eyesight had failed her. Rachel had then set up the audio version of the book so she could enjoy that as well as listen to the movie.

'If she was still here, she'd be coming with us,' Rachel added thickly, echoing what I had thought my grandad's reaction to the trip would have been.

'That she would,' her mum agreed. 'Now come on, you two, you need to go. Heaven knows you've waited long enough; you don't want to waste a single second of this adventure.'

We didn't need telling twice and rushed into our respective seats. I forced myself to not feel guilty that Tori wasn't with us. She'd accepted the situation and wouldn't have been impressed to know that either Rachel or I were feeling anything less than on top of the world about finally heading off.

'Here goes nothing,' said Rachel, tentatively turning the key in the ignition while I crossed my fingers.

The engine sprang into life and we let go of the breath we'd both been holding. When I'd sent Tori a photo of the car the evening before she'd immediately messaged back that we shouldn't have paid four grand for it and Rachel was quick to reply that we hadn't. The old jalopy had been just over half that

amount but insurance, breakdown cover and fuel had earmarked all of the rest. Tori had been mightily amused about that.

'Don't worry,' said Rachel's mum, leaning through the window and fondly patting the steering wheel. 'This'll see you right. I had a VW when I was your age and it just ran and ran,' she reminisced.

'I hope you're right,' said Rachel, clumsily finding first gear. 'Bye, Mum!'

'Bye!' she called after us. 'And if you've got enough phone signal when you get there, don't forget, three rings!'

According to the satnav, the journey from Leeds to Lakeside should have taken far less than three hours, but finding the tucked away property proved quite a challenge, in spite of the detailed directions Catriona had sent us. I wasn't sure if that was because we were too excited to concentrate properly, or if the cottage really was so well hidden.

Neither Rachel nor I really minded the delay as we had the *Hope Falls* soundtrack playing on a loop courtesy of Spotify, and the scenery which lined the road became ever more enchanting and increasingly dramatic with every passing mile. My head was awash with nostalgia and my eyes filled with tears on more than one occasion as lakes, valleys, hills, mountains, woods, drystone walls and picturesque cottages enthralled us while Rachel carefully navigated the twisting roads and narrow lanes.

'There!' I screeched, making Rachel stamp on the brake as I pointed out the pale blue painted postbox and gate which would lead to our dream retreat. 'Oh my god! This is it!'

Grinning, Rachel pulled up alongside another car, wrenched on the handbrake and turned the engine off.

'I don't know why my legs are shaking,' she laughed.

Once we'd climbed out and had a quick stretch, I pulled her in for the biggest hug.

'What was that for?' she asked, when I eventually released her.

'For getting us here, of course,' I said seriously. 'I know how knackered you are and you haven't driven for ages.'

'It was fine,' she said. 'I've got so many endorphins whizzing around my system, I barely worried about making the trip, but thank you for acknowledging that and don't worry, I'll be feeling even better in a few days. As soon as I've got school out of my head, I'll be full of beans.'

'More beans,' I laughed, because compared to earlier, she was already pretty bouncy. 'And that's good, because you know how packed the itinerary is.'

'That I do,' she beamed, giving me another hug. 'Can you believe we're really here?'

'Don't.' I swallowed. 'You'll have me in tears if you're not careful.'

'Well,' she said, giving me a playful shove away. 'We don't want that, do we?'

'I wonder if this is Alex's car?' I then asked, taking more notice of the other vehicle.

It made ours look even more shabby by comparison, but at least it had got us to our dream destination.

'I doubt it,' Rachel reminded me. 'She said she wouldn't be able to get away before three today, remember? And Catriona said we wouldn't be disturbed. I reckon it belongs to a hiker.'

'Oh, yes,' I remembered. 'I daresay you're right. Thank goodness Alex didn't want us to wait to all go into the cottage together. The suspense would have killed me!'

I hadn't said as much, but I was also secretly pleased that Rachel and I would get to explore it alone. I hoped that wasn't mean. I was genuinely on-board with welcoming someone else, especially as their presence meant our holiday could still happen, but there were certain moments I still secretly wanted to keep just for us.

'And at least she'll be here in time to watch the film,' I added, to balance out my selfish thought. The last thing I wanted was to attract bad karma.

Rachel and I looked at one another and squealed again. Watching the film was a first night tradition when staying at the cottage, we had been told, and one we were both very much looking forward to upholding.

'Shall we take our stuff with us now, or go and look around and come back for it in a bit?' Rachel asked, eyeing the path beyond the gate.

There were multiple winding steps down to the cottage, which was completely hidden from view by a thicket of dense trees, so going and coming back again would be a bit of a trek, but I couldn't wait to see the place now.

'Let's just go,' I said, putting a hand on the gate and feeling my heart rate quicken again. I knew dozens of people had opened the gate since the film had been made, but it was thrilling to be doing it myself, rather than imagining it. 'I don't want to arrive weighed down with all our stuff, do you?'

'No,' said Rachel, locking the car. 'I want to savour every second. I'm always telling my students to be aware of their thoughts and feelings when they experience something for the first time, because you never get that chance again.'

'You're absolutely right,' I agreed.

I'd never really thought about that before.

'Come on then,' she said, joining me at the gate and running her hand over the top of it before linking arms. 'Let's go.'

Mindful of what Rachel had said, we didn't race down the steps, but took our time, taking in the view in all directions, savouring the heady perfume coming from the trees, the fresh scent of which was the result of a recent downpour, and admiring the surrounding mountains and hills which seemed to hold the valley beyond in a comforting embrace. It all reminded me of time spent with Nanna and Grandad and as silly as it might sound, I willed them to be watching me.

'Okay,' I said, pulling Rachel closer as we reached the bottom of the first flight of steps and paused for a moment. 'When we turn this corner, we're going to get our first glimpse of the cottage. Are you ready?'

Rachel swallowed and nodded. 'I hope it's as wonderful as we want it to be,' she said, sounding a little apprehensive.

'Having studied the images on the website for literally years,' I reassured her with a knowing smile, 'we absolutely know that it will be.'

And it was. Nestled among the trees and encased in a wrap-around covered veranda, complete with swing seat, fairy lights, pots full of lush green plants and outdoor lanterns, sat the traditional slate roofed, pale blue wooden cottage of our dreams.

'Oh my god,' gasped Rachel. 'Oh my god, Em!'

She rushed forward down the last of the steps, but I was rooted to the spot. It was perfect. Perfect in every possible way and I hadn't got anywhere near the threshold yet. Even from this distance it took my breath away so goodness knows what state I'd be in by the time we went inside.

'Come on!' Rachel called over her shoulder as she ran across the grass to the veranda just as I caught sight of someone standing around the side of the building.

It was a man.

'Rach,' I called back, wondering who it could be. Catriona had given us the code to unlock the box holding the keys and said we could let ourselves in. 'Wait up!'

I rushed to join her just as the man stepped further out of the shadows. He was a little taller than both of us, wearing dark jeans and a dark red shirt with the sleeves rolled up to reveal tanned forearms. His hair was dark too, thick and short and as we got closer still, I could see he had brown eyes. Incredibly kind looking brown eyes, to be precise. Whoever he was, he was extremely good-looking.

'Oh,' Rachel gasped, as she finally became aware of him.

'Sorry,' he apologised, holding up his hands. 'I didn't mean to make you jump.'

'It's okay,' said Rachel, throwing me a quizzical look.

I shrugged in response to indicate I had no idea who he was either. Perhaps the other car on the road didn't belong to a hiker after all.

'I managed to get finished early,' he said, with a small self-conscious smile which made the corners of his kind eyes crinkle. The lines looked to be a permanent feature and suggested he smiled a lot. 'I thought it would be better if I got here in time for us all to go into the cottage together, just like in the book. I wanted us to have the perfect start, so . . .'

'Sorry,' I interrupted, confusion overriding my initial acknowledgement about how handsome I thought he was, along with my excitement about having finally arrived. 'Who are you?'

He looked from Rachel to me, his smile faltering. 'I'm Alex,' he said, stepping further forward while holding out his hand and pinning me with his dark eyes which, close to, I could see were flecked with gold. 'I'm your housemate for the next six weeks.'

Chapter 4

Had it not been for Rachel coming to her senses and giving me a nudge, I might well have ended up standing on the veranda staring at Alex in stunned silence for far longer than the few seconds that in reality it probably was.

'You're Alex?' she asked, unable to keep the incredulity out of her surprised tone.

It was a relief to hear that she sounded as flabbergasted as I felt.

'Yes,' he said, dropping his hand, which I hadn't made any effort to acknowledge even though it had been angled in my direction. 'I'm Alex,' he further confirmed. 'Is everything okay? I know I'm earlier than I said I'd be, but . . .'

'But you're . . .' I started to say, my mouth opening and closing as the words dried up.

'Here now,' Rachel briskly and brightly intercepted, stepping between us. 'Which is wonderful, because it means we can all go in together.'

'That's what I just said,' Alex pointed out, smiling again. 'Is everything okay?' he asked, looking from one of us to the other.

'Of course.' Rachel vigorously nodded, throwing me a look.

'We're just a bit awestruck, aren't we, Em? To finally be here, I mean. I'm Rachel, by the way.'

She stepped aside again and gave me a pleading look when I didn't respond.

'Yes,' I blurted, no doubt making a total hash of hiding what I was really so surprised about. 'Completely overwhelmed.'

'We've waited a long time for this moment,' Rachel beamed, sounding more like herself. 'I still can't believe it's actually happening.'

I wondered if she was talking about finally being at the cottage or meeting *him* rather than the gal pal I knew we had both been expecting. Either way, she was right.

We had waited years for this moment and although I had known that our arrival wouldn't be quite the same as when the three women in the novel had arrived, because two of us already knew each other, being thrown together with Alex – who was very definitely not the person we were expecting – was a total distraction and had turned the greatly anticipated moment into something else entirely.

I had genuinely been looking forward to meeting someone I didn't know since accepting Rachel's solution to Tori dropping out, and further fuelling our alignment with the plot, but Alex was a surprise not even my wildest imaginings had been capable of dreaming up.

'Me too,' Alex agreed, seemingly and thankfully unaware of any of what I was thinking as he looked at the pretty cottage exterior. 'And I know everyone must say this when they first arrive,' he added, with another tentative smile. 'But it looks exactly how it does in the film, doesn't it?'

'It does,' said Rachel, sounding a bit choked. 'I was just about

to say the same thing myself. They couldn't have picked any-where better to represent the cottage in the book.'

If she really had been about to say that, then she'd got her thoughts together far quicker than I had. My head was still processing the shock that Alex was a guy and I'd spent more time looking at him than admiring the cottage. I can't deny, I felt rather resentful about that. My first impressions of the place had been hijacked and right when I had been so determined to focus on them.

'So,' said Alex, looking from Rachel to me. 'Shall we go in?'

My gaze swept over the picture-perfect abode which was to be our home for the next six weeks and I made a concerted effort to take note of as many of the details as I could. I forced myself to remember what Rachel had said about absorbing something the first time you experienced it, and apply it to something other than Alex.

'I think we should,' she said, pulling her phone out of her pocket to retrieve the key code she'd earlier added to her notes. 'No signal here at all,' she commented, waving the phone about. 'So no three rings for Mum.'

'I managed to send a text to my parents back on the road,' said Alex, looking over his shoulder in the general direction. 'If we share the same network, you might be in luck up there too.'

'Your parents wanted you to let them know you'd arrived?' Rachel asked, sounding touched.

'They did,' he said, turning a little pink. 'It was the first thing I did when I arrived.'

'I love that.' Rachel beamed.

'They're as excited about me taking this trip as I am,' he said, no doubt encouraged by her positive comment to further share.

He took a breath and then more sombrely added, 'They know how much it means to me.'

If it meant that much to him, I would have expected him to sound more excited about it, but then I'd already had one lesson about making assumptions that day so reined in my reaction to his solemn sounding words.

'From what you'd written in your emails,' Rachel smiled, 'we could tell you're as big a fan of the book as we are.'

I knew she had said that to remind me rather than acknowledge Alex's passion. My reaction to him wouldn't have gone unnoticed by my observant friend and she was already setting herself up as keeper of the peace. Not that I had any intention of deliberately causing trouble, but there could be no denying that it was going to take me longer than her to process the change of dynamic.

'And the film too.' Alex laughed, rubbing his hand around the back of his neck. 'I'm as obsessed by both as they come.'

That was something positive to cling to, I supposed.

'Good,' said Rachel. 'And thanks for the heads up about the phone signal. I'll see if I can message when we go back to the car for our stuff.'

'Have you got the code?' I asked, thinking we'd been standing about long enough.

'Yes,' she said. 'Here it is. I thought it would be . . .'

'Twenty-nine, zero, five?' Alex and I suggested together and I laughed along with the pair of them in spite of my unsettled feelings.

'Exactly,' Rachel giggled. 'But I guess if it was, the world and his wife would have been able to access the cottage, wouldn't they?'

Alex smiled at me while Rachel keyed the correct random number into the key safe and knowing that his trivia knowledge really was up to scratch if he had memorised a minor character's birthday, I smiled back.

'Here they are,' said Rachel, sliding open the box and reverently handling the three cottage keys as if they were priceless jewels. 'One for each of us. Who's going to do the honours?'

'I think one of you should,' said Alex, taking a step back. 'It seems only fair given that I was very late to this party and I'm only here thanks to you picking my name off the waiting list.'

The irony of that wasn't lost on me. We had picked him.

'Are you sure?' Rachel asked. 'I could use a number generator or something.'

'Not without a phone signal you couldn't,' he reminded her. 'And, I am sure. You two go ahead.'

Rachel smiled warmly as she thanked him and I thought she looked perfectly at ease with him too. She had clearly completely recalibrated her thoughts already. I might have been impressed by Alex's trivia knowledge but I still wasn't sure how I felt about spending the whole of the next six weeks living with him.

'You do it, Em,' Rachel then said, holding out one of the keys for me to take.

'No,' I said, closing her fingers around it and knowing how big a deal it was for both of us. 'Let's do it together.'

With my hand over hers, she slid the key in the lock and we turned the handle and pushed the door open.

'Wow,' the three of us breathed as we peered in the doorway.

'It's . . .' Alex started to say, but stopped himself.

'Just like in the film,' sighed Rachel as we followed her inside. Once over the threshold, we each took our time, exploring

the luscious cottage interior on our own. It was exactly how I hoped it would be, but with a special something extra I couldn't put my finger on. It felt luxurious and yet there was nothing in the whole place which was shiny or new and the resultant atmosphere was warm, welcoming and lived in, with a vintage vibe you'd expect from somewhere set up to tastefully replicate the early nineteen eighties, which was when the book had been published and was set. Not even Alex's unexpected existence could diminish the pleasurable sense of immediately feeling at home among the Laura Ashley inspired interior.

The open plan living and kitchen area housed a squishy sofa complete with floral print cushions, thick throws, matching curtains and two comfortable looking armchairs as well as packed bookcases, deep window seats and a huge wood-burning stove. The patterns which defined the era had been stylishly matched to fit the woodland setting and it took no effort at all to imagine Heather, Laurie and Rose sitting there wrapped in blankets and warming up after their dip in the lake.

The kitchen was authentically rustic. Locally made pottery, ancient Le Creuset, and a wooden dining table and chairs complete with jam jars crammed full of pretty wild flowers. It was cottagecore perfection and I knew that if any of the characters from the book wandered in there too, I wouldn't have batted an eye.

Then there were the bedrooms and bathrooms to swoon over. The twin beds were made up with Laura Ashley Campion pale pink linen and the double ... I stopped on the threshold of the sweet pea patterned double room and its en suite bathroom with the huge tub and my breath caught in my throat.

There were jars of sweet peas on the nightstand and more on

the windowsill. I could pick up their intoxicating sweet scent as it filled the room and I imagined how wonderful it was going to feel to drift into a deep and satisfying slumber, my head filled not only with the scent which permeated the book, but also so much of my childhood thanks to Grandad's horticultural prowess . . .

'I suppose this had better be mine,' Alex said from behind me, cutting through my wistful thoughts and making me jump as he peered over my shoulder. 'Unless you and Rachel want to bunk in here together and I take the twin?'

Even though we had got on so wonderfully well via email we might not have done had we got around to broaching the issue of bedroom allocation.

'Have you seen the size of these towels?' Rachel gushed as she rushed out of the twin room, a huge dusky pink bath sheet clasped in her hand. 'Oh,' she said when she realised what Alex had just said. 'Oh Em . . .'

'So,' I said briskly, turning my back on the dream bedroom and shoving the fantasy of sleeping in it to the back of my mind. 'Alex is going to take the double and you and I can share the twin, Rach.'

'But,' she faltered.

'And it looks like it's going to rain again,' I said loudly, cutting her off and steering us all back towards the sitting room, 'so we'd better start ferrying our stuff, Rach.'

'I'll give you a hand,' Alex offered. 'I've already carried mine down. It's just out on the veranda.'

'No,' I said, perhaps a little too sharply, given the way his eyebrows shot up. 'No need. We can manage. Why don't you make some tea? Or coffee? Either would be great.'

There was no way I wanted Alex ferrying our stuff. I was

going to need the trips to and from the car to purge myself of the unkind thoughts I was now in danger of succumbing to and which if I wasn't careful, would completely eradicate my excitement.

'Oh, Em,' said Rachel, sounding upset as she rushed to keep up with me when I set off along the path at speed. 'Let me talk to Alex about the bedroom.'

'Talk to him about the bedroom,' I laughed as I glanced back at the cottage. 'What can there possibly be to say to him about the bedroom, Rach? You can hardly share the twin with him, can you?'

I bit my lip hard to stop myself from blurting out anything mean about Jeremy having something to say about the possibility of that.

'No, I know,' she tried to soothe me by saying, 'but you've wanted to stay in that room forever.'

'Funnily enough,' I croaked, my breath tight in my chest as I took the steps back to the road too fast, 'I'm well aware of that.'

'Em,' Rachel panted. 'Slow down.'

By the time we'd reached the car, I was bent double with a stitch and in spite of the fact that I'd incoherently muttered most of the way, I still didn't feel any better.

'At the end of the day' – I resignedly shrugged, when I had breath enough to properly speak again – 'it's just a room.'

It was *so much more* than just a room.

'I know it's more than just a room,' Rachel sighed, echoing my thoughts.

She pulled me in for a hug which made more tears spring to my eyes.

'It doesn't matter,' I swallowed, turning away and going

completely overboard. 'The break's most likely already ruined anyway, isn't it?'

'Ruined?' Rachel frowned.

'Yes,' I said, waving my hand back towards the cottage. 'In case you hadn't noticed, Rachel, Alex is a guy.'

'Of course, I've noticed,' she said, sounding cross.

'You can't tell me we would have picked his name off the waiting list if we'd know he was a bloke,' I said bluntly.

Rachel shrugged, but didn't deny it.

'We should have searched for his name online,' I groaned, giving it further thought. 'Or on social media at least, but we were getting on so bloody well in those emails.'

'Oh, you've remembered that, have you?' Rachel then snapped, her patience with me finally finding its breaking point.

'What?'

'That we were getting along fine.'

It was my turn to shrug then.

'It's not Alex's fault we assumed he was a woman,' Rachel pointed out. 'And at the end of the day, he's *still* Alex. He's exactly the same person he was in those emails. There's no difference about him at all.'

I couldn't imagine that Jeremy would feel the same way if Rachel told him she was going to be sharing a cottage for the next six weeks with an attractive man. It was on the tip of my tongue to ask her if she was going to mention exactly who had taken Tori's place, but I bit the words back knowing the resultant row would only make the situation worse.

'That's as maybe,' I said instead. 'But it still changes things. The vibe's all off now.'

Rachel rolled her eyes. 'We knew it was going to be a bit

different as soon as we decided to include someone we didn't know in the trip, whether they were another woman or a man.' She tutted, fiddling with the dodgy boot catch. 'And given the plot of the book, that was actually supposed to be a positive thing, wasn't it?'

I didn't say anything.

'Wasn't it?' she said again.

I couldn't bring myself to say that she was right. 'So, you're still up for skinny-dipping, are you?' I asked her instead.

She jumped back as the boot lid sprang open. 'I don't know,' she said, her cheeks turning pink. 'Perhaps when we know Alex a little better ...'

'I don't want to get to know him better,' I harrumphed. 'He's pinched my room.'

Rachel let out a long breath. 'You said it was *just* a room.'

'You know it's not *just* a room.' I swallowed. 'You just said so yourself.'

I reached into the boot for the first of my bags and Rachel did the same.

'Well, I do want to get to know him better,' she said. 'And not only, in case you've forgotten, because this trip is a dream come true and he's now a part of it, but also because there's a story there.'

'You think?' I sniffed.

'You know there is,' she nudged. 'When he said about his parents knowing how much this trip means to him there was way more implied by the words than him just having a crush on Heather, Rose or Laurie.'

'Perhaps,' I said, pushing back through the gate, the thought of lugging my luggage and sewing machine down to the cottage

making my legs prematurely ache. 'Anyway, hadn't you better message your mum rather than searching for clues about his?'

In the end, because further rain was imminent and there was a distant rumble of thunder, Alex did help us carry our stuff. We'd just got the last of it inside when the first heavy drops fell.

'Thank you,' I said, as I relieved him of the box which contained my sewing machine and set it down carefully on the table.

'I've taken quite a few holidays in my time,' he said, sounding amused as he interestedly eyed the image on the box, 'but this is the first time I've ever known anyone to bring a sewing machine along with them.'

'It's for my work,' I told him.

'Oh, talking of work,' he carried on, ignoring my blunt response. 'I'm going to carry on too. I've just secured a rebranding contract with a small but growing restaurant chain, so I'll be having one day a week working back in my office in Manchester while I get the project up and running.'

'Congratulations,' said Rachel, handing round the mugs of tea Alex had made and which were rapidly beginning to cool. 'That sounds exciting.'

'It is,' he said. 'Thanks.'

'Bad timing though,' I couldn't resist saying. 'No one wants to work on a break, do they? Especially one as special as this.'

Alex did acknowledge my tone then and I was annoyed that I noticed how his face suited the smile far better than the deep frown my comment prompted.

'You've literally just said you've brought your sewing machine with you because it's for your work,' he tersely shot back.

'Yes,' I volleyed. 'But the work I've brought with me isn't

office based and doesn't require internet access which we haven't got here.'

'It's more of a hobby really,' Rachel said disloyally and I shot her a look.

'And beyond a day a week at the moment, neither does mine,' he returned, ignoring Rachel. 'I'm at the planning stage and can actually think better without the distraction of being online.'

'I'm guessing you'll drive down as you've got your car?' Rachel asked, stepping between us again. 'Rather than take the train.'

'I will,' he said, looking around her and directly at me again. 'And it's a bit of a trek. At least two hours each way so you'll be rid of me for one whole day a week.'

I smiled but didn't comment.

'And I had been going to suggest that I could do a big shop on my way back as I've seen online that there's only a small general store in the village here,' he carried on, 'but we'll see how we get on, shall we?'

I could tell from the back of Rachel's head that she was mortified, but I coolly held Alex's gaze.

'Yes,' I said, 'by all means, let's see how we get on.'

Chapter 5

After that, we each went our separate ways for a while. I left Rachel sifting through the contents of her luggage which she had tipped out on her bed and took my time finding the perfect spot to set up my sewing space.

I knew there was a beautiful scrubbed pine table with painted legs in the window of the double bedroom and I had formerly been planning to utilise that, but as I had been denied the room, I would have to set up somewhere else.

In the end, I opted for the table in the corner of the sitting room which had the benefit of windows on either side so the light was probably even better than in the bedroom. Not that I was prepared to acknowledge that because I was still smarting over the switch. However, covered in a patterned oilcloth the table offered plenty of room and as I arranged my sewing box, along with the bags which held the commissions I was currently working on, I pictured myself happily working there for the next few weeks and feeling very much at home.

I settled my hoard of material underneath, making sure Rachel's secret surprise was tucked right at the back. She wasn't likely to go looking through any of it, but I wasn't going to risk

her seeing the project and recognising the fabrics. If she ran true to her usual end of term form, she'd sleep through the next couple of days and I would be able to get ahead with it. The dress was ready to be sewn together but the patchwork panels still needed to be cut out and positioned before being incorporated into the skirt and bodice.

A movement beyond the window caught my attention and I leant further over the table to seek out the source. I was surprised to see Alex sitting outside. It was still raining, the thunder still rumbling but, thanks to the overhanging roof, the veranda appeared to be completely dry. I could tell by the way he was sitting that he was on his phone and I wondered if he was composing 'I hate my housemate' texts to send to friends and family went he went offsite and found a signal. My stomach twisted at the thought.

'What shall we have for dinner?' Rachel asked, when she emerged from the bedroom, stretching her arms above her head and yawning loudly. 'I'm starving.'

'You've been ages,' I said, looking up and smoothing out the kink in my neck and only then noticing the time.

With the cottage to further explore, I had only intended to work briefly on the piece I had been asked to create by a former colleague for his wife's silver wedding anniversary present but, as always, I had become immersed in the design and then the stitching and the time had whizzed by without me noticing. If I did decide to take my sewing sideline further, I felt fairly certain that my passion for it wasn't going to dwindle.

'Oh, Em,' said Rachel, putting her hands on my shoulders and looking at the partly constructed design. 'This is exquisite.'

'Thank you,' I said, holding it at arm's length and feeling a

pleasing glow of satisfaction with how it was coming together. 'I'm really enjoying creating it.'

The design incorporated material and fabric objects which held special memories from the couple's wedding day, including a piece of floral fabric which had been used to make the brides-maids' dresses, a lace-edged monogrammed handkerchief which had served as the bride's something borrowed and something old, as well as some tiny pale blue silk roses and covered buttons. I was integrating some hand embroidery too, to commemorate the date and create a floral edge and the finished piece was going to be mounted inside a box frame that I had already painted in Farrow & Ball Middleton Pink.

'This is all a far cry from what you started out doing, isn't it?' Rachel said admiringly, my *hobby* gaining her approval again.

'Yes,' I agreed, thinking back to the carefully measured cush-ions and baby quilts I had cut my patchwork teeth on. 'It is.'

'And so are your dresses,' she added, kissing my cheek. 'I'd even be tempted to wear one of those myself.'

I was relieved to hear it.

'Hey,' she then said to Alex who had come in via the door next to where I was working. 'Is it still raining?'

'Mizzling,' he said, glancing at what I was doing. 'Nothing like before.'

I slid the panel back into the bag I used to keep what I was currently working on flat and safe.

'I don't know about you two,' he said, looking towards the kitchen, 'but I could go for something to eat. It feels like ages since lunchtime.'

'I agree,' said Rachel, patting her stomach. 'I'm starving. Must be all the excitement.'

'Could be,' Alex responded, sounding as far from excited as it was possible to get.

I had a feeling that my lacklustre response to his presence and subsequent snippiness was most likely responsible for his downbeat tone and my stomach rolled again.

'Either that or the multiple trips to and from the car to collect our stuff,' I suggested, making an effort to join in. 'Thanks for helping with that, Alex. You saved us at least two extra trips.'

'Rain-soaked trips, too,' Rachel added, smiling at me.

'You're welcome,' he said, sounding a bit brighter. 'My legs are feeling it though and I have to admit, I'm already looking forward to falling into that big bed later tonight. That double mattress is the comfiest thing I've laid on in a long time. Have either of you tried yours out yet?'

'No,' I said shortly, my desire to make amends taking flight again.

'I've tried mine,' said Rachel, squeezing my shoulders. 'And it was blissful. Come on then, let's go and have a look at what Catriona's put in the fridge for us, shall we?'

Catriona, at our request, had stocked the fridge and larder with essentials and some local produce including huge swirled Cumberland sausages. Because they were so big, we decided to share two of those between us and serve them with buttery mustard mash and the peas, which were still in their pods and, according to a note on the table, had earlier been picked fresh from Catriona's own garden.

The sausage and mash combo wasn't exactly high summer fare, but then the weather and the temperature felt almost autumnal when compared with the rest of the country. It was classic Lake District weather and exactly as I remembered it from my holidays staying with Nanna and Grandad.

'Bagsy firing up the barbecue to cook the sausages,' said Rachel, sounding way too eager as she extracted the paper-wrapped parcel from the fridge. 'Whenever I go to Jeremy's place, he'll never let me near his. He comes over all hunter-gatherer and I'm left sorting the salad and other sides.'

'I'm embarrassed to say, from what I've heard, that's pretty standard among our sex,' Alex sighed. 'My dad's the same. Once he's got his Griddle King apron on and the tongs in his hand, there's no stopping him.'

I couldn't help but laugh at that.

'You don't fancy fighting Rachel for the honour then?' I asked. 'If your dad is usually the barbie boss, aren't you keen to have a go yourself?'

'God, no,' he grinned, making his eyes crinkle again and I wished he wouldn't. 'I wouldn't want to deny Rachel the pleasure and besides, I burn everything. You don't want me anywhere near that thing.'

'Duly noted,' Rachel said happily.

'But what about the weather?' I asked, wrinkling my nose. 'It's coming down again out there.'

'It's dry on the veranda though,' Alex said, confirming what I'd earlier noticed. 'I was sitting out there for quite a while and never felt a drop.'

'In that case,' I suggested, 'let's eat out there too, shall we?'

'Oh yes,' said Rachel. 'Then we can come back in and fire up the wood-burner. It's certainly cool enough to justify it, isn't it?'

'Definitely,' I agreed.

'And then we're going to watch the film, aren't we?' Alex asked, sounding hopeful. 'We can't miss out on that on our first night here, can we?'

They both looked at me and, even though the dynamic in the cottage felt nothing like I had been expecting, I had no intention of ruining Rachel's first night. Or Alex's. Or mine, for that matter. My previously guilt-riddled rolling stomach was proof that I wasn't going to be that mean, even if I was still in shock.

'Of course, we're going to watch the film,' I said enthusiastically. 'Now, who wants wine?'

It was idyllic sitting outside, wrapped in fleecy throws and sharing out the food. Alex's mustard mash was to die for and I had made a decent job of shelling the peas, dropping them in boiling water and then scooping them straight out again. The rich red wine was good too. It knocked off some of the awkwardness that had been lingering from the moment we arrived and, which I knew deep down, I had done very little to eradicate.

The air smelt fresh and clean and there were birds twittering among the trees which surrounded the cottage. I loved how green and lush everything was and was very much looking forward to taking the path through the garden down to the lake. The cottage had its own private little shore and quite a few of the scenes in the film had been set there to tie in neatly with the descriptions in the book.

'Well, Rachel,' said Alex, pulling me out of my reverie as he sat back in his chair. 'That Jeremy fella you mentioned earlier is certainly missing a trick because you clearly know your way around a barbecue.'

'Why, thank you,' she said, raising her glass and looking a little fuzzy around the edges. 'I will take that compliment.'

'And I'll second it,' I said, clinking my glass against hers.

'Was he going to be the third person in your party?' Alex

asked and I spluttered so hard, a little of the wine I'd drunk shot up my nose. 'I take it that's a no?' he grinned.

'That's a definite no,' I resolutely confirmed and Rachel gave me a look. 'Jeremy is absolutely not the *Hope Falls* type, is he, Rach? But then . . .' I added, cocking a brow at Alex, 'I haven't come across any other men in real life who are.'

I'd chatted with a couple via online forums, but that was it.

'I have,' Alex told me. 'But only recently and only a few.'

'So, what drew you to the book and film originally?' I asked, drinking another mouthful of wine. 'Did you find your own way to it or were you helped along? Coerced even?'

'Oh,' he said, turning red and shifting in his seat. 'That's a story for another night.'

'I sense intrigue,' I said, fixing him with a piercing look. 'I bet there was a woman involved somewhere along the line, wasn't there?'

'Em,' Rachel said.

'It's fine.' Alex swallowed. 'There was, but I'm not getting into it now. I most likely will at some point, just not yet.'

'I wish you would tell us now,' I persisted, the inhibition reducing impact of the wine doing nothing to stop me leapfrogging the boundary he'd just set up.

'Em,' Rachel said again.

'What?' I shrugged. 'I'm just interested. There's no harm in being interested, is there? If we're going to be living together for the next six weeks it makes sense to find out a bit more about one another, doesn't it?'

Rachel shook her head and looked apologetically back at Alex. When she had suggested letting Catriona find us a new housemate, I had gone along with it in the spirit of the book and

on the assumption that having *Hope Falls* in common would be enough for us to properly bond, but was it?

'Jeremy is my partner,' said Rachel, tracking further back in the conversation, most likely to stop me from prying deeper into Alex's personal affairs. Or offending him. Or both.

'And how does he feel about you being away for six weeks?' Alex asked. 'It's a long time. Are you planning to meet up at some point?'

'It is a long time,' she agreed, ignoring the first question Alex had asked, 'but this trip was planned long before Jeremy and I got together and nothing was going to stop me from taking it. I won't see him until September now.'

It was a relief to know that Jeremy's attention seeking and mithering couldn't sabotage Rachel's passion for our getaway and I gave her a virtual high five.

'I'm going to miss him though,' she then said quietly.

'Sorry,' Alex apologised. 'I didn't mean to upset you.'

'You haven't,' she reassured him, as she started to gather the dishes together. 'I'm just overtired and feeling a bit sentimental as a result.'

'She's always like this at the end of term, Alex,' I added, more to make myself feel better for not factoring her feelings about missing Jeremy in, than to reassure Alex. 'You should hear the way she cries over anything on TV, even adverts. She'll be better in a few days when she's caught up on sleep and got Jeremy out of her system.'

'Em!'

'Shit, sorry,' I said. 'I didn't mean that how it sounded.'

It was a classic case of loose lips sink friendships. Especially when they'd already sunk too much wine. Definitely more of a Rose than Heather slip up.

'I know what you meant,' she said.

I hoped she didn't.

'Shall we go in and get set up for the film then?' Alex suggested diplomatically.

'Yes,' I said, standing up too quickly and further feeling the impact of the quickly gulped units, along with a dip in my mood which had just started to lift again. 'Good idea.'

Rather than raise my spirits, getting ready to watch the movie made mine sink further. I had been looking forward to a first night bubble bath in the double room's heavenly tub ahead of curling up to watch the film in the very place where much of it was filmed. Consequently, the shower in the twin room en suite, although high end and surprisingly powerful, was a poor substitute and Alex's confession when I came out of the bedroom didn't make me feel any better either.

'Any chance I could use your shower?' he blithely asked. 'I'm not a bath person.'

'Of course,' said Rachel, while I gritted my teeth. 'No problem.'

'Oh my god,' I hissed when he was out of earshot. 'Can you believe that? I'm broken-hearted here and he hasn't even noticed!'

'Why should he?' Rachel frowned. 'And besides, there was nothing stopping you asking him if you could use the bath, was there?'

That was me told and I supposed she did have a point. To make amends for my waspishness, I made the area in front of the TV as cosy as it could possibly be. I lit the candles, sorted the fire, arranged the throws and curled up with Rachel on the sofa. The scene was beautifully set and my heart was finally back to thumping in anticipation.

While we waited for Alex, we thumbed through our ancient, tatty but treasured paperback copies of the book and when he did finally join us, he was carrying his too. It was exactly the same edition as ours which cheered me even further, as did what he was wearing.

'Oh my god!' Rachel gasped, when she spotted him. 'Where did you get that? I need to get me one of those.'

'Shipped from the US,' he said, standing in front of us and pulling the hoodie, which looked to be not quite oversized enough for his frame, further down.

'Turn around,' Rachel demanded.

'Oh wow,' we said together. 'That's so cool!'

The heather-coloured hoodie had #TeamHeather emblazoned across the back and down one arm and the entwined hearts logo, which matched our tattoos and had been created for the film, on the left breast of the front. Rach, Tori and I had T-shirts, but I'd never seen a hoodie. Not a decent one anyway.

'I love it,' said Rachel. 'We need to get one, Em, don't we?'

'Absolutely,' I agreed, feeling a little choked as I looked at our books lined up together on the coffee table.

'There are different coloured ones with the other two names on,' Alex explained, turning back around again, 'but it had to be team Heather for us. I mean, me.'

The slip of the tongue drew my gaze away from the books and, coupled with the flush of colour on Alex's face which accompanied it, re-sparked my interest in his 'how I came to *Hope Falls*' story, but I snuffed it out. Rachel would never forgive me if I started digging so soon after she'd wrestled the spade from my wine infused grasp.

'I'll get you a Rose or Laurie one for your birthday, Rach,' I said and she frowned.

'And while we wait for it to be delivered,' I quickly carried on, 'we'll have to make do with our matching tattoos, won't we?'

As one, Rachel and I pulled back the sleeve of our PJs and showed Alex our wrists.

'Oh wow.' He smiled, bending to take a closer look. 'They're gorgeous.'

When I looked up, my senses assaulted by the freshly showered scent of him, he was staring at my face, rather than my wrist and I quickly pulled my sleeve down and sat further back on the sofa. For a mad moment, I had wondered what it would feel like if he lightly ran his thumb over the top of the tattoo and looking up and finding his eyes trained on my face, made me wonder if he'd read my thoughts. My cheeks flushed scarlet as a result.

'How about hot chocolate with all the trimmings to really get us in the mood?' suggested Rachel, thankfully breaking the spell as she flung the fleecy blanket right over me and jumped up.

Alex stepped aside as she skipped to the kitchen and I tried not to breathe in the lingering scent of his pine infused shower gel which matched our surroundings to a T.

'I was going to suggest more wine,' I said, forcing myself to sound unaffected as I twisted around to look at her. 'But hot chocolate would be wonderful. Given the weather and how chilly it is this evening, something warming will be far better than wine.'

As hard as I tried, I found I couldn't relax into the film. Rachel cried buckets at all the appropriate moments and I noticed Alex shed a tear too, but not at the same time as my friend. I was eager to ask what had triggered his reaction to certain scenes,

but didn't. Instead, I dabbed my eyes with the tissue I'd put up my sleeve in anticipation of the usual torrent and sniffed when I knew Rachel would be expecting me to.

It was the first time I've ever faked it and the resultant guilt was no doubt the reason why I didn't sleep a wink that night. That and the fact that the single bed, although incredibly comfortable and beautifully dressed, looked to be nowhere near as accommodating as the long wished for double next door.

Chapter 6

With Rachel still out for the count the next morning and, in spite of the fact that I was tired from lack of sleep, I quietly pushed back the duvet and slipped out of the bedroom knowing I would regret it if I didn't curb my desire to run about the cottage comparing the descriptions in the novel to the objects in front of me. For the time being at least, I needed to make more productive use of my time.

I would easily be able to put the main part of Rachel's dress together when she was up and about because that could be a garment for anyone, but the patchwork panels were another matter. She would instantly recognise the fabrics I was using and therefore stealth was required if I was to keep the surprise under wraps until the final stitch was sewn and the dress was complete.

However, before I settled to start, I made myself a coffee and, for just a couple of minutes, quietly admired the silent cottage with the biggest smile lighting up my face. I still couldn't really believe that I was here. I selected another well-thumbed novel from the packed shelves and drank in the lush green view of the surrounding trees which filled every window.

Then, mindful of the minutes ticking by, I sat at the table and readied myself to begin. I kept the anniversary piece next to me, just in case Rachel woke earlier than expected and I needed to grab it to cover up what I was really doing. I tried not to let my annoyance, that had I been in the double room as originally planned and with the door closed it wouldn't have been an issue, sour the moment, and began.

Having selected the patterned fabrics I thought would work best together, and arranged the interlocking shapes, I had just started carefully cutting out the pieces for the sleeve inserts when the rain began to drum on the roof, the back door opened and Alex rushed in carrying a holdall. How I didn't end up cutting more than the material I'll never know.

'Shit!' I swore, my heart racing, but not from the usual excitement associated with the place, as I put the scissors down. 'I thought you were still asleep.'

His bedroom door was shut and, as it was so early, I had assumed he was enjoying the comfort of the coveted double bed.

'Sorry,' he said, as he quickly closed the door behind him, put down the bag and pulled off his jacket.

'Mind,' I tutted, covering the precious fabric with my hands as the raindrops he displaced splattered far and wide.

'Sorry,' he said again.

His voice sounded husky and thick and when I looked up, I could see his expression was wretched. His kind eyes were filled with sadness and there were dark smudges under them, all signs of the smiley crinkles wiped away. Clearly, I wasn't the only one who hadn't had a restful night. So much for his expectation that he was going to crash out. I could have felt smug about that but the sadness radiating out of him tempered the emotion.

'Are you all right?' I frowned, concern about the change in him overriding my preoccupation with where a few raindrops had landed.

His eyes flicked to the bag as he ran a hand through his mussed-up hair before bending over to unlace and pull off his boots.

'Yeah.' He swallowed, standing back up and avoiding my eye. 'I'm fine.'

'Well, you don't look fine,' I said brusquely.

'Thanks.'

'I mean you look tired,' I clarified. 'If it's any consolation, I didn't sleep either.'

If the set of his stubbled jaw was anything to go by, my admission was no consolation at all.

'Would you like a coffee?' I offered. 'I was just thinking about making myself another one.'

'No,' he said, picking the bag up again. 'No, thank you.'

'What have you got there?'

'Nothing,' he said, taking a step away.

'Where have you been?' I asked, taken aback that he sounded so defensive and feeling suspicious as a result.

'Down to the lake,' he said, the words catching in his throat.

'Oh,' I responded, feeling a surprising pang of disappointment. 'I had hoped we might go there for the first time all together. It's another one of the traditions associated with the place.'

His expression suddenly changed from upset to incredulity. 'I'm not being funny, Emily,' he said. 'But yesterday, at times you left me with the impression that doing things together was the last thing you wanted. I know we had a meal together and watched the film, but you seemed hell-bent, on more than one

occasion, of leaving me in no doubt that we wouldn't be doing anything beyond that as a group.'

I knew I had come across as being pleased about him having a day away at work every week and I had also been rather forthright at bedtime when I shared my solo plans for today, but that was because I was determined that Rachel shouldn't feel guilty about catching up on her end of term kip, so I could work on her dress. It had genuinely had nothing to do with me trying to further shut Alex out.

That said, I could appreciate why he had thought it might, especially when combined with the memory of my more than frosty welcome. I chewed my lip as I mulled it all over. As uncomfortable as I still felt about his unexpected presence, I knew I had to make amends for the less than lovely first impression I had clearly made because this was every bit as much his dream getaway as mine.

'The thing is . . .' I awkwardly began. 'And I know it's absolutely not your fault . . .'

'You don't need to explain,' he interrupted. 'I get it. You were expecting another girl to make up the group and you've got lumbered with me.'

'I wouldn't say lumbered,' I rushed to say. 'We did pick you after all.'

'It's fine.' He shrugged, turning away, having picked up my mug. 'I've got my own stuff to do anyway, so don't worry about including me in anything. I'm perfectly happy going it alone. I'll make you another drink.'

I wasn't sure if that made me feel better or worse.

'Do you mean that?' I called after him. 'About going it alone, I mean.'

'Yeah,' he said, looking back. 'I do. You and Rachel are welcome to carry on as if I'm not even here.'

While the kettle came to the boil, he stowed the mystery bag in his room and when he came back to the table, he handed me the freshly made drink and looked at the picture I was working on along with the pieces I had just started to cut out. Some of the gloom he had carried back with him from the lake seemed to have lifted, but he still looked dog tired.

'So, I'm guessing this is why you needed to bring your sewing machine,' he commented, once he had taken it all in. 'Is this your work? Is this what you do for a living?'

'No,' I said, making sure the mug was set down well out of harm's way and not feeling the same desire to put the work away as I had the day before. 'It's not my day job. Like Rachel said, it's just a hobby really.'

'It's beautiful.'

'Oh,' I said, feeling suddenly hot, and not only because he was standing so close. 'Thank you.'

I hadn't been expecting him to say anything like that.

'I mean it,' he continued seriously. 'It's stunning. What's this all about?' he asked, pointing at a specific part of the anniversary commission.

I explained who it was for and what it was designed to commemorate and how every piece of the fabric held a special significance, but that until I had been given them to work with, they had been packed away in a box at the back of a cupboard.

He was listening so intently that I then got completely carried away by his interest and told him all about the skirts and dresses I also made and how some of those included treasured fabrics too.

'I've also been thinking about designing blouses,' I finally finished up, feeling slightly out of breath.

I realised then that I had been prattling on for ages, but he didn't seem to mind.

'I love it all,' he said, sounding sincere. 'What a wonderful gift and I don't just mean that your pieces are unique gifts for the lucky recipients. You have an incredible talent, Emily. The way you've put this anniversary piece together is quite extraordinary.'

My heart skittered and I turned to look at him, just to make sure he was in earnest. His face was unexpectedly close to my shoulder and I felt another rush of heat pulse through me. It pooled much further south than the earlier spike in my temperature.

'Thank you,' I croaked, then turned back to the table.

He straightened back up again, leaving behind a lingering trace of aftershave.

'So,' he said, sounding more composed than I felt. 'If this isn't your day job, what is?'

I took a long breath, but it didn't much settle me as I tried to trick myself into believing that my reaction to him was the result of what he'd said, rather than his physical proximity. It was his kind words and high praise which had caused my body's reaction, I sternly told myself, definitely not his closeness.

'I'm a data analyst,' I told him. 'But I'm currently between jobs.'

'Really?' he said, sounding genuinely shocked. 'That's very different to this,' he added, with a further nod to the table.

I was almost tempted to tell him that it was my intention during our holiday to think about whether I was going to give the patchwork sideline the opportunity to become my main hustle, but fought the urge off. Not even Rachel or Tori knew

what I was considering and I needed to further consider my options before I took on board anyone else's opinion.

Alex's brain didn't get that memo though and he shared his thoughts regardless. 'And I hope you're as passionate about analysing data as you are about sewing perfect stiches,' he said, with a small smile. 'But if you're not, then I'd seriously think about making this your main line of work.'

I risked another look at him. Knowing he was a little further away, it should have been safe, but it wasn't and my heart fluttered in response.

'Not that it matters what I think,' he said, with a shrug and another smile before he turned back to his room. 'But one thing I do know,' he sighed, 'is that we should all follow our hearts. We should all do the things that make us happiest, before we run out of time.'

He quietly closed the door behind him and after a few seconds, I picked up the scissors again. Rather than try to deny how attractive I found him, because that was proving increasingly impossible, I focused instead on what he'd said.

His words had been relevant to the plot of the book, but I had the distinct impression that he hadn't been thinking of either that or the film when he said them. The emotion in his tone suggested that the sentiment came from a place of personal experience and not necessarily a happy one.

It was lunchtime before Rachel emerged from the bedroom looking tousled and sounding groggy. I had made great headway with her dress and had long since packed it away so she found me curled up in the window seat reading the paperback I'd earlier selected from the bookshelf. It wasn't a patch on our favourite, but it made a change.

'Hello sleepyhead,' I smiled, setting the book aside. 'Are you ready for some lunch? Or would you prefer breakfast?'

She opted for a combination of both and we sat at the kitchen counter tucking into bacon and avocado sandwiches and fresh fruit smoothies.

'I'm sorry you've had to spend your first morning here on your own,' she apologised.

'Well, I'm not sorry,' I told her with a wry smile. 'I know it probably sounds selfish, but I've loved it and it was always part of the plan for you to rest up. And besides, I wasn't alone the whole time. I saw Alex earlier.'

'Oh, really?' she said, looking towards his room as she pressed a napkin to her lips. 'I thought he was still asleep.'

'No,' I responded in a low voice, in case he could hear me. 'He was up even earlier than me and he'd been down to the lake.'

Rachel wrinkled her nose. 'Damn,' she said, 'I wanted us to all go down there together the first time.'

'Me too,' I sighed. 'And I'm sorry, but I think it's partly my fault that we didn't get to do that.'

'I'm sure it isn't,' she said unconvincingly.

'He pretty much said it was,' I told her, thinking back over the awful impression I'd left him with the night before. 'Although . . .'

I let the word hang as I thought about the holdall he had carried in with him and the look of sadness he had also brought back from his visit to the lake.

'Although?' Rachel repeated.

'Oh, I don't know,' I shrugged. 'It was probably nothing.'

'But?' she encouraged, raising an eyebrow and leaning in.

'I just got the feeling that he'd gone to the lake alone for a more specific reason than me being a cow to him yesterday.'

'What sort of reason?' Rachel asked, not denying my bovine behaviour.

'I don't know,' I said again, thinking of the look on his face and the tense set of his shoulders and jaw, 'but I don't think it was a happy one.'

'Well, that doesn't sound good,' said Rachel, puffing out her cheeks. 'Was he okay?'

'No,' I told her. 'I don't think he was actually. But given my less than warm welcome yesterday, he was hardly going to open up to me about whatever was on his mind, was he?'

'I suppose not,' Rachel said, still making no attempt to suggest that I hadn't behaved badly which left me in no doubt that I had.

'But he did say,' I carried on, trying to distance myself from my unkind conduct, 'that we were to carry on with our pre-made plans because he'd got his own things to do.' Rachel raised an eyebrow again. 'And I'm pretty sure that wasn't down to my frosty welcome,' I hastily added.

'It seems to me,' she said, reaching for the last of the sandwiches and sounding intrigued, 'that we've all come to Lakeside with secrets.'

I knew I had and was now certain that Alex had too, but the fact that Rachel had a secret was completely fresh information.

'Is that right?' I questioned, waiting for her to spill the beans.

'Uh huh,' she said as she chewed.

'So, what's yours then?' I blatantly asked when she didn't say anything else.

'You first,' she nodded, a mischievous smile appearing before she took another bite.

'All right,' I tutted. 'Touché.'

'I'm sure all will be revealed when it's meant to be,' she said

sagely. 'But in the meantime, I'm going to treat myself to another few hours in bed.'

I willed myself not to waste time trying to guess what Rachel and Alex's secrets might be as I tidied away the dishes, re-laid the wood-burner, courtesy of Catriona's list of instructions, and returned to the cosy book-nook in the window.

I spent just as long that lazy afternoon looking around the beautiful cottage and out at the hills as I did reading what was on the page. I mulled over the kind things Alex had said about my patchwork projects and considered what a future dedicated to it might look like.

It was still pure fantasy, but I allowed myself the luxury of imagining how my website might look, along with my Etsy shop and stalls at trade fairs and festivals. I considered dozens of different dress designs as well as the sort of people who might wear them.

I even thought about the person *I* would be if I decided to go for it. No more smart suits and sleek up-dos for me. I would be able to wear the clothes I loved to design and make and not just at the weekends! In my head it was all perfect, but then I realised there was danger in that.

I had put my time at the cottage on a pedestal and it had turned out that no matter how hard I'd planned, no matter how many lists I'd made, the reality was already turning out to be nothing like I had imagined it would be.

I knew Tori's absence and Alex's presence accounted for much of that, but would something similar happen if I raised my expectations about my prospective business too high? Had my parents got it right after all? Maybe I would be better off sticking to the security of what I knew and keeping my patchwork as a

weekend and evening interest? Why risk potentially spoiling what I already had?

I put the book down and rubbed my temples, grateful that I had six weeks rather than six days to get it all straight in my head, and somewhere I found beguilingly beautiful in which to do it.

'Where's Alex?' asked Rachel when she later joined me again.

Her day in bed had clearly suited her as she was looking much more like her old self, in spite of whatever the secret was that she was holding so close to her chest.

'Still in his room,' I told her, with a nod to the closed door. 'Has been all afternoon.'

'Do you think we should knock?' Rachel frowned. 'Just to make sure he's okay.'

'No,' I said. 'I'm sure he's fine. He'll come out when he's ready. And for all we know,' I added, 'he might be working on that rebranding project he told us about. We wouldn't want to break his concentration, would we?'

'I suppose not,' said Rachel, moving slightly as a shaft of sunlight, the first we'd seen since we'd arrived, shone through the window and lit the room up.

'Would you look at that?' I laughed. 'I was beginning to think the rain was a permanent feature.'

'Let's go to the lake,' Rachel said keenly. 'Make the most of it before it clouds over again.'

'All right,' I said. 'I'll grab a sweater and we'll go.'

It was cool outside in the early evening air, but nowhere near cold.

'We mustn't forget to water all these pots,' Rachel said quietly, mindful we were outside the room Alex was in as she nodded at

the tubs of huge leaved hostas and purple flowering petunias. 'As the rain doesn't reach here, they're bound to dry out.'

'We'll do it when we get back,' I said. 'Come on.'

Beyond the veranda there was a well-defined path which led us through the woods and at the end of that we knew we would find the pebbled shore that belonged to the cottage, with access to the lake.

'Doesn't it smell amazing?' Rachel sighed dreamily, veering off the path to pick up yet another pine cone that had most likely fallen the autumn or winter before.

The pocket on the front of my hoodie was already bulging and I was beginning to wish we'd brought a bag.

'It does,' I agreed, breathing in a lungful of the fresh, cool air. 'If I said it smells green, would you know what I meant?'

It was a smell reminiscent of my childhood.

'Funnily enough,' Rachel laughed, 'I would and I can get a whiff of petrichor too which, given the amount of rain that falls here, is a bit of a surprise.'

'You're right,' I agreed. 'The ground is hardly dry, is it?'

We linked arms just before we reached the end of the path and squeezed close together.

'Here we go,' said Rachel.

It was time for another first impression and I hoped there was going to be nothing to twist or diminish this one.

'Let's do it.' I nodded.

We stepped out of the trees and down the slight incline to the pebbled lakeshore.

'Oh my god,' I gasped, a lump forming in my throat. 'It's huge.'

The lake filled the whole of the view and was surrounded by

dense trees with hills and even mountains beyond. I had known the body of water was vast from scenes in the film and online searches, but it wasn't until I stood beside it that I could appreciate just how huge it actually was.

Even after all my summer holidays spent in the Lake District with Nanna and Grandad, I couldn't remember anything quite as spectacular as this, but then I was looking through the eyes of an adult now rather than a young girl. Perhaps that made a difference?

'Look,' said Rachel, tugging at my sleeve.

Tucked under the canopy of the trees closest to the shore were two Adirondack chairs and a bench. There was a rope swing tied to a tree branch a little further along, as well as the jetty the three main characters had jumped off during the famous skinny-dipping scene. I could also see a small rowing boat moored alongside it.

'This is every bit as wonderful as the cottage, isn't it?' I said, feeling in awe all over again and selfishly grateful that Alex wasn't with us.

I know I had said to him about coming down to the lake for the first time together, but I was pleased it was just me and Rach. It would have been even better if Tori had been with us but that wasn't meant to be. I walked over to see if the chairs were wet and finding they weren't, reverently sat in one, rubbing my hands along the length of the smooth wooden arms.

'In the film, the women really sat in these, didn't they?' I breathed.

'They did,' Rachel confirmed, sitting in the other. 'I wonder which one Heather sat in?'

'Definitely this one,' I said, patting the one I had picked.

'I reckon it was this one,' Rachel grinned back, meaning hers.

I hugged my knees to my chest and looked out over the lake. It was extraordinarily beautiful.

'I'd love to camp out here,' I whispered, swallowing over the lump in my throat which was determinedly hanging about to make up for the fact that the shock of finding Alex at the cottage the day before had ensured it hadn't shown up then.

'I don't know about that,' Rachel beamed, her eyes shining as she nodded to the pebbled shore. 'But weather permitting we could definitely moon gaze.'

I hoped I looked as ecstatic as she did because I certainly felt it. I had no idea what had knocked the wind out of Alex's sails when he'd come down here, because the view was magnificent.

'Moon gazing would be wonderful.' I beamed back.

Wanting to make the most of the sunshine, we then walked arm-in-arm to the end of the jetty.

'Selfie!' I insisted, pulling my phone out of my pine cone packed pocket. 'Come on.'

It took a while to select the best view because there were so many possibilities and then I snapped away, scrolling through the results just as the sun disappeared behind the clouds again and the temperature dropped as a result.

'When I get a signal somewhere,' I said enthusiastically, 'I'll send these to Tori.'

Rachel didn't say anything.

'Unless you think I shouldn't,' I said. 'I wouldn't want her to think I was rubbing her nose in it.'

'Let's sleep on it,' Rachel suggested, sitting down and pulling off her plimsolls and socks. 'Although I daresay she probably would like to see what we're up to.'

'What are you doing?' I frowned, shoving my phone away again.

'Testing the water.' She grinned, dangling her feet over the edge. 'If I'm going to be jumping in here in the buff, I want to feel the temperature first.'

I bit my lip, as she braced herself to plunge her feet in because I knew exactly what she was going to say.

'Fuck!' she screeched, pulling her feet out of the water as quickly as she'd dropped them in. 'That's freezing!'

'Of course, it is.' I burst out laughing. 'What did you expect? We had the wood-burner lit last night and need I remind you, we're in the Lake District, so it was hardly going to be tropical, was it?'

'There's no frigging way I'm swimming in there,' she giggled, massaging her blue toes.

'That's one use we've found for Alex then,' I guffawed.

'What do you mean?'

'We can use the fact that he's a bloke as an excuse for not wanting to strip off, can't we?' I said, giving her a nudge. 'No one need ever know we wimped out!'

'That's not a bad idea,' she said, twisting around to shove her frozen foot in my face. 'Feel that. Not even the promise of a stress-free autumn term would tempt me to go in that water in the nip.'

Chapter 7

Although we were both aware that there was something going on with Alex and consequently a little concerned, I did manage to convince Rachel that we should leave him to it. That said, I wouldn't have done had his mood not lifted a little during our post-lake conversation on Friday. Had he remained as morose then as he had been when he initially arrived back from the lake, then I would have made more of an effort to draw him out and include him.

Having spent more time at the lake and pottering about the cottage, by Sunday Rachel and I were keen to venture further and set our sights on another popular setting in the film, the nearest pub. The information in the property folder backed up what we'd researched online and we knew that The Drover's Rest in the nearby village of Lakeside was just a mile and a half away and could be reached within a brisk thirty-minute walk. As it was so close, we thought we'd risk the weather and go on foot.

'Alex,' said Rachel, having quietly knocked on his bedroom door. 'We're going to the pub for lunch. Will you come with us?'

We'd hardly seen him, but in the brief moments when he had left his room to make a drink and prepare a meal, we'd exchanged a few words and I was still happy to leave him to

it as he'd requested. Rachel, however, was beginning to think that he'd been holed up alone long enough and was increasingly determined to prise him out of his shell again.

'No, thanks,' came his eventual muffled response. 'I might walk down and join you in a while though.'

'Okay,' she said, shrugging in my direction. 'We'll maybe see you later then, but we'll take door keys in case you decide you want to head off somewhere else.'

'I don't think that's likely,' I said to Rachel as we set off, remembering to take our waterproof jackets with us along with the cottage keys.

'Tell me again what he said when he came back from the lake,' Rachel asked once we were out of earshot of the cottage.

'I've already told you a thousand times,' I sighed, throwing her a frustrated look. 'I'm not going over it again.'

'All right,' she shot back. 'There's no need to snap.'

'I'm sure he's fine,' I told her in a more placatory tone. 'I wouldn't be so willing to leave him on his lonesome if I didn't genuinely believe that, would I?'

'I suppose not,' she reluctantly acknowledged.

'And you were happy to leave him alone too, until today, weren't you?'

'I know, it's just . . .'

'We know he's got something going on,' I interrupted. 'But it's not our business to pry, is it? You'd hate it if the boot was on the other foot and he was trying to fix you, wouldn't you?'

'I don't want to fix him.' She blushed.

'Rach,' I said, reaching for her hand. 'You want to fix everyone. It's one of the many reasons why the kids at school love you so much. You're the most nurturing person I know.'

She was partly pacified by that, but I could tell she still ached to know what was going on with Alex.

'Just think how you'd feel if he was trying to winkle your secret out of you,' I then cunningly said, putting her in his shoes. 'You'd hate an intervention, wouldn't you? No matter how well meant. And I'm sure Alex would too.'

'I would,' she said hastily. 'You're right.'

'So come on then, before it starts to rain,' I insisted, pulling her along and feeling relieved that she was going to let it drop again. 'Let's look for landmarks from the film as we walk. The village is left from here, isn't it?'

'No,' said Rachel, checking the directions Catriona had left us. 'It's right.'

I looked first in one direction along the road and then the other.

'But the girls turn left at the gate to go to the village in the film,' I pointed out, my ponytail swinging as I tried to pick out any familiar looking trees or roadside rocks.

'That's as maybe,' said Rachel in her most teacherly tone as she showed me the notes and pointed to her right, 'but IRL, the village is this way.'

'Something else that's not how I imagined it.' I sighed without meaning to.

'Oh now, come on,' she scolded. 'Don't be so dramatic. It's not that big a deal and I bet the village will be exactly what we're expecting.'

Thrillingly, she was right. We walked, following the directions Catriona had left for us and it didn't take us long to reach the tiny village of Lakeside which was partly made up of a postbox, the pub and a small general store and post office combined, all of which looked exactly as they had in the film. There was also

a picturesque telephone box library and a Lilliputian village hall, but nothing more. One sweeping glance was all it took to take in the utterly charming place and it was all instantly and heart-thumpingly recognizable.

'Even the hanging baskets are the same!' Rachel laughed, when we reached the pub.

Set a little way back from the road, which was more of a lane really, there was enough space in front of the whitewashed pub for a couple of benches and picnic tables and the baskets and tubs were filled with bright red geraniums and blue and white trailing lobelia, just like they had been described in the book and depicted in the film.

'And the village store has the same ones too,' I said, pointing out the similarly planted pots which flanked the door.

'Come on,' said Rachel. 'I've got a good feeling about this place. Let's go in.'

I felt nervous as we stepped through the door of The Drover's Rest, even more so when a few heads turned in our direction, but the feeling didn't last long. The interior of the pub felt every bit as familiar as the outside had, only it was perhaps a little larger than I expected and Rachel and I were both mesmerised.

In just the same way as when I'd first stepped into the cottage, it felt like I was walking straight into the pages of the book. As I looked about, my mind started to run through a showreel of the scenes from the film which had been shot there and I felt my shoulders relax.

There were a few up to date touches, but there was also the same oak bar which ran almost the whole length of one side of the pub with a few stools in front of it and wooden tables and chairs grouped together around the huge, but currently unlit

inglenook. There were old-fashioned booths too and framed photos taken during the filming hung on the walls. The atmosphere felt as warm as the welcome we received from a glossy black Labrador who trotted over to greet us, her claws tapping lightly on the traditionally flagged floor.

'Hello you,' said Rachel, bending to give her a fuss. 'Aren't you wonderful?'

'She certainly thinks she is,' said a guy who walked out from a back room and stepped up behind the bar. 'What can I get you? I'm Connor, the landlord,' he continued, with a wide smile and attractive Irish lilt. 'Welcome to The Drover's Rest.'

'Hello Connor,' said Rachel, straightening up again.

'Hi,' I said, with a small wave.

Rachel bent to fuss the dog again and Connor, his gaze following her, appeared transfixed. I practically heard the twang of Cupid's bow as his arrow hit its mark.

Wearing a red and navy checked shirt with a band T-shirt underneath and sporting a thick but closely cropped black beard, Connor wasn't my type and I didn't think he was Rachel's either. Not that it mattered because she wasn't looking for a date or a holiday fling. Her relationship with Jealous Jeremy was one hundred per cent exclusive, so poor smitten Connor was destined for disappointment.

'We're staying at . . .' Rachel started to say when she straightened up again.

'Don't tell me,' Connor laughed, holding up a hand. 'You're staying at the *Hope Falls* cottage and you're the newest arrivals on the book and movie pilgrimage.'

'Is it that obvious?' Rachel laughed in response, stepping closer to the bar.

She was completely oblivious to the impact she was having on Connor's heartstrings, but I knew love at first sight when I spotted it.

'Only to those of us in the know,' he said. His face flushed beneath his beard as she smiled up at him. 'You get a feel for these things.'

'Is that right?' Rachel asked.

'It is, but you usually travel in threes,' he recovered enough to say. 'Sometimes fours. Is there someone missing from your party?'

'Funnily enough,' said Rachel, amazed by his powers of deduction, 'there is.'

'So, I am right then?' He grinned.

'One hundred per cent,' I confirmed.

'And you're planning to visit all the sights and recreate as many of the scenes as you can back at the cottage and down at the lake.'

I didn't bother to feel put out that he was reeling our itinerary off as if it was something he'd been privy to a thousand times before, because he most likely had been. The cottage guests would all visit his pub and, as he had rightly predicted, we would be doing the tour, seeing all the sights and enjoying the occasional re-enactment.

That said, this holiday was inimitable to me, a once in a life-time opportunity and I wanted it to feel special. *Extra* special in fact and, a few moments aside, so far it hadn't quite lived up to expectations.

'Yeah, yeah,' laughed Rachel, taking Connor's observations onboard as stoically and as quickly as she had got her head around Alex being a guy. 'You're right and you've obviously seen and heard it all before.'

Perhaps I needed to take a leaf out of her book, as far as Alex was

concerned anyway. Rachel had been waiting the same amount of time as me to take this holiday and no doubt had the same expectations as I did, but she was still managing to have a completely hiccup-free holiday in spite of our unexpected housemate.

'I sure have,' Connor confirmed. 'But not as many times as I've read the book and seen the film.'

'You're a fan?' I asked, sounding surprised.

'Of course, I'm a fan,' he laughed, his gaze turning to me. 'How could I move here a couple of years ago to run this place and not be?'

He had a point. It was a shame he hadn't been here during the filming though because I would have happily spent hours picking his brains about that.

'The third member of our party will be delighted to hear it,' I told him.

'And where is she today?' he asked, looking to Rachel and then back to me again.

'He,' I corrected, amused that he'd made the same assumption as Rachel and I had, 'is back at the cottage.'

'Hallelujah!' Connor cheered approvingly. 'Another guy! That is a rarity. I'm looking forward to meeting him. It's always good to get another bloke's perspective on certain aspects of the film adaptation.'

Rachel let out a yelp and turned red. The Labrador had given her bare legs a nudge with her wet nose as a reminder that she was still there, waiting to be fussed again.

'Come on, Siddy,' Connor called, but the dog didn't budge.

'Siddy,' said Rachel, relenting and giving her another stroke. 'That's an unusual name.'

'It's short for Obsidian,' Connor explained.

'As in the stone?'

'That's right.' He beamed again. 'The stone that's used for protection, not that my Siddy is any sort of a guard dog and thankfully we don't need one around here.'

His heart might need protecting though because if the continued look on his face was anything to go by, he was going to be heartbroken when he found out Rachel was already spoken for.

'The village looks lovely,' I commented, happy to know it was a safe as well as picturesque place. 'Small, but perfectly formed.'

'My thoughts exactly,' he agreed.

His eyes were back on Rachel again.

'Any chance you could squeeze us in for lunch today, Connor?' I asked as my tummy rumbled and I noticed that most of the tables were already taken.

'Of course,' he said, picking up a couple of menus. 'Follow me.'

Once Connor had settled us in a booth, I was about to ask Rachel if she was aware of the impact she was having on him, when a woman came over and introduced herself as Catriona and I was denied the chance.

'I was going to wander down later to see how you're all settling in,' she said. 'But if everything's okay, I won't intrude. Are you still sure you don't want the cleaning service?'

'Thank you.' I smiled. 'We're completely settled and more than happy to look after ourselves.'

The money we were going to save cleaning up after ourselves and changing our own sheets was even more appreciated now.

'And the cottage is stunning,' added Rachel.

'And so is the lake,' I gushed. 'It's all perfect.'

'And Alex?' she asked, her eyebrows raised. 'How's he finding it? Hard, I would imagine.'

Rachel and I exchanged a look.

'Sorry,' she then said. 'I should really ask him that, shouldn't I?'

'Why would he be finding it hard?' Rachel frowned.

Catriona's freckled face turned bright red. 'Oh, he hasn't said anything,' she groaned. 'Of course, he hasn't. Why should he? I'm so sorry,' she apologised again.

'We haven't actually seen all that much of him,' I told her. 'And no, he hasn't said anything which would suggest he's finding the visit hard, although,' I added, 'he has hinted that there might be more to him being at the cottage than a desire to fulfil a long-held dream.'

Catriona turned even redder then. 'Well,' she said. 'It's not my place to comment on that. I shouldn't have said anything at all. Let's just forget I mentioned it.'

Looking at Rachel's inquisitive expression and knowing how many questions I now had whizzing about in my head, I guessed that was going to be easier said than done.

'You've got my number if you need anything, haven't you?' Catriona carried on. 'I won't disturb you, but you can always call if you need me.' She took a step away. 'Any problems just let me know, and I'll sort them.' She nodded, clearly relieved the conversation was over.

She rushed away and Rachel looked at me, wide-eyed. 'What do you suppose that was about?' she asked.

'Obviously, the baggage Alex has brought with him,' I said, eyeing the menu and thinking again of the bag he had carried back from the lake. 'And which we're not going to speculate over, right?' I reminded her, even though I was desperate to pick it all apart.

'Right,' she agreed, opening her own menu.

'I reckon it has something to do with a woman though,' I blurted out as my eyes scanned the list of meals but didn't take a single dish in. 'That Heather hoodie he wore to watch the film was nowhere near big enough, was it? I wonder if he's pining for an ex?'

'I thought we weren't going to speculate,' Rachel smirked.

'We're not,' I said, sitting up straighter and banishing the image of Alex's kind eyes. 'To be honest,' I said, changing track, 'right now, I'm more interested in the impact you're having on the lovely landlord over there.'

'What?' she tutted, as a deep frown formed. 'Don't be so ridiculous.'

'He's smitten, Rach.' I grinned.

'Don't be daft . . .'

Convincing her further was impossible because her mobile started ringing.

'Oh,' she said, once she'd pulled it out of her pocket. 'Guess who?'

'Jeremy,' I ventured, in a more sarcastic tone than I'd intended.

I knew it must have been killing him not to be in constant contact.

'No,' she retorted sardonically, accepting the call. 'It's Tori.'

Connor was hovering to take our order by the time we'd filled Tori in about our third housemate and what the cottage was like and she insisted that we send her a selfie of the two of us in the pub as well as the shots I'd taken at the lake.

'And that landlord sounds like a total hunk,' she said, sounding very much like her usual self and Rose from the book rolled into one. 'So, get him in the shot too.'

I had resisted telling her how good-looking Alex was.

'You really want to see what you're missing?' I asked, just to be sure she meant it.

'I damn well do,' she said. 'I need something to cheer me up.'

'Have you got any further with your new life plan?' Rachel asked.

'Not yet,' she sighed. 'I'm still readjusting to living back at home.'

'Well, don't readjust for too long,' Rachel said gently, knowing that meant she was sleeping all day and binge-watching Netflix all night. 'The sooner you've got something going, the sooner you'll get your dad off your back.'

'I know,' Tori said. 'Anyway, I better go. He's changed my phone contract and I haven't got unlimited anything anymore.'

'Poor Tori,' I said, after she'd gone and I'd sent her the lake selfie.

'And poor Jeremy,' said Rachel, scrolling through her messages folder. 'Would you look at this lot? He must be really missing me.'

She showed me the ridiculous number of messages and voicemails already stacked up unheard and unread and I willed myself not to make vomiting noises.

'You did tell him that you weren't going to be able to call him all that much while we're here, didn't you?' I frowned.

'I did,' she sighed. 'But he clearly still wants to keep in touch, even if it is all one way. How sweet is that?'

'Saccharine sweet,' I said, clapping my hands as Connor came over carrying two packed plates of the traditional roast beef lunch we'd opted for.

'Oh wow,' said Rachel, abandoning her phone when she spotted the vast Yorkshire puddings.

'Enjoy.' Connor smiled, carefully setting the meals down.

'Hang on,' I said, whipping up Rachel's phone and turning the camera on. 'Can you just take a snap of us for our friend?'

He willingly acquiesced.

'And,' I added, before he headed back to the bar, 'just one more, with you in it.'

'Me?' he laughed.

'Yes, please,' I told him. 'Because for some reason, after Rachel described you, our friend back home thought you sounded like quite a hunk.'

'Oh, well, in that case,' he said, grinning at Rachel who looked mortified. 'You'd better get my best side, hadn't you?'

I made sure most of the screen was filled with him and Rachel and pressed send before she had a chance to veto it.

'Thanks, Connor,' I said, as I turned the phone off and rammed it into my pocket so Rachel couldn't fret over the mountain of messages while we ate.

'Always happy to oblige,' he laughed and sauntered back to the bar.

'Don't encourage him,' Rachel tutted, obviously having processed what I'd said earlier about him liking her. 'And give me back my phone.'

'No way,' I said. 'If you think I'm going to sit here trying to enjoy my dinner, while you scroll feeling sorry for Jeremy, then you've got another think coming.'

'Don't you think I should just let him know we're here, now I've got a decent signal?'

'No,' I said sternly. 'I don't, because it will set a precedent. Now, eat your puddings before they deflate, and maybe you can do it after.'

Chapter 8

Rachel and I chatted about the pretty pub and the perfect village all the way back to the cottage and by the time we'd remembered that I'd still got her phone and she hadn't let Jeremy know she'd arrived, she was out of signal range and the rain had started to pour. I did feel a little bad, but for her rather than him.

'You could walk back up to the road and do it first thing tomorrow,' I suggested as we ran on to the veranda to avoid a thorough soaking. 'It might be dry again by then.'

'I suppose I could,' she said, biting her lip, 'although I do feel bad that I haven't been in touch at all so far.'

Conversely, I was ecstatic about that.

'I should have done it when I messaged Mum three rings the day we arrived,' she carried on. 'But I was so excited to be here, that I didn't think and you know how he worries.'

I wanted to say that I knew how he liked to know exactly where she was every minute of the day and not knowing for once would do him no harm at all, but stopped myself.

'I do,' I said instead, shaking out my coat and hanging it on a hook next to the door to dry, 'but he wouldn't want you catching a cold just to send a text, would he?'

'No,' she sighed heavily, hanging her coat on the hook next to mine. 'I guess not.'

I looked at her furrowed brow and wondered if my discouraging her from messaging was as reprehensible as the behaviour Jeremy resorted to and that she frustratingly hadn't picked up on, but then I reasoned that my actions came from a completely different place, one of love and in this instance, to stop her getting soaked and genuinely risk catching a chill.

'Come on,' I said, finding the door unlocked and guessing Alex hadn't gone out after all. 'Let's go in and get the kettle on. We've got a lot of relaxing to do.'

The next couple of days ran comfortably and comfortingly according to our original plan. I took my time putting the finishing touches on the anniversary picture and Rachel continued to recover from her end of term exhaustion. As far as I was aware, she hadn't ventured back up the road to message Jeremy. An action which I was blown away by but didn't comment on for fear of breaking the spell. I had no idea what Alex's plans had been, but he had finally remembered there was life beyond his bedroom door and that was a relief all round.

By the time Wednesday dawned, he almost resembled the man we'd first met and when he emerged from his room, ready to drive down to Manchester, the dark circles under his eyes had almost completely faded. Whatever had got him so stirred up during that first trip to the lake had clearly taken quite a toll and a long time to recover from and I was certain he hadn't been back, which was a shame because it was such a beautiful spot and of course, integral to both the book and the film.

'Will you be driving through Lakeside this morning, Alex?' I asked, as he checked he'd got his keys, phone and wallet.

'I will,' he said. 'But only for around three seconds. I had another look at the details about the place in Catriona's folder yesterday and it's hardly a sprawling metropolis, is it?'

'No,' I agreed, wondering if he intended to visit the pub. Connor would be delighted if he did. 'One blink and you'd miss it, although it looks exactly like it does in the film. I don't suppose I could blag a lift with you as far as there, could I?'

He looked rather taken aback. 'Of course,' he said, picking up his jacket and sounding nonplussed. 'You aren't planning on carrying shopping back though, are you? It'd be a bit of a trek from there with heavy bags.'

'No,' I said. 'I want to send a parcel and if you don't mind dropping me off, it will save me having to ask Rachel to drive me later. I want to make sure I catch the early collection. Assuming there is more than one.'

'Is it that lovely anniversary picture?' he asked.

'It is,' I told him, showing him a photo of the finished piece in its frame on my phone.

'Wow,' he said, taking in the intricate final details. 'It looks even better than the day I saw you working on it.'

Was it my imagination or did his cheeks colour a little at the mention of that day?

'Thank you,' I said. 'I'm really happy with how it has turned out.'

'I can send it from Manchester if you like?' he then kindly offered.

'That's very kind,' I said, putting my phone away again. 'And thank you, but I'd rather do it myself.'

'That's fair enough,' he nodded. 'And, as we've made it this far into the holiday without further falling out, you can add anything you want to this shopping list, if you like.' He smiled, referring back to another of our earliest interactions, but this time making me blush.

'Thanks,' I said, taking the piece of paper from him.

I wondered if the falling out situation would have been different had he spent more time out of his bedroom and I found myself hoping not.

'That's kind,' I added. 'And much appreciated.'

I'd got over my initial upset that he hadn't turned out to be the person Rachel and I had been expecting to share the cottage with and had no desire to waste more time smarting over it. I had far more important things to think about during my summer than Alex's gender, and took the offer of adding to his shopping list as a metaphorical olive branch. Not that it should have been him who was offering one.

'Do you want anything picking up when I do some shopping in Manchester, Rachel?' he asked, as she wandered out of the bedroom, looking sleepy and dishevelled.

'I do actually,' she said, coming to read what I'd added so far. 'But I don't know how you feel about buying feminine hygiene products, Alex.'

I turned to look at her and felt a rush of tears gather behind my eyes. Not only had she not been rushing to message Jeremy, she'd also got her period. I felt like punching the air.

'I'm sure I'm up to it,' he said. 'It certainly wouldn't be my first time.'

'Thank you,' she said, then frowned at me. 'What's up with you?'

'Nothing.' I swallowed. 'Do you want the usual?'

'Yes,' she said. 'Two packs, please. I've almost run out. I'll pay you later, Alex, if that's okay? My brain hasn't quite engaged yet.'

'Sure,' he said. 'No problem. Are you ready, Emily?'

'Just a sec.' I swallowed, adding a couple more things to the list before handing it back and picking up the parcel, along with my bag and coat. 'Alex is going to drop me at the post office,' I told Rachel. 'I won't be long.'

'Okie doke,' she said, heading back to the bedroom, with a mug of coffee from the pot. 'See you both later.'

'Are you all right?' Alex asked as I watched her close the door.

'Yes,' I said, then cleared my throat. 'Sorry. Let's go. I don't want to make you late.'

During the last couple of days, I had begun to panic that the secret Rachel had come to the cottage with was that she was pregnant. I knew her cycle every bit as well as my own so I was well aware that she was a little late.

The thought of her being tied to Jeremy through a baby had played heavily on my mind, but not anymore. I still didn't know what her secret was, but at least it wasn't that. It was a huge relief and restored my hope that they might not end up together forever after all. Had I thought it through rationally, of course, I would have realised sooner that a baby wasn't on the cards because Rachel hadn't stopped drinking.

'Your car's much smarter than ours,' I told Alex as he held my parcel while I arranged my bag and pulled on my seatbelt.

I noticed he'd put the bag from the lake on the back seat and I was itching to know what was inside and whether it had any connection to what Catriona had indiscreetly said in the pub.

'Thanks,' he said, carefully handing over the parcel before

closing the door and walking around to get in. 'But yours is a classic.'

I wasn't sure about that.

'But,' I countered, feeling thrown by how close we were once he had settled himself into the driver's seat, 'there are no scratches or dents on yours.'

'Thankfully not,' he laughed, the sound filling the car as he turned the key in the ignition. 'Any comments you'd like to make about the weather before we set off?'

'What?' I frowned.

He turned to face me and I didn't know where to look. Not only were we in close physical proximity, we were also eye to eye and I was unsettled by the impact that had on me.

'We've shared the cottage for almost a week,' he pointed out, 'and yet we still know so little about each other that now we're alone you've started talking about the paintwork and condition of my car to keep a conversation going.'

He said it with no rancour, but that didn't stop me from bristling. Or was it his nearness that set me off again?

'Is it any wonder?' I bit back, looking away as my heart thrummed in my chest. 'You've been hiding out in your room for days. We could hardly have a heart to heart with a solid door between us, could we?'

I regretted the harsh words the second I'd uttered them, but I knew deep down why I'd said them. It was my preoccupation with his intensely kind eyes that I resented. I was supposed to be thinking about nothing other than *Hope Falls* and my future during this holiday, but it was proving impossible when he was taking up so much room in my head.

'Sorry,' I choked. 'That was uncalled for.'

He took a breath before answering. 'It's fine,' he finally said. 'And you're right. I suppose I have been hiding out.'

The sadness in his tone, and knowing I was the one who had caused it, fractured my heart.

'You're on holiday,' I said huskily. 'And totally entitled to do whatever you want. I shouldn't have said anything ...'

'No,' he said, cutting me off. 'I'm pleased you did and I think it's high time we started over.'

'You do?' I swallowed.

'I do,' he said, sounding stronger. 'Can we please start again, because in spite of the fact that it might not have appeared that way over the last few days, I do want this holiday to be a success. I *need* it to be a success.'

He didn't say why.

'So, can we start again?' he asked, offering me his hand. 'Hi.' He then smiled. 'I'm Alex and I'm delighted to finally be here.'

I took a deep breath and felt my face flush as I slipped my warm hand into his cool one. The touch of his skin set my insides alight, but I tried my best to outwardly pretend the contact had no impact at all. I was determined to embrace the second chance he was offering and hopefully use it to turn off my feelings and dial down my libido.

'Hi,' I stammered, the word catching. 'I'm Emily and I'm delighted to be here too.'

'What are your plans for the next few weeks, Emily?' he asked, sounding completely unaffected as he released my hand and put the car into first gear.

'Well,' I began, the feel of his fingers holding mine lingering long after he had withdrawn them.

I shrugged the sensation off and in the spirit of our fresh

start, quickly ran him through the schedule Rachel, Tori and I had come up with in the two minutes it took him to drive to Lakeside. I felt better for having cleared the air, but my heart still felt as uncomfortably close to the danger of being hijacked as it had been before.

'Oh, my goodness,' Alex gasped as Lakeside came into view. 'This is . . .'

'Just like in the book,' I laughed unguardedly. 'I know, believe me, I know.'

He pulled up outside the pub and shut the engine down.

'And the film,' he said, looking first one way up the road and then the other. 'Wow.'

'Do you want to get out and look around?' I asked.

'I'd better not,' he said, checking the time. 'I really should get going and I'm meeting my mum for lunch so I need to get as much done as I can this morning. I'll definitely come back later in the week though.'

'You absolutely have to meet the pub landlord,' I told him. 'He's a *Hope Falls* fanatic too and was thrilled when we told him the third member of our party was a guy.'

He turned to look at me again and my heart skittered.

'I am a member of your party then?' he asked.

I fussed about, making a total hash of releasing my seatbelt. 'Of course, you are,' I confirmed, my own eyes tracking back to his even though my brain was trying to resist.

'I'm very pleased to hear it.' He smiled, making those wonderful crinkly lines reappear. 'It might have taken me a few days to get my act together, but now we have five glorious weeks to make the most of.'

'Exactly,' I said on an out breath. 'Five whole glorious weeks.'

I tried not to get het up about the fact that the first of the six had already flown by. I would now put my feelings of attraction for Alex to one side and get us back on track. After all, as Rachel had been so keen to keep pointing out, we'd all got along famously when we'd been emailing each other and at the end of the day, the Alex sitting next to me was still that Alex. The one I had thought would make a fine friend.

'I wonder if Connor, the landlord, might be up for occasionally making our party a foursome?' I said in a show of bonhomie. 'That would even things up for you, wouldn't it?'

If he was, I would let Connor know that Rachel was already spoken for, just to make sure he didn't get the wrong idea or his heart properly broken.

'Yes.' Alex smiled. 'I'd like that. It would be good to chat to another bloke about the book and the film adaptation too.'

'Funnily enough,' I smiled back, 'that's exactly what he said.'

I had quite a wait until the post office opened, so I sat outside the pub and fired up my phone. I only had one message and it was from Tori. She loved the photos taken at the lake, but asked where the snap of the swoonworthy landlord was. I pinged a message back saying I'd sent it from Rachel's phone and that she should ask her to send it again if it hadn't landed.

'Good morning,' said Connor, who appeared with Siddy and a hosepipe and set about dousing the baskets and tubs. 'Are you waiting for me?'

'I'm not,' I told him, jumping up to dodge the splashes from the deluge and almost tripping over Siddy in the process. 'I'm waiting for the post office to open. Although as you're here, there is something I wanted to ask you.'

'Ask away,' he said, turning off the hose.

'I was wondering, if you ever have some free time, if you might like to spend some of it with us?'

'Oh wow,' he said. 'I would. I'd like that very much, thanks.'

I thought I'd better explain about Rachel straightaway in case he thought I was matchmaking, or worse, that she herself had asked me to suggest he should hang out with us.

'It would help even things up for Alex,' I therefore hastily added. 'I feel for him a bit, being lumbered with two women he doesn't know. He wasn't part of our original party, but took the spot when our other friend had to drop out.'

'I see,' Connor said thoughtfully. 'That matches the plot though, doesn't it?'

'It does,' I nodded. 'Though for a while,' I then creatively carried on, 'we thought Jeremy, that's Rachel's partner, might take the place, but it didn't work out.'

'Rachel's partner?'

'Um.'

He was quiet for a moment and I could tell he was recalibrating. 'I'm pleased you've mentioned him,' he then said, ducking his head. 'I could have made a fool of myself there, couldn't I?'

'Knowing Rachel as well as I do,' I told him, 'she wouldn't have let you.'

'Serious, is it?' he asked, reeling in the hosepipe. 'This relationship with Jeremy.'

'Sadly,' I said, knowing I couldn't lie, 'I think it is, yes.'

'Why sadly?' he asked. 'Do you not like him?'

Oops.

'I wouldn't go that far,' I winced, knowing I already had.

'But if it comes up, would you mind not letting on that I put it like that?'

'All right.' He grinned. 'Mum's the word.'

I hoped it was. The last thing I needed was for Rachel to somehow find out that I'd been bad mouthing her relationship or her boyfriend, no matter how mildly, and especially to someone who clearly thought she was the bee's knees.

Chapter 9

'What about cheese?' Mrs Timpson, who ran the post office and general store, asked as she waved a waxed packet about. 'How are you fixed for cheese? This is local and goes down a treat with that fruitcake you've decided on.'

I had posted my parcel and was now being subjected to a sales pitch canny enough to rival any Dragon in the Den by a woman wearing a floral tabard and with a soft grey wash and set. Her grandmotherly appearance had duped me completely and she'd reeled me in the very second she'd handed over the proof of posting receipt.

'I think we're all right for cheese, Mrs Timpson,' I said, trying to put my foot down, especially as *I* hadn't even decided on the fruitcake. *She* had. 'And I haven't got a bag to carry all of this back to the cottage in anyway.'

'You better have one of these reusable jobbies as well then,' she said, adding a jute bag with the name of the store printed on the side to my growing pile of superfluous purchases. 'It'll last you forever. And that will mean you can take the cheese. Yes?'

'Why not?' I feebly caved as she began ringing everything up and I began to fear for my holiday food fund.

I thought my arm was going to drop off by the time I had made it back to the cottage. I'd kept switching hands, but after a certain point it didn't make any difference.

'Where have you been?' Rachel frowned, when I staggered in and dropped the shopping all over the floor. 'You've been gone hours.'

She didn't sound particularly impressed, but in that moment, neither was I.

'I got fleeced in the shop,' I said, scooping everything back up. 'The owner, Mrs Timpson, went in for the kill the second she'd got hold of my parcel and I'm thirty quid lighter now. Anyway, what's up with you?'

'Nothing,' she said, stowing the cheese in the fridge and the artisan bread in the cupboard with an extremely heavy hand and pairing it not with the jar of locally made chutney I'd also got, but with a face like thunder.

'Well, I don't believe that for a second.' I tutted, pouring myself a glass of water and drinking it down in one long go.

'Of course, you don't,' she snapped. 'Because you know exactly what's wrong.'

'No, I don't,' I frowned, rubbing the middle of my chest because the water had been really cold and I'd gulped too much air down with it.

She gave me a look which could have killed and I pitied any of her poor students who found themselves on the receiving end of it.

'You're going to have to fill me in,' I said, putting down the glass with one hand and neatly catching the phone she tossed me with the other.

I hoped she hadn't somehow been in touch with Connor and

he'd already forgotten his promise to keep schtum about my slip of the tongue relating to Jeremy.

'Did you do it on purpose to stir up trouble?' Rachel demanded, her bottom lip trembling.

'Do what?' I asked, beginning to panic.

Rachel and I rarely argued and I had certainly never done anything awful enough to warrant making her cry.

'You may have noticed,' she tearfully told me, 'that I've done as you suggested and held out on Jeremy, to make sure he got the idea that I wasn't going to be constantly available while we're staying here.'

'You have.' I swallowed.

A part of me thought she hadn't been in touch, but another part, a larger part, hadn't dared to believe it. Under other circumstances I would have been thrilled, but I genuinely couldn't account for her current state of upset and that tempered my desire to offer her a high five.

'But I know now the real reason why you didn't want me to call him too soon,' she said, an angry edge replacing the upset in her tone and further baffling me. 'How could you be so mean, Em?'

'I don't understand . . .'

She snatched back her phone, found what she was looking for and held it up in front of my face.

'Now do you understand?' she shouted.

I looked at the screen and found the craftily cropped photo of her and Connor smiling with their heads together in the pub on Sunday looking back at me.

'It's the photo I took on your phone in The Drover's on Sunday,' I stupidly said.

'I know it is,' she seethed. 'And I know who you sent it to!'

'Oh shit,' I gasped, as I realised what I'd inadvertently done. Jeremy and Tori were the top two listings in her favourites. 'That's why Tori never got it. I sent it to . . .'

'Jeremy!' Rachel screeched. 'You sent a photo of me and another man, looking *extremely* happy, to my boyfriend and right at the beginning of when we're not going to see each other for the next month and a half and then talked me into having zero contact with him.'

And, of course, Jeremy wasn't just any boyfriend, was he? Had it been any other boyfriend, the misunderstanding could have been easily explained, there most likely wouldn't have even been a misunderstanding to explain, but Jeremy was the most clingy, jealous and manipulative man I'd ever encountered.

'Shit,' I said again, as the implications – especially having seen and heard how he'd reacted to a guy innocently asking Rachel where the loos in a club were – sank in.

'I can't believe you'd do that,' Rachel carried on, sounding horribly hurt and, even worse, disappointed.

My eyes flicked from the screen back to her face. 'Surely, you're not thinking that I did this on purpose,' I gasped.

She gave me a look which implied that was exactly what she was thinking.

'And as if that wasn't bad enough,' she continued, 'just as I was standing up on the road and in the middle of the conversation trying to smooth it all over because the messages I discovered from Jeremy when I finally turned my phone on had gone from mildly irritated to *"I'm coming to bring you home,"* Connor pulls up and starts going on about you, me, him and Alex making up a foursome!'

'I can explain about that,' I told her.

'No need,' she said, through gritted teeth. 'I've already worked it out. You thought you'd get Jeremy out of the picture and fix me up with Connor who you conveniently, but completely inaccurately, think has the hots for me.'

I knew she was upset but that didn't warrant her thinking quite so badly of me.

'Did Jeremy hear what Connor was saying?' I asked, trying not to show her how much she'd upset me.

'No,' she huffed. 'But he knew I was talking to a man.'

'You are allowed to talk to other guys, Rach,' I pointed out.

'I know that,' she snapped. 'I'm not stupid or anywhere near as under Jeremy's thumb as you and Tori seem to think I am.'

The whole situation was further proof that the relationship wasn't a healthy one and that she was completely wedged under Jeremy's thumb but it wasn't the moment to contradict her about that. For now, I had to let that go, along with my upset over what she'd assumed about me.

'He's not really coming up here to get you, is he?' I tentatively asked.

'No,' she said, letting out a long breath. 'I think I managed to calm him down on the promise that I'd check in every day at a set time from now on and that—'

'You've got to be kidding,' I cut in, unable to stop myself. 'That's ridiculous.'

'Not as ridiculous as you sending someone, who's feeling a bit fragile because I've left them for the entire summer, a photo of me with another man and looking very happy about it, and then,' she raged on defensively, 'set me up with someone else.'

'Look,' I said, unable to hold back now she'd maligned me a

second time. 'I sent that photo to Jeremy by mistake. I genuinely thought I was sending it to Tori and you can look at the message she's sent me, and quite possibly the one she's now sent you, to prove that.'

Rachel shifted from one foot to the other, but didn't comment.

'And yes,' I ploughed on, 'I have asked Connor if he'd like to hang out with us on the odd occasion because I thought that might be good for Alex. I thought having another guy around who loves *Hope Falls* as much as he does, might even things up. Given that you've been on at me to make more of an effort, I thought you'd be all for that.'

Rachel went to speak, but I didn't let her.

'And last, but by no means least, when I was talking to Connor, I made a point of telling him that you're in a relationship, a serious one. And I was right, he does like you, but he's a stand-up guy and has therefore now assigned you to the friend zone.'

I walked away before she could comment and, in lieu of having my own room to flounce off to, grabbed my jacket from the hook by the door and strode down to the lake.

Once there, I sat in one of the Adirondack chairs and hugged my knees to my chest. I stared out across the lake to the hills beyond and willed myself not to cry. So much for the fresh start Alex had been so keen to embrace that morning and which I had done my best to initiate.

Posting that patchwork commission was a real milestone and something wonderful to celebrate. It was the most creative piece I'd designed so far and I had planned to revel in the pleasure completing it afforded me. I had imagined Rachel and I celebrating over a lunch made up of all the things Mrs Timpson had

coerced me into buying, but not now. The magical moment was well and truly lost.

'Em.'

I jumped at the sound of my name a while later and twisted round to see Rachel emerging from the path through the woods carrying a picnic basket and with rugs tucked under one arm.

'Hey,' she said, coming to stand next to me. 'I thought you might be hungry.'

I'd sat for what must have been a couple of hours in the beautiful spot, but I didn't feel much soothed by the lovely location and I hadn't made any headway with my decision-making either because I hadn't been thinking about my future. Rather than channelling Heather and deciding which life path to take, I had fallen to brooding over the unsatisfactory start my fantasy holiday had so far had.

First there had been the presence of Alex to get my head around along with the fact that he had moved into my dream sanctuary without a second thought. And now, my best friend, who had accepted Alex far more willingly than I had, had accused me of trying to sneakily sabotage her relationship with her partner from hell.

'And given how much you spent on all this,' she carried on when I didn't comment, 'I thought we should enjoy it while it's at its freshest.'

I pulled one of the blankets out from under her arm and wrapped it around my shoulders. It was chilly sitting in the shade, but it wouldn't be too much longer before the sun reached our side of the lake and things warmed up a bit. At least it hadn't rained.

'I'm really sorry, Em,' Rachel sniffed, dumping the basket in

the face of my sullen silence. 'I walked back up the road after you went out again and I have had a message from Tori and, having thought back over how Connor was earlier, compared to last Sunday, I know you were right about him, too.'

I looked at her and shook my head.

It was more than a little frustrating that she hadn't mentioned Jeremy in her apology or acknowledged that his reaction to the photo I'd inadvertently sent had been OTT in the extreme. How was it possible that my strong, intelligent, independent friend was so blinkered where that man was concerned? What was it about him that had managed to wrap her so tightly in his web?

I was desperate to get to the bottom of that, but knew that if I risked saying anything else even remotely scathing about him, she'd cut me out and then I wouldn't be able to be there for her when it all came to a head. Because it would at some point. I was certain of that.

'Sending that photo really was a genuine mistake,' I said quietly.

'I know.' She nodded, lowering herself into the seat next to mine.

'And asking Connor to join us really was for Alex's benefit,' I further said. 'He was so keen when I suggested it while he drove me to Lakeside earlier.'

Rachel nodded. 'I know that too.'

'When we first met him,' I told her, 'I would have been happy if he had planned to stay hidden in that precious double room for the entire duration of our stay, but not now. From today on, I wanted to make more of an effort to make the three of us being here a memorable experience for all the right reasons.'

Rachel's eyes filled with tears and I reached across and grasped her hand.

'Oh, come on,' I said, drawing a line under the drama. 'Let's eat. I'm starving.'

The food might have been a bit on the pricey side, but it was delicious. The cheese especially, when paired with the rich fruit-cake in the Yorkshire tradition, was a taste sensation. And the bottle of red we drank alongside it was perfect too. The sun shone long enough to warm the side of the lake where we were sitting and as I sat back in the chair, closed my eyes and lifted my faces to the heat-filled rays, I finally felt as though I was living the *Hope Falls* dream.

This was the nirvana I had been trying to achieve all along. Not the row which preceded it of course, but this moment, this wonderful time-out moment with my friend. I wished again that Tori could have been with us, not that she could sit still and quiet for three seconds together, but we had Alex to make up for her loss now.

His smiling face and kind brown eyes popped into my head and, unbidden, I let out a long and very contented breath. That had to be more to do with the relaxed state the late lunch wine had prompted than the fact that I found him easy on the eye, right? I really did need to take a leaf out of Connor's book and just like he'd shifted Rachel into the friend zone, very quickly plonk Alex in there too.

'Penny for them?' Rachel asked, just as I was about to drift off.

I opened one eye and squinted at her, taking a moment to marshal my thoughts.

'I was just thinking how this finally feels like the holiday I was hoping for,' I said honestly. 'And how happy I am to have sent that commission off. What about you?'

She didn't say anything and I shielded my eyes from the glare of the sun bouncing off the smooth unsullied lake so I could look at her properly.

'What is it?' I asked, my perfect moment disappearing with a pop when I found her biting her lip and looking preoccupied. 'What were you thinking about?'

She rolled her shoulders and I knew she was gearing up to say something important. It was one of her classic tells.

'I'm feeling bad about not knowing what's been going on with you lately,' she said. 'I've been so immersed in the end of term and . . . some of my own stuff, that I haven't been here for you as much as I should have been and I'm sorry about that.'

'What are you talking about?' I asked, wondering what she meant by her own stuff. 'You've been a total rock since I was made redundant.'

'Well,' she shrugged, 'that's kind of you to say, but if I really had been a good friend, then I would have known you'd interviewed for another position with a different firm already, wouldn't I? You should have told me, Em.'

'How did you know about that?' I frowned, sitting up.

'I spoke to Mum earlier as well as Jeremy,' she said, sounding hesitant but a little happier. 'I understand congratulations are in order. Why hadn't you said anything?'

'Congratulations?'

'Mum went to check on the flat and there was a message light flashing on the phone,' Rachel explained. 'She wasn't going to listen to it, but then started to worry that it might be something important and what with us being away for so long . . .'

'What was it?'

'Confirmation from someone called Greg,' she said with a

small smile, 'that your contract would be waiting for you to sign when you got back from your holiday and that he and the team were looking forward to you starting with them in September.'

'Oh.' I swallowed. 'I see.'

'Congratulations!' she said again.

She sounded thrilled, but I wasn't. It had been my intention to keep the new job under wraps so I could reach a decision about my future without her knowing about it. Rachel, like my parents, very much favoured a safe career path and was all for Team Employee. If I was going to make a well-balanced decision about my next step, I didn't need anyone cheerleading more loudly for one option than the other.

Rachel might have loved the new direction my patchwork had taken, but she wouldn't have been so keen to discover that I was considering sacrificing a regular pay cheque to make a business out of it. She'd already called my sewing obsession a hobby since we'd arrived and that confirmed that she would try to talk me out of taking it on full-time, so I hadn't planned on giving her the chance.

'You're a dark horse,' she continued, sounding happier than she had all day. 'And even though I feel bad for not knowing you'd interviewed, I'm absolutely thrilled for you and,' she added, 'I'm not going to lie, I'm relieved too.'

'Just because you need the security, Rach . . .' I started to say.

'It's not that so much . . .' she said, turning red.

'What then?' I asked.

She wriggled in her seat. 'I haven't said anything before,' she began, sounding cautious again, 'because I was going to use the holiday to think it through further.' That was beginning to sound incredibly familiar. 'Although actually, because you didn't

currently have a job, I knew it wasn't really a feasible option, but now . . .'

'Oh, Rach,' I cut in as a knot began to form in the pit of my stomach. 'Will you please just spit it out?'

'All right,' she said, taking a deep breath. 'The thing is, a few weeks ago, Jeremy asked me to move in with him.'

The tiny knot turned into a huge one as I felt every last bit of oxygen leave my lungs. I knew Rachel absolutely loved Jeremy's two bedroomed flat and private balcony, which was just a stone's throw from Roundhay Park. She loved its proximity to the wonderful green space as much as its square footage and it was conveniently close to her school. It was just a shame that she seemed to love him, too.

'And even though I thought I really did want to move in with him,' she carried on, as I began to feel giddy, 'I didn't say yes straightaway because I didn't want to make a final decision when I was so tired out by the summer term, but also because I was worried about how you'd cope financially after you were made redundant . . .'

'I see.' I swallowed.

'But,' she then cheerfully added, 'now you've got this new job, I don't need to worry about the financials, do I? You could manage it alone, or at least until you find another flatmate, so now I can focus solely on how I feel about the prospect of cohabiting with my boyfriend.'

I wasn't usually lost for words, but this had been the last thing (now I knew she wasn't pregnant), that I had expected her to come out with. If Jeremy got her living in his flat, then Tori and I would have an insurmountable struggle to get her out again.

'I've still not completely made up my mind,' she carried on,

'but this new job of yours has definitely given me a nudge in the right direction. And,' she added, sounding thrilled, 'if it turns out that you can afford to live in the flat on your own, you could turn my room into a designated space for your patchwork, couldn't you? That way, you wouldn't have to keep packing it away all the time. It would make the ideal hobby room.'

There was that word again and how thrilled she sounded to have it all worked out.

'That's true,' I croaked, looking out over the lake and blinking hard. 'What a great idea.'

'I'm guessing, this job was the secret you've come here with, wasn't it?' she nudged, her eyes shining. 'I'm sorry I've found it out, but it was down to Mum, not me.'

'It's fine,' I said, neither confirming or denying that it was my secret. 'And I don't mind you knowing if it helps you make up your mind about moving in with Jeremy.'

Obviously, that was a lie, but what else could I say? If I told her about my plans to set up my own business now, she'd most likely assume that I'd just come up with the idea and announced it to stop her moving out because I didn't like Jeremy. From now on, I was going to be walking on even thinner eggshells where anything to do with him was concerned.

'You really are a true friend.' She beamed, pouring out the last of the wine. 'Let's drink to the future.'

'Yes,' I echoed shakily, holding my glass aloft. 'The future.'

Sadly, it didn't have quite the same ring to it now.

Chapter 10

As if my commitment to making a fresh start hadn't already been churned up enough, I could tell from the moment Alex arrived back from Manchester that he had something on his mind and surmised that he was gearing up to make a revelation too. However, rather than hit us with the details that evening, he waited until the next.

'You go,' Rachel insisted, when we spotted a handwritten note inviting us to join him at the lake for a campfire supper. 'And I'll come down in a little while. I need to check in with Jeremy at six first.'

'Okay,' I said lightly, swallowing down the words about a daily check-in not being a good habit to succumb to and especially one that I'd now discovered had to happen at a Jeremy specified time every day. 'We'll see you in a bit. Try not to be too long, if you can help it.'

I took my time walking through the woods and thought about what Rachel had said about moving in with Jeremy. It was just as well I hadn't already decided to start my own business, because her potential change of address was having a huge impact on my thoughts about it all.

Knowing Rachel as well as I did, I was horribly aware that if I told her now that I had decided to turn the job down, then she wouldn't leave because she would be worried about how I'd manage, even though she knew I had a bit of money put by and, even though her not moving in with Jeremy was the very thing I wanted the most, it would be terrible if my actions stopped her going, because I could tell that she wanted to.

I was also worried that having not told her about my alternative plans when I had ample chance the day before, there was a very genuine possibility that she really might assume I had simply come up with the idea on a whim to sabotage her decision and that I hadn't properly thought it through at all. What a mess it all was.

Fortunately, what Alex had created at the lake distracted me from my tangled thoughts.

'Oh, wow,' I gasped as I reached the end of the canopied path and took in the transformation in front of me. 'This is amazing!'

Stepping into the dramatic lakeside vista was always a breath-taking moment, but what Alex had spent the afternoon setting up made it doubly so.

'You recognise it?' he asked, a smile lighting up his face as he turned to look at me.

He was wearing a dark sweater with a light shirt underneath, jeans and big boots and he looked every inch the classic romantic hero. Even his jaw was seductively stubbled. I knew he hadn't created that particular aesthetic on purpose, but the more I saw of him and the more I got used to the fact that he was part of mine and Rachel's party, the more attractive I found him.

It was wholly inconvenient. Falling for someone had never formed part of my summer plan and I had recently pledged not to, but I couldn't seem to stop myself.

'Of course, I recognise it,' I said, the words catching as I took in the details of what he'd so cleverly and painstakingly recreated. 'This is an exact replica of the big revelation scene in *Hope Falls*, isn't it?'

As soon as I said the words, I knew that I had been right about him coming back from Manchester with something on his mind and that he had gone to great lengths to set the scene to share whatever it was with Rachel and I.

That would make two lakeside revelations in as many days. I wished I had spoken up when Rachel and I were talking and made it a triple, but it was too late now. In the face of what Rachel had shared, my own secret had the power to be horribly misinterpreted and I wasn't going to risk that.

'It is,' Alex said, ducking his head as his cheeks flushed. 'I was hoping you were going to get it.'

'How could I not?' I said admiringly, making him colour further. 'It's absolutely perfect.'

He'd set a campfire going in front of the bench and there were storm lanterns dotted around as well as an old tin bucket full of beers on ice. He'd even thought to carry down the blankets and throws Rachel and I had used during our lunch the previous day. There was something cooking on the fire too.

'Where's Rachel?' he asked, looking over my shoulder. 'Isn't she coming?'

'She'll be here in a few minutes,' I said, taking the chilled bottle of beer he scooped out of the ice bucket, wiped on a towel and offered me. 'She just had to make a quick call.'

I hoped it was going to be quick.

'Okay,' he said, raking a hand through his hair, before turning back to the fire. 'Good. That's great, because I really only want to have to do this once.'

'Well, I'd appreciate it if you did it every night.' I smiled, as he carefully lifted the lid on the enamel pot which was nestled next to the raked-out embers at the side of the fire. 'Because it all looks and smells amazing.'

'Sorry,' he said, stirring the pot and releasing more of the wonderful aroma, 'I meant, I only want to have to say what I'm going to tell you and Rachel once.'

'Oh,' I said, taking a swig of the ice-cold beer. 'I see. That sounds intense.'

'It is,' he said. 'Intense but necessary, I think.'

I didn't know what to say to that.

'This is almost ready,' he said, saving me from having to find the words.

'What have you got cooking in there?' I asked, leaning in for a closer look.

'It's campfire stew,' he said, replacing the lid and straightening up before nudging the pot a little further away from the fire with the toe of his boot. 'It's always been a tradition in my family and made mostly from whatever happened to be left in the fridge the day we went camping.'

I already knew he was close to his parents and having now confirmed that he was an outdoorsy type, I found myself falling for him even harder. Kind, considerate and a bit rugged was a winning combination as far as I was concerned.

'This is the veggie option,' he added. 'And I commandeered the bread that was in the cupboard too. I hope that was okay?'

'If it tastes even half as good as it smells,' I told him, 'then going forward, please feel free to help yourself to whatever you fancy.'

Heat flooded my face and I became engrossed in the label on my beer.

'Crikey.' He grinned, making me feel even more embarrassed. 'I'll bear that in mind.'

While we waited for Rachel and made inroads into more of the beer, I filled him in about how I'd been fleeced in the shop, making him laugh with my description of the deceptive looking Mrs Timpson and he told me more about the project he was working on to rebrand the small restaurant chain in Manchester.

In spite of my gaff about helping himself to whatever he fancied, it was the most relaxed I'd felt in his presence, however, I wasn't sure he felt the same about being in mine.

He laughed and nodded in all the right places, but I could tell he was on edge. His eyes kept flicking back to the path while we waited for Rachel and a couple of times, he had to ask me to repeat what I'd said. I found myself hoping that his jitteriness wasn't down to us being alone but more about whatever it was he had decided to tell us.

'And Connor said he'd be more than thrilled to join us when he can,' I finished up as I heard Rachel's footsteps growing closer. 'So, you won't be outnumbered the whole time.'

'Well, that's something.' He smiled as my friend gasped in the same way I had when I'd first seen what he'd organised. 'Not that I mind being outnumbered now things are settled between us,' he carried on and when I looked at him, I found his eyes fixed on my face.

'Oh, Alex,' said Rachel, as she stuffed her phone in her pocket. 'This is amazing. I had no idea you'd gone to all this trouble. There's no doubting which scene this is. Have you got something to reveal to match it, or is it just a coincidence?'

'I have got something to tell you actually,' he told her, sounding tense again. 'But let's eat first.'

Rachel gave me a look as he turned back to the fire and I shrugged to let her know that I didn't know what it was he was gearing up to share.

'It smells amazing,' she told him. 'I was getting a waft right back along the path and hoped it was coming from down here.'

The veggie stew was a total triumph and all three of us enjoyed soaking up the last of the thick, rich smoky sauce with great chunks of bread. I could imagine Alex's family camping trips were full-on Enid Blyton style adventures rather than glamping and gastro-pub dining affairs. That was another tick in his box.

'The sticky bits on the bottom always taste the best, don't they?' said Rachel, dipping her bread back in. 'That,' she then laughed, as she pulled her soaked chunk out again, 'is a weird sentence.'

Clearly, the beer had got to her.

'That was outstanding, Alex,' I told him, having practically licked my tin plate clean. 'I hope you've got a few more family recipes tucked up your sleeve. Feel free to cook for us again during the next few weeks, won't you?'

'I will,' he said. 'Gladly.'

'Yes,' Rachel agreed, with a wink. 'Please do if you can, just to keep Em out of the kitchen, Alex. You'll be doing us all a favour.'

'Hey.' I pouted, embarrassed to have had my lack of culinary skills flagged up. 'I'm not that bad. Those peas I boiled the day we arrived were wonderful.'

'And remember, I'm no barbecue king,' Alex laughed, 'so we all have our own skills.'

We piled the dishes together, then Alex threw a couple of extra logs on the campfire and we settled back down with more

beer. Rachel and I snuggled close on the bench and Alex perched on the edge of one of the chairs.

We fell into silence for what stretched into minutes and when I looked at Alex, I found he was staring so intently at the flames, that I began to think he'd changed his mind about sharing with us whatever it was he had so perfectly set the scene to say. But then, he struck up, making me jump.

'Okay,' he said loudly, as he sat back and gulped down the last of his beer. He took a breath before carrying on. 'I can't believe I'm about to do this,' he said, shaking his head. 'But then, I still can't really believe that I'm here.'

Rachel and I exchanged a look and I wondered if the depth of concern showing on her face was also etched across mine.

'I always said that if I ended up here with other people,' Alex carried on, 'rather than on my own, then I would explain the real reason behind my *Hope Falls* journey, because it's so much more complicated than just being a fan of the book.'

'I think we established in the emails we exchanged that you're actually a superfan,' I reminded him, trying to ease some of the tension I could see building up in his shoulders.

He smiled at that, but didn't visibly relax.

'And you don't owe either of us any kind of explanation, Alex,' Rachel said kindly. 'Does he, Em?'

'No,' I said. 'Of course not. Whatever the reason behind your being here is completely your business. No one else's.'

That said, I was eager to know what had prompted his desire to stay and what had caused Catriona's discomfiture in the pub. It was clearly more than a firm fondness for the book and a desire to walk and sleep where the film was set.

'Well,' he said, thankfully not put off by mine and Rach's

suggestion that he could keep it all to himself, 'I'm going to tell you. I need to, to be honest, although I'm doing it sooner than I expected to.'

'You're not doing it now because of our rocky start, are you?' I winced. 'Because if that's the case . . .'

'It's not that,' he said, holding up his hands.

'That's a relief,' I breathed.

'If anything, it's the opposite.' He carried on, 'I'm doing it now because we're over that and I feel comfortable with you both and because, having spoken to Mum yesterday, she thought it would be good to get it off my chest.'

Knowing his mum had an opinion about whatever it was he was going to say made me feel rather guilty about being so privately but dreadfully keen to hear it.

'And,' he said, having closed his eyes for a moment, 'given the toll my first trip to the lake took on me, I know she's right. If I'm going to enjoy my time here, there's something you need to know because I can't possibly be my true self around you, if you don't.'

Rachel and I looked at one another again while he reached for the last of the beers and then handed them out. I couldn't have told you what she was thinking for all the patchwork commissions in the world and I daresay I looked every bit as confused as she did.

'Can you remember the first time you saw the film?' Alex asked, once everyone's bottle was open.

'Yes,' Rachel and I said in perfect synchronicity, which made us laugh.

That was a no-brainer. I knew we'd both spent our early teenage years repeatedly reading the book, so the arrival of the film was more eagerly anticipated than, well, anything.

'Well, I can't,' Alex shrugged and Rachel and I raised our eyebrows.

'I'm not sure that's something a superfan should admit to,' Rachel advised him.

'But I have a good reason,' he said, defending his admission.

'Go on,' I encouraged.

'I can't remember the first time, because once it came out on DVD it was *constantly* playing on a loop in our house.' That struck a chord. 'My older sister, Gracie' – at the mention of her name, he stopped to take a swig of beer – 'would literally finish watching it, either in the sitting room or in her bedroom and then immediately start it again, or pick up the book.'

'That sounds right.' Rachel beamed, clinking her bottle against mine in solidarity. 'Holidays, weekends, after college, even before college,' she reeled off. 'Yes?'

'You got it,' Alex agreed.

I already liked the sound of Gracie.

'I felt like I'd seen all of the film in snatches, practically absorbed it by osmosis, but one day,' he reminisced, 'Gracie press-ganged me into sitting with her and watching the whole thing properly. From the opening scene to the closing credits.'

'And?' Rachel demanded, wide-eyed.

'And I was hooked of course.' Alex smiled. 'But I wasn't going to let Gracie know that. There was no way I was going to let her know she'd won. We were siblings after all. Competitive ones.'

I had cousins with a similar competitive streak and it used to drive me nuts. Neither of them was willing to come second in even the simplest of competitions and many family Christmas board game sessions had ended in a meltdown as a result.

'But,' Alex continued, 'she knew anyway. Within days of

watching the film together she'd ordered me a copy of the book and even when we were apart, we'd spend hours on the phone reading passages aloud to each other or critiquing the film as we watched it in tandem, the miles between us not mattering at all.'

He blushed as he told us, clearly aware that it was an unusual thing for siblings to do.

'You're obviously close.' I smiled, to let him know I understood. The book had forged an even stronger link between me and Grandad and I knew the same could be said of Rachel and her nan, too. 'What a wonderful thing to bond over.'

'So close.' Alex nodded and then I realised Rachel wasn't smiling like I was. What had I missed? 'We made a pact that one day we would come here to Lakeside together. We had plans to do everything: see the locations, row on the lake, share a meal around the campfire, just like the three of us have done here tonight.'

My smile faltered and I felt a prickle of disquiet take its place.

'Eventually we'd got it all booked.' Alex swallowed, his voice losing some of its former strength. 'We were packed, literally just a couple of weeks away from coming and then ... we had to cancel.'

'Why?' I whispered, even though I didn't think I wanted to know the answer.

'Gracie was diagnosed with breast cancer,' Alex choked. 'And she needed immediate treatment.'

'Oh, Alex,' Rachel gasped beside me.

'We made two more bookings to come here over the next three years,' he carried on, the words sounding as though they were being ripped from him, 'but we weren't able to honour

either of them. Each time Gracie had a setback and we had to let the trip go.'

'I'm so sorry,' I whispered, forcing the words out because the shock of what he was saying could have quite easily silenced me. 'For you and for Gracie.'

Rachel didn't say anything.

'Before Gracie died,' Alex then stoically said, confirming the outcome I had already guessed, 'she made me promise that I would still come. She said that when I felt ready, I should come here and do all the things that we had planned to do together.'

I reached for Rachel's hand and squeezed it. Had I known the circumstances as to why Alex had joined our party as opposed to coming with his own, I never would have reacted to his presence the way I did or stupidly sulked over who was sleeping where. No wonder Catriona had coloured in the pub when she let slip that Alex had come to the cottage with more baggage than most.

'To be honest,' he further said, 'I didn't think I was ever going to be ready, but when Catriona emailed to say there was a short notice opportunity, I told myself I just had to go for it otherwise, I might never have made it here.'

'I'm so pleased it was us, Alex,' I said emotionally, thinking we were even more like the three thrown together characters in the book than I had initially realised. 'I'm so pleased you were able to come here with us.'

'I'm not sure your friend who couldn't come would agree,' he smiled ruefully, 'but I appreciate that.'

'She would,' Rachel said kindly. 'She would.'

'What happened here at the lake that first day, Alex?' I asked, knowing it was somehow connected to Gracie. 'You were so sad after you'd come down here that first time.'

He looked at me, then away again. 'Gracie also made me promise,' he shudderingly said, 'that when I did finally get here, I would scatter her ashes from the end of the jetty, out over the lake.'

I felt the tears I had so far managed to hold back start to fall as I imagined him standing alone looking into the deep, calm water and letting his sister go.

'I hadn't planned to do it so early in the trip,' he swallowed, 'but I realised that if I didn't do it straightaway, I never would and she wouldn't have forgiven me for that. Gracie always wanted to be here,' he said, looking out over the lake. 'And now, she is.'

'And you're here too,' Rachel said thickly.

'And the three of us are going to do your sister proud,' I followed on. 'We're going to make this the most memorable visit to the cottage and Lakeside any group has ever had.'

Alex's gaze flicked to mine and he nodded. He looked absolutely forlorn, but there was a light in his eyes and an appreciation of our words. I hated myself for ruining the start of his stay and making him feel awkward, unwanted and out of place. He was already carrying the weight of intense grief when he arrived and I had made him feel even worse.

'I know what you're thinking, Emily,' he said, still looking at me. 'And it doesn't matter. We've made our peace now, haven't we? So, let's move forward from here on. Yes?'

'Yes,' I said simply. 'Yes.'

We were all quiet for a moment.

'So,' Alex finally said, with a smile I was grateful to see. 'Now you know why I was wearing a slightly too small hoodie when we watched the film.'

'It was Gracie's.' Rachel smiled back.

'Yep,' he nodded. 'You must have thought I was a total idiot, squeezing myself into it.'

'It wasn't that small,' I laughed, even though it had been a pretty tight fit.

'You wear that hoodie, and you sleep in that bed,' Alex said, counting on his fingers. 'They were just two of Gracie's stipulations. Thankfully it made sense for you two to share the twin room, so I didn't look too selfish bagsying the double, did I?'

Rachel squeezed my hand and I thanked every star in the cosmos that I hadn't gone to battle over that bedroom.

'You didn't look selfish at all,' I told him.

We sat by the lake, each of us lost in our own thoughts as it started to get dark and the fire burnt low, then Rachel and I each shared with Alex our own stories about how we'd been introduced to the book. I got teary again talking about Grandad and Rachel was the same when talking about her nanna.

'To absent, but much-loved family,' Alex smiled as he gave a toast before we carried everything back up to the cottage.

Once inside, Rachel and I sorted the dishes so he could go and call his parents. He'd promised that he'd let them know when he'd told us the tragic reason behind his coming to the cottage and as he set off in the near darkness along the path to the road, my heart broke for him and the sister he'd so dearly loved and tragically lost.

Chapter 11

It took me hours to get to sleep that night and I know Rachel couldn't nod off either because every time I turned over and thumped my pillows into a different shape, I could see she was staring at the ceiling with her eyes wide open.

Neither of us spoke, but it was obvious that we were both mulling over what Alex had revealed at the lake. Thoughts of Gracie's tragically early death pushed all thoughts of my potential new business idea or Rachel's announcement that she was seriously considering moving in with Jeremy, right out of my head.

Consequently, the early morning hollering which roused me after what had felt like no more than a handful of seconds of sleep was a shock to the system.

'Come on, you two!' Rachel shouted from somewhere in the cottage. 'It's time to get up and at 'em!'

She sounded absurdly chipper as I rolled over and pulled the duvet over my head. I could hear the rain drumming on the cottage roof, so why she thought it was necessary for any of us to be out of bed so early was beyond me.

'Come on!' she called again, her voice even louder because

she'd flung open the bedroom door. 'I have coffee and warm pastries.'

I peeped out from under my cosy nest and discovered it was lighter than I had assumed it would be and therefore most likely later, and I knew Rachel wasn't lying about the coffee and pastries just to get me up – a ruse she'd tried once too often in the past – because I could smell both and so, with a groan, I pushed back the warm duvet with my feet and swung my legs out of the bed.

'Oh, for pity's sake, look at the pair of you,' Rachel sniggered as Alex and I appeared in our respective bedroom doorways at exactly the same moment.

He gave me a small wave and I nodded back, refusing to acknowledge how snuggly he looked as he tiredly rubbed his eyes.

'Need I remind you,' I said, my voice thick with sleep as I honed in on Rachel instead, 'that we have been here just over a week?'

'A week and a day, today,' Alex yawned, confirming the fact.

'And therefore, Rachel,' I continued, 'you should only now be coming out of your end of term coma. You should most definitely *not* be bouncing off the walls, bribing us with breakfast treats and looking wide awake, especially when I know for a fact that, like me, you barely slept a wink.'

Alex looked between us and I instantly regretted mentioning the lack of sleep.

'Sorry,' he mumbled. 'That was my fault, wasn't it? Do you think it would have been better if I had said something about Gracie in our emails? That way you could have processed it before we met. I've been thinking . . .'

'Oh, be quiet, the pair of you,' Rachel said in her trademark

teacherly tone. 'No more ifs, buts or maybes Alex, okay? In fact, don't even answer that because I don't want to hear another peep from either of you until you've eaten these pastries. They're already on the cusp of turning soggy.'

I didn't need telling twice and rushed over to the kitchen. Sitting side by side with Alex at the counter, Rachel plied the two of us with calories and caffeine until we were both looking and feeling more awake.

'I like your hair like that.' Alex smiled at me after he'd polished off his second croissant. 'You should wear it like that more often.'

My hands flew to the nest on my head. My bed hair was legendary and whereas Alex's own hair was attractively mussed up, I bet mine looked backcombed beyond redemption.

'Leave it,' said Rachel, batting my hand away. 'It's fine.'

Alex smirked and I stuck out my tongue, grabbing the last pain au chocolat before he had the chance.

'Now then,' Rachel said, coming to the heart of the matter once she considered us compos mentis enough to compute. 'I don't know about you two, but I can't help thinking that the first few days here have been cathartic for all of us.'

I very nearly snorted pastry out of my nose when she said that. They'd certainly been intense, but cleansing? Purifying? I wasn't so sure about that, not for me anyway. More like emotional and exhausting.

'And,' she carried on, as if she hadn't noticed my reaction, 'as a result, they've set us up for a thoroughly fabulous holiday.'

'Really?' Alex and I said in unison.

Without the benefit of a system full of beer, we both sounded doubtful and I felt annoyed with myself for feeling so absurdly

lacklustre when I had waited so long to be sitting in this very spot. For years, I had put this adventure on a brightly polished pedestal and, as tired as I was and as unsettled about my feelings of attraction for Alex which were taking up far too much of my headspace, I knew that if I didn't buck my ideas up, I was in danger of knocking the entire holiday even further off its perfect plinth.

'Yes,' Rachel firmly said and I could see her point even before she gave her explanation. 'Really. We've got to know each other now and revealed our secrets early enough to be able to really focus on the next five weeks without the preoccupation of worrying that we're going to blurt them out or not mention them at all.'

If only she knew.

'We have?' Alex frowned, looking between us.

'Yes,' Rachel said again. 'Let me bring you up to speed, Alex.'

'Okay,' he said, pouring himself more coffee.

He was going to be buzzing all day, especially if it carried on raining and we couldn't kick him out to burn off some energy.

'The day you were in Manchester,' Rachel began, 'I told Em that my boyfriend had asked me to move in with him and, thanks to her own bit of news, I know I might really be able to take him up on his offer now.'

'Congratulations,' Alex warmly smiled. 'That's wonderful.'

If only *he* knew!

'Thank you.' Rachel blushed and I swallowed down my reaction.

Talk of her moving in with Jeremy didn't sound any better second time around. In fact, it was beginning to sound like a *fait accompli*, which was even worse. My stomach twisted, not

only because of the thought of that, but also because her words confirmed my fears for my business idea.

'So, Em,' said Rachel. 'Why don't you tell Alex your news and then we'll all be in the know about what's going on with each of us?'

I didn't want to have to discuss it, but in the spirit of the fresh start all three of us were supposed to be embracing I said the words out loud.

'I've been offered a new job,' I said, failing to inject any enthusiasm into my tone, not that I'd really put much effort into trying.

Alex looked at me and narrowed his eyes. 'So, you're not quite between jobs like you said then,' he frowned.

'I am,' I said, thinking back to our conversation the morning he'd been to the lake. My face flushed when I thought of what he had gone there to do. 'I've been offered another one but I haven't started it yet.'

'Another data analyst position?' he asked, wrinkling his nose and sounding as keen as I was.

'That's right,' I said lightly, glancing at Rachel. 'I'll be starting in September.'

'Isn't that wonderful?' said Rachel, clapping her hands.

'I guess.' Alex shrugged. 'But what would have been really wonderful was if you'd just told me you'd decided to—'

Given his glowing opinion of my patchwork skills, I knew exactly what he was going to say next and raised my voice to cut him off. 'And taking that job will mean Rachel won't have to worry if I'll be able to manage to pay the rent and keep the lights turned on,' I said meaningfully.

Understanding thankfully dawned in Alex's eyes as he looked

from one of us to the other and the cogs whirred in his head as he realised that my taking the job would enable Rachel to do what she wanted.

'Oh, well, yes then,' he said, with a rather over-enthusiastic nod. 'That really is wonderful news. Congratulations to you, too.'

Rachel picked up the used mugs and plates and while she was distracted, I shook my head at Alex.

'You shouldn't be faffing about with graphs and statistics,' he said in a low voice. 'You should be focused on growing your patchwork business.'

Intuitive as well as attractive. He really had it all. Not that his intuition was going to be appreciated if it resulted in him putting his foot in it.

'I'm flattered you think so,' I whispered back. 'But this job will offer me some real security.' I ignored the fact that I'd been made redundant from my last one. 'And a regular income too. I'm going to need that when Rachel moves out.'

I felt a lump form in my throat as I realised I wasn't just saying that to fob Alex off. It was the reality of the situation I now found myself in. The money I'd saved to support myself through the next year didn't allow for Rachel's missing contribution to the household budget and therefore, my plans to grow my patchwork business, as Alex had put it, really would have to go on hold.

Suddenly, I didn't have to give myself time to think about what I was going to do because there was no choice. With my head planted firmly in the real world, I knew I had no alternative but to take the new job.

'But you're so talented, Em,' said Alex, as Rachel walked to open the window in the sitting room and stepped further out of

earshot as a result. 'You could make your own sewing business work full-time. I know you could.'

'Oh, Alex, you barely know me,' I reminded him. 'So, you can't possibly know that. A week and a day, remember?'

'That's as maybe,' he said, 'but I know enough and I've seen your work. You really should think about setting up on your own.'

I shook my head.

'I'm serious,' he said and he certainly sounded it.

'It's just not feasible . . .' I began.

'I know you're just saying that to try and help Rachel, and that's admirable of you, but don't waste any of the time you've got,' he then urgently cut me off. 'There's precious little enough of it in a lifetime. Believe me. That much I do know. And yes,' he said with a wry smile. 'If playing the deceased sister card is what it takes, then I'll bring Gracie's name out, whenever I need to, to make you see sense.'

My mouth opened and closed and he laughed.

'What?' he said challengingly, lifting his chin.

'You're mad,' I said, louder than I intended.

'Who's mad?' Rachel asked, picking that exact moment to come back over to the kitchen and bringing her beloved paperback copy of *Hope Falls* with her.

'According to Em,' Alex mischievously said, 'I am.'

'Don't you dare,' I said, my lips barely moving.

He had been clever enough to work out that my motives for keeping my patchwork as a hobby were for Rachel's benefit, but was he puckish enough to expose them? I hoped not.

'Why?' Rachel asked. 'What did you say?'

Alex looked at me and I silently pleaded with every atom of my being.

'I said a walk in the rain to the pub for a lunchtime pint would be worth it,' he blinked. 'But Em said it wouldn't be. She'd rather go in the car.'

I felt my shoulders drop and some of the tension which had been holding my spine rigid relax. It felt good to hear him call me Em. A little too good.

'Oh, Emily,' scolded Rachel, 'I won't tell Connor you said that. How about we go for a pint *and* some lunch? That'll justify a walk in the wet, won't it?'

'I suppose,' I said, slipping shakily off the stool. 'But I better see if I can do something with my hair first.'

'Good idea,' Alex winked, so I poked him in the ribs on my way by.

'I reckon,' said Alex as we turned the last bend in the road before we reached Lakeside, 'that's it's rained every day since we arrived.'

I thought back over the last eight days. 'I think you're right,' I agreed. 'But if we'd wanted sun, we would have gone south rather than north west, right?'

'We would,' he said. 'But we didn't want sun, did we?'

'No,' I said, shaking out my umbrella and giving him a further soaking. 'We wanted to embrace everything our book-based getaway had to offer!'

'Hey!' he protested, jumping out of reach. 'Aren't I wet enough?'

'You are now!' I laughed.

He carried on to the general store and Rachel and I ducked into the pub. She'd spent most of the walk lagging behind and glued to her phone as Jeremy had set a different time that day to

touch base, but at least that meant she had missed what felt like a flirtatious shift in mine and Alex's budding friendship. The last thing I needed was her radar picking up on the fact that I fancied the pants off him.

'Everything all right?' I nudged, when she didn't even notice Siddy skipping around her feet in the pub doorway and looking for a fuss.

'Yes,' she said, sounding strained. 'All good.'

We left our dripping coats hanging in the porch and headed further inside.

'I wondered when I might see you two again.' Connor beamed, his smile lighting the place up.

He'd got a fire burning in the inglenook and the wall lights were dimly glowing. Coupled with Connor's cheerful greeting, it was a warm and cosy welcome after the wet walk. The pervading smell of woodsmoke made the day feel more like autumn than high summer, but I didn't mind.

'Us three actually,' I told him. 'Alex will be along in a minute.'

'Even better.' He nodded. 'What can I get you, or do you want to wait for the third musketeer?'

'We'll wait,' said Rachel. 'But we'll grab a table if that's okay? We thought we'd stay for lunch.'

'Perfect,' said Connor. 'And I've got staff in today, so I might even join you as it's not too busy.'

For some reason, Rachel didn't look too sure about that but given that I'd asked him to make up the numbers with Alex, I wasn't about to object.

'Are you sure you're all right?' I frowned at Rachel as we slipped into one of the booths. 'You were full of the joys when you dragged Alex and I out of bed this morning.'

I'd taken the seat opposite her so I could easily see she didn't look anything like the sunny version of herself who had suggested we should eat out.

'I'm fine.' She smiled tightly. 'Might have a bit of a blister forming. I knew I should have spent longer breaking these new boots in.'

I was about to remind her that she'd been wearing them for weeks so that explanation didn't wash, when Alex stumbled through the door weighed down by not one, but two of Mrs Timpson's jute bags.

'She got me,' he said, staggering over and dripping all over Connor's flagged floor.

'What on earth have you got there?' I laughed, aware he'd only been gone a couple of minutes. 'I did try and warn you, didn't I?'

'She thought this might keep us amused if the rain keeps up,' he panted, pulling a thousand-piece jigsaw of a view of Lakeside out of one of the bags.

'There are jigsaws back at the cottage,' I guffawed, laughing all the harder when he pulled out an ancient looking Ludo to go with it.

'You must be Alex?' said Connor as he wandered over with Siddy at his heels. 'Or should I say Mrs T's latest victim?'

'Got it in one,' Alex laughed. 'And you're Connor, right?'

'I am,' he said. 'Do you want put that lot in the back room?'

'That might not be a bad idea,' he said, giving Connor one of the bags. 'What can I get you two to drink?' he asked Rachel and I.

We decided on bitter and the two men spent a while with their heads together at the bar while Connor poured our drinks.

I could tell from the change of expression on the usually cheerful landlord's face that Alex had most likely taken the plunge and filled him in on the details as to what had led him to Lakeside and the cottage.

'Poor Alex,' I sighed. 'You can't even begin to imagine what he's been through, can you?'

'No,' said Rachel, following my gaze. 'It must have been a hellish few years for him and his parents.'

He had told me, as we walked into the village, that Gracie had been gone almost two years now. If time really was a great healer, I would have hated to see how much he had suffered when she first died.

'I'm so relieved I wound my neck in over the bedroom allocation,' I said quietly, shifting along the seat as the two men came over, with Connor carrying the tray of drinks.

'Yes,' Rachel nodded. 'Me too. Can you imagine how things might have played out if you hadn't?'

I didn't want to.

'It would have been even worse,' she added.

I ignored the reminder that I had got us off to an awkward start.

'Are we going to order lunch?' I asked, once the glasses had been distributed and Alex had taken the seat next to Rachel which put Connor next to me. 'I don't know about the rest of you, but I'm famished. I reckon it must be all this extra fresh air I'm enjoying.'

'That and the extra walks,' Rachel smiled, reminding me that Alex had told her I had said I'd wanted to come out in the car, but he'd done it for a good reason. 'I'm on my feet all day at work, but I'm never usually moving as much as I have been since I got here. My legs are aching today and we haven't even had a decent hike yet.'

I couldn't help thinking that she would cut down on at least half her daily steps if she didn't now have to keep running up the road to find a phone signal, but I kept the uncharitable thought to myself knowing my silly muddle over the photo was the cause of it. She had told me she was sticking to messaging Jeremy once a day at his preordained time, but I was certain she'd been in touch with him more than that.

'Talking of hikes,' said Connor, as he beckoned over the guy serving behind the bar, 'you should do the walk to Star Shine Falls tomorrow. The weather's going to be perfect.'

'What can I get you?' the guy asked.

'I'm going to have the goat's cheese and warm beetroot salad,' Connor smiled, 'and if you three trust my judgement, you should too. The cheese comes from a farm just a couple of miles away and it is sublime and the crackers which complement it are made locally, too.'

With a recommendation like that we could hardly refuse.

'So, I'd be up for that hike tomorrow,' said Alex as the guy went to put our lunch order in at the kitchen. 'What about you three?'

'I can't, I'm afraid,' said Connor. 'Saturdays are too busy, but I went a couple of years ago, so don't put it off on my account and as I say, the weather will be perfect. You have to see it in the sunshine . . .'

'Or by moonlight if you're a real book and film aficionado,' I corrected. 'The place looked magical in the film with the moonlight catching the water.'

We all knew that the real waterfall called Star Shine Falls had been picked to represent Hope Falls and it was one of the most beautiful of all the outdoor settings. That said, had we been

sitting in the rowing boat in the middle of the lake and admiring the full moon as in one of the other scenes, I daresay I would have claimed that as the most picturesque too.

'We'll still go and see the waterfall on a clear night,' said Rachel. 'Even if we do go in the sunshine tomorrow.'

'Sadly, you won't,' sighed Connor.

'Why not?' Rachel frowned.

'Because over the last year or so,' he told us, 'there have been a few too many night-time call outs for the emergency services, so the site is locked at sunset now.'

'Oh no,' I wailed. 'I didn't know that. Are you sure?'

'I am,' he said. 'And as the falls are located on private property the owner has gone to great lengths to make sure no one can get in at any point around the boundary once the gates are locked at the end of the day.'

'That's such a shame,' I huffed as I consigned the image of myself, rather than Heather, leaning out and running my hands through the moonlit flow of water to the 'dream unfulfilled' category in my head.

I didn't have too long to pout over the reclassification though because our lunch was served and feeling so famished, I dived straight in. The cheese was extremely creamy with a delicious tang and that of course made it the perfect partner for the sweet beetroot and seed coated crackers.

'This is amazing, Connor.' Rachel smiled and I was relieved to see her looking more relaxed than when we'd arrived.

She had been so tense earlier that I was worried that Jeremy's reaction to the photograph of her and the lovely landlord was still rumbling on.

'I'm pleased you approve,' he said, addressing us all but with

his gaze fixed mostly on my friend. 'It's my aunt who makes the cheese at her farm up the road, but I didn't want to mention that until I knew what you thought of it.'

'It's wonderful,' I said, adding my own praise to Rachel's.

'How long has your aunt been making it?' Alex asked, as he pushed his empty plate away. 'I wonder if any of the cast or crew got to sample it when they were filming here?'

'She's been making it for as long as I can remember,' Connor explained. 'I used to visit here as a lad, many years before I had the chance to move here, and she was producing it then. And yes, they did. There are loads of photos hanging in the farm shop from when a couple of the actors visited. The connection is very good for business.'

'That's amazing.' I smiled.

'What a wonderfully lucrative endorsement for her goats!' Rachel laughed.

'You're not wrong,' he agreed as he carried our dishes out to the kitchen and then came back with Siddy and more drinks.

'You'd better give her a stroke this time,' I said to Rachel. 'You missed her when we came in.'

Rachel didn't comment, but slid out of the seat and gave the Labrador the overdue fuss that she loved.

'Now,' said Connor, rubbing his hands together, 'who fancies taking part in a quiz?'

'What sort of quiz?' I frowned.

It was a truth universally acknowledged that my general knowledge (unlike my cache of literary quotes) was woefully lacking and I had no desire to be shown up in front of Rachel who was a well-rounded clever clogs, or Alex, who I happened to fancy. A dual humiliation would be too much.

'A *Hope Falls* quiz,' Connor said, rushing back to the bar and returning with three sheets.

'Oh, goody,' I said, jiggling in my seat and knowing I'd fare far better if the book and the film were the specialist subjects. 'Count me in.'

If I was an expert on anything it was *Hope Falls*, but then I remembered, so were the others seated at the table ...

'Where did you get them from?' Alex asked Connor.

'I made the questions up,' he told him. 'And I have to warn you, there are some really tricky ones. This sheet is designed to separate the fans from the superfans.'

'I should be all right then,' Alex grinned, pulling one of the pages towards him.

'When do you use them?' Rachel asked as Connor slid a sheet over to her and another to me.

'Whenever there's a *Hope Falls* coach tour party booked.' He smiled. 'They go down an absolute storm.'

'A coach party!' Rachel laughed.

'You'd be amazed by the number of fans who come here,' he said.

'Given the book and film's enduring popularity,' I observed, 'I think it's pretty amazing that the place hasn't been turned into some sort of theme park.'

'We'd never allow that,' Connor said seriously as he handed out some pencils. 'Now, you've got half an hour to answer as many of these as you can.'

He walked back to the bar and Alex said he'd sit at another table so he had 'more room'.

'You don't need to worry about me cheating,' I told him, as he wrapped an arm around his paper like a schoolkid during a test. 'I know everything there is to know.'

It turned out I didn't, and neither did Rachel. Alex got the highest score but not even he was able to answer everything and claim the coveted superfan status. Connor refused to give us the missing answers but let us keep the sheets so that when we re-read the book and watched the film again, we could try and spot what we'd missed and if we found it, report back.

'I think we should watch the film tonight,' I suggested as we collected Alex's shopping and set off back to the cottage in the, thankfully much lighter, rain.

'Me too,' the others agreed.

'I'm getting withdrawal symptoms,' said Alex, who hadn't gloated when the ticks had been counted because he was so disappointed with himself for not getting everything right. At least none of us had got anything wrong. That would have been mortifying. 'I'm reading the book at night again,' he told us, 'but it's been days since we watched the film.'

'You're right,' said Rachel. 'This has to be the longest any of us has gone without seeing it.'

'But,' I said, in a singsong voice, 'that's because we're actually living the dream.'

'So we are,' Alex laughed, joining in when Rachel began singing the theme tune.

The three of us ended up singing all the way home.

Chapter 12

Having re-watched the film together, skimmed through the book and found some, but not all, of the missing answers, we checked Connor's weather prediction and then agreed on an early night. We knew that with it being the weekend, and a sunny one too, the queue to visit Star Shine Falls the next day would be a long one, so a punctual start was required.

'Here you go, Rach,' I said, tossing the pack of blister plasters on to her bed as we settled down for the night.

'I don't need these,' she said, picking them up and frowning at the packet.

'Earlier in the pub, you said you had a blister forming,' I reminded her. 'You said that's what accounted for . . .'

'Oh, yeah,' she said, heading into the en suite, but not before I noticed she'd turned bright red. 'You're right. Thanks. I'll make sure to put one on before we leave tomorrow.'

I watched her close the door and cursed Jeremy under my breath. I would have bet all of my savings on him being the only blister blighting my friend's dream getaway.

*

We took our old jalopy the next day, to give it a run rather than because it was the perfect vehicle for uphill terrain, and the three of us were feeling suitably smug as we rushed to the Star Shine Fall estate gates and found ourselves at the head of the queue. In fact, looking properly around, we were the queue.

'Connor was right about the weather,' said Rachel, squinting up at the unusually cloud-free sky.

'This is going to be perfect,' I squealed excitedly, giving her a squeeze.

'And we're going to be first in too, which is a bonus,' said Alex, who looked as ecstatic as I felt. 'We're going straight to the falls and then the gift shop after. Yes?'

'That's the plan.' I nodded and Rachel gave him a double thumbs up.

I'd only been able to look at the website for the dream location en route because there was no Wi-Fi at the cottage and oddly enough, Catriona hadn't included any info about it in the welcome pack. All of the other places available to visit on the *Hope Falls* trail were listed so its absence was a surprise but everything looked good online. I wondered if someone might have taken the info and it hadn't been replaced. I resolved to pick up a few leaflets in the shop later and add them to the folder for future visitors.

'Here we go,' said Rachel, standing back so the security guard who was carrying a huge bunch of keys, could open the gate.

'You three are keen,' he grinned. 'In you come, before the rush.'

'Is it usually this quiet?' I asked, looking over my shoulder and finding there were still no other cars or coaches in the car park.

'It is at this time of day,' he informed me, standing aside to let us through.

I assumed he meant because we were so early.

'How much?' I heard Rachel gasp, as the woman in the kiosk told her how much entry cost. 'Is that for all of us?'

'No,' said the woman, sounding embarrassed. 'It's twenty-five each.'

'My treat,' I jumped in, taken aback by the cost, but not wanting anything to mar the magical moment. Funnily enough, the entry price hadn't been listed online either.

'No,' said Alex, stepping up. 'Let me.'

In the end, we each paid for our own ticket and with a slow trickle of people starting to arrive, we rushed over to the gate which led to the path which would take us up to the wonderful waterfall.

'Are you absolutely sure you want to go up now?' asked the security guard who hadn't yet unlocked it. 'You only get to go up once per ticket.'

I thought it was a rather odd question, but didn't waste further time considering it.

'Yes,' Alex urged him.

'All right,' the guy shrugged. 'It's a one way only walk. You follow the trail to the top, take your snaps and come back down the other side. And watch your step. It's a bit slippery in places after all the rain we've had.'

He wasn't wrong. We slid along some parts of the muddy track and slipped around others, but it didn't deter us. We'd set off at such a pace that, getting on for twenty minutes later, we were all panting for breath. Fortunately, the summit was in sight by then and the sound of water crashing over rock spurred us on.

With the last corner ahead of us and no one behind, we took

a moment to let our heart rates settle, knowing that a dream fulfilled was just a few short steps away. It was imperative that we were all at our physical best to take in the unique moment and I prepared myself to take a lasting mental snapshot of my first impression. I was so pleased Rachel had flagged the importance and significance of that the day we arrived at the cottage. I ducked between my two friends and took half a dozen smiling selfies in anticipation of the spectacle to come.

'Ready?' said Rachel, readjusting her sun hat.

'Ready,' Alex and I said together.

We let Alex go ahead, knowing the trip to see the falls had been on Gracie's bucket list and therefore meant even more to him than it did us, then Rachel was next with me last. I took a deep breath, expecting to hear cheers and whoops ahead of me, but there was only the sound of the waterfall. I guessed the others had been stunned into awed silence.

I let my breath slowly release and stepped around the corner to join them. The viewing platform was narrower than I would have expected and it was a bit of a squeeze for three so I had to watch where I put my feet. Once we'd settled into the space, none of us spoke for quite a while.

'I can't believe it,' Alex finally said, bending so far over the barrier that Rachel instinctively reached for the straps of his rucksack to stop him toppling over.

'This can't really be it, can it?' I croaked, also shifting my position to get a better view. 'We can't have just parted with seventy-five quid for this.'

'Is this how it looked on the website?' Rachel asked.

'No,' I said. 'Nothing like. But,' I added, pointing out what looked like a path on the hill opposite the falls and which was

directly above where the crashing water pooled, 'I reckon the promotion photos used online were taken from over there.'

The inadequate platform we were standing on only offered a side-on view of the torrent and a very narrow one at that. Standing at the side of the cascading water, rather than face on, completely altered the perspective and there was nothing recognisable from the scene in the film at all. In all honesty, we could have been standing next to any waterfall in the world.

'The sunlight isn't even hitting it,' Alex groaned. 'There's no sparkle.'

As one we looked up and realised that it would be quite a while before the sun would be in a high enough position to hit the water and make it magically shine as its name suggested.

'No wonder no one was in a rush to get up here so early,' Rachel sighed.

'Not that anyone will see much whatever time they choose to come up,' I huffed, wondering how the scene where Heather and then Rose had run their fingers through the flowing water had been filmed.

Had that close-up even happened here?

'That security guy must have known,' said Alex, sounding cross. 'Why didn't he give us a heads up?'

'Probably wanted to stagger the stream of visitors,' I charitably said. 'Either that or not fall foul of his employer by putting people off and to be fair,' I remembered, 'he did ask if we were sure we wanted to come up now. This must have been why.'

I had noticed the gift shop and courtyard area in front of it was teaming with merchandise, so knew the estate were keen to cash in on what should have been a stunning setting. I daresay staff putting visitors off wouldn't have gone down well at all.

'So much for Connor's reaction to your comment about not turning the area into a theme park,' said Rachel, sounding bitter. I guessed she'd clocked the merch too. 'He should have warned us about this place rather than recommended it.'

'But didn't he say,' Alex pointed out, 'that he'd visited here a couple of years ago? He must have had a very different experience to ours to suggest it.'

'Yes,' I said, clicking my fingers. 'And now I think about it, he did say we'd want to see the falls in the sunshine, in lieu of the moon, didn't he?'

'Oh,' said Rachel, sounding chastened. 'In that case, I take it back. Sorry, Connor.'

'You're right,' Alex sighed, agreeing with me. 'He did say something about seeing it in the sun. That was why he suggested we came today.'

'And in our rush to be first here to enjoy the so-called spectacle alone,' I tutted, 'we forgot that, didn't we?'

'We'd better give him an updated review of the place next time we see him,' said Rachel. 'If he's suggesting people come here based on an experience he had before the changes, then he needs to be told what it's like now, doesn't he?'

'Or come and see it for himself,' I suggested. 'Although I wouldn't really want him to waste all that money just to tell his customers not to bother. To be honest, I'm surprised no one's been back and told him it's a sham.'

I wished I'd looked at some online reviews while we were en route, but I had been so sure that we were in for a treat, rather than a fleecing, I hadn't bothered.

'What a let-down,' Alex said sadly. 'Gracie would be devastated.'

That made it all even worse and we didn't bother taking any

further photos because there was nothing we wanted to remember. We walked dejectedly back down the hill and slipped even more because it was downhill all the way – mentally and physically – and harder to get a footing. We trudged along in near silence and I felt my frustration with the set-up bristle further when the path led us straight into the café and then through the tacky gift shop.

'I might be gasping for a drink,' said Rachel, shunning the packed shelves, 'but I'm not falling for that old ploy.'

'And my tummy's rumbling,' I put in. 'But not for an amateurishly iced cookie.'

'Don't worry,' said Alex. 'I've packed us a decent picnic so we can eat that and have a drink back at the car.'

'How did you find it?' asked the security guard when he spotted us stepping out of the shop and no doubt looking hot and bothered.

Given our glowering expressions, I was surprised he approached us let alone spoke.

'It's a total waste of money,' Alex said forthrightly, making a few heads turn.

It was much busier than when we'd headed up the hill and I had the strongest urge to give the people poised to pay at the ticket kiosk a heads up about what they were really going to see versus what they imagined they were going to admire. Surely someone must have had a moan online? Or were other fans more easily pleased than we were?

'You can't see bugger all, can you?' said the guard in a near whisper.

'You could have told us that before we parted with so much money,' Rachel scowled.

'More than my job's worth, my love,' he sighed, looking fed up. 'You used to view the falls from a path directly opposite them and it was magical.' His face took on a dreamy expression I wouldn't have thought it capable of and I realised he was referring to the path I'd spotted. 'But the footfall took its toll,' he further explained. 'And rather than pay the bill to repair it, my boss – who quite recently inherited the estate – took the cheaper option and moved it. He reckons we can get twice as many visitors through the gate now.'

If the path we'd walked was considered safer, then the other one must have been treacherous.

'And shaft the *Hope Falls* fanbase in the process,' I grumbled. 'He's not even updated the photos on the website so you get a proper idea of what you're actually parting with all that money to see. Or not see.' I scathingly added.

'Em,' said Rachel.

'Well, I'm right, aren't I?'

'That you are,' agreed the guard, looking around nervously. 'Not that you heard me say that if anyone asks. Given the enduring popularity of the book and the film, the new estate owner reckoned folk would still pay to come wherever the path led them and that's all he cares about.'

I felt relieved that no one else we'd encountered seemed to hold the same opinion when it came to making money out of fans, but wondered why none of them had intervened. Connor might not have known about the altered path, but someone in the vicinity must have heard a grumble from at least one disgruntled fan.

'If I were you,' the guard then quietly confided, 'I'd pass on the gift shop and head straight over to Archer's Force. That'll

fulfil your waterfall fantasy. My other half makes me drive her there all the time.'

'Hey, Charlie!' someone shouted, making us all jump. 'Are you coming, or not?'

'Where's Archer's Force?' Alex asked.

'Google it,' said the guard, now identified as Charlie, as he backed away. 'It'll come up and it's totally worth the drive.'

Back in the car park, which by then was more than half full, we didn't waste time berating the Star Shine Falls experience any longer, even though I could tell all three of us were bitterly disappointed that our first trip further than the cottage, lake and pub had been a colossal, and expensive, let-down.

So much for running my fingers through the icy falls and in the magical moment imagining myself as Heather. I hadn't even properly seen the falls, let alone got close enough to touch them.

'I thought we agreed to turn notifications off,' Rachel tutted from the driver's seat when my phone pinged with an incoming message as we sat in the car and considered the rest of our day while Alex did battle with the dodgy catch and fetched the picnic from the boot.

'Sorry,' I said, pulling the phone out of my pocket and feeling bad because I had moaned about her constant screen checking. 'I thought I had.'

In truth, I hadn't bothered turning mine off because I hadn't been expecting any messages.

'I'll do it now,' I told her.

'You might as well check it first, now it's gone off,' she said generously as Alex climbed back in and handed her a wrapped packet of sandwiches.

'Yes,' he said slyly, when he spotted my phone in my hand

as he passed me a packet too. 'It might be another commission request and you wouldn't want to miss out on that, would you?'

I didn't answer him, but he was right.

'It's a message from Hugh,' I said, unwrapping the cheese and chutney filled sandwich while waiting for the accompanying image to download.

At least my and Alex's extravagant purchases from Mrs Timpson's expensive deli range had been put to good use. The sarnie was delicious.

'Who?' Rachel frowned.

'No,' I quipped. 'Hugh.'

'Ha, ha,' she said, rolling her eyes.

'Hugh's the guy who wanted the anniversary picture for his wife,' I elaborated. 'Oh, wow,' I gasped as the image finally popped up. 'Look at this.'

I held my phone up so we could all see the ecstatic expression which my work, and Hugh's thoughtful gesture in commissioning it, had prompted. The smile on his wife's face was, according to the message, even wider than it had been on their wedding day and two guests at their party had asked if I would also consider making something for them. One was for a milestone birthday and the other to commemorate a christening.

'Crikey, Em,' said Rachel, sounding properly pleased. 'That's phenomenal. Congratulations!'

'Thank you,' I said, trying to take it in. 'I wasn't expecting that.'

'Well, maybe you should have been,' Alex said astutely. 'We've both already told you how exquisite we thought that piece of work was and there's no better form of advertising than word of mouth. You only have to look at that woman's face to see the impact your picture had.'

'As you liked the picture so much, you should see the clothes Em makes,' Rachel kindly told him. 'They're exquisite too and every bit as bespoke as the pictures. That's where I reckon the real money is, Em. You could make a fortune from those clothes.'

'Steady on, Rachel,' Alex stopped her. 'At this rate you'll be putting ideas in her head and she'll be thinking about turning down that new job and starting her own business.'

'Yes,' she said, biting her lip as a frown knitted her brows. 'You're right, Alex. Sorry, Em. I guess with me thinking about moving out, that's the last thing you should be considering, isn't it? That would be far too risky, in the current economic climate and with the cost of living still soaring.'

Alex didn't look at all happy that his tongue-in-cheek comment had backfired and her words meant I couldn't even take comfort in the fact that she had said she was still thinking about moving out rather than having completely decided to do it.

'It is,' I agreed, acknowledging that she was right and Alex was wrong.

'Well,' Alex doggedly carried on, as I sent a message thanking Hugh and saying that I'd be in touch for further details after my holiday. 'If you keep pulling the commissions in at this rate, you won't have to worry about the cost of living, will you? There'll be more than enough work for you to make ends meet.'

I ignored him, but could tell Rachel had taken on what he had said.

'So,' I quickly asked. 'As I'm on my phone, shall I have a quick search for this Archer's Force place, the guard suggested?'

'No need,' said Alex, holding up his own phone. 'I've found it and it looks spectacular.'

'More spectacular than Star Shine Falls?' Rachel mockingly asked.

'Anything would be more spectacular than Star Shine Falls.' Alex frowned.

'You're not wrong,' she sighed. 'What a gargantuan let-down that was.'

'Let's not dwell on it,' I said stoically, in an effort to save the day. 'How far is it to this Archer's Force, Alex?'

'About forty minutes by car,' he said. 'And there looks to be some pretty spectacular scenery on the way. What do you think?'

I was keen, but Rachel was a bit dubious. 'Let me have a look at it first,' she said, trying to catch a glimpse of the images on Alex's phone.

'No way,' he said, turning it away. 'I've read some reviews and double-checked the views, so I'll vouch for it. If we do decide to go, I want your first sighting to be a surprise. A good one,' he hastily added before Rachel said she'd already had one too many.

'All right,' she finally agreed. 'We'll go, but only if you drive. I'm not used to these narrow roads and twists and turns.'

'What makes you think I am?' Alex asked, sounding apprehensive.

Alex was right about the scenery. The closer we got to Archer's Force, the more rugged and dramatic it became and I found myself breathing in every time we passed another vehicle or turned a corner and found the road blocked with sheep. I was amused to remember that the tight roads hadn't bothered me at all when I stayed with Nanna and Grandad and I guessed the whole world had looked different to me then.

'Did you know your knuckles could go that white, Alex?' I asked, after a particularly close encounter with a woman in an

off-road vehicle who refused to put so much as the edge of a tyre on the verge.

'I didn't,' he said, eyeing the drystone walls which lined the way. 'And I didn't know I could hold my breath for so long either.'

'Are you sure it's around here?' Rachel asked, after we'd squeezed along another mile or so. 'There aren't any signposts and it doesn't exactly look like the usual tourist hotspot, does it?'

Alex pulled over and checked his phone. 'I'm pretty certain we're heading in the right direction,' he told us as the signal flickered in and out. 'It's not far now and I promise it'll be worth it.'

The only indication that there was anything magical or otherwise carved out of the hillside was a wonky wooden sign that we would have missed had we not had two pairs of eyes trained solely on looking out for it.

'There!' I shouted from the back, making Rachel jump and Alex stop sharply. 'You'll need to back up a few yards, but I definitely saw it.'

He carefully manoeuvred the car back and there was the sign.

'I can't believe I missed that.' Rachel blushed, from her vantage point in the front.

'No harm done,' said Alex, sounding relieved we'd finally arrived. 'We're here now.'

The car didn't sound all that happy about the steep ascent and when we pulled in to the car park, there were only two other cars.

'I hope this isn't a wild goose chase,' Alex cringed, suddenly full of doubt.

'Well,' I said, opening the back door and jumping out. 'You're

the one who has seen the photos and said you'd vouch for it, so this is all on you, my friend.'

'Don't wind him up,' said Rachel. 'Not when he's gone through all of that dramatic driving to get us here!'

We put on our jackets and rucksacks – complete with the obligatory Kendal mint cake which we all admitted we didn't like but felt was a necessary component to any Lakeland trek – and set off again.

'Afternoon!' said a smiling couple who were coming back down the hill and most likely accounted for one of the other cars in the car park.

'Is it worth the climb?' I asked them, already starting to feel out of breath.

'I should say so,' grinned the woman. 'Keep going. You're almost there.'

We reached the summit and descended into woodland neither Rachel or I expected to find on the other side and Alex said he only knew it was there because he'd seen it online. The firs quickly gave way to more native trees, and a fern lined path – not all that dissimilar to the one back at the cottage – took us the rest of the way. There was no sign of anyone else and it felt as if we'd stepped into another time.

'I don't know what to say.' I swallowed, mesmerised by the sheer perfection of the view in front of me as we rounded the final corner to the falls.

'Me neither,' said Rachel, reaching for my hand.

'It's a twenty metre drop into that pool, according to the internet,' said Alex, coming to stand next to me.

The water looked crystal clear and the sound of it pouring over the precipice above was intense and yet the water in the vast

pool below was calm and still. There were verdant overhanging branches and moss and lichen of every shade which contrasted beautifully with the granite rocks and boulders they grew on.

'Oh, my goodness,' Rachel gasped as the sun broke through the cloud and overhanging canopy and hit the water as it plunged down to the pool.

'This,' I said, unable to stop a tear escaping as the water sparkled in the rays, 'is Star Shine Falls.'

'No, it's not.' Rachel sniffed. 'It's Archer's Force.'

We both giggled.

'You know what I mean.' I nudged her.

'It's perfect,' said Alex, sounding every bit as moved as we were. 'This is what Star Shine Falls should have looked like, isn't it?'

'It is,' I agreed, reaching for his hand too and squeezing it without overthinking whether or not I should.

He gripped mine tightly and the three of us stood for ages just looking around and taking it in. Mindful again of Rachel's comments about first impressions I wanted to take as many mental pictures as possible before we started to explore.

'Keep your eyes peeled for any movement in the trees,' said Alex who, compared to me and Rachel, was quite the expert on the place. 'Apparently there are red squirrels in the area.'

Sadly, we didn't get to see my childhood favourite, Squirrel Nutkin or Old Brown, but the fact that there wasn't another person in the vicinity was a bonus. Our time at the Force felt all the more magical because we had the entire place to ourselves.

Time seemed to stand still as we climbed to the top and looked down, then climbed back down and looked up. There

were a million and one photo opportunities and I snapped loads on my phone, including lots of Rachel and Alex when they weren't looking.

It was late in the afternoon before we settled on a rock to eat a few chunks of the mint cake and drain the dregs of our drinks to give us enough energy for the hike back to the car.

'I don't want to go,' I admitted. 'I'm so pleased you insisted we came, Alex, and that you didn't let us see the photos before we arrived.'

'It's quite something, isn't it?' he said wistfully. 'Gracie would have hated this morning but she would have loved this every bit as much as we have.'

'I think we would have got along with Gracie very well, don't you, Em?' Rachel smiled.

'Without a doubt,' I agreed.

Alex nodded.

'And I'm so grateful to Charlie the guard for suggesting this place.' I further said.

'Yes,' said Rachel. 'He totally saved our day.'

'And our humour,' Alex added.

The walk back to the car seemed to take far less time than the scramble up to Archer's Force and I didn't think it was entirely due to the downhill terrain. My head was full of distracting thoughts of what I'd seen and how my memories were going to inspire me for a long time to come.

Rachel opted to sit in the back for the return journey and was asleep almost before Alex had pulled out of the car park.

'What a wonderful day,' I sighed, twisting around for one last look at the hill which held such a precious secret just over its summit. 'If you'd told me after the travesty of this morning

that I'd end the day feeling like this, I never would have believed you.'

'I know what you mean,' Alex agreed, as I turned back and made myself comfortable in the seat next to him again.

'But then,' I thoughtfully added, 'perhaps I shouldn't be all that surprised.'

'Why's that?' he asked, laughing at my sudden and contradictory change of heart.

'Because if this holiday is teaching me anything, it's that shocks and unexpected twists and turns can have the loveliest outcomes.'

'Oh.' He swallowed, his Adam's apple bobbing as his eyes fixed more intently on the road ahead. 'Is that right?'

'Yes,' I dreamily sighed. 'It is.'

Chapter 13

The next day, after taking care of a few domestic chores, I was still feeling inspired by our wonderful trip to Archer's Force and as a result, set about designing a calf-length full skirt which would incorporate the wonderful green cotton fabrics I had accumulated and thankfully decided to bring with me in one of my many bags of material bundles.

The sparkling water as it rushed over the falls had been beautiful, but it was the lush greenery I most wanted to emulate as I mulled over how I could make the patchwork pieces look like unfurling fern fronds, starting at the hem and appearing to grow upwards, just as they did in the natural world. I had plain as well as patterned scraps and a few ends of rolls to work with and could see the finished garment clearly in my mind's eye, so hopefully I would be able to turn the idea into reality.

'Are you going to want to measure me?' Rachel asked as she pulled the bed linen out of the dryer and I began to match up the different fabrics to create my vision.

'Not today,' I told her. 'But it would be a great help if you could measure me.'

She dropped the sheet she was folding back into the basket. 'You're actually making something for yourself?' she gasped.

'I am,' I confirmed.

'Well, I never!' She beamed. 'About time.'

She was always telling me I should be wearing my own designs but the truth was, having started making the clothes and putting the memory pictures together while working full-time, I hadn't had the opportunity. Not that I really minded. I knew how lucky I was to have people waiting for me to make something for them and the clothing orders had quite quickly racked up after a work colleague wore a dress to the office that I had creatively patched up after she'd torn it. Thinking back, that had been what had prompted the move into garments. It had been my very own Kintsugi moment.

'What are you going to make?' Rachel asked, leaning over the counter for a closer look.

'A skirt,' I told her. 'Inspired by our trip yesterday. I'm going to make it a full one with the patched sections resembling those wonderful fern fronds I took so many photos of.'

'How wonderful,' she beamed. 'You're going to have to tell me how to do the measuring though, because I've only ever been on the receiving end of the tape measure ...'

Our conversation was interrupted by Alex who came bursting out of his bedroom looking flustered.

'Whatever's up with you?' Rachel frowned, picking the sheet up again.

'I'm late,' he said, pulling on his jacket.

'Where are you off to in such a rush?' I asked, not that it was any of my business.

'I'm heading to The Drover's,' he puffed. 'Connor invited me

for lunch when we were there on Friday and I said yes. I thought I could fill him in on the state of the Star Shine Falls attraction, or lack of, while I'm there too.'

'Good idea.' I nodded. 'He really needs to stop recommending that place to his customers or he might find his own business ends up suffering as a result.'

I had briefly wondered if we'd had too high expectations about the attraction, but we hadn't. It really was a commercial rip-off.

'Quite,' said Alex, almost upsetting a chair as he flew about.

'You need to slow down,' Rachel said soothingly. 'I'm sure Connor won't mind if you're not there on the dot. He's a pretty chilled guy. He's not going to hold a few minutes' tardiness against you.'

'I know,' said Alex, still rushing around like a tornado in human form. 'But it's rude, isn't it? Not being on time when you've been given a time.'

He didn't give us time to respond.

'Also, I had another look at the list Gracie left me relating to this trip last night and there's something else I want to book us on. I thought I could take advantage of Connor's Wi-Fi to find it. Are you two up for another adventure tomorrow if I can find what I want at such short notice?'

He stopped for a whole three seconds to take in our reaction to his suggestion.

'If it's as wonderful as the adventure we ended up having yesterday, then count me in,' I was quick to say, lest I held him up.

'And me,' Rachel keenly added. 'The forecast looks pretty good, so . . .'

'Oh, you won't need to worry about the weather,' Alex waved

her comment away, which rather tweaked my curiosity. 'I'll see you both later.'

He banged out the door and Rachel and I let out a breath in the silence that followed.

'Goodness,' she laughed. 'That was intense. What do you think he meant about the weather?'

'Must be something we can do inside,' I shrugged, thinking that was the most obvious explanation. 'Now,' I added. 'Let's get measuring.'

I was standing on a chair – to save Rachel having to kneel down – in my slightly too short T-shirt and a pair of cotton knickers when Alex came bursting back into the cottage.

'Keys!' he shouted. 'I got all the way to the car and realised I hadn't got . . .'

His words trailed off as I yelped and awkwardly jumped down, but not before he'd seen me. I ineffectively covered myself with the cushion Rachel had grabbed off the sofa and hurled in my direction. I don't know who was reddest, him or me.

'Sorry,' he mumbled, bumping into the table and wincing from the resultant pain. 'I didn't realise you'd be . . .'

'Half-dressed,' Rachel unhelpfully giggled and I threw her a thin-lipped look. 'Almost naked,' she infuriatingly carried on. 'Practically in the raw.'

'Rachel was just . . .' I began to gabble.

'Found them!' he yelled, jangling the keys to prove the point before heading back out with one hand practically covering the side of his face closest to where I was cringing and curling in on myself.

Rachel started to properly laugh and fell onto the sofa in a

happy heap as I swatted her with the cushion and Alex disappeared back up the path. That time, hopefully for good.

'Damn,' I swore, feeling mortified as I watched him practically pelt away. 'Damn, damn, damn, damn, damn.'

Rachel wiped her eyes with the sleeve of her sweater and sat back up.

'You're only cussing because he saw you in your Sunday pants,' she teased, holding her stomach.

'I'm bloody not,' I said, biting my lip to stop my mouth curling into a smile.

It wasn't funny. It was crushing. Though she was right about the undies scenario. They were definitely not my best.

'Come on,' I said, throwing her the tape measure. 'Let's get this done quickly in case he comes back for something else.'

'Like a second look, you mean,' she giggled again, twirling the tape around.

'Don't be so stupid,' I said, suddenly unable to hold the laughter back. 'I mean it,' I tried to sternly say. 'Come on.'

It was so late by the time Alex came back to the cottage that I had begun to wonder if he was going to come back at all. I hadn't dared comment about the time to Rachel for fear of being on the receiving end of further teasing, but I was getting a bit concerned when evening had almost turned to night and there was still no sign of him.

'Can I come in?' he called when he eventually returned, having made a rousing rumpus on the veranda before peeping around the door with his eyes tightly closed. 'Are you decent, Em? Have I stayed away long enough?'

I rolled my eyes, which he, of course, couldn't see, and which

turned Rachel's laugh into more of a snort. I couldn't believe he was going to brazen the moment out by making me the butt of the joke. I would have been far happier if he'd just ignored it.

'Yes,' I said. 'You can come in and yes, I am decent.'

'Sure?'

'Oh, for pity's sake,' I said, wishing he'd just come in, 'don't set Rachel off again. She's only stopped going on about it in the last five minutes.'

He came in, sniggering, and hung his jacket by the door.

'I thought you might fancy these,' he said, putting an insulated bag down on the kitchen counter. 'Assuming it's not too late to eat. I didn't expect to stay so long, but Connor's a good bloke to talk to.'

I wondered if he'd spent more time talking to him about Gracie.

'What are these?' Rachel asked, eyeing the bag.

'Two portions of sticky toffee pudding that Connor had left over,' Alex temptingly revealed. 'They're cold, but the custard is still warm.'

'Oh yum,' said Rachel, diving in. 'My favourite. Thank you.'

I grabbed us a couple of spoons and, moving to sit on the sofa, gratefully tucked in. I was appreciative because not only was the sweet treat absolutely delicious, eating it was also a distraction from wondering if Alex was thinking about me standing in front of him in my pants. Well, it should have been a distraction. It was a great way to make up for embarrassing me again, anyway.

'So,' said Rachel, as she speedily polished off her serving of the scrumptious pudding, 'How did Connor take the news about the not quite star attraction?'

I smiled at the almost pun.

'He was gutted,' Alex told us and I wasn't surprised. 'He wanted to compensate us for the amount we'd spent to get in, but I wouldn't let him.'

'Did you suggest he recommended Archer's Force from now on instead?' I asked.

Alex shook his head. 'I almost did,' he said, 'and then I felt a bit guilty that I hadn't, but I'd hate the thought of being potentially responsible for making it too popular. Some of its appeal was wrapped up in its wonderful solitude, wasn't it?'

'It was,' Rachel agreed.

'Well, I wouldn't worry,' I said, scraping out the last bits of sponge from the pot. 'Connor's a local. I'm sure he already knows about the place so he can decide whether or not to suggest it to *Hope Falls* fans, can't he?'

'That's true,' said Alex, sounding happier.

'And how did you get on booking tomorrow's adventure?' Rachel asked him.

'Very well,' he said, unfolding three sheets of paper which had been in his jeans back pocket. 'We're all set. It'll be another early start, but totally worth it.'

I took one of the sheets and handed the other to Rachel. I didn't look at mine, but noticed the colour draining from Rachel's face as she read hers. What on earth had he booked for us to do?

'Everything all right?' Alex asked, also aware of her peaky pallor.

'No,' she said shakily. 'I can't do this, Alex. I'm sorry, but this isn't for me.'

I abandoned the last mouthful of my pudding and perused the sheet in front of me.

'What even is ghyll scrambling?' I frowned, skimming the details, but still not getting the gist because there was no explanation.

'Throwing yourself off waterfalls.' Rachel shuddered. 'Sliding down fast flowing rocky river paths, that kind of adrenaline junkie stuff.'

'What?' I frowned, looking at the paper again. 'You're kidding.' She shook her head. 'You're winding me up, right?'

'I'm not,' she said, her pastiness suggesting she wasn't fooling around. 'I'm all for swimming in the lake, should it miraculously heat up twenty degrees in the next few weeks, but this stuff, no way. Sorry, Alex, but I had a near-death experience on one of these so-called adventures during a team-building exercise with some staff from my school and I swore then, never again.'

'Near death?' Alex gasped.

'It was not near death,' I cut in, halting the drama. 'It was a momentary scare.'

'Which had a lasting impact,' she said, handing Alex back the booking sheet. 'If you're so blasé about it, Emily, you can do it.'

I didn't want to do it either. No way was I going to go bowling down waterfalls into the freezing pools below.

'It's perfectly safe,' Alex said to me, picking up on my hesitation.

The fact that he wasn't including Rachel in the pep talk told me he knew he'd lost her and I was his last hope for a wild water companion.

'It's more of a splash and a slide than a full body immersion,' he not so temptingly carried on. 'Unless you want a full body immersion.' I vehemently shook my head. 'Kids do it,' he said, as if that would be the clincher. 'The place I've booked us in with even allows seven-year-olds to take part.'

Maybe he could borrow a willing child to accompany him because I wasn't going to do it. Full body, with armbands or otherwise.

'Gracie loved this sort of thing,' he carried on, letting the implication hang in the air.

'Are you pulling the—'

'No,' he said, cutting me off. 'I'm not. Absolutely not. I'd just rather not do it alone but if I have to, I will.'

There was no denying the disappointment in his tone and I could see from the bill that he'd already shelled out a hefty amount, even though it was listed as a last-minute bargain. Given the money we'd wasted at Star Shine Falls the day before, he would have been better off emptying his wallet into an obliging well and making a few wishes. Then I remembered why he was doing the wet and wild adventure in the first place along with what he'd most likely wish for if he did find a well.

'No wonder you said the weather isn't going to matter,' I tutted. 'I'm going to get soaked, aren't I?'

'You'll do it?' he shouted, jumping up.

'You're not serious,' Rachel gasped.

'I can hardly let him do it on his own, can I?' I grimaced.

'I would,' she said, with no hint of remorse.

'Well, I can't,' I said. 'How bad can it be?'

Alex pulled me to my feet and into a hug. The feel of his firm body pressed close to mine sent a shockwave of pleasure coursing through me and I reluctantly eased myself away.

'Really bad,' Rachel warned me. 'It could be really, really bad.'

Around fourteen hours later, Rachel's prediction had come horribly true.

'You're going to have to let go!' yelled the instructor. 'You're holding everyone up!'

'I can't,' I screeched, hanging on to the slippery rocks either side of me as if my life depended on them. Which it quite possibly did.

'Just fold your arms over your chest and relax into it,' Alex yelled from below.

He and Connor, who had happily stepped in to take Rachel's place, were having a fine old time of it. They'd already thrown themselves into the icy water with abandon and high-fived each other when they resurfaced. I, on the other hand, was terrified that I wouldn't resurface. The massive helmet kept slipping down over my forehead, my hands were scratched to hell from where I kept trying to cling on to the rocks and I was already thoroughly soaked, in spite of the fact that I hadn't gone for full immersion.

I looked up at the visitor centre where I could see Rachel watching out of the floor to ceiling window and nursing a mug of steaming coffee. She was dry, warm and completely safe. She gave me a thumbs up with her free hand and as I went to flip her the bird, my other hand lost its grip and I plunged down the rock face into the icy pool below where Connor hauled me to my feet and Alex whooped and cheered.

'Come on,' he said, dragging me along. 'It's a longer drop next.'

I would love to say I had some sort of life-changing epiphany halfway through the experience. If I could have had my way, I would have been transformed from terrified, squealing woman into a rampaging water warrior, complete with a powerful, guttural roar.

But the only sounds I made were terrified shrieks and my throat was soon so hoarse, that I gave up on even making those.

I had always considered myself reasonably fit, but on the back of the double hike the day before, my legs shook like not quite set jelly and if at any point I did have an adrenaline rush, it must have been a really, really small one.

'That's it,' shouted Connor. 'You're getting the hang of it.'

I wasn't getting the hang of anything. I was just flinging myself down the last few drops to get it over with as quickly as possible.

'Go you!' Connor called, as I spluttered my way to the surface unaided.

'Go you,' I muttered back, when I had enough breath.

Had I known Alex had arranged to meet him at the centre after Rachel had backed out, I would have paid Alex for my share of the so-called fun and could have been enjoying coffee with my so-called friend, but I'd already been suited up and lashed to a rope for the first descent by the time Connor arrived and there was no going back then.

'This is the last one!' yelled another fresh-faced instructor. 'And it's a biggie. Brace yourselves, guys!'

I submitted to my fate and threw myself off the edge before the other two had even moved. The drop was far further than I expected and I did indeed manage complete immersion. It was some minutes before I had pulled in enough oxygen to speak, but that was fine because if what I was thinking had actually come out of my mouth, I don't think Alex, Connor or anyone else present would have had a very high opinion of me.

'Oh my god!' cried Rachel, when I finally emerged from the changing rooms, already aching all over. 'How the hell did you do that?'

Neither Alex or Connor were in sight so I didn't feel like I had to pretend I'd had the time of my life as she helped my limp

shell of a body into a chair and did up my shirt buttons for me because my hands were shaking so much. I couldn't decide if that was because I'd caught a pernicious chill or was still terrified. Time would tell, I supposed.

'Here,' said Rachel, 'eat this. I bet your blood sugar has dropped like a stone.'

'*I* dropped like a stone,' I bleated as I crammed the chocolate and raspberry muffin into my mouth, barely chewing before I swallowed it down.

'And drink this,' she said, helping me bring the mug of hot chocolate to my lips without spilling too much of it.

'You can laugh,' I said tiredly as the last iota of energy upped and left before the sugar rush had a chance to hit. 'I must have looked a total twit.'

'I'm not laughing,' said Rachel and she really wasn't. 'I honestly have no idea how you did that. I couldn't have even made it down the baby drop.'

'But you've had a near death experience at one of these things,' I sarcastically reminded her.

'Hardly,' she conceded. 'You were bloody brilliant.'

I hadn't felt bloody brilliant. I still didn't feel bloody brilliant but at least I knew ghyll scrambling was something I would never, ever have to do again.

'At least I got changed before Alex and Connor,' I weakly smiled, looking around.

'Sorry, my love,' said Rachel, pointing towards the adventure centre lobby. 'But you didn't. They came out ages ago.'

As if they knew we were talking about them they turned and gave us a cheery wave. I couldn't lift my hand to wave back. Not even one finger.

'You're changed,' Alex beamed, as they rushed over. 'Look what we've found,' he excitedly added, shoving a leaflet under my nose with the word canyoning in large font across the top. 'They've got vacancies for next week, if you fancy it.'

I pressed my lips together and reached out to Rachel who helped me to my feet.

'Em?' Connor called after me as I shuffled away.

'She said she'll think about it,' said Rachel, keeping me moving. 'We'll meet you at the car.'

Chapter 14

Not surprisingly, I went out like a light that night and slept long into the following day. If there was any justice in the world, my (naïve) willingness to literally throw myself into the activity should have been rewarded with a warm glow, a heightened sense of well-being and the satisfaction of an act of kindness well done, but there was no reward, only a world of pain like I'd never experienced before.

'Rachel!' I screeched, a few seconds after I'd woken up. 'Rach!'

'Whatever's wrong?' she gasped, pounding through the cottage and into our room.

'I can't move,' I sobbed. 'I think I must have broken every bone in my body.'

Her shoulders dropped and she let out a long breath.

'What are you doing?' I protested. 'Why are you relaxing? Did you not hear what I just said? Call a doctor. I need help!'

She came and sat on the edge of the bed. Even just the slight movement of her sitting down caused me to wince.

'You haven't broken anything, you numpty,' she said with a sympathetic smile. 'Your muscles are just a bit stiff from the ghyll scrambling, that's all.'

'If you use the words *just a bit*, or *that's all* again,' I sobbed, 'I swear, I'll swing for you. I'm in agony here.'

'So, how are you going to muster the energy to do me such monumental harm with your little broken body?' she asked, a mischievous smile lighting up her face and a twinkle sparkling in her eye.

'Why are you not taking this seriously?' I cried, because my voice was the only physical thing I had at my disposal with an iota of strength left in it. 'It really hurts.'

I would have turned on the waterworks but held the tears back in fear that the effort might cause further pain.

'I'm actually not surprised it hurts,' she then said, reaching for my hand which slightly improved her previously appalling bedside manner. 'I've watched the video this morning and I still can't believe that you're the person in that yellow suit with the slightly too big red helmet bobbing along the rapids.'

'The kids' helmets were too small,' I sniffed, before her words sank in, 'and the adults a tad too big.' I wondered for a moment if I had an odd sized noggin. 'But hang on,' I then gasped, gingerly inching myself into a more upright position and worrying that the activity of the day before had somehow impaired my processing skills. 'What video is this?'

Rachel looked to the door and lowered her voice.

'Alex paid extra to have the whole thing recorded,' she told me. 'I knew you hadn't taken that in when we were talking about it on the journey back from the activity centre.'

Not to be too melodramatic, but I was pretty certain I'd spent most of the journey home drifting in and out of consciousness and I had absolutely no recollection as to how I'd made it from the car, down the long path and into my bed at all.

'Why would he do that?' I groaned, horrified to think that there was actual recorded evidence of what I'd been through. 'Why on earth would he think I'd want a memento of such a traumatic and humiliating experience?'

'He didn't do it for you,' she said quietly. 'He wants it so he can show his parents that he'd ticked something spectacular off Gracie's list after the disappointment of Star Shine Falls.'

'Oh.' I swallowed, as I heard Alex come out of his room. 'Right. Of course.'

'And between you and me,' Rachel whispered, 'you don't look either traumatised or humiliated in that recording. You look like a total bad-ass.'

'You said you couldn't believe it was me.' I pouted.

'Only because I know you and it's the last sort of thing I would ever expect to see you doing,' she laughed. 'Not because you looked like a—'

She cut off whatever choice adjective she was going to end her sentence with as Alex knocked on the door.

'How's my ghyll scrambling companion feeling this morning?' he asked, looking around the frame. 'Afternoon actually,' he added, checking his watch.

'Marvellous,' I said, then continued, with an attempted smile for fear that I might have come across as sarcastic, 'Or I will be when I can move again.'

'Oh dear,' he grimaced.

'I'm pretty sure I'm pinned to this bed.'

'I'm feeling it a bit myself today,' he admitted. 'But another bath has helped.'

'I think it's going to take more than a bath to help me,' I joked, although I wasn't actually joking.

'But how about a hot bath filled with Epsom salts courtesy of Mrs Timpson?' he suggested.

'Mrs Timpson actually stocks Epsom salts?' I laughed, though the pain around my ribs soon put a stop to that.

'I can't believe you're even asking that, Em.' Alex grinned. 'You should know by now that she stocks *everything* as I was reminded when I went down there earlier looking for something to relieve the aches and pains.'

'But even so,' I said. 'Epsom salts?'

'Apparently,' he informed me, 'we aren't the first adrenaline junkies around here . . .'

'I'm not an adrenaline junkie,' I quickly countered.

I suddenly remembered the word canyoning coming up the day before and there was no way I was getting roped into anything high octane again, by either him or Connor.

'Well, we're not the first visitors to overdo it on the outdoor pursuits front apparently,' he carried on, 'and she saw a gap in the market and got a suitable stock of products in to ease our collective pain.'

'She's the ultimate data analyst,' Rachel giggled. 'She reads the terrain, puts in the orders, then pounces.'

'You're right,' I laughed. 'I should get the firm taking me on to employ her.'

'But then you'd do yourself out of a job,' Rachel nudged.

'Might not be a bad thing,' said Alex, steering us towards tricky territory.

'What else did Mrs Timpson have?' I asked him. 'I bet she didn't stop at a few bags of salt, did she?'

'Radox Muscle Soak,' he reeled off. 'Freeze sleeves in various sizes and every painkiller on the legal market along with their gel form counterparts.'

'Covering all bases then?' Rachel snorted.

'Very much so,' Alex said, rubbing his wet hair with a towel and making it stand up on end. 'And I for one am feeling grateful for that today.'

The ease with which he rubbed his hair suggested that he had far more movement in his muscles and limbs than I had in mine. I wondered if the fact that I'd been as tense as a tightrope throughout the experience was partly behind the uncomfortable consequences. I knew I had more readily thrown myself into it, to get it over with, towards the end but the damage had most likely been done by then.

'How about I run you a bath?' Rachel offered.

'I was going to suggest that too,' said Alex. 'Feel free to take advantage of my terrific tub and the extra Epsom salts I picked up to come to your aid, in case you needed them.'

'And then we could settle down and watch the video of your outdoor adventure together,' Rachel smilingly added.

'And I have something planned for the three of us for later tonight,' Alex finished up as if that was the clincher which would prise me out of my bed.

'Oh no,' I said, gingerly shaking my head. 'I've had enough of your plans to last me a lifetime, thank you very much.'

'You'll love this one, I promise,' he said, looking at me so intently, I felt my heart skip. 'It won't raise your heart rate at all.'

Given the tattoo that was currently beating in my chest, I didn't believe that for a second.

As well as running the bath, I got Rachel to help me into it and she even came back halfway through with a mug of soothing chamomile tea and topped the water up.

'If it gets too cool,' she said, in a mumsy tone, 'that could be counterproductive, so you'll have to get out soon.'

Laying in the water, and doing my best not to feel bitter about the fact that the beautiful bathroom with its view of the woods wasn't my usual wash spot, I couldn't tell if the salts were having any impact at all.

But then I remembered I had once worked with a woman who had gone through a few hours' labour in a birthing pool and hadn't thought the water was doing anything until she climbed out and had a contraction with one leg cocked over the side. I hoped I would feel a longer lasting benefit than that when I eventually got out, otherwise I was going to take up residence in Alex's bath and no doubt turn into a prune as a result.

'Better?' Rachel asked, when I later emerged, wrapped in my fluffy towelling robe, softest pyjamas and fleecy bed socks.

'Heaps.' I nodded. 'But be warned Alex,' I said to the back of his head when I spotted him sitting on the sofa, 'if I start to tense up again, I'm diving straight back in.'

'You would be more than welcome,' he said, twisting round and giving me a heart-warming smile.

Rachel caught my eye and winked.

'I've resolved to do the same myself,' he said, turning away again.

'Then we'd better not need it at the same time, had we?'

'Oh, I don't know,' he pondered. 'I'm pretty sure that tub's big enough for two.'

Rachel didn't wink that time, but she couldn't have done even if she'd wanted to because her eyes were like saucers. I didn't say anything but I could feel my face had gone bright red.

'I think I'll just get dressed.' I swallowed.

'No, don't,' said Alex. 'Stay as you are. You look comfy, and besides, I can't wait any longer for you to watch this.'

'And I'm making bacon, halloumi and salad sandwiches and they're so much nicer eaten warm,' Rachel recovered enough to say.

'Oh yum,' I said. 'My favourite.'

'Sit down then,' she urged. 'And I'll put them on a lap tray.'

'And don't forget that fig relish Mrs Timpson sent me back with,' Alex piped up.

'I had a feeling you wouldn't have got away with just buying salts,' I laughed. 'But I'm very grateful that you got enough of them to include a bath for me.'

I might have initially been reluctant to watch, but Rachel was right about the recording of my once in a lifetime ghyll scrambling experience. Fortunately, whoever was filming hadn't been able to get close enough to zoom in on my abject terror and the noise of the crashing water meant the sound of my terrified screams was barely noticeable at all.

That said, I could see there was a definite difference between how I went into the first drop compared to the last few and Alex picked up on that too.

'Look at you,' he said, flicking my arm with the kitchen towel Rachel had supplied us with while we ate her delicious sandwiches. 'You're really going for it on that last drop.'

'I think she just really, really wanted it to be over,' Rachel corrected him.

'I admit there was a certain element of that written into my technique,' I laughed. 'But watching this now, I am pleased I did it. Not,' I severely added, 'that that's any sort of hint that I'd like to do it, or anything like it, ever again.'

'Noted,' Alex grinned, rewinding again to the last drop.
'Fuck, that was a long way down,' he whistled, making me
splutter and Rachel choke.

'Right?' I said, that time swiping him.

'The instructor guy did say it was a long one, but it did take
me a bit by surprise, especially given how willingly you'd seemed
to launch yourself off.'

'Believe me,' I told him, 'I was not willing and it was as much
of a surprise to me as it was to you!'

Having watched our watery escapade at least half a dozen
times, Alex and I offered to do the dishes as Rachel had cooked
and I was relieved to find that my muscles were still feeling
much soothed when I stood up from where I'd been curled up
on the sofa.

'Are you all set for tomorrow?' I asked Alex.

It was Wednesday the next day so he would be driving down
to Manchester to work.

'Yes,' he said. 'I think so. I'm meeting the new client to
sound out my initial ideas for their rebrand. I'm really looking
forward to it.'

'You're obviously excited about the prospect.'

'I am.' He nodded. 'It's quite a radical change that I'm thinking of, which will reflect the alterations they're making to
their menus.'

'Sounds good,' I said. 'And it's lovely to hear you sounding so
enthusiastic about your work.'

'Likewise,' he said. 'About your patchwork anyway. I haven't
heard you waxing lyrical over your new data analyst role since
Rachel flagged it up.'

I really didn't want to talk about that.

'I guess it's easier to be excited about something when you don't have to rely on it to pay the rent,' I therefore said.

'I wouldn't say that,' he objected and given that his job did pay his salary I couldn't contradict him. 'But I'll let you off the hook because I have a feeling that you've got something more to do with your lucrative sideline going on in your head.'

I kept my lips locked, neither confirming or denying that he was right.

'And I'm excited to show Mum and Dad the recording, of course,' he told me. 'I'll be seeing them at the end of the day and filling them in. Although I might not mention the whole Star Shine Falls travesty,' he added, with a shake of his head.

'I don't blame you,' I agreed. 'But Archer's Force and even yesterday's adventure more than made up for that, so just tell them the good bits.'

'I will,' he grinned.

'So,' I said. 'Tell me what's on the new menu at this restaurant you're working with.'

'I only know the opening taster menu, but you'll have to wait to find out what's on it.' He winked. 'I'm planning to invite you and Rach over to Manchester, and your other friend, if she'd like to come, for the grand unveiling and the meal which will follow it.'

'Oh wow,' I said. 'Thank you.'

'You're welcome.'

'It will be something to look forward to when the time comes to leave here, won't it?' I rather liked the thought of seeing him for longer than just the next few weeks, but I felt the words catch as I said them.

'Oh, don't,' Alex responded, also sounding choked. 'I can't even bear to think about not being here.'

'Me neither.' I nodded, grateful that we still had more time ahead of us than behind.

'I'm having such a wonderful time,' he further said. 'And even though some if it is, not surprisingly, tinged with sadness, you and Rachel are making it so much better than it might have been.'

'Even after our rocky start?'

'Even after that,' he said softly, his eyes finding mine. 'I couldn't have been thrown together with two better people to honour my promise to my sister.'

'Oh, Alex,' I said, swallowing hard. 'That's so kind.'

'I don't know what I expected to find when I came here, Em,' he tenderly said, 'but it wasn't . . .'

'Aren't you two finished yet?' Rachel frowned as she came back in from where she'd been sitting on the veranda.

Alex and I instantly sprang apart. I hadn't realised how close we'd got during our heart to heart and I can't in all honesty say what might have happened if Rachel hadn't walked in when she did. I could feel her eyes on the pair of us and so turned away to dry the last of the dishes.

'Almost,' said Alex, coming across as far more composed than I felt as he leant to look out of the window. 'And looking at the sky, it won't be long before I can treat you both to the next part of my water-based plan.'

'Oh goodness,' I groaned, feeling thoroughly doused. 'Not more water.'

Chapter 15

Alex refused to share what it was that he had lined up for us to do that night, but he did promise most sincerely that it would be worth going out in the dark for and that it didn't involve us dipping even so much as a toe in the water. Rachel and I were all for that. Or we were until she came back from her unusually late daily roadside chat with Jeremy and told us she'd got a raging headache.

'You two should still go,' she insisted when I suggested putting the excursion off. 'I'm just going to take some tablets, drink plenty of water and call it a night. I'll be fine.'

'Are you sure?' I frowned, frustrated the phone call had had an impact on Rachel's health and Alex's efforts.

'Absolutely,' she said again.

'We really don't have to do it today,' Alex kindly joined in. 'There's still plenty of time for what I have in mind.'

'No, please don't put it off,' she begged. 'Not when you've gone to the trouble of arranging something, Alex. You pair carry on, otherwise I'll feel guilty about scuppering the plan and that won't help clear my head at all, will it?'

Alex looked at me and raised his eyebrows. 'Do you think we should?' he asked, wrinkling his nose.

'I think it will annoy her if we don't,' I answered, resolutely trying not to notice how scrunching up his nose also made his eyes attractively crinkle at the corners.

'It most definitely will,' Rachel confirmed.

'Come on then,' I said, before I gave in to temptation and asked her if there was anything in particular that had sparked the headache. 'Let's go. Do I need to bring anything?'

'Just a warm jumper,' Alex told me. 'Nothing else.'

He had already snuck out to do something which was connected to his plan while Rachel was on the phone and it was still just about light and he had also packed a bag for whatever it was that he'd got in mind, which he then picked up. The second the two of us stepped off the veranda, I realised we were heading into the woods and therefore most likely down to the lake.

As we walked among the trees, our path through them lit by the torch usually kept in the cottage, I couldn't help wondering if Rachel really did have a headache triggered by something that cock-weasel had said.

She did look a little pale so she most likely was suffering, but I pondered, if she wasn't, had she feigned the pain after walking in on mine and Alex's earlier 'almost but not quite something' moment, to give us some more time alone?

'Are you okay?' Alex asked, twisting around to look at me.

'I'm good,' I said.

'Only you just let out a *really* long breath,' he said, 'And in my experience that often means a woman is feeling anything but good.'

I had to laugh at that.

'But you're okay?' he asked again. 'Legs not aching too much now?'

'My legs are fine and I am good,' I repeated, then lunged forward to grab him as he tripped over a tree root because he was eyeing me and not the path. 'And I'll be even better when you start watching where you're walking again.'

He bypassed the lakeside benches and chairs when we arrived on the pebbled shore and headed straight for the jetty.

'You did say we were going to stay dry,' I said, stopping a few paces behind him. 'You're not going to spring skinny-dipping on me, are you?'

'No way,' he laughed. 'You can trust me, Em. I always keep my word and I promise, you are going to be staying dry tonight.'

I put my faith in him and followed him along the jetty to where the little wooden rowing boat was moored. I could see there were a couple of pillows already arranged, along with a hurricane lamp and some blankets.

'What's all this?' I asked. 'I'm not sure there's going to be room in there for us and all this stuff.'

It would have been a really tight squeeze if it had ended up being the three of us.

'Yes, there is,' Alex said, confidently climbing down, depositing the bag and holding out his hand for me to join him. 'Come on.' He smiled. 'It's completely safe.'

The boat might have been watertight, but as far as the good ship Alex was concerned, I was in danger of being sunk. My defences were fast being breached and the feel of his fingers securely holding mine as I cautiously stepped down were all the proof I needed that if someone didn't throw me a life jacket soon, I was going to slip under.

Had we been in any other setting at any other time, that would have been fine but there was no way I was going to let

our relationship shift beyond the friend zone. I had set a specific agenda for this holiday, along with a definite idea about how it was all going to pan out and a holiday fling with a man who also had precise ideas about what the retreat should include as well as his own trauma to work through, was not a part of the plan.

'Steady,' he said, his other hand coming to rest lightly on my waist for the briefest moment as he stilled me while I found my sea, or should that be, lake legs.

The lake was as calm as a millpond, but I felt heady enough to be riding the waves in a force five gale as he held me.

'All right?' he asked.

'Yes,' I said again, only this time breathlessly. 'I'm good.'

'Okay.' He nodded.

I could still feel the warmth of his touch, his fingers resting on my waist, even though they weren't there anymore.

'Now,' he said. 'You make yourself comfortable on the blankets up that end and I'll work out how to start this thing.'

I must have looked stricken.

'I'm kidding,' he laughed. 'I've rowed before. Dozens of times. Relax, Em. The last thing you need is to tense up and start aching again.'

I sat as instructed and as I watched him competently ready the oars and untie the rope, I did begin to relax. He clearly did know what he was doing and as he slowly, calmly and steadily set our course for the middle of the lake, I admired the view. Not the one of the surrounding landscape because it was too dark to see it, but the one directly in front of me, softly lit by a solar hurricane lantern.

It was headily hypnotic watching Alex sweep the oars back and forth, the muscles in his arms and chest flexing with each stroke. At one point, his gaze met mine. I cleared my throat and

looked towards the pinpricks of light coming from the cottages along the hillside.

After a while, there was a gentle thud against the side of the boat and we came alongside what Alex told me was the mooring buoy. He secured the boat to it using the rope which had previously attached it to the jetty.

'It will stop us drifting while we watch,' he said.

'Watch what?'

He pointed to the sky and I looked up.

'Oh, Alex,' I gasped.

I had never seen the sky so beautifully lit. There were myriad stars and countless constellations. Having been so distracted by his perfect strokes, I hadn't noticed the sky as he rowed across the lake and on other nights it had been too cloudy to really see anything beyond the occasional twinkling glimpse.

'It's stunning,' I sighed.

'And it's going to get even better,' he said, smiling at my reaction.

'What do you mean?'

'We're going have a drink and then we're going to lay down,' he told me. 'And then you'll see.'

I shot him a look. I wasn't sure that sounded like a good idea when my defences had already been weakened.

'Trust me,' he said again and my senses tingled with more than the evening chill.

After pouring us each a coffee, which was deliciously laced with a little rum, and moving the bag and blankets to make more space, we shuffled around until we were able to comfortably lay side by side.

It took more fidgeting on my part than it probably needed to

but that was because I was keen not to let any part of me touch any part of him and that wasn't easy in the confined space of a small rowing boat. As I wriggled to get more comfortable, I couldn't make up my mind if I felt relieved or exasperated that Rachel wasn't with us. Had she been present Alex and I could go have gone top to toe.

'Gracie taught me,' said Alex, as he turned off the lamp and plunged us into inky darkness, 'that when it comes to stargazing for any length of time, this is the best way to avoid a stiff neck and aching shoulders.'

'Wise, Gracie,' I praised, as my eyes tracked from left to right and scanned the skies. 'I can see even more stars now you've turned the lamp off. It's incredible.'

'That's one of the real treasures of this area,' Alex sighed. 'No light pollution.'

I had admired the stars here with Nanna and Grandad in the past but certainly not while reclining in a boat in the middle of a lake. It was by far the most spectacular outing anyone had ever arranged for me and I hastily reminded myself that this wasn't some sort of romantic liaison or sweet seduction. After all, Rachel was supposed to be here too and that put a very different complexion on things. That should have made me feel better, given the talking to I'd earlier given myself but annoyingly, it didn't.

'I hope this makes up for what I put you through yesterday,' Alex said and I could tell he was smiling.

'It most definitely does.' I smiled back. 'But please don't ask me to go ghyll scrambling again. Or anything remotely like it,' I hastily added. 'Even if this sort of spectacular reward is likely to come after it.'

'I won't,' he laughed.

'Was stargazing on Gracie's list for this trip, too?' I asked, after a second had passed.

'No,' he said. 'This is my idea, inspired by the full moon scene in the book.'

'Well,' I said, feeling it was even more special because it was something he'd arranged. 'Thank you. I love it. And Rachel would love it too..'

'Can I ask you something, Em?' Alex then asked and my heart began to race.

'Of course,' I said, turning my head a little so I could see his face.

I could just make out his profile in the darkness but no distinguishing features which, given the intimate proximity, was probably just as well. Had those kind eyes been discernible I don't know what I would have done.

'What's the deal with this Jeremy guy?' he asked, still staring skywards.

'What do you mean?' I swallowed, trying not to feel disappointed that it wasn't the sort of question I had been both longing for and dreading.

'What is it about him that you don't like?'

Absolutely everything, I wanted to blurt out, but didn't.

'What makes you think I don't like him?' I asked instead.

Alex turned his head to look at me and I shifted my gaze back up to the stars.

'Well,' he said. 'Whenever his name comes up, your shoulders stiffen and you look like you're chewing a wasp.'

I laughed out loud at the mental image that conjured. It sounded louder in the silence of the lake than it would have done inside the cottage and I felt my cheeks flush.

'I'm sure that's not true,' I said, in a whisper to make up for my noisy outburst.

So much for making my dislike of Jeremy less obvious. Clearly, I hadn't dialled my reaction to any mention of him down anywhere near enough and if Alex had noticed, then Rachel was bound to have picked up on my continued dislike too.

But then, given that Jeremy had been such a knob over the photo of her and Connor, and was now impacting on her days out with his demands to be in touch at specified times, it was hardly surprising that I hadn't changed my mind about him and offered to help her pack for the probable move to his flat, was it?

'I promise you it absolutely is true,' Alex said sincerely. 'I'll take a photo next time if you like, so can see your face for yourself.'

'I'd rather you didn't,' I sighed, knowing I wouldn't really like to see that expression written on my features, even if the thought of it had momentarily amused me.

'So,' Alex nudged. 'What's going on? Why is the idea of Rachel moving in with this guy so abhorrent to you?'

Abhorrent was a very strong word, but in this instance, Alex was right to use it.

'Because he's not good for her,' I said on an out breath, then found I couldn't stop. 'And not good enough for her. He's controlling and manipulative and she just can't see it. She's always making excuses for his behaviour and when Tori or I flag up some over-the-top reaction he's had, or how he's deliberately sabotaged something we've planned, she just cuts us off.'

'What sort of over-the-top reaction?' Alex asked, sounding concerned.

I gave him the lowdown on the near bar brawl and Alex whistled under his breath.

'So, he's physically *and* mentally abusive.'

It turned my stomach when he put it like that. I was pretty certain that it was all mind stuff where Rachel was concerned, but that was sickening enough.

'He even went nuts about a photo I sent him of me, Rach and Connor by mistake,' I said, as tears filled my eyes. 'It was supposed to go to Tori's phone, but I was distracted and sent it to his instead. That's why Rachel's now speaking to him every day. Originally, they weren't going to have much contact during this holiday at all.'

'So as far as he's concerned,' Alex surmised, 'Rachel isn't supposed to even be in the vicinity of other guys, let alone have male friends?'

'You've got it.' I swallowed, swiping away a tear. 'And I just know that if she moves in with him, it's going to get even worse. I'm so angry with myself for sending that photo because I thought being apart from him would help give her some perspective.'

'But it was an accident,' Alex reminded me.

'An accident which has caused further damage,' I shot back. 'I had hoped that being away from Jeremy and getting to know Connor, who clearly isn't a self-centred, gaslighting prick, might make her see Jeremy for what he really is, but my mistake has given him the leverage to keep her wrapped up in him right when she had the chance to distance herself.'

The words had tumbled out in a rush and I stopped to draw breath. I hadn't expected to say even half of what I'd blurted out, but it was said now and I couldn't take it back. Not that I wanted to.

'So, maybe,' Alex slowly said, 'you shouldn't accept this new job offer. When you told me about it before, you implied that it would enable Rachel's move, so maybe you should pull the plug on it?'

'But that would make me every bit as manipulative as Jeremy, wouldn't it?'

'Perhaps,' Alex pondered. 'But with a completely different motive.'

'But if Rachel guessed why I'd done it, or worse, Jeremy did,' I said, voicing my fears about being found out, 'then I'd most likely end up losing her friendship anyway, because he would use it to turn me into the bad person.'

'He does sound like the kind of guy who would enjoy twisting the situation to suit him,' Alex said astutely.

Alex hadn't even met Jeremy and yet he'd already got the measure of him. Oh, how I wished Rachel could see the situation for what it really was too.

'Exactly,' I sighed.

'And you're going to need to be there for her when this relationship goes really wrong, aren't you? From what you've told me, I'm pretty sure it will at some point.'

'I'm sure it will, too,' I agreed, acknowledging that I had thought the exact same thing just a few days ago.

I focused my attention back on the stars, wishing that when the end came for Rachel and Jeremy's twisted relationship, I would still be considered enough of a friend to be allowed to help her pick up the pieces and move on.

'And you're really not thinking about turning your passion for patchwork, which should totally be your business name by the way, into a career?' Alex then asked.

He had completely turned the conversational tables and right at the point when I was least expecting it.

'No,' I said firmly, but nonetheless loving his clever name idea. 'Absolutely not.'

There was no lie in that. I might have come away with the intention of seriously considering it, but Rachel's bombshell had put an end to that. I might still mull it over at some point, but my immediate future was now filled with more pressing preoccupations.

'Well,' said Alex, 'I think that's a shame.'

'I know you do.'

'And I'm also sorry that I haven't got a solution for dealing with Jeremy.'

'I didn't expect you would have,' I told him. 'But I do appreciate the listening ear. I know I said far more than you bargained on hearing, but sometimes we just need to vent, don't we? I'd usually talk to Tori about it, but she's got her own stuff going on and given my recent track record I'd most likely make the call to her, holler for half an hour and then realise I'd picked up Rach's phone and dialled Jeremy's number.'

'I guess that would be one way of taking action and dealing directly with the situation.' Alex laughed. 'And at least he'd be in no doubt about how you felt after that.'

I laughed myself then, imagining Jeremy puce and dumbstruck on the end of the line. Perhaps it wasn't such a bad idea should a dramatic intervention become necessary.

'Don't tempt me,' I nudged. 'It might end up coming to that.'

'I'm sure it won't,' Alex said. 'You're doing the right thing, just quietly being there for Rachel and I totally get it about the listening ear. After Gracie died, even before then actually, people

were always encouraging me to talk, which was great but then they kept trying to come up with strategies to fix me and lessen my grief and guilt, but that's not what I needed. I just wanted someone to listen while I was going through it.'

'I understand that.' I swallowed.

Sometimes we all needed to get things out of our system without a solution or advice being offered, even if it was well-meant.

'In that case,' Alex nudged, 'I shouldn't have apologised about not having a solution for dealing with Jeremy. But here's a thought, do you think he knows I'm a bloke? Do you think Rachel's told him I'm a guy?'

'Absolutely not,' I said, feeling my stomach twist as I imagined his reaction. 'There's no way he knows you're a bloke. If he knew Rachel was sharing the cottage with another man, he would have talked her into leaving by now or come and picked her up on some trumped up pretence himself.'

'Well,' Alex said. 'Let's hope he never finds out.'

'Yes,' I said, chewing my lip. 'No more photo faux pas from me, that's for sure. Had I taken that damn photo of Rachel and Connor on my phone then the mix-up wouldn't have happened.'

'You're telling me Jeremy isn't one of your contacts?' asked Alex, pretending to be shocked, and I laughed.

We were quiet for a few seconds then as we looked back at the stars.

'Can I ask you something else?' he then asked. 'It's about your patchwork.'

'Oh, Alex,' I grimaced, feeling frustrated.

'I'm not going to nag you about taking it more seriously again,' he promised, putting up his hands in a gesture of

surrender, which looked a little strange given that he was laying down. 'It's a commission request, actually.'

'Oh?'

He sat up and shifted around so he could look down at me. My stomach stopped twisting and flipped completely over as my brain began to think of him looking down at me from that angle in a very different scenario. I put a hasty stop to it.

'What sort of commission?' I asked, just about regrouping.

'I was wondering if you would consider making a memory picture for my parents using some of Gracie's things connected to *Hope Falls*,' he said softly. 'I know they'd love to have something they could keep close by like that and having seen that anniversary . . .'

'Oh, Alex,' I said again, shifting up on to my elbows and even though we were now inches closer, I was so taken aback by what he'd requested that all sensual thoughts were entirely banished. 'I'm not sure if I could. It would be such a huge responsibility. I'd be so worried about getting it wrong.'

'You wouldn't get it wrong,' he insisted, moving closer still. 'You couldn't.'

'Well . . .' I faltered.

'Don't give me an answer now,' he pleaded. 'Think about it for a few days and then let me know. No pressure, but it would be wonderful to be able to give them something like that for Christmas. We've all promised to make more of an effort for it this year, and one of your pictures would be perfect.'

I was about to further object when something over his shoulder caught my eye.

'What was that?' I gasped.

Alex twisted around and the boat rocked a little. Given the

intensity of what we'd been talking about I'd almost forgotten we were in the middle of the lake.

'What?' he asked. 'Where?'

'In the sky,' I said. 'I thought I saw a shooting star, but I must have imagined it.'

'No, you didn't,' he said, laying back down. 'That's what we're really here for,' he told me as he got comfy again. 'It's almost the peak time for the Perseid meteor shower. I thought this would be the most wonderful place to watch it and fingers crossed we're going to strike lucky.'

'I've never seen a shooting star before,' I told him as I also laid down properly again. 'I can't believe it.'

'Look!' he said, as another sparkling trail blazed across the sky above our heads. 'And there's another!'

'This is amazing!' I gasped, as I watched them whizz over us.

'I hope you've got enough wishes to make on all of these, Em,' he said, reaching for my hand.

I laced my fingers through his, my insides lighting up as brightly as the night sky. I'd never shared something so spectacular with anyone, not even my two best friends.

'I'm pretty certain I can come up with something,' I told him.

Chapter 16

Alex had already set off for his day's work in Manchester by the time I was gushing to Rachel about our night-time trip to the lake. I knew he had taken the recording of our ghyll scrambling experience to show his parents and wondered what they would make of it.

'There's still plenty of time for you to see the meteor shower for yourself.' I beamed at my friend, having described practically every piece of cosmic dust and debris which had blazed a sparkling streak across the sky. 'And you absolutely must. It's utterly mesmerising.'

I stopped to flick the kettle on and draw breath and realised she hadn't said a word or made a sound since I had started the retelling of mine and Alex's ultimate night out, however, when I turned to look at her after arranging mugs for our morning coffee, I found her gaze fixed firmly on my face.

'I'm sorry,' I grimaced. 'I forgot about your headache. How is it this morning? I shouldn't have got so carried away. You know I always get shouty when I'm excited about something.'

Rachel shook her head and smiled.

'It's fine,' she said. 'I woke briefly in the early hours and it was already feeling much better by then.'

'What is it then?' I asked, spooning coffee and splashing milk. 'Why are you so quiet this morning? You're freaking me out. Is it just because I haven't let you get a word in edgeways?'

'It is,' she laughed. 'I'm enjoying hearing you talk about last night and I'm so happy for you!'

'What do you mean, you're happy for me?' I queried, sliding one of the mugs over to her and reaching into the bread bin.

'You know exactly what I mean,' she said, with a wicked grin.

'No, I really don't,' I maintained, as I dropped bread into the toaster.

I did though and I wished I'd never got so carried away describing the effort that Alex had gone to, to make the evening such a success and the boat so comfortable. I had told Rachel it was Gracie's genius idea to stargaze laying down, but the soppy expression on my friend's face told me that she believed that every bit of it was all Alex.

'I don't think I've ever heard of anything so romantic,' she said dreamily. 'Apart from when Jeremy turned up at work last December and whisked me off on that trip to the Christmas market in Nuremberg. Do you remember?'

How could I forget? It would have been a truly romantic get-away had it not coincidentally started on the very evening that Rachel and her colleagues had finished term and were planning to let their hair down and have a wild night out in the city.

Knowing the crowd she worked with, it wouldn't really have been anywhere near wild, but Jeremy had put paid to Rachel participating in it by turning up at the school gate and presenting her with a luxury trip to Europe the moment the bell rang at three fifteen.

I also couldn't forget how just a couple of weeks before

the event, when Rachel had reeled off the names of everyone she was planning to party with, a certain history teacher had been mentioned and Jeremy's back had stiffened and his brow had furrowed.

Rachel had graduated with Kevin Cunningham and they'd been firm friends since and Jeremy couldn't stand their association. It didn't take a genius to work out that the impromptu romantic getaway had been organised to ensure Rachel's end of term blow-out, with Kevin among the party, never happened.

Tori had bravely suggested as much to Rachel when she arrived back from Germany weighed down with bags of festive trinkets and Lebkuchen, and had been told she was both deluded and paranoid. Apparently, Jeremy had only been able to get away that weekend and so that was when they had to go. Rachel was one of the most intelligent people I knew and yet he'd somehow managed to do a real number on her.

'Of course, I remember.' I smiled, determined not to look, thanks to Alex's flagging, like I was chewing a wasp. 'But this wasn't a romantic thing with Alex. It was planned for both you and me, remember?'

Rachel shook her head, a look of disbelief written across her face.

'Well, whatever.' She shrugged, sipping the still hot coffee as the toast popped up. 'Whoever it was organised for, I can tell it won you over. You're totally smitten.'

'That's absurd,' I shot back, hotly denying her astute observation.

'It is not,' she countered, thickly buttering the hot toast. 'I've known something was brewing between you for days and then yesterday when I walked in and interrupted what I can only

assume was going to be a first kiss, I knew it wouldn't be long before you properly got together.'

I shoved two more slices of bread into the toaster with more force than was necessary.

'I can't believe you're saying this,' I snapped, feeling aggrieved.

But of course, I could believe it because I had already predicted it was exactly the conclusion she would jump to. I felt my face flush as I remembered that Alex had started to tell me that he had found something unexpected on the trip and even though Rachel was right, and I was smitten, I hoped his discovery was to do with coming to terms with losing Gracie and nothing to do with me.

I might have liked him more than I should, but it would be hugely inconvenient if he liked me back and our mutual attraction ended up turning the holiday into something different to what I had planned for or worse, if it didn't work out, something horrid that none of us would want to remember.

I could just about keep my feelings in check if I knew they weren't reciprocated and given that Alex hadn't said anything further in all the time we were alone on the lake, they had to be, didn't they? If he was falling for me then surely, he wouldn't have wasted that opportunity to tell me?

'You're kidding?' Rachel laughed.

'No,' I said, picking up my mug in an attempt to hide behind it. 'I'm not.'

'Well, in that case,' she grinned, 'you'd better tread carefully because it's more than obvious that he's falling for you.'

Alex arrived back at the cottage extremely late that night and laid in bed long into the next morning which meant I was able

to avoid him for practically the entire day. I wasn't sure making myself scarce was the right course of action, but I didn't know what else to do until I'd processed what Rachel had said, drawn my own conclusions and come up with a plan.

'Hey, Emily,' Connor said welcomingly when I turned up at the pub for lunch. 'Where's the rest of the clan?'

'Alex is recovering from a long day in Manchester yesterday,' I told him, bending to fuss Siddy who was as effusive in her welcome as always, 'and Rachel's gone for a walk down to the lake.'

'Is she okay?' Connor frowned.

'As far as I know.' I shrugged, having not given her solo wander any deep thought. 'Unless you know different.'

Connor suddenly became very interested in polishing the pumps with the tea towel he always had thrown over his shoulder and which were already spotless.

'Connor?'

'It's probably none of my business,' he said, clearly trying not to make a thing of it. 'And she hasn't said anything specific, but . . .'

'But?'

'I can tell there's something going on with her,' he sighed, sounding sad. 'You're her best friend, I assumed you'd know.'

I felt a prickle of unease creep across the back of my neck because, headache aside, from what I'd been able to work out, she was on cloud nine and looking forward to moving in with Jeremy. However, Connor's look of concern suggested otherwise.

'When have you spoken to her long enough to have got this feeling?' I asked, because as far as I was aware Rachel hadn't seen Connor since the ghyll scrambling debacle and she'd been too busy nursing me to have a deep and meaningful with him then.

'She's been here a few evenings over the last couple of weeks,' Connor told me, making my stomach drop. 'Didn't you know?'

'No.' I swallowed.

'Didn't you miss her at the cottage?' he asked, sounding surprised. 'Or do you all do your own thing in the evenings?'

'Yeah,' I said, not entirely truthfully. 'We tend to do our own thing after supper.'

The thing I had assumed Rachel had been doing was spending hours on the side of the road talking to Jeremy, but what she'd actually been doing, for some of that time at least, was chatting to Connor in the pub. It was a bit of a shock and one which elicited mixed emotions.

'Has she been glued to her phone when she's been here?' I asked, trying to get a clearer picture of what was really going on.

'I've never seen her with it,' Connor said, shocking me further. 'She comes in and has a drink. Then we chat for a bit and she heads off again.'

'That sounds like what I'd expect every customer to do,' I pointed out. 'What is it about Rachel's visits that makes you think there's something wrong?'

Apart from not telling her best friend about them, I thought, but didn't say.

'Call it my landlord's sixth sense,' Connor said with a wry smile. 'You kind of get a feel for these things. You, for example—' he started to say.

'Never mind me,' I said, holding up a hand to stop him. 'I'm just here for a glass of Coke and a seafood sandwich.'

'In that case,' he laughed, 'grab yourself a table and I'll bring it over.'

'Thanks.'

I made myself comfortable and turned my phone on. It had been ages since I'd been in touch with Tori so I fired off a message to apologise and ask how she was adapting to life back home. I felt bad that Rachel and I had all but abandoned her since we'd arrived in Lakeside and moved into the cottage, even though she had told us that she was happy for us to do exactly that.

'This looks great,' I said as Connor carried over my lunch. 'Thank you.'

'You're welcome.' He smiled, then nodded at my phone as it pinged with an incoming message. 'Don't spend the whole time on that thing. You're on holiday, remember?'

He was right. I was on holiday, but a holiday with a mission which had gone completely awry since Rachel had told me about Jeremy's invitation for her to move in with him. Was I really going to set my dream aside because of that? For Rachel's sake, I most likely was, and it would doubtless be something else I would end up resenting Jeremy for.

I took a bite of the delicious sandwich and unlocked my phone again. Along with a flurry of emails, there was a message from Tori and it turned out it was just me who hadn't been in touch, because Rachel had apparently been messaging her every few days.

Our ditzy friend admitted she wasn't much further forward with her New Life Plan but she had worked out a few things about her life – she didn't specify what – and was confident that she'd get into her stride soon. I kept my return message upbeat and breezy and when she asked how I was doing, I didn't mention that Rachel had said Alex was falling for me or that I'd discovered there was something mysteriously amiss with her.

I later left the pub having placed an order for metres of cotton

fabric to be delivered to the cottage thanks to an unexpected word of mouth dress commission – which had unhelpfully ended up in my spam folder and which meant it was now a rush order – and thinking I needed to get my getaway back on track.

I might not need to further consider setting up my own business, not in the immediate future anyway, but I did need to make the dress in double quick time *and* find out what was going on with my best friend. I also needed to keep a closer eye on my relationship with Alex and make sure it didn't shift any further out of the friend zone.

'Here she is!' Rachel called out when I arrived back at the cottage.

So much for making a discreet entrance and sloping off for a nap.

'Where have you been?' she practically demanded.

'To the pub for lunch,' I told her, thinking she looked and sounded so much like her usual self that Connor's landlord's intuition must have been off. 'I didn't realise we had to account for our comings and goings,' I added with emphasis, but she didn't bite.

'Look what I've found for us to do tomorrow.' She beamed, pulling me into the kitchen the second I had slipped my plimsolls off. 'I've no idea if I'll be any good at it, but it should be a laugh. I've booked each of us a place for the whole day.'

Knowing that she'd booked the three of us to do something together made me feel thankful for the unexpected dress order. At least I wouldn't have to lie to get out of spending time with Alex. Whether Rachel had been right about his changing feelings for me or not, I didn't think it would do any harm for us to spend a few more hours apart.

'Oh, Rach,' I therefore said. 'I'm really sorry, but I can't do anything tomorrow.'

'What?' she said, looking at me with such dismay I was almost tempted to change my plan. 'Why not?'

'Has Rachel told you we're going to be treading the boards tomorrow?' Alex asked as he came out of his room. 'It's not my thing at all, but if you were willing to throw yourself down a waterfall for me, then I suppose the least I can do is recite a few lines in the dry.'

'I was most definitely not willing,' I reminded him and he grinned.

I looked away.

'What do you mean you can't do it?' Rachel asked, tugging at my sleeve.

'I checked my emails while I was at the pub,' I told her, 'and there was an order for a dress, complete with all the measurements I need, stuck in my spam folder. I've got a parcel of fabric coming first thing and then I'll need to make it and get it sent off as quickly as possible to make up for the lost time.'

'No way,' Rachel pleaded. 'Just tell them you're on holiday and can't do it.'

'I can't,' I said. 'I've already confirmed and I can't go back on my word.'

'Of course, you can't,' Alex said kindly. 'You have a reputation to build and if the clothing line is going to become the main part of what you do, then you want to see as many people walking about in your garments as possible, don't you?'

'Exactly,' I said, grateful for his support.

'I didn't realise building a reputation was such a priority right now.' Rachel frowned. 'Surely you're going to be

too busy settling into your new job to seriously think about more sewing?'

'Well,' I said. 'I'm not settling into my new job right now, am I? And I have promised to get this dress made and delivered within the next few days. It's for a wedding.'

Rachel still didn't look impressed. 'But guests have outfits arranged months in advance of a wedding,' she said, wrinkling her nose.

'I know, but this person has changed their mind about what they've already picked out,' I explained. 'And they'd seen the first dress I made because they're a friend of the person I made it for, so they know my design is just what they're after.'

'Oh, well,' Rachel sighed. 'I suppose if it's for a wedding then you really can't back out, can you?'

'And you never know,' said Alex, 'if the wedding photos get shared online, then you might get even more business from it as a result.'

'That's true,' I said.

If he was right, and I did get more commissions on the back of it, then I was going to be working every hour because there was no way I'd turn them down.

'If I start early in the morning, as soon as the fabric arrives,' I told Rachel who still looked upset, 'I could have it ready to post first thing the next day and then I'll be back on the holiday track.'

'I suppose,' she sighed.

'So,' I said. 'What exactly are you two going to be doing tomorrow?'

She picked up a leaflet and a printed sheet and handed both to me. 'I bumped into this woman while I was walking around the lake,' she explained, some of her former enthusiasm returning.

'We got chatting and I told her we were here on the *Hope Falls* journey of discovery and she told me that she's a drama teacher and a huge fan of the book and that she's running some themed workshops over the summer, based on it.'

The leaflet featured the Little Lakeside Theatre which was located just a couple of miles away from the cottage. We had considered watching a performance there during our stay, but the opportunity to take part in any workshops had never come up.

'We're going to read through some of the book and compare the passages to how they were adapted for the film, then read aloud the scenes as if we're acting them out in a pre-filming read through,' Rachel said excitedly, properly back up to speed.

'A table read,' Alex knowledgeably interjected.

'And then she'll cast us in the roles and we get to act them out on stage in costume.'

'Oh my god,' I breathed, looking back to the sheet.

It sounded amazing. The ultimate book-based holiday experience and exactly the sort of thing I would have loved to do, but I couldn't back out of making the dress now.

'And the best part is . . .' Alex encouraged Rachel to carry on.

'Oh, yes,' she squeaked, 'I almost forgot. There are actual props from the film for us to use at the theatre. I don't know what they are yet but there's every possibility that by this time tomorrow, I might well have sat in another of the chairs that the women curled up in to make one of those all-important life-changing decisions.'

'Wow.' I smiled, feeling jealous as hell. 'That's going to be amazing.'

I could have done with more time doing exactly the same thing myself.

Chapter 17

Rather than wait for the arrival of the main dress fabric the next morning, I made a start on planning the panels that evening and had made good progress while Rachel and Alex chatted away about their itinerary for the following day. In fact, I was so organised by bedtime, having tacked the pieces together using the patchwork material I already had, I thought that if I ended up completing the dress sooner than expected, then I would be able to use Rachel's absence to finish her surprise. I was very much looking forward to presenting it to her before the end of our holiday, which her Mum had given me her blessing to do.

'Hey, Alex,' I said, purposefully slipping out to the veranda the second I heard Rachel singing in the shower early the next morning.

'Hey,' he said, looking up from the book he was reading and taking off a pair of dark framed glasses which my traitorous heart would have very much liked him to keep on. 'How's it going? Do you need me to try something on to check the fit?'

I rolled my eyes. 'Best not,' I said. 'I don't think your broad frame would do much for my seam allowance.'

Cue more blushing.

'Fair enough.' He smiled.

'What are you reading?' I asked, as if I couldn't guess.

He held up Gracie's tatty *Hope Falls* paperback. It was a wonderfully well-worn copy, complete with cracked spine and more than its share of creased pages.

'Just as I suspected.' I smiled. 'It couldn't possibly have been anything else, could it?'

'I just wanted to run through a few lines,' he explained, 'and it felt fitting to read from Gracie's copy today. As you've seen, mine's in better condition.'

'Which one will you take with you today?' I asked.

'Mine,' he immediately said. 'I couldn't risk anything happening to this.'

'Would Gracie have been keen to take part in the workshop?'

'Oh, yes,' he nodded, with a wry smile. 'She would have absolutely loved it. She was quite the drama queen herself.'

'And which role do you fancy yourself in?' I asked.

'I'm going to try for Laurie,' he said, with another smile. 'Assuming the wig fits.'

'You'll make a great Laurie,' I told him, thinking of their matching his and hers fresh starts and just about managing to keep a straight face. 'And I wish I was going to be there to see you rise to the challenge.'

'Me too,' he said, looking deep into my eyes and I realised I had allowed us to stray into dangerous territory again. Given that just the day before, I had been committed to keeping my distance, this sort of thing was most definitely not allowed. 'But this commission is important for you,' he added. 'I get that.'

'It is.' I swallowed.

Mindful of Rachel's four-minute shower rule, I dismissed the banter and headed for what it was I had really come out to say.

'I've actually disturbed you because I wanted to ask you a favour,' I said, sitting in the rattan chair opposite the sofa he was stretched out on.

'Oh,' he said, putting the book and glasses down properly.

'It's about the other night on the lake.'

'That was such a great night,' he said, his voice as thick as honey and a faraway look in his eyes.

'It was,' I sighed, also thinking back to the enthralling spectacle. 'It was perfect and again, thank you so much for arranging it.'

'You want to go again?' he asked hopefully, his gaze coming back into focus. 'I really want to row Rachel out there at some point, so I hope you'll come along too.'

The thought of a repeat performance was most appealing and perfectly proper if it was going to be the three of us.

'Yes,' I said, 'that would be wonderful. We shouldn't waste the opportunity to see it again, should we?'

'No,' he agreed. 'We shouldn't. So, was that what you wanted to ask me about?' he quizzed, his eyebrows raised.

'No,' I said, full of frustration that I'd got side-tracked yet again. 'No,' I repeated. 'It wasn't that. It was actually to do with what I said to you' – I lowered my voice and leaned in closer – 'about Rachel's partner, Jeremy.'

'Okay,'

'You remember what I said about him being—'

'A total dick.'

'Yes.'

'What about it?'

'I just wanted to ask you not to say anything to Rachel about any of that.'

'What?' He frowned, sitting back.

'I'd rather you didn't mention anything we'd said about him while we were out on the lake,' I expanded.

Alex's face took on an appearance I hadn't seen it wear before. It was a mixture of bewilderment, disappointment and anger. I couldn't really accept that it could contort into any of those expressions.

'I can't believe you thought that I would,' he frowned, making me feel awful. 'Why on earth would you think that I would even bring it up, let alone repeat it verbatim?'

'I just wanted to be certain that you understand . . .'

'Of course, I understand,' he said, sounding hurt. 'What you said was shared in confidence. I'm not a total imbecile.'

'I didn't mean to offend you,' I said, as my hands started to sweat. 'It's just that there's something more going on with Rachel and until I work out . . .'

'It's fine,' he said, dismissing my bungled explanation, but it clearly wasn't. 'I get it.'

'I only meant . . .'

'I know what you meant,' he shot back. 'You don't know me particularly well and you wanted to make sure I wouldn't blab.'

'No,' I said. 'That's not how I meant it. It's not that at all.' I choked. 'How could it be after everything we've shared during these last couple of weeks?'

'I don't know,' he said, sounding more sad than cross which in turn made me feel even worse. 'Maybe I've been reading things wrong between us, Em.'

'Hey, Alex!' Rachel called from the house. 'Are you all set? I'm almost ready.'

'Coming now!' he called back, standing up and pocketing the glasses and reverently picking up the book. 'I'll see you later.'

I kissed Rachel on the cheek at the door and the two of them went off to enjoy what I knew would be a truly memorable experience. At least, I hoped it would be. I hoped I hadn't blighted it for Alex. One thing I was certain of, given how keen he was to get away, was that I had sent him off thinking that I didn't know him at all and, as a result, had probably got him thinking that he didn't know me either.

Once the fabric – which I waited at the roadside for in case the delivery driver didn't fancy the walk down to the cottage and dumped it on the damp verge instead – was safely delivered, I focused on making up the dress as quickly, but as professionally as possible and having wrapped it ready to send, I set about completing Rachel's after a very late lunch.

As the weather was mild, the earlier gusty wind had dropped and I was in no danger of her catching me at work, I set myself up to pin and stitch outside until I needed to use the sewing machine. The dress was perfect and I knew my friend would be a vision wearing it.

'Beautiful,' I sighed, holding it up before I headed back into the cottage to turn the individual pieces into one complete garment. 'Quite beautiful.'

As the day wore on and I continued to stitch and sew, completely immersed, the full force of my passion for my craft again hit me with the impact of a ten-tonne truck. I was more than competent, my skills were exemplary and the finished results,

faultless. I didn't think I was being arrogant in thinking that, because the dress I was holding was proof that I deserved each and every one of those accolades.

Ever since Rachel had told me that she was considering moving in with Jeremy and that it was a relief to know that I had a job waiting to pay a monthly salary into my bank, I had done everything in my power to convince myself that taking it was the right thing to do. The *only* thing to do if I didn't want her assuming I had turned it down to stop her moving on with her life because I didn't like her boyfriend.

And for a while, that had been enough for me to set my dreams aside and confine sewing to the hobby compartment she had also wedged it into, but as I considered the two completed dresses, I knew it wasn't going to work in the long term. My star was genuinely rising and there was increased interest in my work and that had to be too good an opportunity to let pass by, hadn't it?

Towards the end of the afternoon, I walked down to the post office and, as Rachel and Alex still weren't home by the time I arrived back, I completed my fern skirt which was a verdant vision. The pair had talked of having dinner with the other workshop participants if the day went well so, to make myself feel better about missing out on such a wonderful experience, I slipped on the skirt and ate my supper sitting next to the lake.

The skirt had turned out even better than I hoped. I loved the way the weight of it swished around my legs as I walked and I knew I would certainly be adding more of them to my reper-toire. I later drifted off to sleep with my current favourite fantasy, which involved potential branding and website ideas, whirring around my head. However, there was a new twist to my dream

and it involved Alex. I imagined myself asking him to design my branding for my empire which I, of course, had named Passion for Patchwork. It was a wholly satisfying way to nod off.

'Let's see this dress then,' Rachel yawned late the next morning, when she joined me on the veranda.

For a moment I thought she'd somehow worked out that I was making one for her, but then realised she was talking about the wedding outfit.

'You can't,' I told her. 'I've already put it in the post.'

'Crikey,' she said, sounding impressed. 'You must have got a wriggle on. That has to be your speediest make yet.'

'It was,' I agreed, still thinking about how I was going to explain that I might well be making them even faster once Passion for Patchwork was up and running. 'Now come on,' I added, knowing it all needed further thought and shouldn't be rushed, 'I want to hear all about how you got on at the theatre.'

She flopped down on the sofa and let out a long breath. 'Oh, Em,' she said. 'It was amazing. I really did feel like Heather up on that stage.'

I smiled to myself as I again imagined Alex as Laurie.

'I wish you'd been there.'

'I wish I'd been there, too.' I swallowed. 'What were the props?'

By the time she'd finished telling me, I wished I'd never asked.

'I've already signed up to do it again,' she said excitedly.

'Before we go home?'

'Sadly not,' she said. 'But Sophie, that's the woman who ran the workshop, gave me a heads up about another session happening in November and I've signed you, me and Tori up for that.'

'Oh, that's great!' I said, feeling slightly better. 'Thank you.'

'Consider it an early Christmas present.' She winked. 'We'll come up for the whole weekend and stay at an Airbnb or something.'

'Will that mean keeping hold of the car?'

'We'll decide about that once Tori's sorted,' she laughed. 'You never know, she might get to keep the Range Rover, after all.'

She stood up again and stretched out her back and I wondered if Jeremy would allow her out of his sight again so soon. At least knowing that she'd booked the workshop already meant she hadn't spent time worrying about what he would think of the idea.

'I need coffee,' she said.

'What about Alex?'

'I don't know,' she said, looking through the window. 'I'll ask him when he gets up.'

'No,' I giggled. 'I meant, has he signed up for the workshop, too?'

'Oh,' she laughed. 'No, but he's going to do it today. He wasn't going to, but then when we stopped at the pub and told Connor about it, Alex said he'd enjoyed it in spite of the fact that he'd been the only bloke there and Connor said he'd go with him next time to balance the numbers, so they'll both be treading the boards.'

I would look forward to seeing that.

'Sophie will be thrilled,' Rachel said happily. 'She told us the workshops often lacked a male perspective.'

'They'll be extra popular then.'

'Oh,' she said, flopping back down and abandoning her desire for caffeine. 'I can't believe I almost forgot to tell you!'

'Forgot to tell me what?'

'We're all set for a great night out tomorrow.' She beamed. 'It won't be the usual Friday night drinks with Tori, but it's going to be brilliant nonetheless.'

'It is?'

'Yep,' she explained. 'Connor has a book-lovers' coach tour booked in for supper so he's doing the quiz *and*,' she said, 'you'll love this, Em.' Here she paused for dramatic effect and I held my breath. 'He's also organising a soundtrack karaoke and cosplay competition.'

I couldn't stop a groan escaping. The quiz and cosplay I was totally up for, but not the karaoke.

'You're going to sing, aren't you?' I grimaced, cradling my head at the thought.

'Of course, I am,' she said, slapping my leg a little too hard in her excitement. 'When have I ever let not being able to hold a note stop me singing along to the soundtrack? And this time,' she added as if it made the unappealing prospect more palatable, 'I'll have a microphone.'

That was what I was afraid of.

Chapter 18

I had, meanly I know, hoped that Rachel's theatrical exertions at the drama workshop might have impacted on her voice to such an extent that it would stop her singing by the time Saturday dawned, but my hopes were dashed when I woke to her crooning – if you could call it that – in the cottage kitchen.

She never sounded quite so bad when she was in the shower because the din was muffled by a door, a shower screen and running water, but unfiltered it was almost painful. Think Bridget Jones at the office Christmas party combined with nails on a blackboard and you've almost got the gist. And what made it worse, or perhaps better depending on your disposition and how many drinks you'd downed, was that she didn't give a flying fig.

I did, however, and I hastily squashed my pillow over my ears determined to drown her out for at least a few more hours.

'I think I'm getting better,' she said, bounding in, wrenching the pillow away and shoving a mug of hot coffee under my nose. 'Come on,' she said, 'we've got chores to do and then we need to start getting ready.'

It was eight o'clock in the morning.

'Why don't you go and rouse Alex,' I suggested, 'and then come back to me?'

'I can't,' she told me as she set the coffee down on the nightstand. 'Because he's already gone out. He left about seven after he'd cleaned his room and watered all the pots on the veranda, but said he'd be back in time for tonight.'

'Where's he gone?' I asked, pushing myself up on my elbows.

'I don't know,' she said, flouncing out jauntily, 'I'm not his keeper.'

I collapsed back down and pulled the duvet over my head, shutting Rachel's reedy notes out again and closing my eyes. Alex and I had barely spoken since I'd upset him the morning before and I couldn't deny, I didn't mind that he'd gone out for the day because I had no idea how to make amends. I'd already tried to apologise but I don't think he'd accepted it and I didn't know what else I could do.

'Come on!' Rachel called. 'Drink that coffee and get your butt in gear. We've got makeovers to attend to.'

'I really don't mind driving us in,' I listened to Alex say for the hundredth time early that evening while I was putting the finishing touches to my outfit in the bedroom.

He'd been back a while and we'd exchanged a few stilted words, but nothing beyond pleasantries.

'I hear you,' Rachel responded, also on a loop. 'But if you do, you won't be able to have a drink and Connor has promised some truly killer themed cocktails tonight, so as the weather's all right, we might as well walk and he's arranged for us to have a lift back.'

I heard Alex sigh, even though I wasn't in the same room.

'And you're going to walk all the way there in those heels, are

you?' he rather sceptically asked. 'I might as well take my car and leave it there.'

That sounded good to me.

'Of course, I'm not walking in these,' Rachel tutted. 'I'm going to go in my trainers and change into the heels when we arrive. I appreciate the offer of the car, but there's limited parking in the village and Em and I have been indoors all day, so we could do with the fresh air.'

She had a point.

Our outfits were based on those featured in one of the night out scenes in the film and I was pleased we'd decided to bring them with us. Not that packing them was ever really in question. Even if Connor hadn't been putting on an event, we still would have worn them at some point, even if only to curl up in the window seat and read the book or sit on the sofa and watch the film.

Rachel was wearing a red sleeveless satin top with plunging neckline (think Farrah Fawcett) and mid-length shorts with a tie waist which showed off her tanned legs and I was dressed in a soft pink satin cami, which made the most of my paler complexion, and blue jeans. I had made the silk tops in the style of those in the film and loved the way mine draped and felt cool against my skin. Teamed with three necklaces of different lengths, it was perfect, but I wasn't sure about not wearing a bra.

'You have great boobs,' Rachel had insisted when we were getting dressed, 'and you'll ruin the look if you wear a bra because you'll see the straps.'

Once she'd gone out, I turned this way and that in front of the mirror and then pulled the top back over my head. It was no

good. I'd never relax if I was worrying about my nipples being on display all night. I had a gorgeous lace triangle bra from La Redoute which would make on show straps look perfectly pretty and more importantly, make me feel comfortable.

'Rach!' I screeched as she came bowling back into the bedroom, leaving my near nakedness exposed to the entire cottage.

'Sorry,' she said, quickly closing the door. 'I just came to see what's taking you so long.'

'I'm almost done,' I said, slipping the bra on.

'Alex nearly got a look at the top to marry up with his view of the bottom then, didn't he?' she giggled.

'Not funny,' I hissed. 'I'm going to wear this.'

I knew she wasn't wearing anything under her top and I had no issue with that at all, but the no bra rule wasn't for me.

'Oh, that's cute,' Rachel said, cocking her head to one side. 'That works and I know you'll feel better wearing it. And you're going to faint when you see what Alex is wearing,' she added in a mischievous whisper.

I gave her a look and pulled the silk top over my head, then she teased the curls she'd spent ages styling for me back into place. She kissed my cheek and we looked in the mirror, gauging how we appeared standing side by side.

'I think you're definitely going to pull tonight,' she giggled again.

'I think you're definitely going to pull tonight,' I said straight back and we both laughed.

It was something we had been saying since the very first Friday night drinks session getting on for a decade ago. She wrapped her arms around my waist and rested her head on my shoulder.

'Sometimes,' she said dreamily, 'I still can't believe we're actually here, can you?'

'I know,' I said, blinking hard to rid myself of the sudden rush of tears which could easily threaten my mascara and liner. 'It's amazing, isn't it?'

She nodded and blinked too.

'Come on then,' I said. 'Let's go before Connor runs out of those killer cocktails you've been banging on about all day.'

Alex was already waiting by the open cottage door when we came out of the bedroom and Rachel was right, I did almost pass out when I got my first glimpse of him. I faffed about, picking up our jackets and checking our bags until I recovered.

'You okay, Alex?' Rachel asked, pulling my attention back towards him and finding he was looking at me.

'Yeah,' he said, closing his mouth and opening it again. 'Great.'

Rachel gave me a nudge.

'You two look amazing.' He swallowed. 'For a second there I thought the real Heather and Rose had just walked out of the bedroom.'

'You didn't say that when you saw me earlier,' Rachel teased him and I nudged her back.

'Well,' he blushed, 'it was seeing the pair of you together that really did it.'

'Thank you, Alex,' I said, not wanting to give Rachel further opportunity to rib him, especially when I was so keen for us to fall back into step. 'You look great, too.'

'Thanks,' he said, blushing deeper. 'But just to be clear,' he qualified, 'I would never in real life wear my shirt unbuttoned this low.'

I felt my own face flame as I thought that was a shame, about

the shirt anyway, because the extra open buttons gave the world a glimpse of the broad, firm chest that I had only previously guessed at when he had rowed me across the lake. Coupled with his toned arms, it made for quite a tantalising tableau.

'Shame.' Rachel winked, embarrassingly echoing my thoughts. 'Because you look hot. Doesn't he, Em?'

'You're incorrigible,' I tutted, rolling my eyes.

'What?' she objected. 'I'm simply stating a fact.'

'Well,' said Alex. 'I think we all look hot and the sooner we get to the pub, the better.'

'Amen to that,' I agreed, digging Rachel in the ribs again and following Alex out of the door. 'But just for the record, Alex, you really do look great.'

The pub was heaving by the time we arrived and lots of people were wearing outfits similar to ours. There were a few floaty, floral frocks too, though, and I wondered if *Hope Falls* had been responsible for inspiring me in ways I hadn't really considered before.

'At least there's no chance of me losing you two,' said Alex, his voice close to my ear as Rachel clung to my arm while she slipped into her heels.

I had decided not to bother with mine. I was most likely going to be spending most of the evening on my feet, so my faithful plimsolls would comfortably suffice.

'Very funny,' I said, leaning back so he could hear me and almost falling into him as a result.

'I wasn't being funny,' he said, putting his hand on the small of my back to steady me. 'No one else in here is wearing the look quite like you two.'

His warm palm felt reassuring and my heart thumped hard in response to the feel of it through the thin fabric of my top. I twisted around to check his expression and, finding he was genuinely in earnest, experienced a rush of relief surge through me because it felt like we really were back on an even keel again.

'I mean it,' he said, his warm, woody aftershave caressing my senses and making me feel like I'd already drunk a cocktail or three.

What was wrong with me?

'That's because Em made the tops,' Rachel said, straightening back up and smoothing hers down. 'And she spared no expense on the fabric.'

I didn't point out that I'd packed her top in the case with mine so it wouldn't be irreparably creased by the time we arrived at the cottage.

'I should have known.' Alex smiled, his kind brown eyes fixed on mine.

In that moment, my awareness of him cranked up yet another notch and I realised I was going to need to keep a check on the number of cocktails I downed, because it wouldn't take many to completely send my inhibitions and reservations packing.

'I never skimp where fabric is concerned,' I said throatily and then burst out laughing because it had to be the most unseductive few words I had ever uttered. 'I can't believe I just said that.'

'Me neither,' Rachel guffawed. 'I take back what I said about you pulling tonight. There's no hope.'

'Well, I can believe it,' Alex said, then hastily added, 'Not that you won't pull, but about the fabrics. I can't imagine you'd ever skimp on material, Em because it's something you feel so passionate about.'

'That's very noble of you, Alex,' said Rachel, before I could respond. 'At least we know she's passionate about something.'

I was suddenly feeling passionate about a whole lot more than swatches, bolts and fat quarters. I put it down to the outfit. I must have been directly channelling carefree Rose rather than more cautious where romance was concerned Heather.

'Hey!' Connor called from behind the packed bar, thankfully coming to my rescue before I made even more of a twit of myself. 'I was beginning to wonder where you three had gone to. I don't suppose any of you know how to pull a pint or mix a cocktail, do you? One of my bar team has called in sick.'

Alex and I both shook our heads, but Rachel keenly hopped around the counter and up behind the bar.

'I know how to pull a pint,' she said, looking along the length of the pumps. 'Or at least, I used to know. One of my first jobs was working in a bar.'

'My saviour,' said Connor, kissing her cheek and making my eyebrows shoot up.

'Don't get too excited yet,' I warned him. 'Rachel's time pulling pints is a very long way behind her.'

'It's like riding a bike,' he told me, with a grin. 'You never forget.'

Alex and I left him running through everything Rachel was going to need to know and bagged ourselves the last available booth which, looking around, I could see was also pretty much the last available seat anywhere.

'This is amazing,' Alex said, raising his voice above the level of excited chat as everyone exchanged bookshop and cinema memories and resultant real-life related anecdotes.

'It is,' I agreed, also looking around and listening in.

Our words dried up then and I had to resist the urge to turn on my phone and scroll rather than acknowledge that things felt a little awkward.

'Can I just say again,' I quickly plucked up the courage to say before I could change my mind, 'that I'm truly sorry for what I said before you and Rachel went out yesterday?'

'No,' Alex vehemently said, shaking his head and for an awful moment making me think that I'd kicked the row back off again. 'You can't.'

'But . . .'

'You can't say it because you've got nothing to apologise for,' he said firmly. 'I shouldn't have reacted the way I did. I should have known that you were just trying to ensure that I wasn't going to let anything slip and make things difficult between you and Rachel. I can understand where you were coming from now.'

I wilted with relief and wondered what, if anything, had prompted the change of heart.

'That was exactly what I was trying to do,' I said, feeling thankful that he now understood. 'I'm so desperate to keep her close because I think she's really going to need me, and Tori, before too long.'

'I agree.' Alex nodded.

'That's also why I've stopped saying anything to her about Jeremy,' I further said. 'I don't want to say or do anything which will push her further into his grasp and pull her out of our friendship.'

'I get that,' he said.

'Did she say anything about him yesterday?' I asked, checking she was still behind the bar.

Alex looked too. She was lining up glasses and looked like she didn't have a care in the world. It was a joy to see because she hadn't looked like that all too often of late. Not even when we were at the cottage. She'd successfully shrugged off the end of term exhaustion, but taking in her carefree expression then, I realised that something else had snuck in and replaced it.

'During one of the improv sessions, we fell to talking about relationships,' Alex told me, 'and pretty much everything she said backed up your concerns.'

I groaned in response.

'But don't fret,' he said, before I could ask for details. 'With so many friends in her corner, and I count myself as one of them now, she's going to be fine. No harm's going to come to her when we've all got her back.'

That sounded like fighting talk to me and I loved it. Tori and I might not have so far been able to make an effective frontline assault, but knowing that we now had Alex on the team and that we were all alert in the wings and primed for action was reassuring. When the time inevitably came, I knew we'd be able to count on Connor, too.

'Cocktails!' Rachel excitedly announced, as she arrived at our table with a packed tray.

'These can't all be for us?' I gawped as she began to line them up.

'They are,' she said. 'Connor gave me a quick crash course and I've made you one of each.' Which added up to four for Alex and four for me. 'But I have made them a little stronger than he suggested because I don't know when I'll be able to get back to you.'

'You're not joining us?' I frowned, taking in the queue at the bar.

'Connor needs me.' She smiled as she walked away. 'But I'll stop serving when the singing starts.'

'Heaven help us,' Alex and I said together, then collapsed into giggles.

'You know then?' I asked.

'Of course, I know,' he said, pushing the first cocktail in the line towards me. 'Your bathroom wall backs on to my bedroom. I've heard her murdering the film soundtrack in there more times than I care to mention.'

'Come on then,' I laughed again, as I raised my glass and tinkled it against his. 'We better get these down us to help dull the pain.'

We knocked back the first one almost without it touching the sides.

'There was definitely gin in that,' Alex said appraisingly, smacking his lips.

'And some sort of soft fruit?' I suggested. 'Strawberry, perhaps?'

'And mint,' he finished up. 'Next!'

The next one was a classic Negroni and within a couple of minutes of finishing it, I knew Rachel had made it more than double strength.

'I think,' Alex lazily smiled, 'that we should have something to eat before sampling the rest, don't you?'

'Definitely.' I nodded, feeling the full strength of the alcoholic hit. 'I think food would be a very good idea.'

We each polished off a classic burger and fries as also featured in the book and Rachel joined us in time for pudding. The black forest chocolate mousse was to die for but it didn't have much impact on soaking up all the alcohol units we had downed in the

rest of the cocktails. Rachel was pleasantly merry, but Alex and I had tipped over the edge of that as our later vociferous objection to coming third in the quiz proved.

'I need air,' I said, slipping out of the booth, once our answers had been counted again and our third place conclusively confirmed.

'And I need to come with you,' said Alex, sliding along the seat.

'No, no,' I said, grabbing his arm. 'You stay here and keep our seats because I don't think I can stand for the rest of the night or hoist myself up on one of those stools if we lose the booth.'

'Hey,' Alex laughed. 'That rhymes.'

'I know,' I giggled, stumbling but only very slightly.

'I'm definitely coming with you,' Alex laughed again.

'You're such a gent,' I said, familiarly slipping my arm through his. 'Just going to get some air!' I yelled to Rachel, but I'm not sure she heard me.

The fresh air made me feel more awake, but no less tipsy. Although I couldn't have been that gone, because I had sense enough to realise that I didn't have the added stress of trying to walk along the uneven road in heels.

'Come on,' I said to Alex, pulling him along with me.

'Where are we going?'

'No idea.'

We stopped at the gated entrance of the field which signified the end of the tiny village of Lakeside and where the more rugged landscape once again took over.

'I think it's the Perseid peak tonight,' Alex said, leaning on the gate and tipping his head back to look at the stars.

'That sounds a bit rude,' I giggled.

My sober self would have cringed.

'There, look!' he said, pointing to the sky, but by the time I'd spun around, I'd missed the starry spectacle.

'Do you think we should lay down?' I suggested, looking about us for a suitable spot.

'Absolutely not,' he said. 'It's way too damp and ... there ... look. Another one.'

I missed that one too. Alex stopped looking up and looked at me instead.

'If you keep looking at me,' he laughed, as he realised I was staring, 'you're going to miss everything.'

I carried on gazing, but not at the constellations. In that moment, *he* felt like everything and I didn't think it was just Rachel's fully loaded cocktails which were making me believe that. I stepped in front of him, leaning in between his legs which he'd positioned slightly apart to balance himself while he was looking up.

'What are you doing?' he asked, his Adam's apple dipping as he swallowed, his eyes taking the whole of me in.

'I'm not sure,' I said softly.

'In that case,' he said, the words catching in his throat as I inched closer, 'you definitely shouldn't do it. Em ...'

'Don't say anything,' I begged as the silk of my top pressed against his chest and my hips pushed against his.

We were so close I could feel his breath and his heart beating as fast as mine as the heat from his body met the bare skin of my chest and arms. He rested his hands lightly on my waist to try and ease me away but I resisted.

'If you really don't know what you're doing,' he began, 'then you really shouldn't be ...'

'It's all right,' I brazenly said, brushing my lips lightly against

the side of his neck and feathering his tanned skin with soft, butterfly kisses. 'I'm getting surer with every second.'

He let out a sultry moan and his hands held my waist more firmly, pulling me closer and making my own breath catch. Desire pulsed through me as a warm and longing ache began to build. I drew away for the briefest moment to reposition myself and he pulled me straight back. Our eyes locked and then my mouth was on his.

His lips were soft and full and the kiss, which was tentative to begin with, quickly intensified as I dipped my tongue into his mouth and he groaned again. He spun me around so my back was against the gate and then his mouth was on my collarbone and throat as he leaned into me.

'Don't stop,' I begged, pulling him closer. 'Don't stop.'

With his eyes on mine again and his chest rapidly rising and falling, he slipped his hand under the silk of my top. He brushed the lacy cup of my bra, making me gasp and my nipples harden. His touch was tantalisingly light and it fuelled my desire. I pushed myself into him feeling his want match mine.

'Kiss me again,' I breathed and he did.

Harder that time and the strength of his caress matched it. I was crazy with desire, arching against him as his mouth tracked lower.

'Oh, Alex.'

A sudden shaft of light illuminated the road back towards the village and we sprang apart, chests heaving and sweat pooling.

'Fuck,' I groaned as the sound of heels met my ears.

'Em!' came Rachel's voice. 'Alex! Are you out here?'

'Yes!' I called back, albeit a little shakily. 'We're here.'

I couldn't look at Alex. I couldn't bear to see the desire I

couldn't quench in his eyes or worse, the regret that he had succumbed to my tipsy seduction.

'What are you doing all the way up here?' Rachel asked, when she finally reached us. 'It's freezing.'

I didn't think it was cold at all.

'Perseid reaches its peak tonight,' said Alex, pointing at the sky.

'Sounds a bit rude.' Rachel grinned and I burst out laughing. 'What?' She blinked.

'Nothing,' I said, linking her arm through mine.

'You haven't really come down here to avoid my singing, have you?' She pretended to pout.

'Of course not,' I said. 'I'm looking forward to it.'

'Come on then,' she said, pulling me back towards the pub. 'It's about to start.'

I caught Alex's hand and we walked along in a wobbly line.

'And I've put you two down for the duet,' she said. 'You're singing "Love Will Find a Way".'

'It bloody better,' Alex whispered, squeezing my fingers and I laughed again.

'What was that?' she asked.

'I was just saying,' he cleverly replied, 'that will be the perfect end to the day.'

Chapter 19

More of Rachel's double strength cocktails, coupled with a few hours' karaoke, did not make for a passionate end to the day and love, or perhaps more accurately lust, most definitely did not find a way.

It was a miracle that we even made it back to the cottage because the taxi driver Connor had booked didn't want to take us anywhere when he realised we were all a little worse for wear.

'No one's going to hurl, Tony,' Connor reassured him. 'They're not that far gone, but here are a couple of carrier bags just in case.'

Connor had been right, none of us did hurl but, lying in bed staring at the ceiling a few hours later, cursing the strength of the light peeping around the curtains and not at all impressed by the layer of fuzz coating my tongue, I thought I might then.

The rolling sensation in my stomach had little to do with the killer cocktail combo though. The nausea was almost entirely the result of guilt and regret, which was a wholly different sort of concoction.

I had shamelessly thrown myself at Alex and of course, given the amount he had also drunk, he had responded. It would have

taken a will of iron for him not to. Had he not been three sheets to the wind I knew he would have stepped away because he was a stand-up guy but he, like me, had been the wrong side of a few of the killer brew combos by then and both our inhibitions had been flattened in the alcoholic stampede.

Not that I was using that as an excuse or justification for my bad behaviour which had shamelessly continued in the pub after Rachel had dragged us back inside. A sultry rendition of 'Love Will Find a Way' followed by some hedonistic dirty dancing had cranked things between us up even further, but the drive back had tamped the flames down again.

The journey back to the cottage, with the car windows down and the chilly breeze stopping us from falling asleep, had gifted me with the sense to head straight to my own room rather than Alex's and I was relieved he hadn't questioned that. The last I'd seen of him before I closed the bedroom door, he was sensibly downing a pint of water in the kitchen.

As my head pounded, I released a long, drawn-out breath and wished I'd had the wherewithal to do the same.

'Are you dying?' came Rachel's muffled voice from her side of the room. 'Because I am.'

I didn't answer.

'Are you even there?' she croaked, shifting under her duvet. 'Or are you loved up and enjoying some pre-breakfast sex in the bed next door?'

'Of course, I'm here,' I mumbled. 'And I am dying, but I don't think from quite the same affliction as you.'

I rolled on to my side to face her and suppressed an unexpected smile.

'What?' She frowned.

'The Alice Cooper look suits you.'

'Shit,' she groaned. 'I didn't wash my make up off, did I?'

'Nope,' I said, feeling virtuous in that department at least. 'I told you to. I even offered to do it for you, but you wouldn't let me. You pretty much passed out as soon as your head hit the pillow.'

'Call yourself a friend,' she said, easing her head off the bed and sighing at the sight of the mascara-streaked pillowcase. 'I'll have to wash this quick. It's vintage Laura Ashley for crying out loud. You should have slapped a wipe over my face when I flaked out.'

'You're a big girl,' I told her. 'And besides, you were face down to begin with.'

'How's Alex this morning?' she asked, gingerly lowering her head back down.

'No idea,' I said lightly. 'I haven't been up yet. I can't imagine he's any more alive than we are though.'

But I was wrong about that. When I found the courage to get out of bed and the ground didn't sway beneath my bare feet, I found him at the cottage front door, pulling on his trainers.

He looked remarkably sprightly and I found myself hoping that it was the pint of pre-sleep water which was responsible for his chipper demeanour rather than my wanton behaviour and the implications of what he thought might end up happening between us as a result of it.

'Good morning.' He grinned.

'Hey.' I weakly waved.

'I've poured you and Rach a pint of water apiece, lined up some painkillers and there's tea in the pot,' he reeled off.

'Thank you.' I nodded. 'I think that's about all either of us can handle right now.'

'I thought it might be,' he laughed.

'I can't believe you're so Pollyanna though,' I said enviously, then added in case our embrace was the reason behind his chipper demeanour and knowing I needed to face it straightaway. 'Look Alex,' I sighed. 'About last night . . .'

'Wasn't it fantastic?' he happily reminisced after a moment's hesitation. 'Let's talk about it when I get back.'

'From where?' I frowned. 'Where are you going?'

'Just up to the road,' he told me. 'Connor promised he'd drop off some of his famous hangover helper breakfast rolls at eight.' He glanced over at the kitchen clock. 'So, I better get going. It's almost five to now. You'll manage one of those, won't you?'

'I daresay by the time you get back, I'll be capable of mainlining some protein and carbs.'

'What about Rachel?'

'I'm sure she will too.'

'Great,' he said, pulling open the door. 'I'll be back in a bit.'

I watched him jog up the path, the rolling sensation in my tummy fast turning into a tight knot.

'You're going to break his heart, aren't you?' came Rachel's voice behind me and I jumped.

I turned to find her standing in the doorway, *still* wearing last night's make-up, although not in any of the right places, and wrapped in the duvet from her bed.

'What are you talking about?' I sighed, peeling a false eyelash from her forehead before walking over to the kitchen and finding everything set out as Alex had said it was.

'I know I interrupted something when I came to find the two of you,' she said, her tone suggesting she wished she'd left us to it.

'Only our stargazing,' I lightly said back, handing her one of the glasses of water and two painkillers.

'Don't lie,' she tutted, downing both and handing the glass back again.

'I'm not.'

'Yes, you are.'

'We were watching the meteor shower,' I said, turning away and swilling her glass out before pouring the tea.

'Your top would not have got creased like that from watching the bloody stars,' she pointed out.

She'd got me there. It was pretty ruffled.

'Your necklaces were tangled too and your curls were definitely dishevelled,' she carried on in a sing-song voice. 'That sort of disarray only comes from close contact.'

I felt my traitorous cheeks flush.

'Skin to skin contact,' she sexily added.

'All right,' I said, putting up my hands.

'Ha!'

'I admit it, I did kiss him.'

'*You* kissed *him*?'

'Yes,' I confessed. 'It was definitely all me. Poor Alex didn't stand a chance.'

'Poor Alex my arse,' Rachel said crudely. 'I bet he wasn't thinking poor Alex or anything like it. I bet he couldn't believe his luck. Haven't I been saying . . .'

'Yes,' I loudly responded. 'But can you please stop?'

She looked as if I'd slapped her.

'Sorry,' I said, shaking my head and making it thump. 'I didn't mean to snap.'

'What's going on?' she asked, then immediately said, 'Oh god, you really are going to break his heart, aren't you? I was kidding before, but that's what you're going to do, isn't it?'

'That kiss was a mistake,' I sighed. 'One which I most definitely will not be making again and one,' I perhaps unfairly added, 'that I blame you and your triple strength bloody cocktails for.'

'They were double strength actually,' she corrected. 'And, for what it's worth, I don't think it was a mistake.'

'It was.'

'No,' she said, as if she knew my mind better than I did. 'It wasn't. You're so well suited. You're both creative, you have so many common interests and you look great together . . .'

'I get what you're saying,' I conceded, because I couldn't contradict her on any of those points, 'but I haven't come on this break with the intention of either starting a relationship or having a fling.'

'I appreciate that,' she carried on, 'but neither of us were expecting to share it with Alex either, were we? Not this Alex, anyway. Him being who he is has been a total game changer. You have to admit that.'

'I just haven't got the headspace for a relationship right now,' I told her. 'I've got other things on my mind and I've come here with the sole intention of making sense of them.'

'What things?'

'And I can't afford to get side-tracked,' I more calmly said, knowing I'd regret it if I blurted out what I had been considering just to stop her going on about Alex. 'We've already got a third of our time here behind us and I'm not about to go off-piste and waste what's left.'

Rachel looked shocked. 'Starting a relationship with Alex would not be a waste of anything,' she said crossly.

'You know I didn't mean it like that,' I tutted. 'I just need to keep focused and he would be . . . a distraction.'

'So, what exactly is it that you need to be so focused on?' she directly asked. 'I thought you'd made up your mind about the new job. Is it something else or are you still not sure about that?'

'It's not that,' I quietly told her. 'That's all settled.'

That was partly true. Thanks to my alone time in the cottage and the opportunity to completely immerse myself in my work and the resultant joy that sprang from it, I had suddenly settled on a decision. Just not the one she thought. What a moment to conclusively realise it!

I didn't know how I was going to convince her that I could manage on the financial front when she moved in with Jeremy, but I wasn't going to let that put me off making the leap. Perhaps I could work both jobs part-time and gradually increase the hours working on my business until it became my entire working week? That way, I'd calm Rachel's worries *and* have a safety net.

'Em?' Rachel said sharply. 'Are you listening?'

'Yes,' I said, coming to. 'Of course, I am.'

'Well, that's a relief,' she huffed. 'About the job, I mean, but it doesn't alter the fact that you're going to break Alex's heart, does it?'

'What?'

'You're going to break his heart and send him spiralling right back to where he was at the start of the holiday.'

'That's not fair,' I said indignantly.

This was exactly the sort of drama I had been wanting to avoid.

'And it's not true,' I carried on, but with less conviction than I would have liked. 'I'm putting the brakes on things before they get out of hand and I'm putting us firmly back on track. I want us to go back to being three friends enjoying their book-lovers' getaway, just like we'd always planned, with no strings and no

complications and long before anyone's heart is in danger of being damaged.'

'I think you might find it's too late for that,' she said as we heard Alex bounding back up the path and full of beans that I was still hoping our embrace wasn't responsible for. 'You've crossed a line, Em, and there's no going back now.'

She accepted the fully loaded breakfast roll Connor had so kindly supplied and then retreated back to bed.

'Is she really feeling that bad?' Alex asked once she'd closed the door. 'Or is she trying to give us some space?'

I had just picked my roll up, but his canny comment curbed my fledgling appetite and I put it down again. It was a shame because it had looked and smelled so delicious when he offered it to me.

'Aren't you going to eat that?' he asked, already tucking into his.

'In a minute,' I said, sitting back on the sofa. 'Perhaps. How was Connor?'

'Full of the joys.' Alex smiled. 'I think his theme nights are good for business.'

'They're certainly good for emptying out his optics,' I said, rubbing my temples.

'Are you still feeling rough?' He frowned. 'I read somewhere that rubbing your neck and shoulders is better than your temples, for relieving a headache.'

Having experienced a little of his technique last night, I'd bet the whole of my savings that Alex was a dab hand at giving neck and shoulder massages.

'I'm feeling a lot of things right now,' I told him, forcing myself to stop thinking about his hands and trying to find the words to let him down gently. 'Alex . . .'

'It's all right,' he said. 'You don't need to say it.'

I looked at him and he unwaveringly met my gaze. Somehow, I knew that he knew exactly what I was about to say.

'That's as maybe,' I softly said, 'but I still want to. Is that all right?'

'I suppose.' He shrugged. 'I was just trying to spare you.'

'You really have read my mind, haven't you?'

'Yeah,' he sighed. 'I have. But it wasn't until this morning that realisation dawned. I went to bed thinking we were going to pick up where we'd left off at that field gate, but when I saw you before I went to meet Connor, I knew.'

'How?'

He put the remains of his roll down on the paper bag it had come wrapped in and also sat back.

'Well, let's put it this way,' he ruefully smiled. 'You don't say to someone you've been passionately kissing "About last night" the next time you see them if you're still pumped up with lust for them, do you?'

I dropped my gaze to my lap as my face flared.

'If you're really still feeling it when you first clap eyes on them again,' he carried on, 'you leap straight on them, don't you?'

I knew he was trying to make light of it and was grateful for that.

'And right now,' he carried on, 'you don't look inclined to leap in my direction at all.'

'Oh, Alex,' I said. 'I'm so sorry.'

'Don't be,' he said. 'It's fine. I thought about it while I was waiting for Connor and it's probably for the best. We've both come here with baggage, so it's hardly the ideal time to be starting something up, is it? Even if that kiss was . . .'

'Unforgettable,' I breathed.

'Oh.' He shrugged, funnily feigning nonchalance. 'I was going to say all right, but if you want to put an ego boosting label on it.'

I picked up one of the sofa cushions and threw it at him. He caught it and grinned.

'We got carried away in the moment,' he said kindly. 'After three too many cocktails.'

'I think we'd only had two at that point,' I cut in.

'That's not helpful,' he laughed. 'And you're wrong. Given Rachel's ridiculous measures it was actually more like six.'

'Fair point,' I conceded.

'It was a moment of holiday madness,' he said, and I wondered if he really believed that. 'That should definitely not be repeated.'

I didn't say anything because I wasn't sure if his willingness to pretend it hadn't meant anything was making me feel better or worse. I didn't think I would have minded if he'd fought for us the tiniest bit, which I know was a complete contradiction.

'Not that I don't like you,' he carried on when I didn't say anything, 'because I really do and if this had been any other time, I wouldn't be feeling anywhere near as willing to give you or that unforgettable kiss up.'

That went some way to making me feel a bit better.

'But . . .'

'But,' I said, picking up the thread he'd started to pull, 'we're on a once in a lifetime holiday with loads to see and do and get straight and no desire to overshadow the real purpose behind our trip with a romantic complication.'

'Exactly.' He nodded along. 'Although to be honest, I was

just hoping for three weeks' amazing no strings sex and a wave goodbye at the end of it.'

'I don't believe that for a second,' I said, picking my roll back up. 'If there's one thing you're not, Alex, it's that guy.'

Our eyes met for a moment.

'Very true,' he said, screwing his serviette into a tiny tight ball. 'I am most definitely not that guy.'

Chapter 20

Ultimately it was a relief that Alex was so willing for the two of us to slip back into the friend zone because it meant there was no ill feeling between Rachel and me and we were all able to carry on in the groove that we'd so comfortably started to slip into before cocktail-gate.

As a result, we spent more time at the lake, plenty of time in the pub and also enjoyed the peace and quiet at the cottage where Alex worked on his restaurant branding, Rachel read all the novels she didn't have time for during term-time and I designed two more skirts, thanks to the extra fabric I'd ordered, and completed the second picture I needed to send off to the eager recipient.

The peace and settled atmosphere gave me plenty of time to further consider the possibility of a part-time soft launch which, I hoped, wouldn't jeopardise either Rachel's plans or our friendship. On paper, it looked like the ideal compromise and I hoped the reality would live up to the planning and I could find a position in my field which offered the twenty or so hours I thought would be the perfect fit.

Even though I was extremely curious and mildly concerned,

I hadn't tackled Rachel about the time she had recently been spending alone in the pub. Time I had thought she was messaging Jeremy during his strictly prescribed schedule. We'd come through me letting Alex down unscathed and I didn't want to risk upsetting the apple cart. And to be honest, even though she had kept her trips to The Drover's to herself, any time she wasn't messaging Jeremy was warmly welcomed whether I was privy to the details of them or not.

We were getting closer to the mid-point of our getaway when Alex set off for his office in Manchester that week and, even though I didn't like to dwell on how I was going to feel when there was more of the trip behind than ahead of us, I was feeling optimistic and in a celebratory mood when I got back from posting off the second picture commission.

'You've been gone ages,' Rachel pointed out when I arrived back late into the afternoon. 'Did Mrs Timpson collar you again?'

'Of course, she did,' I laughed, placing my shopping bag down on the counter.

Considering I had only walked to Lakeside with the intention of emptying it, it was very heavy and very full for the walk back, but I didn't mind because it was packed with ingredients I could utilise to, hopefully, cook us a special dinner. In that carefree Rose-inspired moment, I didn't even mind that I'd blown my weekly food budget on it.

'Well, you don't sound too upset,' Rachel said, peering into the bag, before I could whisk it away. 'You haven't forgotten Alex is bringing a shop back with him, have you?'

'I'm not upset,' I told her. 'And no, I haven't forgotten.'

'What's going on then?' she asked, catching my upbeat mood.

'I popped into the pub for a lemonade when I got to Lakeside because I was feeling hot,' I told her, 'and my phone updated while I was chatting to Connor.'

'Good news?'

'Just a bit.' I grinned.

'Go on,' she said. 'Don't leave me in suspenders!'

'Well,' I slowly said, savouring the magical moment. 'As well as those two picture commissions I got off the back of the anniversary present for Hugh's wife, I've now had orders for three more dresses as well.'

'That's amazing!' Rachel gasped, her eyes every bit as wide as mine had been when I read the emails. 'Who are they from?'

'It's another friend of a friend recommendation,' I explained. 'And even though I can't make the body of the dresses up now because I haven't got the measurements, I can start putting the patchwork panels together in the colours the client has asked for.'

'Get you,' said Rachel. 'Clients! How professional does that sound?'

'I know,' I said. 'It's just as well I registered my earnings with HMRC, isn't it?'

'Surely you haven't already earnt enough to pay tax on what you've been doing?'

'No,' I said. 'Well, I don't think so, but you still have to declare it as a second income.'

At least having some basic knowledge about that side of things would be a help when I got going properly.

'Crikey,' said Rachel. 'I didn't know that. At this rate, you'll be jacking in the day job and expanding this sideline in no time.'

'About that . . .' I began, thinking there would be no better

opportunity to explain what I was planning, but there was a knock on the door and the opportunity was lost.

'Hello Catriona,' said Rachel, when she answered it. 'Come in.'

'I'm not stopping,' she said, having a quick look around, 'but I was passing and thought I'd just pop down and make sure everything's okay? As you know, I don't intrude as a rule, but as you're here for such a long time ...'

'Everything's absolutely wonderful,' I told her, feeling relieved that Rachel's mascara hadn't done any lasting damage to the pillowcase. 'Although you might need to employ some heavy-handed tactics to turf us out when the time comes.'

'Em's right,' Rachel laughed. 'This place is beginning to feel more like home than home.'

'I knew you'd feel like that.' Catriona smiled. 'I've hardly had any visits that have lasted as long as yours. I could get used to it though. It's rather nice not to have the tight turnaround of a weekly or fortnightly handover.'

'I can believe that,' Rachel said.

'Have you time for tea?' I asked. 'I was just about to make a pot.'

'No, no,' she said. 'As I said, I just wanted to check in and as everything's ticking over okay, I'll leave you to it.'

Rachel walked back up to the road with her and I filled the fridge with some of the treats I'd picked up in the village as a way to distract myself. Catriona's visit had prompted me to think about the time constraints of our trip again and I really didn't want to get caught up counting down the days as opposed to living in the magnificent moment.

By the time Rachel got back, I'd changed my mind again

about mentioning my business plan. That could be something special for the future. For now, I would remain focused on the present.

'So,' she said, sounding a little perturbed as she eased her feet out of her Converse without fully untying the laces. 'What's on the menu for tonight?'

'Something tried and tested that I can't get wrong,' I reassured her, knowing her cautionary tone was the result of some of my more disastrous culinary experiments.

'Beans on toast?'

'No,' I said, swatting her with a tea towel. 'Risotto.'

'Oh, yum.'

'And I'm using some lovely ingredients courtesy of Mrs T to make it extra special.'

'Such as?' Rachel asked, her eyes shining because she knew she was safe with my risotto.

'Well,' I said. 'There's pecorino to stir through it from Connor's aunt, who keeps sheep as well as goats, and some smoked pork lardons and also fresh peas to pop in right at the end.'

'My mouth's watering already,' said Rachel, licking her lips. 'Sweet, salty and savoury. I can practically taste it and you must let me pay half. Connor's given me some cash for my stint in the bar the other night.'

'No,' I insisted. 'This is my treat and I'm not going to start it too early, so snack now if you need to. I'm going to try and time it so it will be ready for when Alex gets back and we can all eat together.'

'He's been a good sport about everything, hasn't he?' she said, broaching the subject we'd both previously been avoiding.

'The best,' I said, 'but then I knew he would be. We both

agreed we didn't want to plunge ourselves into a relationship, not even a short one, when we were supposed to be making the most of our book-based retreat.'

I didn't mention our extra baggage, but hoped she would be accepting about me putting a halt on things now she knew for certain that he was as onside about it all as I was. Her nod suggested she was.

'What time is he usually back?' she asked.

'Not much before eight,' I said, suddenly aware that I was very in tune with his weekly comings and goings, 'but he said it'll definitely be nearer seven tonight.'

'I'm not sure I'll last until then,' she grimaced, clutching her stomach.

'That's why I said you should snack,' I laughed, presenting her with a box of cream cakes. 'And that's why I picked up these. They should tide us over for a while.'

The risotto was timed to perfection for Alex's arrival around seven, but unfortunately, he didn't appear.

'I think we should get on and have ours,' said Rachel as she lit the scented candles which I had dotted about the room and her tummy, in spite of the earlier cakes, gave the loudest rumble. 'I'd hate for it to spoil,' she added, giving the air an appreciative sniff.

'You're right,' I said, turning off the heat and sliding two small warm baguettes out of the oven before breaking them apart and generously buttering them. 'I hope he's okay.'

'I daresay he got held up in the office or maybe stuck in traffic coming out of the city,' Rachel suggested, eagerly passing me two bowls.

'You're probably right,' I agreed. 'It's a shame though.'

I had thoroughly enjoyed cooking the risotto. It was a simple dish but one I knew well and always took my time over. I knew some people added all the liquid at the beginning, but I liked to stir and tend right from the moment I added the rice to the melted butter, then poured in a glass of wine. Once that had been absorbed, I patiently added a ladle of stock at a time, stirring all the while.

I didn't have many recipes in my repertoire but this was a favourite and definitely the most soothing to follow. Not that I was feeling all that soothed as the peas began to lose their fresh green colour and Alex still wasn't back.

'Are you fed up?' Rachel asked, as she poured the wine I'd already opened to cook with, into two glasses.

'I am a bit,' I said. 'But not with Alex because I know it won't be his fault. I just don't want his dinner to spoil.'

It had turned chilly as the afternoon gave way to early evening so we had lit the wood-burner again. It wasn't something we had really been expecting to use much when we made the booking for the height of summer but the close proximity of the trees and the geographical location kept the cottage cool on cloudy days, so it was a justified treat.

Rachel curled up in the armchair, balancing her bowl on a cushion.

'Pecorino?' I offered, holding out a dish of the grated salty cheese. 'There's plenty stirred through, but would you like some on top, too?'

'Yes, please,' she said, holding the bowl out Oliver-style so I could sprinkle another helping on top.

I gave my own portion the same garnish and sat cross-legged

on the sofa, my bowl wrapped in a tea towel because it was hot to the touch.

'*Bon appétit*.' I smiled. 'I hope it tastes as good as it looks.'

'And smells.' Rachel appreciatively sniffed again. 'And don't you mean, *buon appetito* as it's risotto?'

'Probably,' I laughed. 'Anyway, enjoy.'

We each took a first taste and then nodded at each other as we chewed, savoured and swallowed.

'Oh, yeah,' said Rachel.

'Good?'

'Perfect,' she said, appreciatively diving back in.

We didn't speak as we ate but the yummy noises we made and the nods and smiles spoke volumes.

'Best ever,' said Rachel, wiping the last of the crusty buttered bread around the inside of her bowl to soak up every last morsel.

'It's probably arrogant to agree,' I admitted as I reached for my wine, 'but yeah, best ever, for sure.'

'Cheers.'

'Don't you mean, *saluti*?' I winked.

'Yes,' she laughed. 'That too. Is there any more?'

'Wine or risotto?'

'Risotto.' She grinned.

'I'm sure I could find you another half ladle,' I said, holding out my hand for her bowl.

'Don't leave Alex short though,' she said, stretching out in the chair as I walked back to the kitchen.

'I won't,' I promised. 'But he's missed out on a full glass of the wine and all of the bread.'

'What's that noise?' Rachel then asked. 'Is it raining?'

The heavens instantly answered as the rain began to drum down, drowning out the sound of everything else.

'Just a bit,' I laughed, but as I listened more intently, I thought I could hear something else too. 'And thundering, maybe,' I added, straining to separate the rumble from the rain.

It wasn't thunder though, it was the sound of pounding feet. I was just about to say as much when the cottage door was flung open and Alex fell inside laughing and soaked through, closely followed by a sopping wet, but equally amused, Tori.

Chapter 21

Time seemed to stand still for a second, then Rachel sprang out of the armchair and ran, squealing, over to the door.

'Oh my god!' she shrieked. 'What are you doing here?'

She pulled our friend in for a hug, receiving a soaking in the process.

'I can't believe it!' she said, giving Tori a shake by the shoulders. 'Can you believe it, Em?'

I was still standing in the kitchen with the risotto-filled ladle in my hand poised somewhere between Rachel's bowl and the pan. I put it back down, wiped my hands on the towel and joined the three of them at the door.

'No,' I said, trying to sound excited as Alex pulled off his jacket and gave it a shake, soaking us all with freezing droplets of rain. 'I can't.'

'I've come to stay.' Tori beamed, still looking beautiful in spite of the fact that her hair was plastered to her head.

'She's come to stay,' Alex echoed, pulling off his boots.

'I'm here for the holiday,' she said, looking from Rachel to me.

'She's here for the holiday,' Alex repeated, then giggled.

'Are you drunk?' I frowned, as he swayed towards the doorframe.

'A little,' he said, holding up his forefinger and thumb to demonstrate the size of his inebriation.

He was way off, as men so often are with their measurements. Rachel looked at me and raised her eyebrows. Clearly, she was as taken aback by the unexpected turn of events and surprise guest as I was, but far better at pulling the shock off. And not for the first time since we'd arrived at the cottage.

'Well, come in, the pair of you,' she said, encouraging Tori out of her dripping coat. 'I have a feeling this is a meet-cute I'm going to want to hear all about.'

I turned back to the kitchen feeling irrationally niggled by Rachel's choice of words, but then remembered my manners.

'Would you like some dinner while you fill us in?' I offered, thinking I might be able to stretch what was left to two if they weren't that hungry.

'What's on the menu?' Alex asked, wandering over and leaning so far across the counter he was right in my face. 'It smells amazing.'

He drew the word out but I didn't feel the same glow of satisfaction hearing him say it as I had experienced when Rachel had pointed out the delicious aroma.

'Risotto,' I told him, feeling further surprised that his piercing dark, but somewhat unfocused gaze no longer reached me in quite the same way as it recently had.

'Oh, yum,' said Tori, pulling off what I could see looked like brand-new Dubarry boots. The Barbour she had been wearing looked fresh out of the box too. 'Em's risotto is legendary.'

'It's got bacon in it,' I said, for some reason unable to acknowledge the compliment.

'Oh no,' she said. 'I can't have it then. I'm vegetarian,' she added for Alex's benefit.

'Had I known you were coming,' I swallowed, 'I would have left it out.'

'It's fine.' She shrugged. 'We ate in the pub anyway. What a find The Drover's is and that Connor is an Irish hunk and a half, isn't he?'

It was a classic Tori slash Rose comment, but it rankled with me as did the fact that they'd already eaten. It shouldn't have annoyed me because Alex hadn't known I was making something special, but it did.

'Did you have a big meal in the pub?' I asked him, while Tori made herself at home in front of the fire and in my usual spot on the sofa.

'I did.' He frowned. 'I didn't know you were going to cook.'

'I know you didn't,' I said, trying to smile. 'It doesn't matter.'

'But I could definitely go for some of that risotto, if there's enough left.' He smiled, making me feel a bit better. 'Now I've smelt it, I can't resist.'

'Give him all of it,' Rachel insisted. 'I don't think I've got room for another helping now my brain has registered my tummy's full.'

I filled a bowl for Alex, then fetched a towel from the bathroom for Tori to rub her wet hair on and we congregated in front of the fire. Alex took the armchair and tucked into the risotto without uttering a word, Rachel sat next to Tori on the sofa and I perched on the pouffe next to the wood-burner.

'So, come on,' said Rachel, nudging Tori's long legs. 'Tell us what's going on. How come you're here?'

'Have you run away?' I asked, then felt cross with myself for sounding so snippy.

'No,' she laughed. 'It's nothing like that. I'm no Laurie, am I?'

'So . . .' Rachel encouraged, while Alex slurped.

'Dad's gone away on business with my eldest brother and the others are away now, too,' she told us.

'And your dad didn't trust you to stay home alone?' Rachel cut in, because it wouldn't have been the first time.

'Harsh,' Alex muttered while Tori looked hurt.

'Perhaps,' I told him, 'but Rachel's only going on past experience.'

'That's a fair supposition, I suppose,' Tori allowed. 'But I actually didn't want to stay home alone. I've been toeing the line since I moved back and found I didn't want . . .'

'To be tempted to throw another all-nighter?' Rachel put in, before I could.

'No,' Tori tutted, sounding further deflated. 'I really have changed, you know. I've been doing a lot of thinking and the truth of it is, I didn't want to be in that big house all on my own for the next few weeks.'

'So, you phoned your dad and he gave you his blessing to come here and join us while he was away,' Alex knowledgeably said, rattling his spoon in the empty bowl.

'Exactly.' Tori nodded, throwing him one of her devastating smiles. 'He transferred me a little spending money and arranged my travel to get me here too.'

'So how come you ended up in The Drover's?' I frowned, thinking she really must have been behaving herself if her dad had relented to that degree. 'And how come you know so much about it?' I asked Alex.

'I got a taxi all the way from the railway station, which Dad had booked and must have cost a fortune,' Tori told us, further

confirming that she was still without her beloved Range Rover. 'But the driver couldn't find the cottage and because I'd backed out of the trip at the last minute, I didn't have the detailed directions to find the place that Catriona had given you. It's very tucked away, isn't it?'

'It's one of its many charms,' I told her.

'You should have messaged us before you set off,' Rachel said. 'I could have sent you the directions then.'

'I wanted it to be a surprise.' Tori beamed.

'Mission accomplished then.' I hesitantly smiled back.

'So, what happened when you couldn't find us?' Rachel eagerly asked.

'The driver dropped me at the pub,' Tori carried on. 'And when I told the lovely landlord who I was and where I was heading, he said he'd drive me here. I was just deciding whether or not I should finally message and give you a heads up in case you were out somewhere, when Alex walked in . . .'

'And the rest is history,' Alex winked, sounding thrilled.

'So how come you were in the pub?' I asked him, most likely sounding like a nag, but not meaning to.

'I'd finished work early, so called in,' he explained, 'to see if Connor had any more desserts going spare. I thought it would be a bit of a mid-week treat.'

'Em had already gifted us one of those,' Rachel said, pointedly looking at the bowl on his lap.

'And then Connor introduced me to Tori and obviously, I said I'd drive her here . . .' Alex further elaborated.

'We weren't going to stay long,' Tori giggled. 'But Connor had this new beer on that he wanted us to sample and things got a bit fuzzy after that, didn't they, Alex?'

Alex bit his lip and shook his head to suppress another laugh.

'Since when have you been a beer drinker?' I asked Tori.

'Since about six o'clock this evening,' she tittered and Alex couldn't hold his mirth in a moment longer.

Rachel looked at me and she was laughing too, but I couldn't see the funny side. I wondered if the pair of them had also taken a walk along the lane but shut the thought down before I started to visualise it. Tori was far less inhibited than me, even without a belly full of guest beer and she certainly had form. It wouldn't be the first time she'd bagged a bloke who had once been on my radar. Not that she had known Alex had ever been on mine.

I had been dating a guy for a couple of months just after Rachel and I had graduated and when I finished things because I realised we didn't have anything in common, Tori had immediately asked if she could ask him out. I knew I shouldn't have been so put out considering I had been the one responsible for the break-up, and given that she had asked me, rather than just jumped straight in, but it had upset me more than I let on.

I knew it was my own fault because I should have said no when she asked. She wouldn't have pursued him without my blessing. But now, she wouldn't be paying me the courtesy of checking if I minded her flirting with Alex, and potentially more, because she hadn't been privy to everything that had happened before her rain-soaked arrival.

'So, did Connor have any desserts to spare then?' Rachel asked.

'Do you know,' Alex said, wiping his eyes, 'I never got around to asking.' That set him and Tori off again. 'The second I was introduced to Tori and she started telling me all about you two and your lives away from here, sticky toffee pudding went clean out of my head.'

'I hope you didn't tell him too much,' said Rachel, giving Tori another nudge.

'Only the good stuff.' She winked. 'The poor sod already knew all about your singing, thanks to the *Hope Falls* karaoke night, so I couldn't spill the beans about that.'

I felt my face grow warm as I wondered if that conversation had led on to sharing a few of the more intimate details about that night. At least if it had, then Tori would be in the know that Alex and I had form.

'And the conversation wasn't all one way,' Tori carried on, making me feel hotter. 'Alex told me about all the things you've been doing here, too. It sounds like a fabulous place, even better than we imagined it would be. I can't wait to curl up in one of the window seats like the girls did in the book and I'm thrilled I haven't missed the skinny-dipping.'

Her knowledge of the book sounded more detailed than when Rachel and I had left her and I wondered if she'd picked it up again in our absence.

'You won't be saying that if you go down to the lake and dip a toe in,' Rachel warned her with a shudder. 'I did when we first arrived, didn't I, Em? And it was glacial.'

'Oh, I don't mind that,' Tori said. 'When I used to go to the spa, I loved the sauna into ice bath experience. It really gets the blood flowing.'

'I'll bet,' said Alex, puffing out his cheeks.

'Who wants coffee?' I asked, jumping up too quickly and almost toppling into the hearth.

I covered the wobble, by holding out my hand to grasp Alex's empty bowl.

'Did you get the milk and the rest of the shopping?' I asked him.

He looked up at me, all puppy dog eyes. 'I did,' he said, 'but it's in my car, which is back in the village. Obviously, I couldn't drive here after all that beer, so Connor gave us a lift home and I didn't think to get the bags before we set off.'

'Oh, Alex,' Rachel laughed.

'I've left my keys with him so he can put the perishables in his fridge,' Alex continued, trying to make amends. 'Apparently, he's not allowed to put them in the pub one. Health and safety or food standards or something. How weird is that? A fridge is a fridge, right?'

I let out a long breath. I didn't give two hoots about the rules and regulations which governed running a pub kitchen, I just wanted to make us all a drink.

'And Connor is also looking after my bags tonight,' Tori then said, 'because they're all back in the bar, too.'

She'd obviously had a right old time of it if she'd forgotten her luggage. I could just imagine the three of them with their heads together, laughing and getting better acquainted. I knew that sounded childish and it shouldn't have rankled, but it did.

'That's probably just as well,' I told her. 'Because I don't think you'll actually be able to stay here beyond tonight, Tori.'

'Of course, she will,' said Rachel, throwing me a look.

'The booking was for three people,' I pointed out. 'Tori makes the party four.'

'Catriona won't mind,' said Rachel. 'I'll walk up to the road in the morning and call to okay it with her. If I tell her it's Tori, who was a member of the original booking we made, I can't see it will be an issue. We've paid the same amount of money to be here, whether it's three or four of us, haven't we?'

'If you say so.' I shrugged.

'I'm really sorry,' Tori said, sounding upset. 'I didn't think it would be a problem. I was just so excited to see you guys and finally live the *Hope Falls* dream. Emily's right, though. I shouldn't have just descended. Perhaps I haven't changed as much as I thought I had,' she sighed, blinking back tears. 'I suppose I could see if Connor lets out rooms, or knows someone in the village who does, although I haven't got all that much cash . . .'

'Oh, for pity's sake,' I said, pulling her up off the sofa and giving her a one-armed hug. 'I'm sure it will be fine. Ignore me,' I insisted. 'I was just thinking aloud and wondering how we could work things out, that's all.'

I really did feel rotten. It wasn't her fault that I'd had such an adverse reaction to seeing her and Alex fall through the door. The look on her face now reminded me very much of the one that Alex had worn when we first arrived and I'd made things difficult because he wasn't the person I'd been expecting.

If things had turned out all right with him, a man who just a few short weeks ago had been a total stranger, then I should be able to get my head around being reunited with one of my best friends, shouldn't I?

Calling a truce with Alex had only enhanced the whole extended getaway experience, so the sooner I got used to Tori being with us, the better. If I gave the change a chance and quickly got my head straight again, then this very special summer now had every possibility of becoming even more magical.

'Well,' she said, hugging me back. 'As long as you're really sure.'

'Of course, I'm sure,' I told her.

'Of course, she's sure,' said Alex.

I rolled my eyes, hoping he wasn't back on the tipsy repetitive loop again.

'But Em does have a point,' Rachel then surprised me by saying.

'I do?' I frowned.

'Yes,' she said. 'What are we going to do about the sleeping arrangements? There are only two bedrooms here, aren't there? The twin we're in and the double.'

'That's all right,' said Alex, standing up. 'Tori can have my room.'

I felt my heart lurch and my face flush.

'But then where will you sleep?' Rachel asked him.

'I can kip in here,' he shrugged. 'I don't mind. As long as I can still use one of the bathrooms, I'm not bothered.'

Hadn't he been the one waxing lyrical about the joys of that double mattress and how he was fulfilling Gracie's dream and now he was giving it up to sleep on a sofa that wasn't even a pull out?

'Well,' Rachel tentatively said, 'as long as you're sure.'

'Absolutely,' he nodded.

I couldn't believe that Tori was going to take over the room, that exquisite room, that I had coveted for so long. In the grand scheme of things, it shouldn't have mattered, but it did. It really hurt. I could feel Rachel's eyes on me, but I didn't trust myself to look at her.

'That's settled then,' Tori said happily, clapping her hands. 'Any chance I could borrow a T-shirt, Alex?' she asked with a winning smile. 'Only all of my clothes are back in the pub and I'm not sure it's warm enough to sleep au naturel, or appropriate, if you're going to be popping in and out to use the bathroom.'

Rachel shook her head and I turned away. It was all classic Tori. I bet Connor had come in for the same flirtatious

treatment. I knew that she didn't even know she was doing it half the time, but seeing her having everyone eating out of her hand grated a bit sometimes. And this was one of those times.

'Give me a minute,' said Alex, clearing his throat, 'and I'll see what I can find.'

Chapter 22

In the end, Rachel lent Tori her old Snoopy nightshirt which, of course, she looked impossibly cute in and I spent the night tossing and turning and feeling put out. The fact that I had no right to feel put out, coupled with the fact that Tori had done nothing to deserve the negativity I had already told myself I needed to banish, made its lingering presence all the more bitter and frustratingly harder to dismiss.

I was exasperatingly close to tears as I lay in bed listening to her and Alex talking next door. I couldn't hear any of what they were saying, but they chatted away long after we'd all decided to turn in. Rachel had wasted no time in nodding off, but with my ears straining to hear, even though it was impossible to make out a single word, I couldn't get anywhere even close.

'I'm going for a walk around the lake and then I'll call and sort things with Catriona,' Rachel informed me when I woke later than planned with a fuzzy head and bleary eyes the next morning. 'Are you all right? You look really rough.'

'Thanks,' I said grumpily.

'Did you not sleep?'

'How could I with the slumber party going on next door?' I complained. 'They were yapping on half the night.'

'Were they?' She shrugged, looking at the dividing wall. 'I never heard a thing.'

'Yes,' I said. 'They were. They seem to be getting along famously, don't they?'

Rachel looked at me for a second, taking me in. 'I suppose so,' she said. 'But that's all right, isn't it?'

'I guess,' I huffed, adding my own shrug to the conversation.

Rachel narrowed her eyes.

'Oh, ignore me,' I said, sitting right up and pushing my tangled hair out of my face. 'I'm just in a fug because I didn't sleep.'

There was so much more to it than that but I couldn't bear the thought of Rachel launching into a 'well, you didn't want him so don't go minding if someone else does' speech. Especially as we'd been there before and that was not what this was about.

'Why don't you try a hot shower?' she suggested in response to my explanation for sounding so sulky the second I'd opened my eyes. 'That might soothe you a bit.'

'What, and then go running down to the lake and jump off the jetty, Tori style?' I said, with a wry smile.

'It seems to work for her,' Rachel laughed.

Everything seemed to work for her. Even though her father had pulled the plug on her holiday, she'd still ended up on it. I nipped the desire to talk about piles of poo and roses firmly in the bud.

'I'll give it a go,' I said instead, pushing back the duvet with my feet. 'The shower, that is, not the swim in the lake.'

I'd finished my shower and made a pot of coffee when there

was a knock on the cottage door. There was still no sign of Tori and if the softly snoring pile of blankets on the sofa was any indicator, it would be a while before Alex surfaced too.

'Hey, Connor.' I smiled, opening the door and finding him surrounded by a mountain of designer luggage. 'Are you moving in?'

'Someone is,' he laughed. 'Where do you want this lot? There's more in my car.'

'More luggage?' I squawked, wondering where it was all going to go.

Tori had never travelled light but a suitcase for every week we had left at the cottage felt rather excessive, even for her.

'No, don't panic,' he said. 'It's just Alex's shopping in the car and a parcel for you. I took it off the hands of a poor delivery guy who couldn't find the cottage and was at his wits' end to find the post office shut. I hope that was okay?'

'Oh, yes, thank you,' I said, knowing it would be more fabric I had ordered, but hadn't had a specified delivery time for. 'Let's leave this lot here, next to Miss Tori's Birkin,' I added, wheeling one of the heavy suitcases inside, 'and I'll come with you to grab the rest.'

'You don't have to do that,' said Connor, manoeuvring the other two cases through the door and into a position that wouldn't cause too much of a trip hazard.

'It's fine,' I told him as I pulled on my plimsolls and wondered how he'd managed to get all three cases from the car to the cottage in one go. 'I could do with the fresh air. I'm feeling a bit groggy this morning.'

'Is it a Tori hangover?' he laughed.

'Something like that,' I sighed, following him out.

'She's quite something, isn't she?' he commented as we set off along the path.

'Yep,' I said. 'She's definitely something. Have you fallen under her spell, too?'

'Me?' Connor laughed. 'I've only got eyes for one girl this summer, and sadly, she's already spoken for.'

I linked my arm through his.

'I'm sorry about that,' I told him. 'If we're talking about the same girl, that is, then I'd far rather she—'

'Don't finish that sentence,' Connor cut in. 'Because that way lies madness.'

'Fair enough,' I said, squeezing his arm closer to mine.

'So,' he then asked. 'Who else has fallen under Tori's spell?'

'Most likely everyone who was drinking in your pub when she landed last night,' I reeled off. 'Oh, and Alex, of course.'

Connor burst out laughing.

'What?' I frowned.

He looked at me and shook his head. 'I'll give you everyone who was in The Drover's,' he said, 'because she made quite an impression.'

'She always does,' I sighed.

'But not Alex.'

'No?' I said disbelievingly.

'No,' Connor insisted.

'Well,' I huffed. 'You wouldn't say that if you'd seen and heard the pair of them after you dropped them off. They stayed up talking half the night in the bedroom next to mine and Rachel's.'

'They're sharing a room?' Connor asked, wide-eyed.

'No,' I said, relieved that they hadn't gone for that option,

but still feeling put out. 'Alex has given up his room, so Tori can have it. He's now sleeping on the sofa.'

'What a gent.'

'Yes.' I swallowed. 'Isn't he just?'

'So, what were they talking about for so long?'

'No idea,' I sighed. 'All I could hear was them rambling on, but I've no idea what about.'

I wondered if Alex had taken the opportunity to explain to Tori about why he was on the holiday. Did she know all about Gracie now, too?

'No wonder you're in such a grump,' Connor said teasingly.

'Exactly,' I shot back. 'I need my sleep. Always have. Anything less than seven hours and I'm not nice to know.'

'Telling me,' he quipped and I thumped his arm. 'But I didn't mean that,' he said, playfully shoving me back.

'What then?'

'I meant, you're in a grump because you think Alex likes Tori,' he said sagely.

'No, I'm not,' I hotly denied, dropping his arm.

'Yes, you are,' he nudged. 'But you're completely wrong.'

I shook my head.

'He probably does like her,' Connor carried on, 'because anyone who knows her must like her, right? But he doesn't like her, like her.'

We'd reached the road by then and I helped him unload my bulky parcel and the shopping Alex had picked up but then forgotten the day before. There was quite a lot, definitely more than usual, which was just as well as we now had an extra mouth to feed.

'I don't know why you'd think I'd be bothered that Alex

likes Tori,' I said, unable to let the subject drop as we headed back down to the cottage. 'Not that I am, but it makes no difference to me.'

Connor rolled his eyes and stopped to swap the bags he was carrying from one hand to the other. They were all heavy, so I didn't bother redistributing mine.

'What?' I snapped.

'I saw you at the cocktail and quiz night.' He smiled. 'We all did. You're obviously into each other.'

'You hit the nail on the head there,' I told him, quickening my pace. 'The cocktails had a lot to do with what went on that night.'

There was no point denying that we had been 'into each other' when we'd downed Rachel's double strength concoctions, because the dancing and the duet, not to mention the rousing roadside embrace – not that anyone else had seen that – were all proof enough.

'Maybe they did,' Connor said, 'but Alex likes you, Em. He likes you a lot, even without the cocktails.'

'You don't know that,' I tutted, shrugging off what I already knew. Or thought I knew until Tori turned up.

'Blokes talk,' Connor shrugged.

I threw him a sceptical look.

'Especially to a landlord after a few drinks,' he said, adding weight to his words. 'And Alex talks about you, a lot. Too much really and even without the beer. It's quite boring. Sometimes when he leaves, I feel like I've got Em overload.'

I biffed him with the bags.

'Well, whatever,' I said. 'Though I daresay he hasn't mentioned me this week, because after cocktail hour, we had a deep

and meaningful and both agreed that a relationship is the last thing that either of us needs right now.'

I let out a long breath wishing I felt better for saying that, but I didn't. If anything, I felt worse.

'You did?' Connor frowned.

'We did,' I firmly said. 'From our hangover onwards and for fear of possibly ruining our summer if things went wrong, we've agreed to be just good friends.'

We'd both been very grown up about the whole situation and it was now resolved. Sort of.

'Well, I hate to be the one to break it to you,' Connor said, chewing his lip, 'but I've spoken to him quite a bit this week and I don't think that's sunk in with him at all. It certainly hasn't shut him up anyway.'

'It hasn't?' I swallowed, as a fluttering sensation in my chest made my breath catch.

'Nope,' he said. 'So maybe Tori showing up will turn out to be a blessing. She might be just the tonic he needs if you're so determined that the pair of you shouldn't be together.'

If Alex did end up jumping straight into Tori's arms, especially as we'd jointly agreed that we *both* needed to be relationship-free on this holiday, then I would not be impressed. Even just the thought of it was putting me in an even grumpier mood.

'Oh yes,' I said, putting down one of the bags so I could open the cottage door. 'Tori's a tonic all right.'

I offered Connor a mug of the coffee I had made before he arrived, but he declined because he had to get back to The Drover's in time for a delivery. I was just thanking him again for his taxi service, when Rachel arrived back from her walk

around the lake. In complete contrast to me, she looked the picture of health.

'Can I offer you a coffee?' I asked her, holding up a mug.

'Yes, please,' she said. 'Are you having one, Connor?'

'No,' he said. 'I'm now away.'

'In that case,' she said, 'hang fire with the coffee, Em. I'll walk up to the road with you, Connor, because I need to call Catriona.'

I watched the pair of them head off, wondering if Rachel had any idea that Connor still had romantic feelings for her. I hated the thought of her moving in with Jeremy in just a few weeks' time. Or at any time for that matter. And especially when there were far lovelier men who thought so much of her in the world.

'They make a cute couple, don't they?'

'Oh, bloody hell, Tori!' I spun around to find her standing right behind me. 'Where did you spring from?'

'Sorry,' she giggled. 'You should see your face.'

I looked back at Connor and Rachel just as they disappeared out of sight.

'He's so much nicer than Jealous Jeremy,' Tori said dreamily.

'He is,' I agreed. 'And unfortunately, I need to talk to you about Jeremy.'

'There's no need,' she sighed sadly. 'I already know all about the big moving in extravaganza and the massive photo muddle.'

I felt a shiver run through me as she said the words out loud.

'I'm so worried about her, Tor,' I said, my voice catching again. 'She hasn't been in touch with him as much as I thought she had since we've been here, but . . .'

Tori laid a hand on my arm and shook her head. 'Don't worry about it,' she whispered. 'I have a plan.'

'You do?'

'I do.'

'What is it?'

'I'm not going to tell you.' She winked. 'But you'll find out soon enough.'

'But maybe I could help,' I offered, keen to get involved.

'You can't,' she said. 'I can manage. It's all in hand.' Her expression changed to one of concern. 'It might end up costing me,' she added, 'but it'll be worth it.'

'What do you mean by that?'

'No more questions,' she firmly said, smiling again. 'Now, do I smell coffee? I've just had a swim in that tub and it's given me a thirst. Isn't that bathroom heaven?'

'Yeah,' I said, pouring her a mug. 'Celestial.'

'Ugh,' she grimaced after the first mouthful. 'This has gone over. Shall I make some fresh? What a novelty to have an old-fashioned pot instead of a pod machine.'

'It's all part of the being faithful to the book aesthetic,' I told her, stunned that she was offering to make the coffee herself.

'You'll have to show me how to work it,' she said, eyeing the pot as if it was from another time.

Which I supposed, given the age of the book, it was.

'Here,' I said, reaching around her. 'This is where the coffee goes.'

By the time Tori had finished clattering about in the kitchen, over-filling the coffee pot and slightly singeing some toast, Alex was starting to come to and Rachel was back from calling Catriona.

'All sorted,' she announced, rushing in because it was starting to rain in spite of the promises made by the forecasters that we were in for a few dry days.

I was beginning to realise that in this part of the Lake District there was no such thing. Either that or we had been particularly unlucky on the weather front. No pun intended.

'Catriona was thrilled that you've joined us, Tori.' Rachel beamed at our friend. 'And, you'll be pleased to know, Alex,' she added as his mussed-up head appeared over the back of the sofa – he looked as good as I felt, 'that sofa is a pull out. But there's a bit of a knack to setting it up, so Catriona's going to come over later and show us.'

'Great,' he said huskily, then cleared his throat and tried again. 'That'll be more comfortable.'

'And I've been thinking about the sleeping arrangements,' Rachel carried on, leaving her Converse on the mat and coming further in. 'I think we should all take a turn on the sofa.'

'Except Em,' Tori immediately said.

'Why except me?' I asked, wondering why I had been singled out.

'Because when I drifted off to sleep last night in that delectable double,' she said, coming to stand next to me, 'I remembered that we'd drawn straws for that room and that you were over the moon to have won it because you've been dreaming of sleeping in there forever!'

I shook my head.

'You have?' Alex frowned.

'She has,' Tori confirmed, with one of her widest smiles. 'She hadn't shut up about it in literally months. Didn't you know?'

'I had no idea,' Alex said, sounding upset. 'Why didn't you say anything, Em?'

Tori looked between us. 'Oh,' she said, 'have I put my foot in it?'

'No,' I said, reaching for her hand. 'It's fine, Tor. I didn't say anything, Alex, because there was no point. With the three of us here it made sense for Rachel and I to share the twin and for you to take the double. It was no big deal.'

'Except it was,' Alex tutted. 'I'm so sorry. I just kind of assumed that's what would work best.'

'And it does,' I said, dropping Tori's hand. 'It did, and don't forget, it helped you fulfil something on that special list you came here with,' I quietly added.

It really wasn't my place to bring either Gracie or her list up, but I wanted Alex to know that I genuinely hadn't minded about the room allocation, especially under the circumstances.

'I know,' he said smilingly, 'and it's kind of you to say so, but you're moving in there today, Em. Right, Tori?'

'Right,' she said, rushing over and giving him a high five.

'That sounds like a good idea to me,' said Rachel, also walking over and joining them.

I opened my mouth to argue but Tori shook her head and I knew she meant business, so closed it again. I wasn't sure how much she had really changed during the last few weeks, but her father's denial of her previously easy life seemed to have instilled in her a will of iron and a determination I hadn't seen before.

Combined with whatever she'd come up with to scupper Jeremy's plan to further bind Rachel into his web, it made her one very powerful woman and I found myself feeling excited about how her plan was going to play out in spite

of my misgivings about her obvious fondness for our other housemate.

'I'll help you move your stuff,' she insisted. 'I'll even change the bed.'

Rachel took a step away and turned to gape at her. 'Who are you?' she gasped, 'and what have you done with our friend, Victoria?'

I couldn't help but laugh.

'I told you guys,' Tori pouted, giving Rachel a look. 'I'm a changed woman.'

Had I not heard her make the offer with my own ears, I never would have believed it, but she genuinely was sounding less like footloose and fancy-free Rose with every passing minute.

Chapter 23

My astonishment at Tori's transformation was given another nudge when she kept her word and did help me move my things from one room to the other. She even stripped and remade that fabulous double bed, just as she said she would.

'I cannot believe you know how to work a washing machine,' Rachel commented, also looking surprised as Tori bundled in the bed sheets and set the program.

'And I can load a dishwasher,' Tori said smugly, standing back up again, 'and I'm getting there with the ironing, too.'

'It's a miracle,' Rachel teased, but I knew that really, she was as pleased about Tori's down to earth and back to basics transformation as I was.

We both loved her to bits, but the way she had been cossetted and pandered to for so long hadn't made her the most well-rounded adult in the world.

'Your housekeeper will be out of a job soon,' I told her.

'I wouldn't go that far,' she said. 'I'm still thinking about what I'm going to do for a career so I'll need help at home when Dad hopefully signs the new lease and lets me move back into my apartment, won't I?'

'Oh, yes,' said Rachel, rolling her eyes. 'Just like Em and me. We need domestic help too, don't we?'

'Absolutely,' I laughed, pleased to hear that our friend was at least still thinking about the world of work. 'We just don't get it.'

'Well,' Tori further surprised us by saying, 'I'm rather enjoying getting stuck in to some of the domestic stuff. There's a sort of satisfaction in it, isn't there?'

'In that case,' said Alex, who had been listening in and was wearing an amused expression, 'you can carry the bin bags down to the road this week. The refuse van can't get to the cottage so we have to lug them up the path.'

'Steady on,' Tori tutted, sounding more familiar. 'Don't go mad, although I suppose it would be a good arm and core work-out,' she thoughtfully added.

We ate supper next to the lake that evening and I tried not to mind that Alex and Tori shared both the bench and a blanket, when it started to get chilly. Given that I was the one who had instigated the whole *nothing can happen between us* situation with Alex, it was hardly fair that I should object to their closeness.

However, the fact that Alex had cited his own baggage as justification for accepting the non-start situation between the two of us meant that the apparent speedy transferral of his affections and willingness to get to know Tori better did grate a bit. Had he somehow miraculously emptied his bags or was I reading too much into it?

Even though I was still trying to puzzle the Tori and Alex situation out, I made my excuses early and headed back to the cottage alone. I held my breath as I stepped into the bedroom and closed the door behind me. Thanks to the lingering scent of sweet peas it was easy to imagine myself tucked up in another

room, in a different house in the Lakes, with the voice of Grandad describing everything that I could now see around me with my own eyes.

The room was every bit as perfect as I had always imagined it would be. The large windows overlooking the trees, the smooth warm floorboards underfoot, the patchwork cushion filled rocking chair, the old-fashioned dressing table and of course, the inviting double bed. This had been Heather's sanctuary in the book and now it was mine. Coupled with walks in the wonderful landscape, she had puzzled out her life's purpose in this very room and I was determined to do the same.

After a long bubble filled bath (which I enjoyed even more than when I had aching muscles after the ghyll scrambling), and as I slipped between the deliciously cool cotton sheets, I strove to get on track again and keep everything else that was now happening in perspective.

I again reminded myself what I had come on this holiday to do and in a spirit of renewed bonhomie and letting bygones be bygones, drifted off to sleep thinking that the next day would be the perfect time to present Rachel with her dress and maybe offer to make transformed Tori an outfit of her own.

'Like a log,' were the first words I heard Alex say when I reluctantly left the beautiful bedroom the next morning.

'And you're not just saying that?' Rachel asked.

'No,' he said. 'I really mean it.'

'Alex says he's going to sleep on the sofa every night,' Rachel told me.

'That's hardly fair, when he's paid all that money to be here,' I pointed out.

'I'll have to share with either Rachel or Tori if I don't,' he

explained, 'and that's not ideal either, is it? I'm really not concerned about the money.'

My heart further lifted to know he wasn't jumping at the
chance to bunk in with Tori. So much for perspective!

'I hadn't thought of the dynamics,' I said, scratching my head.
'Maybe you and I should swap, Alex . . .'

He quickly put up an objecting hand.

'Nope,' he firmly said. 'No way. I've long since fulfilled
Gracie's dream of sleeping in that room. Now it's your turn, Em.'

'Who's Gracie?' Tori yawned, stretching her hands above her
head and showing off a smooth and tanned midriff in the process
as she drifted out of her and Rachel's room.

I couldn't resist a quick look at Alex and found he hadn't
noticed the flash of flesh at all.

'It's a long story,' he said. 'I'll tell you another day.'

Given the amount of time they had already spent chatting,
especially the night Tori had arrived, I was surprised Gracie
hadn't come up. Rachel looked at me and raised her eyebrows
and I wondered if she was thinking the same thing.

'So, what's the plan for today?' Rachel asked.

'I wouldn't mind watching the film tonight,' Tori suggested.
'Unless you guys have worn the DVD out already.'

Given the choice, she always went for the movie over the book.

'I've read the book three times since you guys arrived here and
I've worked some stuff out about myself as a result,' she then said,
completely contradicting what I had just thought. 'And I'd like to
see if I still feel the same way after I've watched the film again.'

'Well, I never,' gasped Rachel, who was clearly as surprised as I was.

'The DVD is still intact,' I told Tori, pleased that I hadn't been

the one to display such blatant shock. 'And I don't think there's anything specific on the schedule, but Rach,' I added, turning to her, 'I do have a surprise for you.'

'You do?' she asked, spinning around to look at me and forgetting all about Tori's surprise revelation.

'I do,' I confirmed.

'What is it?' she demanded, excitedly clapping her hands.

'If she tells you,' Alex laughed, 'it won't be a surprise, will it?'

'Quite right,' I agreed and Rachel pouted.

Knowing what she was like in the run up to Christmas and birthdays, I realised I should never have mentioned that I was going to give her something ahead of the event because she then nagged her way through the whole of breakfast and during every minute we were watering the veranda pots and making plans for the weekend.

It felt impossible that another week had flown by and we now were at the mid-point of our time at the cottage. In fact, when I checked the calendar and made a quick mental calculation, I realised we really did now have more of the holiday behind us than ahead. I went to say as much to the others, but then decided not to. If they hadn't worked it out for themselves, I didn't want to bring the mood down, especially when I was about to give Rachel her dress.

'Come on then,' I said, when I couldn't bear her plucking at my sleeve and following me around wearing a pleading expression a moment longer. 'Sit there and I'll get it.'

She bounced over to the sofa and held out her hands.

'It's not that big,' I laughed when I came back with it and she moved her outstretched palms closer together.

'Is this a private moment?' Alex asked, going to stand up.

'Not at all,' I told him.

'Boys allowed?' he chuckled.

'This boy is always allowed,' Rachel grinned.

'Cheers to that,' Tori agreed, raising her mug of tea.

Alex sat back down looking very pleased with himself and obviously lapping up the attention being lavished on him. I wasn't sure it was quite what Gracie had in mind when she'd made him promise he would make the trip to Lakeside and stay in the cottage to honour her memory and long-held wish.

'Okay,' I said, feeling nervous as the moment came to hand Rachel's dress over. 'This is from me and your mum, Rach, with love. And yes, she's given me permission to let you open it while we're here. In fact, she insisted, but on the promise that we'd FaceTime her at some point with your reaction.'

'This sounds monumental,' said Alex.

'And intriguing,' added Tori.

'It's both.' I nodded, while she grabbed her phone.

Rachel looked puzzled, but wasted no time in pulling the ribbon and ripping into the soft tissue paper I'd carefully wrapped the dress in. I held my breath as she held it up, one hand covering my mouth to stop me talking her through the moment. I needed to give her time to take it all in without interruption or explanation.

She didn't need time though, because she took one look at the painstakingly put together panel on the front and burst into tears. Tori and Alex exchanged a glance and my heart thumped so hard in my chest I thought it was going to stop me breathing.

'These are all Nanna's,' Rachel whispered, the look on her face conveying all of the emotion I felt times ten.

I nodded, but couldn't get the words out over the lump in my throat.

'Oh, Em,' said Tori, cottoning on and also starting to cry as she snapped away on her phone, recording the treasured moment for posterity.

'I don't know what to say,' Rachel sobbed.

'It was your mum's idea,' I told her. 'And you don't have to say anything, just go and take a minute and then try it on. I want to check the fit. Although it should be fine. I've created enough frocks using your figure as a guide now to know your measurements better than my own.'

'Oh, you,' she laughed through her tears, balling up the tissue paper and throwing it at me.

'I'll help,' said Tori and the pair disappeared into the bedroom.

Ideally, I would have liked Rachel's mum to witness her daughter's delight first-hand, but I had known it would be an emotional moment and one better suited to the privacy of the cottage as opposed to the potentially packed pub.

'What was that all about?' Alex asked, once the door had closed behind Rachel and Tori. 'And did you really make that beautiful dress from scratch, Em?'

'I did.' I nodded, feeling proud.

It was the first of my dresses that he had seen. He had admired the anniversary picture and my fern skirt but hadn't seen the dress I'd quickly made because he'd been off treading the boards and it had had to go in the post practically as soon as the last stitch had been sewn.

'And the patchwork panels are all made up of fabrics which belonged to Rachel's nanna, who died a short while ago,' I further explained.

'Oh,' he said, sounding touched. 'The nanna who was also a book-lover?' I nodded. 'Well, that explains the tears.'

'Exactly.' I swallowed, trying not to succumb to my own. '*Hope Falls* became her favourite after Rachel introduced her to it.'

'Well, I love the dress every bit as much as the picture,' Alex praised. 'What a wonderful keepsake.'

'I think so.' I smiled. 'And Rachel's mum wanted her to have the dress on this holiday because of the book and film connection.'

'And their shared love of both,' Alex added, just as the bed-room door opened again and Rachel stepped out.

'Oh, Rach,' I gasped, both hands covering my mouth this time.

She gave a twirl and then came over.

'It's perfect,' she said, reaching for my hands. 'It fits like a second skin.'

'It really does,' said Tori. 'I had no idea you were so skilled, Em. This is couture quality.'

'Goodness.' I blushed. 'I don't know about that.'

'Well, I do,' Tori said seriously. 'And it is.'

'This coming from a woman who spends hours looking at couture and spends endless amounts of money on it,' said Rachel, as she turned this way and that and made the fabric of the skirt swish about her legs.

'A woman who *used* to spend endless amounts on couture,' Tori corrected. 'I might have kicked the habit, but I do still know what I'm talking about. I know a good thing when I see it and this is most definitely it.'

'She's been commissioned to make a couple more of these too,' Rachel told Tori. 'And all through word of mouth.'

I turned Rachel around so I could examine the side seams of the bodice a little closer.

'That's wonderful,' Tori praised. 'But to be honest, I'm surprised it's not more. Are you sure your social media accounts and online presence is working at full stretch, Em?'

I looked at her and laughed and then realised she was being serious.

'You see,' said Alex, wagging a finger in my direction. 'I'm not the only one who thinks you should be taking this more seriously, Em.'

I began to feel hot and imagined my neck turning blotchy as they ganged up on me. At this rate, I wouldn't need to explain my business plan because they would goad me into launching and assume the resultant success was solely down to their encouragement!

'Please tell me you have social media accounts for ...' Tori frowned.

'Passion for Patchwork,' Alex then blurted out. 'That's what I told Em she should call her sewing empire.'

'I like that,' said Tori, cocking her head to one side. 'And of course, I know you don't have accounts to champion your work because if you did, I'd be following you, wouldn't I? Oh, Em,' she scolded. 'You really need to get your butt in gear.'

'Well ...' I feebly said.

'Have you got anything else with you?' she then demanded, cutting me off. 'Any other garments?'

'A skirt,' Alex told her, answering on my behalf. 'She made it last week.'

I gave him a look and he shot one straight back, making me feel even hotter.

'Go and put it on,' Tori insisted, waving a hand towards the bedroom. 'And then we're going to go down to the lake and I'm going to photograph you and Rachel and get you online.'

'I hardly think now's the time . . .' I began to say but they carried on talking over me and the words trailed off.

'You'll never have a better backdrop,' she prudently pointed out as I went to get changed.

'It's ridiculous that she isn't already online, isn't it?' said Alex, throwing further fuel on to Tori's fire.

'She needs no encouragement from you, thank you very much,' I tutted, but I didn't really mean it and the grin he gave me told me he knew it.

I might not have been willing to admit it, but I was actually feeling pretty excited about their enthusiasm and excitement. Or I was until it dawned on me that Rachel hadn't joined in with the conversation at all.

I turned to look at her, worried that she didn't think Tori's plan to launch me online was a good one. However, when I caught sight of her face as she examined the panels around the bottom of her dress, I realised she hadn't heard a word of what was being said.

She was utterly mesmerised, miles and years away, lost in a plethora of happy memories and I felt extremely proud of what I had created from a bag of fabric that might otherwise have never seen the light of day.

'Now this time, you stand on the left, Em,' Tori shouted, eyeing us through half-closed eyes. 'And Rachel, you look out across the lake.'

Rachel puffed out her cheeks.

'I hope the dress is worth this,' I muttered under my breath and risking Tori's wrath because I had momentarily abandoned my pose.

When Tori had said we should come down to the lake to take a few snaps, I thought she had meant literally just that, but my assumption had been wrong. The few snaps, taken on her phone, had required complete makeovers for us both and we were now in full make-up and sporting carefully styled hair. It had taken a surprising amount of time to achieve the relaxed and casual, I've just popped out for a walk down to the lake, aesthetic. We'd got props too. An artfully draped blanket and vintage flask and enamel mugs had been utilised to complete the idyllic composition.

'It totally is.' Rachel beamed, which made Tori snap away even faster. 'I love it. And believe it or not, I'm rather enjoying this.'

'Em!' Tori then yelped. 'Why the look of surprise?'

'Sorry,' I giggled and Rachel properly laughed. 'I've just had a bit of a shock.'

'Well, get your act together,' she tutted. 'There's not long to go before we'll lose the best of the light.'

Rachel gasped as she realised the time, but didn't say why. I wondered if she was panicking about missing one of Jeremy's assigned call times, but didn't ask. A few shots later, the familiar rain clouds began to gather so Tori said Rachel could go, but she wouldn't let me follow her.

'You'll need a profile pic,' she told me, rushing over to tease out my casual curls and touch up my lip gloss. 'And I've had a brainwave, but we'll need Alex.'

'I'm not sure he'll be up for being photographed,' I warned her.

'I don't want to photograph him,' she told me. 'Although he would make a wonderful subject. I need him for his manpower.'

'As beautiful as they are,' Alex shouted as he approached, having been summoned by Rachel who Tori had sent off with a request for him to join us, 'I'm not sure Em's dresses are quite my style.'

Tori rolled her eyes.

'No modelling required,' she said. 'I just want you to steer this thing.'

Her big idea for my profile pic was to snap me sitting on the end of the jetty, looking into the lake with my bare feet dangling over the edge and the fern skirt fanned out around me. In order to achieve it, she needed Alex to row her into position so she could take the picture facing me on the water.

'What do you think?' she asked Alex, showing him the images, once she'd taken a few.

'Beautiful,' he said huskily. 'You look beautiful, Em.' He smiled, looking up at me and making my heart skitter.

'Thank you,' I said, feeling my face flush.

'Although,' he said, 'you do look a bit mean and moody. You could cheer up a bit.'

Tori looked furious and I burst out laughing as she gave him a sharp nudge which rocked the tiny boat and almost made him drop an oar.

'And that's a wrap!' I said, jumping up and shoving my feet back inside my plimsolls.

'Indeed, it is,' Tori said, looking down at the final moment she'd captured.

By the time Alex had retied the boat to the jetty and we'd walked the path back through the woods to the cottage, a few fat raindrops had started to fall and Rachel had changed out of her dress and was making dinner. I was relieved she hadn't rushed off to answer a summons from Jeremy.

'I know I said I wanted to watch the film tonight,' said Tori, scrolling through the endless shots on her phone, 'but I think we should focus on getting you set up online, Em. The sooner the better as far as I'm concerned.'

She was certainly keen.

'I appreciate that,' I told her. 'But you'd need Wi-Fi to do it, wouldn't you?'

'Oh, damn,' she said, wrinkling her pretty nose. 'I forgot we're in the wilderness. So, where around here can we go to get online?'

'The pub,' the three of us said together.

'In that case,' she said, putting down her phone and picking up the DVD case, 'let's do the film tonight and then marketing tomorrow.'

'And you could FaceTime your mum then, Rach,' I suggested.

'I was already planning to.' She smiled back.

Chapter 24

Alex ducked out of watching the film with us that evening.

'I've just had a lightbulb moment connected to something I've been working on,' he explained, when all three of us objected to his absence. 'And I'd really like to get it drawn up tonight before the idea does a bunk.'

'So, are you heading to the pub to do that?' Tori asked.

'No,' he told her. 'I've got all the components I need already downloaded to my laptop, so I can adapt them and put them together here and then upload them when I'm back in the office again.'

He wouldn't be swayed to put the work off, so it was just the three of us watching that night. He set himself up to work in what was now my room, so our reciting the actors' lines ahead of them, laughing and then blubbing at the saddest bits wouldn't disturb him or tempt him to abandon whatever it was he was doing to watch. I curled up in his armchair and Rachel and Tori stretched out on the sofa.

I missed his presence more than I cared to admit that evening, but no one else seemed to mind that it was just the three of us.

'So,' said Rachel, as the closing credits began to roll and we

all had a stretch. 'Does the film back up what the book told you, Tori?'

The look on our friend's face was a mixture of surprise and delight.

'Yes.' She nodded. 'Thanks to Dad's intervention, carefree Rose has taken a backseat and, now I've realised I've spent years running away from reality, Laurie is in the driving seat. Hold on to your hats, girls,' she added with a giggle, 'because it's all about to kick off!'

I knew her father's actions and Tori's willingness to accept them hadn't always sat easy with Rachel and me, but credit where it was due, he had known what he was doing and Tori had obviously realised she had needed it to happen.

'I don't believe it,' Rachel gasped. 'I hope you haven't completely eradicated all your Rose traits though, Tori, because she had a fresh start, too.'

'That would be impossible,' I laughed.

'Don't worry, there's still a bit of Rose in me,' Tori beamed. 'And you might not believe this either, Rach, but had Dad not called time on my spending, I would have done it myself. He's got me to this point faster than I would have done, mostly because he said Mum wouldn't have been happy with how he'd always pandered to me, but I was actually getting bored with living the high life and having nothing to show for it.'

'Curiouser and curiouser!' Rachel laughed, then pretended to pass out.

When I returned to my idyllic refuge, I tried not to think too deeply about what Tori meant by things being about to kick off, but when I saw what she was victoriously holding up the next morning when she stepped out on to the veranda, I didn't need

too deep a dive to work it out. She already had Alex wrapped around her finger.

'I don't believe it!' Rachel gaped. 'How have you wangled that?'

It was Alex's expensive laptop Tori was holding aloft. He must have had extremely strong, and trusting, feelings for her if he was willing to lend her that.

'Just last week I asked him if I could borrow it,' huffed Rachel, sounding hurt. 'And he looked as if I'd asked if I could buy his baby or something!'

'What can I say?' Tori shrugged, stroking the bespoke case. 'Maybe I asked more nicely than you did, Rach.'

'I don't even want to think about what you might possibly mean by that,' Rachel tutted, standing up. 'Are we going or what?'

I didn't want to think about it either.

'Is this really the best you could do with all that money I raised by parting with my treasured Tom Ford clutch?' Tori groaned as we pootled up the road from the cottage to Lakeside in our almost clapped-out car.

We could have walked, but Tori had insisted it would be safer to transport Alex's laptop by four wheels rather than on two legs. A suggestion she almost retracted when she remembered which car we'd be traveling in.

'Not all of the money went on the car,' Rachel, who was wearing her special dress again, reminded her. 'There was fuel and insurance and tax to pay too. Remember?'

'You're going to have to teach me about all that sort of stuff, Rach,' Tori surprised me by saying seriously rather than further scoffing. 'Dad's always taken charge of that sort of thing, but if

I ever end up with enough in the bank to buy a car in my own name, then I'll need to know, won't I?'

It didn't sound like she was expecting to see her Range Rover again after all.

'That you will,' said Rachel, winking at me in the rear-view mirror. 'That you will.'

She parked as close to the pub as she could get and Tori jumped out.

'Are you open?' she called to Connor, who was just finishing watering the plants in the baskets and tubs and which had grown enormously since we'd moved into the cottage.

'Not quite,' he said, checking his watch and then spotting Rachel. 'But I suppose I could make an exception for you three.'

'You are a love,' said Tori, standing on tiptoe and giving him a kiss on the cheek.

'I know,' he said, blushing. 'My generosity will be my downfall one of these days.'

Rachel and I gave Siddy her usual fuss while Connor fired up the coffee machine, admired Rachel's outfit and Tori set up her office – as she called it – at a booth furthest away from the main bar area.

'Don't you like dogs, Tori?' Connor asked, when she rushed back and asked him for the Wi-Fi code, while giving Siddy a wide berth.

'Love them,' she said, giving the friendly hound a smile. 'I just don't want to get her doggy smell on my hands.'

'Poor Siddy,' I said, giving her an even longer fuss which she lapped up. 'She's perfectly fragrant. Not at all smelly.'

'Well, whatever,' said Tori. 'Hurry up, you two. We've got work to do.'

We didn't settle down to it immediately though, because

Rachel FaceTimed her mum after Tori had sent her the snaps and video of Rachel's first glimpse of the dress and explained that she'd finally made it to Lakeside and would be with us for the rest of the holiday.

When the call to her mum's phone connected, Rachel stood up and did a twirl at a distance before leaning closer to the screen to show off the patchwork panels.

'Oh, Emily,' her mum sniffed, pulling a tissue out of her sleeve. 'It's perfect. Absolutely perfect and the look on your face when you ripped into that parcel was priceless, Rachel. Thank you for capturing the moment, Tori.'

'Wait until you see the panels in real life,' Rachel sighed dreamily. 'Em's done Nanna proud.'

'I can already see that.' Her mum beamed. 'But I am looking forward to seeing it up close.'

'Thank you,' I said, feeling relieved that I'd so effectively fulfilled her brief. 'I'm so pleased you like it.'

'I love it,' she said. 'Well done you. Next stop, a catwalk in Paris!'

'Well,' I laughed, 'I don't know about that . . .'

'I do,' said Tori.

After Rachel signed off, Tori explained what her vision for my online launch could look like. She had based her ideas on both the aesthetic of the film and the photos she'd taken at the lake, along with my actual range of clothes, of course. It struck me again how *Hope Falls* had influenced my designs without my even realising it. Tori had almost finished dazzling us with her ideas when Rachel's phone began to ring.

'Oh, blast,' she tutted, sliding out of the booth having checked the screen. 'It's Jeremy.'

'Why's he ringing now?' I frowned. 'Surely he should be at work.'

Rachel shook her head.

'Really?' Tori frowned as she went to press accept call. 'You're really going to answer? We're in the middle of something extremely important here.'

'I know,' said Rachel, sounding embarrassed, 'but if I don't pick up now, he'll just keep calling so I might as well get it over with.'

She headed for the door and Tori tutted.

'You know, I really do think he's got her tracked,' she muttered. 'And the second she falls within signal range, he pounces.'

'I know,' I agreed, but I was smiling.

'That's not a good thing, Em.' Tori tutted again. 'He's enemy number one, remember.'

'Oh, I haven't forgotten,' I told her. 'I haven't forgotten that for one second, or that you've got a plan to take him out.'

'Is that why you're smiling?' she asked. 'You're so certain that my plan will work, even though you've no idea what it is?'

'No,' I told her, then hastily added, 'although I'm sure it will help things along. But I was just appreciating Rachel's choice of words. If you're in love with someone and they call you, you do not say "oh, blast", or that you want to get the conversation over with, do you?'

Tori took a second to process that, her eyes flicking to the left as she recalled what Rachel had said.

'Well spotted, comrade.' She nodded, offering me a high five, which I willingly accepted. 'Now,' she demanded, 'back to business.'

She was still waxing lyrical when Rachel returned. I didn't

immediately know if Tori noticed that our friend's eyes looked a little red, but I did. I went to ask if she was all right, but Tori pressed her leg against mine and I stopped myself. Clearly, she had noticed.

'So,' she said, taking a breath, 'to sum up. What I'm thinking, is that you should go for the Cottagecore slash pioneer aesthetic. The landscape around here fits that perfectly, Em, and you could even make a trip back here to take the photos for your website a regular event when the collection is updated, because it would be a tax-deductible expense.'

Rachel blinked a couple of times and I turned to look at Tori.

'How do you even know this?' I asked her. 'When did you become such an expert?'

Tori looked well pleased. 'You might think I'm always faffing on my phone' – she smiled – 'or that I always *used* to be faffing on my phone, but I've realised recently that I actually picked a lot of stuff up about the way the things I was buying were marketed, presented and packaged. I might have been buying stuff from the accounts I was continually scrolling, but I also took on-board how they worked. And I know this will work for you, Em. I've come up with the perfect strategy to get the orders rolling in.'

'I'm impressed,' I said, as Connor came to replace our coffees.

'Everything all right here?' he asked.

'Everything will be fine,' Tori told him. 'As long as your Wi-Fi signal holds out.'

'I can't guarantee that' – he smiled – 'but I'll keep the coffees coming, shall I?'

'And if you've got any of those pastries from the bakery,' I said, 'a few of them wouldn't go amiss.'

'I'll see what I can do,' he chuckled.

'My only concern,' Rachel said, biting her lip, 'is if your plan to introduce Emily's designs to the world works too well, Tori, she won't be able to keep up with demand. She's starting this new job next month . . .'

'What new job is this?' Tori cut in.

I brought her up to speed about the offer I'd had just ahead of the holiday and how I was supposed to be joining the new company in September. By the time I'd finished explaining, she was looking at me in disbelief.

'Are you seriously telling me that you'd rather be analysing data than designing dresses?' she gasped, before I had a chance to fill her and Rachel in about the working part-time idea I'd recently come up with as a compromise.

'Well, no,' I said, avoiding looking at Rachel and thinking again of the pleasure I'd felt in making her dress and my fabulous fern skirt. 'I wouldn't rather be doing that.'

'So why in god's name are you taking the job then?' Tori asked, sounding aghast. 'I know I've never taken much interest in your patchwork before, Em, but I am now and I'm telling you, *this* is where your future lies.'

'Well,' I rushed to explain before Rachel had the opportunity to say something sensible about job security and company pension plans, 'I have recently been wondering about working part-time and sewing part-time. I thought it might be . . .' My words trailed off as Tori vehemently shook her head.

'That won't work,' she said. 'You need to commit, one hundred per cent, Em. You need to give Passion for Patchwork your absolute all.'

'But I also need to not be stressing about paying the rent,' I

pointed out. 'With Rachel moving in with Jeremy, a regular income, be it full or part-time, will give me some security.'

'That's true,' Rachel said and I wondered if the compromise would keep me in her good books and not give Jeremy the ammunition to take a pot shot at our friendship.

I was also interested to note that she had said nothing to contradict my assumption, nothing which suggested she was having doubts about the move or still considering it, as opposed to getting on and doing it.

'Rachel!' Connor shouted, beckoning her over before I could ask her to once and for all properly clarify the situation.

'Don't say anything important,' she insisted, as she slid out of the booth and went to see what he wanted.

'You do realise,' Tori immediately said in a frustrated whisper, 'that not taking that job and not finding something part-time would in effect put an end to Rachel's plan to move in with Jeremy because she'd be too worried about your fragile finances.'

'Of course, I realise that,' I said, keeping one eye on Rachel at the bar.

Tori threw up her hands. 'Then why the hell have you accepted it?'

'I've accepted it for now,' I patiently explained, 'because the last thing I want is to give Jeremy another reason to drive a wedge between us. If I don't take that job, he'll make Rachel believe that I turned it down to stop her leaving. You know how manipulative he is.'

Tori's shoulders dropped as she realised the truth in what I was telling her.

'He'll pour more poison into her and she'll end up thinking

the worst of me as a result,' I carried on to really drive the point home.

'Yes, yes,' Tori said, nibbling the end of her thumbnail. 'I can see that now.'

I batted her hand away. 'But I have genuinely been thinking about the part-time scenario,' I carried on, even though she didn't think that would be a good idea. 'I really do want to launch this business. I even came on holiday with the intention of deciding whether I dared go for it and I've got savings in place to help while I get going.'

My explanation gathered speed, for fear of Rachel coming back before I'd told Tori everything. It felt good to share what I had been thinking about, even though the moment didn't match the one I had imagined.

'And I had pretty much made up my mind to go for it,' I said in a rush, 'when Rach mentioned moving out and I panicked. I can't lose her, Tori.'

'But don't forget I'm on the case now,' she reminded me. 'And I really do have a plan. Whatever else you do end up doing and however you end up doing it, we're getting you online right here, right now. It's what we came here to do today.'

'Look out,' I hissed as Rachel walked back, carrying a plate of sweet treats and an envelope which she then put in her bag.

'So, did you?' Rachel asked.

The smell of the warm pastry made my tummy rumble. The pain au chocolat looked particularly good and I immediately reached for one.

'Did we what?' I innocently asked, through a buttery, sweet mouthful.

'Say anything important?'

'We did rather,' Tori recklessly announced. 'I've told Em that as I'm going to be finding myself a job soon, I'll move into the flat when you move out, so that way she won't need to fret about money, you won't need to worry if she's managing and she can focus on properly launching Passion for Patchwork. All of which,' she carried on before either of us could register our surprise or Rachel could form a cautionary response, 'leads me nicely on to this . . .'

She tapped a few keys, then turned the laptop round to show us a logo bearing my dream business name.

'What on earth?' I gasped, leaning closer to the screen and momentarily forgetting that she had come up with a plan which should keep Rachel happy and save me poring over more spreadsheets.

The logo layout featured a hexagonal patchwork background with the words Passion for Patchwork laid over the top. The background shapes were made up of gingham, polka dot and ditzy floral patterns and the lettering was in solid colour, which made it stand out. It had an almost 3D quality to it and was extremely stylish.

'There are four,' Tori explained as Rachel came around to our side of the booth to take a closer look at what was making my mouth open and close like a trapdoor. 'And each one represents a different season.'

She scrolled down and the summer colours changed to shades of orange, yellow and red for autumn. Then red, white and blue for winter and finally pretty pastels for spring.

'Same great logo,' she said, scrolling up again so we could see all four together. 'But with a seasonal twist. There are banners for all social media platforms, too.'

'Where did you get these?' Rachel asked as I carried on admiring the exquisite details.

I noticed that each of the letters was edged with tiny stitches and at the end of the word patchwork there was a tiny needle and thread, making it look as though the words had been sewn rather than typed.

'Where do you think?' Tori laughed.

'Alex.' Rachel grinned, returning to her seat.

'Alex made these?' I gasped, looking at Tori.

'Of course, he did,' she nudged. 'This was the lightbulb moment he finished last night while we were watching the film. He told me he's been secretly working on them for a while in the hope that you might see sense.'

I put the half-eaten pastry back on the plate and wiped my fingers on a paper napkin.

'Tori, what exactly did you say to convince him to lend you his laptop?' Rachel asked, tracking back to what we'd been saying before we left the cottage.

'Nothing.' Tori shrugged. 'He knew I needed more than a phone to get Em up and running today, so rushed to finish the logo last night and then offered me the laptop first thing this morning. I think he'd do anything for you, Em,' she finished up with a nudge, half serious, half teasing.

'He's certainly a wonderful friend,' I finally found voice enough to say and not daring to fully take in her words and the implication that went with them.

My other two friends rolled their eyes.

'So,' said Tori. 'Do you like these? Do you want to go ahead with this look Alex and I have in mind?'

'I absolutely love them.' I swallowed. 'They're perfect, aren't

they? Exactly what I would have asked for had I commissioned them myself, so yes, I want to go ahead. I don't know how much he charges, but these are worth every penny.'

'He won't be billing you, you dozy mare,' Tori nudged me again. 'Now, let's get you up and running.'

By the end of the morning, she had set up accounts on every popular platform for my new business and was making inroads into designing a website too. The profile picture she insisted we use was the one taken with me sitting on the jetty, but not of me looking into the water. We had all agreed that the lucky shot of me laughing when Alex told me to cheer up was by far the best. As I examined it, I thought I looked rather good and that was something I never said.

'You can launch without a website,' Tori insisted, as she typed away, 'because prospective clients can message you via the socials, but we might as well do as much as we can to set one up now. And,' she added, clicking her fingers, 'I'm going to get you a business email address too.'

Rachel looked at me and mouthed 'wow' and I responded with 'I know'. Fortunately, I wasn't too stunned by our friend's savvy knowledge and online prowess to feel stumped about how I could repay Alex for his hugely generous skill sharing.

He had given me something related to his work and in return I would create the picture for his mum and dad, made from things Gracie had loved, for free. It would be the ultimate labour of love and I couldn't wait to get started on it to show him how much I appreciated what he had so kindly done for me.

Chapter 25

Once we'd finished up at The Drover's, Rachel drove us back to the cottage and I walked down to the lake to see if I could find Alex. It dawned on me as I wandered along the now familiar path, that my decision about whether or not to go for it on the business front, the idea of which I had planned to spend the whole six weeks of my time away mulling over, had now been irrevocably and excitingly made. More than that, it was actually happening!

Tori's no-nonsense approach had cut through my procrastination and shone a light on the very heart of the matter, that I did still want to give my venture a full-time chance, and in spite of the fact that I was scared that my timing, given the whole Rachel moving out debacle, couldn't have been trickier.

Had Rachel not told me about moving in with Jeremy then I most likely would have already followed the yearning in my heart. It was pussyfooting around their relationship which had held me up, but Tori had ripped right through that. I wondered what Rachel thought about our friend's plan to move in to the flat and pay her share of the bills while I got the business going and, more to the point, what did I make of it? I loved Tori to bits, but could I live with her?

'Alex!' I called out, when I spotted him walking along the edge of the shore beyond the jetty.

He turned around and waved, then waited while I caught him up.

'I wondered when you'd be back.' He smiled, but I couldn't help thinking he looked a little sad, in spite of his attractively upturned lips. 'How have you got on?'

'Absolutely brilliantly,' I told him. 'And it's all thanks to you and Tori.'

'You like the branding and logo idea?' He blushed.

'No,' I said, reaching out and pulling him into a hug, 'I love it. Absolutely adore it.'

'Really?' he said, as I loosened my grip a little and he looked down at me. 'Because it was just an idea. My interpretation of what I thought you might like. We can alter anything you're not happy with, so don't say you love it if there's something you want to change, because it will be easy enough to fix.'

'Alex,' I cut in, halting his rush of words. 'I really do love it. All of it. In fact, I love it so much that, if you go online and search for Passion for Patchwork, your summer logo and the banners along with Tori's clever words will come up. You might have to scroll a bit because of the unfathomable algorithms, but you'll find me for sure, represented by your beautiful artwork and Tori's clever spiel.'

Not only had Tori created the pages for my social media accounts, she'd also written up some wonderful descriptions along with a bit about me and my vision for my clothes to go with them, all based on a quick chat we'd had while we ate lunch.

I had just twittered on as we ate, assuming we were having a regular conversation but it turned out she was interviewing me

and then used what I had said to put together the lovely pieces for the pages. It wouldn't have sounded anywhere near as good had I known what she was doing because I would have felt too self-conscious to come up with the vivid descriptions which she had then turned into perfect prose.

'Already?' Alex laughed.

'Already,' I confirmed.

'Crikey,' he said, as he started to walk again and I fell into step. 'Tori doesn't hang about, does she?'

'No,' I said. 'She doesn't. Once she sets her sights on something, she has to have it. Only on this occasion,' I thoughtfully added, 'it wasn't something for her, it was something for me.'

Her kindness in sharing her skills and getting me set up was further proof that she really had changed and, remembering how buoyed up she'd been and how focused, I knew she'd enjoyed doing it.

'You sound surprised,' Alex said, carrying on towards the benches and campfire.

'I am,' I laughed and he gave me a disapproving look. 'You needn't look like that,' I told him. 'If you knew Tori as well as I do, then you'd know that she's currently going through a total transformation. She's always been lovely, but pretty self-absorbed and until recently, her wealthy father has given her everything she's ever wanted on a plate so she's never much had to think about other people, but now ...'

'He's pulled the plug,' Alex put in. 'Yes, she told me all about her sudden change in circumstances and how she's going to have to become better acquainted with the real world and pay her way to get along in it.'

I wondered if that was some of what they'd spent half of

Wednesday night – the evening Tori had arrived at the pub – talking about.

'She does seem to be making headway with introducing these dramatic changes, doesn't she?' he further said.

'Yes,' I said, probably sounding more amazed than I intended given the second slightly censorious look Alex then bestowed on me. 'She does. Rachel and I are both stunned.'

I hoped that coupling Rachel's reaction with mine, might make him realise that it wasn't just me who was surprised that Tori was getting her act together so quickly. The last thing I wanted to sound was bitchy and bitter.

'Well,' said Alex, 'I like her enormously already, so I'm really pleased for her and I'm pleased I'm getting to know her after her father cut her off because I'm not sure I would have had all that much in common with her before.'

My stomach dropped and I found myself immediately, and selfishly, wishing that they hadn't met at all. I might not have wanted to turn mine and Alex's gate-side kiss into something more lasting and serious but I couldn't bear the thought of him possibly pairing up with Tori. Not that he really would, would he?

Surely not if he was still carrying the baggage we'd both cited as one of the reasons for not taking things any further between us and, given the nature of his, I couldn't really believe he would be able to empty it all out in one clean sweep just because Tori was on the scene, even if I had previously wondered.

But then I further tortured myself by thinking that if I was finding our dream holiday so transformative, there was no reason why he wouldn't be too. Perhaps he was suddenly feeling footloose, fancy-free and ready for a fling and Tori had arrived

just in time to wedge herself into prime position as the person to indulge in it with after I'd turned him down.

'Perhaps not.' I swallowed. 'She really is a completely different person now. In fact,' I rushed on, trying to use her transformation to my advantage, 'her actions have helped me offload practically all of that baggage we talked about just a few days ago. I feel like a weight has been lifted and I can really focus on having some fun now.'

I held my breath, wondering how he would interpret my blatant declaration.

'Well, that's great.' He beamed. 'And further proof of what a wonderful woman Tori is, or has recently turned into.'

'Uh huh,' I sighed, frustrated that he hadn't caught on.

'Do you fancy a beer?' he then offered. 'I've got a few in a cool bag.'

'Nah.' I smiled. 'But thanks.' Then, tracking back to the original reason why I'd come to find him in the first place, added, 'I just wanted to say thank you for creating my logo. It's a beautiful interpretation of my vision and I'm truly very grateful.'

'Well,' he nodded, blushing again as he shoved his hands in his jeans pockets, 'I'm delighted you like, I mean, love it.'

'I really do.'

'Are you sure you don't want that beer?'

'I am,' I said, taking a step towards the path. 'I kind of got the impression that I'd broken into your thoughts when I interrupted your walk.'

'You had,' he confirmed, but then seeing my smile falter, added, 'but that was probably no bad thing.'

'Oh?' I queried, then found myself rooted to the spot in spite of my previous decision to leave him to his musings.

'I was thinking about Gracie,' he sighed, looking out over the lake. 'Sometimes now, I can think of her with nothing but joy and gratitude for the fact that I had such an incredible sister, but other times, like today, it all gets tangled up in my head and I lose sight of that and end up feeling bitter and angry that she was taken so soon.'

He pulled his hands out of his pockets and ran them through his hair. His nostrils flared as his exasperation with the injustice of his sister's life being cut so cruelly short ignited again.

'You know what,' I said, stepping back to the bench. 'I will have that beer.'

Alex narrowed his eyes. 'It's not a pity beer, is it?'

'No,' I laughed but when Alex looked disbelieving, I reiterated the point. 'It's not,' I said again. 'There's something else I wanted to tell you, but until you mentioned Gracie, I hadn't been sure whether to suggest it to you today.'

With a bottle each, we sat together on the bench and looked out over the lake which was as smooth as a millpond. I didn't immediately mention my desire to create the memory picture as a thank you for designing my branding and for a couple of minutes we sat in companionable and comfortable silence taking in the spectacular view.

'When it's so still like this,' Alex said, with a nod to the water, 'I always think it looks like you could walk from one side all the way to the other.'

'I would love to see you test that theory,' I laughed, the bubbles from the beer going up my nose and making my eyes water.

'I haven't forgotten about our email exchanges discussing the skinny-dipping, you know,' he said, raising an eyebrow and looking more like the mischievous version of himself I'd previously seen glimpses of.

'Well,' I said, reluctantly pulling my gaze away from his. 'You can forget all about Rachel and me joining you. Rachel reckons her toes still haven't recovered from the tentative dip she gave them off the end of the jetty when we first arrived.'

I had been about to add that he might be able to tempt Tori, but stopped myself. We'd already discussed it once and I wasn't about to jog his memory by suggesting something that would make him think about her again, especially with no clothes on.

'Gracie would have been up for it,' he said impishly.

I looked at him and shook my head. 'Oh no,' I admonished, but with a smile. 'Don't be dropping Gracie into the conversation again the second you want to rope me into doing something I don't want to do. That's how I ended up throwing myself down the rapids, remember?'

'How could I forget?' he laughed and I gave him a shove.

'But talking of Gracie,' I said, after I'd taken another swig of beer, 'I've been thinking about the picture you asked me to make for your parents.'

'I haven't forgotten about that,' he was quick to say because it was a while since it had been mentioned.

'I didn't for a second think you had,' I hastily told him. 'But what I was thinking was that as you've been so kind to create and design my logo and haven't billed me for it, I could do the same with Gracie's picture. Will you let me make it as a thank you?'

He was quiet for a moment and looked back at the lake again.

'I'm pretty sure the patchwork picture will take many more hours to create than I spent on your logo.' He then frowned. 'Not that I skimped . . .'

'Alex,' I interrupted, lightly laying a hand on his arm. 'Please

let me do this. I really want to and I think it would be a lovely way for us to share our skills.'

'A tax beating bartering system but with a personal touch,' he said, with a wry smile.

'Something like that.' I smiled back.

'All right,' he said. 'I'll agree to that.'

'Good,' I said, clinking my bottle against his as the chilly condensation ran down my fingers, 'because I was going to do it anyway.'

Alex shook his head. 'In that case,' he said, putting his bottle down and wiping his hands on his jeans, 'I'd like to show you this.'

He reached into the bag of beers again, but this time presented me with a wooden box about the size of a shoebox, rather than a bottle.

'What is this?' I asked, taking it from him, after also putting down my bottle and drying off my hands.

'It was Gracie's,' he said, the words sticking in his throat. 'And it's filled with some of her favourite things. You might be able to use some of them in the picture. I carried it down here to look through, but then got a bit maudlin and left it. I'd like to show you though.'

I carefully opened the lid, a hint of floral scent escaping as Alex reached inside and picked up a bundle of photos tied together with a length of pink ribbon. Along with the pictures, I could see cinema stubs (including multiple viewings of our beloved film, of course), a tiny teddy bear, letters, holey stones, silk flowers and a random assortment of trinkets which had all been a treasure trove to their owner.

Alex fondly explained everything, sometimes with laughter

on his lips, other times with tears in his eyes, but always with love in his heart. I was entranced by the images of the beautiful woman who had Alex's eyes and smile, but a feminine grace and elegance which took my breath away. I didn't say much as we looked, happy to listen to Alex's descriptions of everything and the heart-warming anecdotes which accompanied them and explained their coveted place in Gracie's most special memories. Many of the things had a connection to *Hope Falls* and felt even more special as a result.

I don't know how long we spent looking through everything but the light had begun to fade as I handed Alex the box and he carefully put the lid back on.

'You're right, Alex,' I told him, already imagining how I could make the picture look. 'I will be able to use lots of these in my design and I'm privileged to have had the honour of getting to know Gracie through some of her favourite things. Thank you for sharing them with me.'

The shuddering breath Alex took told me he appreciated my words. I only wished Gracie herself could have shared her memories with me.

'Thank you,' Alex said softly, returning the box to the bag. 'I know the picture will be beautiful and Mum and Dad will love it.'

'It will be stunning,' I confirmed. 'I can promise you that. And then we'll be even.'

Alex shook his head. 'No, we won't,' he said, turning to look deep into my eyes. 'I'm still in your debt.'

'You are?' I swallowed.

'I am,' he told me.

'How so?' I frowned. 'I don't understand.'

'Yours *and* Rachel's actually,' he said, and I felt even more confused. 'You've helped me prepare for my next step in life and introduced me to a potential new partner and I'm not sure what the going rate for that is.'

'Oh,' I said, clumsily standing up as realisation dawned and I thrust my half-drunk bottle into his hands. 'No charge. You can have that one on us.'

'That's very generous.' He frowned, clearly taken aback by my reaction as I took a step away from the bench. 'You're not going, are you?'

'Yes,' I said, turning to walk off. 'I've just remembered I promised I'd help Rachel with dinner and it's getting late. I'll leave you to your thoughts again and see you back at the cottage in a bit.'

Chapter 26

I kept to the periphery of the conversation that evening, thanked both Alex and Tori for their hard work in helping to launch my business online then, feigning a headache, had an early night. I had expected to feel on cloud nine, what with it being such a monumental day on the business front and having been gifted the privilege of getting to know Gracie a little better through her collection of saved treasures, but I couldn't get anywhere near close.

The kindest thing I could do for myself that night was put a bit of distance between me and my friends, but there was no chance of that happening the next day. And actually, I was so excited to see if I'd had any interest online, I was able to put what Alex had said about a potential new partner, for most of the time at least, almost to the back of my mind.

'We'll take my car,' he offered, as we were getting ready to head to The Drover's for Sunday lunch. 'That'll get you there quicker, Em,' he added, catching my excitement.

'There's no rush,' Rachel pointed out. 'Because we've agreed not to look online until we've eaten.'

'But the earlier we get there, the earlier we can eat,' Tori cleverly said.

'Not that I'm going to be able to eat.' I dithered, wiping my hands down my shorts. 'I'm too nervous.'

'Excited,' Alex said hearteningly. 'You're not nervous, Em, you're excited.'

'Potayto, potahto.' I shrugged, rubbing my tummy. 'Either way, I still feel nauseous.'

'In that case,' Tori announced, 'I'm sure you'd benefit from some fresh air and I'd like to walk to the pub, if that's all right with you three.'

Rachel and I looked at each other and gasped.

'What?' Alex asked, looking between us. 'What have I missed?'

'Tori has just said she wants to walk somewhere,' Rachel said in a tone laden with teasing drama and genuine shock. I hoped her reaction would make Alex realise that what I'd said about Tori the day before was nowhere near wide of the mark. 'That's *never* happened before.'

Tori poked her tongue out.

'Before my father confiscated my funds,' she said to Alex, ignoring Rachel flagging up her former refusal to ever walk anywhere when she could be driven, or drive herself, 'I'd picked up a few bits and pieces for the holiday and it would be a shame not to try them out now I'm here, wouldn't it?'

That explained the lovely Dubarry boots and pristine Barbour.

'What sort of things?' Alex asked.

'These walking boots for a start,' she said, holding up a pair of boots which were most definitely not from Mountain Warehouse.

'Fair enough,' said Alex with a smile as he returned his keys to the kitchen counter. 'In that case, we will walk. It's not that far.'

Tori had barely made it a few minutes into the short trek to Lakeside before she was complaining about the beginnings of a blister and wanting to limp back to the car.

'We're not going back for the car,' I tutted.

'There's only one thing for it then,' said Alex, crouching down in the middle of the road. 'Hop up.'

Tori literally jumped at the chance.

'You won't be able to give her a piggy back all the way,' Rachel laughed. 'You should have broken those boots in, Tori.'

'And where would I have done that?' she asked as Alex hitched her higher and set off at a pace.

'Do you think she really is going to move in to the flat?' Rachel asked, the second they were out of earshot.

'She seemed pretty serious when she suggested it yesterday, didn't she?' I pointed out.

'Was that the first you'd heard of it?' she then demanded, taking me by surprise because she sounded so suspicious.

'Yes,' I said, trying to gauge her expression but it was hard as we were striding out side by side.

I didn't want to unwittingly say anything now which might scupper either her plans or mine and waited for her to carry on.

'Well, in that case,' she then bluntly said, which suggested her mood was no longer the sunniest, 'don't get your hopes up.'

'What's that supposed to mean?'

'You know what she's like,' she said, sounding mean.

'I know what she used to be like,' I corrected, jumping to Tori's defence. 'This new version of her is a whole different ballgame.'

One, unfortunately, which appealed to a wholly different man, but I wasn't going to dwell on that.

'Don't get arsey,' Rachel tutted. 'I was just saying.'

'I'm not getting arsey,' I shot back. 'But even if she doesn't move in, I can manage. I've got savings, so there's no need for you to worry about that side of things.'

I knew they weren't enough to pay for everything if Tori did change her mind about moving in, but I wasn't going to back down now I'd come so far. I'd already got commissions lined up and that was without the benefit of the clever online campaign. I'd manage somehow, even if I did end up living on beans and bread for a while. Needs must if I wanted this to work, and now I'd finally made the decision, I really did.

'I can't help thinking that you've been planning this business launch for a while,' Rachel said, sounding further put out.

'It was something I planned to think about during our holiday,' I admitted, knowing there was no need to keep it under wraps now. 'And yes, I have been making plans for the financial side of it, for a while, just in case I found the courage to go for it.'

'It sounds to me like you had every intention of going for it whether you had time to dither over the pros or cons or not.'

'I didn't realise that myself until very recently,' I admitted, further taken aback by the harsh trajectory of her mood swing, 'but I think you're right.'

'So why did you let me think you were taking the other job?' she burst out.

'What on earth's the matter with you, Rach?' I frowned.

'I just don't understand why you didn't tell me before,' she said, sounding upset as well as angry.

'I was going to tell you what I was considering,' I told her. 'Quite soon after we got here actually, but then you said about moving in with Jeremy and I knew that if you thought I was

going to turn the job down and take a risk to become self-employed you'd worry that I wouldn't be able to manage and you'd feel obliged to stay.'

'I thought you'd jump at the chance to stop me moving in with him,' she said cruelly.

Clearly, she didn't need Jeremy pouring poison in her ear about me, because she'd concocted a draft of her own and in spite of my determination to protect her from, rather than include her in, my recent soul-searching.

'Thank you so much, Em,' I said sarcastically. 'For generously putting my feelings ahead of your own.'

She didn't say anything.

'I just want you to be happy.' I sighed. 'Aren't you happy?'

'Perfectly,' she said, picking up the pace again. 'I just feel a bit of a fool that I didn't know what was going on for all this time, that's all.'

'I would have told you everything once I'd fathomed it out,' I said, matching her stride. 'But when Tori arrived and bluntly stated the obvious about me going for it, I could see what she was getting at and as a result it all fell into place far sooner than I expected it to and in a way I didn't really think it would, either.'

'So, you hadn't talked to her about it before?'

'No,' I said. 'I hadn't. The only person who has known about it all along is me!'

'Well, I'm thrilled for you,' she said, still sounding anything but as we rounded a bend and Tori and Alex came into sight.

Alex was bent double nursing a stitch and Tori was sitting on the verge untying her walking shoes. Had I not just had such an unexpected dressing down, I would have laughed.

'I'm sure the two of you will make every success of your new

business,' Rachel choked with a nod at Tori, before she marched off, 'and be very happy living together.'

'Thanks,' I called after her, feeling put out that I was having to justify my decision to the one person I had hoped would be thrilled it had been so well thought through and with her life-changing situation at the heart of it. 'I'm sure we will too.'

The pub was busy by the time we arrived and with Connor short-staffed again, Rachel offered to help him out, rather than sit with us while we waited for our lunch. Tori and Alex sat on one side of the booth and I sat on the other, wondering if gooseberry was on the menu or if my existence made it present enough.

'So,' said Tori, pulling her mobile out of her pocket once we'd finally eaten – or in my case half-eaten – our lunch, 'let's turn on and see what's happened, shall we?'

We'd agreed not to walk into the pub with our phones switched on, mine in particular, so we wouldn't be distracted by the (hopeful) influx of notifications when they connected to the Wi-Fi.

'Here goes,' I said, taking a big breath and, with shaking hands, turning mine on.

'Put it on the table,' Alex laughed. 'Before you drop it.'

I turned it face down and then let it stay there while it went through the motions of starting up. It was some minutes before it stopped pinging and my nerves had shifted from worrying that no one would have found me to stressing that too many people had.

'Don't panic, Em,' said Alex, reaching across the table and squeezing my hand. 'I'm sure they won't all want you to make something.'

'Well, she won't have to worry about paying the bills if they do,' Tori laughed.

'I thought you were chipping in with those,' Rachel tersely reminded her.

'Go on,' said Alex, letting my hand go again and not picking up on the icy edge in Rachel's tone. 'Have a look.'

'Start with Insta,' Tori advised. 'That's where I reckon you'll have had the most interest and interaction.'

I opened the app and looked at the number of followers I'd gained, along with how many likes and comments the photo of Rachel and I standing on the rocks next to the lake had received.

'That's good, right?' I said, looking at Tori, who was also looking at the same thing on her phone.

'That's phenomenal,' said Alex, his head close to Tori's as they shared her screen.

Rachel leant over to look at mine. 'Crikey,' she said. 'I thought Insta was a slow and steady kind of platform.'

Tori was scrolling through the comments far faster than I was.

'I can see what's happened.' She beamed. 'There are a couple of big influencers who have shared you to their stories, Em, and that's what has kicked it all off. People have found you through them.'

'Thanks to you.' I grinned. 'It's your name that will have made the difference, Tor.'

'Have you got to reply to all of these?' Alex frowned.

'I have.' I beamed, wriggling in my seat. 'It's going to take ages, but I don't care about that.'

'Especially the influencers,' said Tori. 'You certainly want to make a connection with them and maintain the relationship.'

'Will you tell me what to put?' I asked, feeling nervous about messing it up.

Tori shook her head.

'Nope,' she said. 'Just be yourself. Your authentic self, Em. Not the person you might think they want to connect with. Be yourself right from the start and everyone will love you for it.'

I could see the sense in what she was saying, even though it terrified me.

'You don't have to tell everyone what you had for breakfast,' she further said. 'These are business accounts, after all, but be yourself. Let prospective clients know who they're working with right from the start.'

Her knowledge of how to do things clearly ran deeper than the nuts and bolts of setting the accounts up.

'You're going to have to keep up with this every day from now on, aren't you?' Rachel said, sounding almost resentful. 'So much for the rest of our holiday.'

It was on the tip of my tongue to bite back about her constantly being in contact with Jeremy at random hours of the day, but then I remembered she hadn't been as much as I thought and then Tori took her to task anyway.

'Oh, stop moaning, Rachel,' she tutted. 'I thought you'd be pleased. Em needs orders to make her business work and by the looks of it, she's already got enough here to keep her busy right to the end of the tax year. That makes one thing less for you to have to worry about, doesn't it?' she pithily added.

Rachel took a moment to let that sink in. 'Of course,' she said more happily but with a smile that didn't quite reach her eyes. 'I'm really pleased for you, Em.'

'Thank you,' I graciously said, then turned back to Tori. 'You're

a genius,' I told her. 'By the looks of it, the other platforms haven't been quite so quick on the uptake but there are still a few likes and messages. I'm going to need a system to keep track.'

Tori smoothed down her hair, looking delighted.

'Em's right,' said Alex, looking adoringly at her. 'You are a genius.'

I tried not to let his admiration taint my excitement.

'I'll ask Connor if he's got a notepad and a pen you can borrow, Em,' he then said, 'so you can make a note of everything as you go through it.'

'Thank you,' I said, as he dashed off.

Tori followed his gaze and gave a sigh.

'What?' Rachel frowned.

'I've never been called a genius before,' she said wistfully.

'Em called you it first,' Rachel reminded her.

'I know,' she said, looking back at us. 'Twice in one day. How amazing is that?'

Rachel went back to the bar when Alex returned with a note-book Connor said I could keep, and a pen.

'I'm going to be a while,' I told him and Tori. 'You don't have to wait if you want to get back to the cottage.'

I didn't much want to be the conduit which facilitated them spending time alone together, but it was hardly fair to manipulate them into staying where I could keep an eye on them. I had made my bed as far as Alex was concerned and I would just have to lie in it. My attempt to point out to him the day before that my holiday baggage was now finally unpacked and that I was 'up for fun' had fallen on deaf ears and I would have to accept that and try to forget about my feelings for him by focusing more on my fledgling business instead.

My heart rate quickened as I thought what a success it already was. With Tori's help and Alex's encouragement I had gone for it and if the interest recorded on my phone was any indicator, it had paid off. I was going to have to seriously think about putting Tori on the payroll because she clearly knew her stuff and had all the right contacts to boot.

Perhaps Alex's ignorance of my attempt to hook him again was no bad thing. If I was going to do Tori's clever social media strategy justice, I was going to need to fully engage both my head and my heart and not split focus anywhere or for anything.

'Your very first afternoon in the office.' Tori beamed.

'And it's a Sunday,' said Alex. 'You'll need to watch that, Em,' he jokingly added. 'Don't let the work life balance go to pot in your first month.'

'And don't forget,' said Tori, nudging him along so she could get out, 'to email that company you're supposed to be starting with next month and tell them thanks but no thanks.'

'You don't think I should wait . . .' I started to say but she gave me a stern look.

'You're right.' I nodded, thinking of my nest egg sitting safe in the bank and which would see me through for a while at least. 'I really do need to give this my all, don't I?'

I could imagine both Nanna and Grandad standing behind Tori and Alex and nodding their heads. They'd both be so proud, especially if they knew which part of the country I'd launched the business from. Both them and *Hope Falls* had played a far larger part in inspiring me than I had previously realised, and I was so grateful.

'If you can afford to,' said Alex, sounding more level-headed than Tori as he sat back down, 'then you should. My business

was a shoestring start-up and it worked for me. There's less to lose with a small start and, for me at least, that gave me the confidence to keep moving forward. If I'd borrowed big time from the bank, I would have been totally stressed.'

With Alex's experience and Tori's passion, I knew I didn't need to go further than them for advice. They made the perfect team. Alex would provide the sense and the facts and Tori would keep drumming up the energy and enthusiasm.

'You and Em sound like a match made in heaven,' said Tori, making me blush because that was exactly what I'd just been thinking about her and Alex. 'I reckon she'd feel exactly the same if she had a big bank loan weighing her down.'

Alex shuddered. 'I certainly didn't want that sort of pressure,' he said. 'I wanted to be in total charge of how the business would grow and not having payments to make meant I could pick and choose the projects I really wanted to work on and selectively build my portfolio.'

'Yep,' said Tori, making my cheeks further flame. 'Peas in a pod.'

'At least we know we're compatible in one respect,' Alex smiled at me.

Tori looked between the two of us. 'What have I missed?' She frowned.

'Nothing,' I quickly said and glanced back at my phone as it pinged again. 'Now, let me get on, otherwise I'll never catch up.'

'She's right,' said Alex, giving Tori a look as he stood up. 'Now, how are we going to get you back to the cottage?'

'Save your back and ask Connor if he's got a wheelbarrow,' I teasingly suggested. 'Then you could push her. It's downhill most of the way.'

'Hey!' Tori yelped. 'I've only put on a couple of pounds. I can't help it if I've developed a fondness for Kendal mint cake, can I?'

Alex shuddered again and I pulled a face and laughed.

'Don't tell me,' Tori tutted. 'Something else you both have in common.'

With them finally gone and Rachel still helping out behind the bar, and seeming to get on far better with Connor than she currently was with me, I turned my attention back to my phone. I acknowledged every comment left on every account and replied to every commission enquiry, writing down the details as I went, along with messaging my thanks to the influencers.

I also drafted out the email to send to the company I wouldn't now be joining, but I didn't send it. I thought it had been enough of a monumental day and I wanted to get the wording just right. Not that I supposed it mattered as I wouldn't be joining them now, but that was how I felt.

'How are you getting on?' Rachel asked and when I looked up at her, I winced.

'Damn,' I said, stretching out my neck and moving my head from side to side, before rolling my shoulders.

'No wonder you're stiff,' she said, putting down two plates of cheesecake. 'You've been at it for two hours straight.'

'No way,' I gasped, but she was right. 'Oh, my god,' I said, glancing around and finding the place considerably emptier than when I'd started. 'I had no idea.'

'How's it all looking?' she asked, sliding on to the seat opposite.

'Really good.' I grinned in spite of the crook in my neck and her former mulish mood. 'I've checked my banking along with all the accounts Tori has set up and I've been paid for everything

I've sent off so far. I really think I'll be able to make a go of it, for a year at least.'

'Don't let Tori hear you say that.' She smiled. 'She's got you down for the long haul.'

'I think you're right,' I agreed. 'She's going to keep pushing me on, isn't she?'

'And I will too,' she said, sounding choked. 'I'm sorry I was a cow earlier. I have a horrible feeling that I've ended up sounding just like your parents and that was truly never my intention.'

I hadn't wanted to point it out, but she had. They would be quaking in their boots if they knew I was passing up a perfectly decent job to start my own business, especially with the world in such a volatile state. They were risk-free all the way and I suppose with Rachel's job at the school, she was similar in that respect herself.

'I am excited for you,' she said, offering me the slice of lemon cheesecake, even though it was her favourite. 'And I didn't mean to be such a bitch about Tori moving in either.'

'It hasn't happened yet,' I pointed out, switching plates. I would be more than happy with the cherry. 'Everything is all right with you, Rach, isn't it?'

I didn't want to have to say the 'J' word unless it became absolutely necessary.

'It is now we've cleared the air,' she said a little too brightly as she handed me a fork. 'Now, let's see if Connor's cheesecake really is all that. He's been going on about it all afternoon.'

I wasn't sure I believed that everything was all right with her, but for the moment I let it drop and a couple of minutes later, I was puffing out my cheeks as I pressed the fork into

the last few crumbs on the plate and ate them even though I was stuffed.

'Well?' said Connor, swaggering over, looking very pleased with himself. 'Marks out of ten.'

'Eleven,' I immediately said.

'Rachel?' he asked.

Hers was the opinion he really wanted.

'I think eleven's a bit mean,' she said, flashing him a hundred-watt smile. 'I'd say a definite fifteen.'

'Wow,' I said, as Connor blushed bright red. 'And from the cheesecake connoisseur, that is quite something.'

'I'm honoured,' was all he could say as he gathered the plates and returned to the bar.

Rachel and I looked at each other and laughed. I gathered my notes together and checked my phone one last time, while she settled our bill and Connor again insisted on paying her for the pints she'd pulled.

There were already likes on the new pic I'd posted on Instagram, but mindful of what Alex had said about it being a Sunday, I thought I would come back to the pub, or head somewhere else with a signal, and respond to them during the official working week.

Rachel and I walked back to the cottage arm-in-arm and I had the strongest feeling that everything was suddenly right in the world. Or it was until we opened the cottage door and found Tori and Alex wrapped in each other's arms.

'Shit,' Alex swore as they sprang apart and Tori made a beeline for the bedroom.

'Oops,' said Rachel, trying to cover our embarrassment but making the situation worse. 'Sorry. We should have knocked.'

'No,' Alex said, running his hands through his hair. 'We were just . . .'

'There's no need to explain,' I said, heading out the side door on the pretence of watering the pots as I felt a forceful wave of déjà vu wash over me. 'It's none of our business.'

Chapter 27

For the next couple of days, I went into denial overdrive. I didn't know that's what it was at the time, but my fixed smile, cheerful can-do attitude and constant busyness must have been painful to watch, let alone live with. I was overly nice to everyone; sickeningly sweeter than even the mint cake Tori had developed a fondness for and more full of cheese than Connor's fifteen out of ten cheesecake.

I threw myself into keeping up with social media via regular trips to Lakeside. I was as keen to avoid the sight of Alex and Tori together as I was to keep on top of responding to notifications. Not that I'd caught the pair in any further clinches, but they either had their heads together in the cottage or were taking long walks around the lake, so it didn't take a genius to work out the direction their recently formed friendship had taken.

The Passion for Patchwork order book (aka currently the notebook Connor had given me), was bulging by the middle of the week as I'd drawn up and sent off quotes for every enquiry and the majority of clients had confirmed receipt and requested I should go ahead as soon as possible.

I'd even found time to make another skirt. Creating that had

gifted me the perfect excuse to stay hidden in my room because that was where my sewing station was set up and I claimed the light was better in there too, even though it wasn't, to further ensure no one objected to my absence.

Just as Rachel feared would happen, for the next couple of days, I completely abandoned our holiday and as a result of me hiding away, she spent even more time in the pub than I did. As mid-week rolled around again, we were a fractured little group and I knew I wasn't the only one who had noticed the change.

'So, about tomorrow,' Rachel announced as we settled to eat lunch, for once all together, on the veranda. 'I've checked the forecast and it's going to be damp in the morning but sunny in the afternoon so I thought we could have a lazy start, maybe watch the DVD . . .'

Tori started to shift in her seat and I hoped she wasn't going to say she wasn't ready to watch it again. She claimed to be, had even proved herself to be a fully paid-up member of the *Hope Falls* fandom now and therefore should know that was not how it worked. Watching – and reading – on a loop was perfectly acceptable and I thought Rachel would combust if she suggested otherwise.

'And then take a picnic to the island in the afternoon,' Rachel carried on, in spite of Tori's wriggling. 'I can't believe we haven't explored it yet.'

'That sounds like a wonderful idea,' I quickly said to try and divert her attention from Alex who had also started to look antsy. 'It is ridiculous that we haven't been over there, although I don't suppose it's hurt to eke things out a bit, has it?'

The island was almost in the middle of the lake and beyond a dense copse of trees at its centre, there wasn't anything to see but

a couple of the pivotal scenes in the movie had been filmed there and that was enough to make it a mecca for us book devotees.

It had been high on our list of places to visit, but just as I had known would happen, our time at the cottage had started to run away with us. I needed to keep a check on that. I couldn't let what was now happening between Tori and Alex impact on my summer dreams because if I did, in the long run I would feel nothing but regret that I hadn't squeezed the most out of each and every day and I would be letting Rachel down too.

'What do you think, Alex?' Rachel asked. 'I know you're a proficient rower, but we wouldn't expect you to take us all the way. We can all pull our weight too, can't we?'

Tori didn't say anything and I could only nod as thoughts of Alex rowing the two of us out on to the lake to watch the meteor shower filled my head. His prowess with the oars had been as impressive as the stars, but I wasn't supposed to be dwelling on things like that. I'd spent the last few days forcing myself not to, but clearly, I wasn't out of the woods yet.

'That sounds wonderful,' Alex regretfully said, 'but it's Wednesday tomorrow and I won't be here. I'll be heading off to Manchester first thing.'

Like Rachel obviously had, I'd also forgotten about him going to work, but the fact that he was sticking to his routine suggested he wasn't too obsessed about staying glued to Tori. The thought cheered me more than it probably should.

'And I'm going with him,' Tori then said, cutting me straight back down to size.

'What are you going for?' Rachel demanded, sounding angry. 'You don't just duck out of a book-lovers' dream getaway, you know, especially when you've only just got here!'

Tori looked contrite but didn't say anything.

'I know for a fact you haven't got funds to go shopping,' Rachel goaded.

'There's just a couple of things I need to do,' Tori eventually and evasively said.

Rachel still looked thunderous, but made no further comment.

'Well, never mind,' I cajoled. 'I'll come with you, Rachel. I think it sounds like a wonderful way to spend a sunny afternoon. In fact, I'll head down to the village after lunch and pick up some extra treats from Mrs T for our picnic.'

'And I'll pay for half of them out of my wages from Connor,' she insisted.

With that settled, I took the opportunity to wolf down my lunch and shoot off to Lakeside faster than a gazelle who'd spotted a lion.

'What about this salmon mousse?' Mrs Timpson suggested temptingly, holding it up. 'That's always good for a picnic.'

I had been thinking more along the fancy dips and classy crisps route, but Mrs T, as always, had ideas which reached way above her customers' expectations. And budgets.

'And these gooseberries?'

'Yes, to the salmon,' I said, even though the price tag made me flinch. I was relieved I'd recently been paid for the latest commissions. 'But no to the gooseberries.'

That was one summer fruit I still wasn't keen on.

'You'll want a packet of these all-butter crackers to go with the mousse then and how about a hot water crust pork pie to fill you up. The mousse is very light and the pie is made by the same farmer who supplies the Scotch eggs, so you know that's a winner.'

She whirled about the tiny shop, adding the extras to the bag of apples and chocolate chip cookies I'd already picked out and before I could object.

'And this cream cheese mixed with chilli jam is delicious for dipping celery and carrot sticks into,' she suggested. 'If you like that healthy sort of thing.'

The cream cheese did look delicious, but hardly healthy.

'I do like it,' I told her. 'But I think we've got enough now. The little boat will sink at this rate and I'll never manage to carry it all back, let alone down to the lake.'

'Nonsense,' said Mrs Timpson. 'That boat is as safe as houses. My brother, Sidney, checks it over every spring. Oh, I almost forgot, you're going to need something to drink. Don't worry about lugging it all back, I'll get Sid to run it down later.'

I walked back to the cottage wishing she'd mentioned Sidney's delivery services weeks ago and feeling in a total daze. This whole avoiding Tori and Alex shenanigan was costing a fortune.

I lay in extra late the following morning, eager to avoid bumping into the housemates who were heading off for the day, and when I eventually got up once the coast was clear, I was surprised to find Rachel still fast asleep. Had it been the start of the holiday, when she was worn-out by the gruelling end of term teaching, I wouldn't have thought anything of it, but heading towards the end of August, it was wholly unexpected.

'Hey you,' I said, when she finally joined me in the kitchen. 'Is everything all right?'

As the forecast had predicted, the damp morning was giving way to a sunny midday and we would need to set off to the island soon, unless Rachel had plans for us to picnic at teatime, rather

than lunch. We'd already missed the chance to watch the film again, but I had read a few scenes from the book while she slept.

'Yes,' she said brightly. 'All good. I just fancied a lie in and thought I'd make the most of not having to listen to Tori snoring. You need to get yourself some earplugs before she moves in, because . . .' she added, her words trailing off.

When I looked up to see why she'd stopped, I could see her eyes had filled with tears and her bottom lip was wobbling. I resolved there and then to use our alone time at the island to get to the bottom of whatever was going on with her.

'I'm fine,' she said, waving a hand in front of her face. 'I thought I was going to sneeze. My hay fever's hell at the moment.'

Hay fever, my eye.

'Um,' she later said when we were standing on the side of the jetty and looking down into the boat. 'Are you sure it's safe?'

'As safe as houses,' I told her. 'According to Mrs T, Sidney keeps it shipshape and seaworthy and it was fine the night Alex took me out to watch the meteor shower.'

Having been a combination of both busy and distracted Alex hadn't rowed Rachel out in it, so this was going to be her first on board experience.

'But you didn't have all this extra weight then,' she said, nodding at the heavy, packed hamper. 'And who is Sidney?'

'Mrs T's brother,'

'Oh, well,' she said, gingerly stepping down and making the boat rock. 'I suppose that's recommendation enough.'

I passed down the rest of the provisions and then, having given Rachel time to check for leaks, climbed in myself.

'Shall we take it in turns to row?' I asked. 'Or grab an oar each?'

There was just enough room for us to squeeze in sitting side by side so we decided to try and row together. It took us a few minutes to get the hang of it and stop giggling as we went around in circles, but we finally found our stroke and set off on a haphazard course towards the island.

'That took longer than I expected,' Rachel puffed as we took off our sandals to hop out and pull the boat further up the pebbled shore.

'And the jetty looks a long way away, doesn't it?' I frowned, shielding my eyes from the sun as I looked at how far we'd come. 'I hope we'll be able to get back.'

'Let's not worry about that now,' said Rachel. 'I'm starving. Let's eat.'

We braced ourselves then plunged our feet in the icy water. It only reached our ankles, but it took our breath away.

'Geez,' Rachel gasped. 'It hasn't warmed up, has it?'

I shook my head, unwilling to speak because I knew the only thing that would come out of my mouth would be a string of expletives. Rachel laughed and then stood on a sharp stone which made her swear enough for both of us.

With the boat and oars secure, we unloaded the hamper, rug and our shoes and carried it all further up the beach. We soon forgot how cold our feet were as the sun burnt off the last remnants of cloud and we tucked into the fabulous fare.

'When you said picnic,' said Rachel, holding her glass out so I could further fill it, 'I had no idea you'd gone all posh on me. This is a total treat. No wonder there was no money left over.'

'I'm pleased you're enjoying it.' I smiled. 'Though I can't take the credit. We need to thank Mrs T for talking me into buying quite a lot of this and you of course for footing half the bill,' I admitted.

Rachel shrugged. 'It wasn't money I knew I was going to have,' she smiled, 'so god bless Mrs T and her persuasive ways,' she added, raising her glass and I did the same. 'And more fool Tori for heading off with Alex,' she finished up, giving me a side-eye that she probably thought I wouldn't notice. 'She's really missing out today.'

'Oh,' I sighed, thinking of her spending the day alone with Alex, 'I wouldn't say that exactly.'

Rachel put down her glass and leant back on her elbows, tipping her face up to absorb the warmth of the sun.

'Careful, Em,' she said softly. 'Nothing tastes, or sounds as bitter as regret.'

'I don't regret anything,' I said back, reaching into my bag for the sunblock.

I loved my freckles, but in spite of the usual cloud cover, they had got a bit out of control this summer. I squeezed a blob of factor fifty into my palm, slightly too much as was usual, and nudged Rachel who then scooped some of it up and applied it to her own face, while I covered mine.

'Are you sure about that?' she then further probed. 'Only I've got the impression over the last few days, that regret is your current go-to emotion, where Alex is concerned, that is.'

I looked out across the lake and pulled in a breath.

'Well,' I said, in as carefree a tone as I could muster, 'I don't know where you've got that idea from because you've hardly seen me.'

'Exactly,' she said sagely. 'I'm not an idiot, Em. I know you've been keeping yourself extra busy and tucked away with more reason than launching your business.'

I felt my face grow warm as I wondered if Tori or Alex had

worked that out too. Then remembered that given how wrapped up in each other they currently seemed to be, it wasn't likely.

'You're a fine one to talk about staying tucked away,' I batted back, twisting around so I could gauge Rachel's reaction. 'I know you've been spending more time with Connor than you've let on.'

She reached up and pulled the claw out of her hair so it swung down and forward, covering the side of her face.

'And I also know you'd been messaging Tori before she turned up,' I forged on, throwing caution to the wind, 'but for some reason you let me assume that it was Jeremy you were in contact with every day. Everything is all right between you two, isn't it?'

'Yes.' She swallowed, tucking her hair behind her ear. 'Of course. It's just a big thing, deciding to move in together. It's a huge life change and it's given me a lot to think about.'

I couldn't help wishing that her thinking had resulted in her turning Jeremy's request down as a crystal-clear vision of the future popped into my head. I could imagine Rachel living in Jeremy's flat, Tori settled in Rachel's room and Alex coming to stay for weekends and all with me not quite fitting in anywhere. The thought made me gasp.

'Em?' Rachel frowned. 'Are you all right?'

'Yes.' I vigorously nodded, as I tried to shake the unbearable images off. 'Too much rich food at the wrong time of day,' I bluffed. 'Let's go for a wander, shall we?'

We tidied the remains of the picnic away and then pulled our plimsolls back on and set off to explore.

'I can't believe we've got the whole place to ourselves!' Rachel called over her shoulder as she wove her way, book in hand, through and between the stand of pine trees growing at the centre.

They provided some shade from the sun which hadn't felt warmer on any other day of our holiday. I stuck to the edges, keen to soak up the vitamin D, now I'd applied the sun cream, as we walked around.

'Here, Em!' Rachel called again. 'Look!'

I followed her voice and found her looking from her phone and the book back to the trees and then turning around to look towards the cottage.

'This is it,' she beamed. 'The exact spot.'

She held out her phone and I compared the screenshot to the view in front and behind us. I already knew it fitted the fictional description the author had so beautifully written.

'Oh my god,' I laughed. 'You're right.'

She'd found the very spot where the island campfire scene had been filmed. We both looked around for any evidence of what had occurred there, but there was nothing and I was pleased about that.

'I'm so pleased there isn't a sign or anything,' said Rachel, echoing my thoughts. 'It's so much nicer to find it for yourself, isn't it?'

'It is,' I agreed, sitting down cross-legged on the pebbles in the spot I imagined Heather had sat in before me.

Rachel did the same only in the position where Laurie had perched. She took loads of photos, some with us in, some without.

'I'll send you these when we've got a signal again,' she said.

'Thank you.' I nodded, still looking around. 'In the book,' I quietly said, pointing at the treasured title, 'and in the film, this scene by the fire was a full circle moment, wasn't it? Heather, Rose and Laurie had almost come to the end of their journeys. Do you think we have too?'

Rachel thought for a moment. 'No,' she then said. 'No way. I think ours is just beginning, especially yours with your new business. I know I didn't make a very good show of it at the weekend, but I really am pleased for you, Em. I think you're really brave. It's not something I could do, but I do admire you for making it happen. I hope you know that.'

'I do now,' I said, reaching for her hand and wishing I'd been able to find a way to tell her about it all sooner. 'And I admire you too.'

'For moving in with Jeremy, you mean?' She wryly smiled, squeezing my fingers.

That was exactly what I meant.

'For moving in with anyone,' I said, to soften the inference.

She still didn't look as excited by the prospect as I thought she should and even though I wanted to see my earlier resolution, to find out what was wrong with her, through, I didn't want to risk spoiling what had been a holiday highlight either. It had been a truly perfect afternoon and therefore I let the subject drop.

'Come on,' I said, standing up and pulling her to her feet as the sun went in and the temperature dropped. 'We should think about heading back before it rains again.'

'It's not going to rain again,' she said, looking around wistfully. 'It wouldn't dare.'

We'd barely made it halfway back before the heavens opened, but we were laughing too much to care.

Chapter 28

Tori arrived back with Alex looking like the cat who had got the cream that night. Not that I could blame her because no matter how hard I tried to stave the feelings off, ever since Alex and I had shared another precious moment looking through Gracie's treasures at the lake, he had become an even more attractive prospect, in every sense of the word.

As a result, I couldn't resent Tori for snapping him up and looking smug about it. I wasn't even all that shocked, given what had happened in the past, but I did feel guiltily bitter about missing out myself on what could have potentially been something very special indeed.

However, having considered what I thought was smugness, when I caught Tori creeping back into the cottage early on the Sunday morning, having got up to fetch myself some water from the kitchen, she looked as far from feeling that as it was possible to get.

'Where had you snuck off to?' I whispered, scaring her half to death because she hadn't spotted me before I spoke.

If I'd expected to find her sneaking anywhere it would have been to cosy up with Alex on the pull-out, but he was very much

alone and sleeping soundly. Although he had shifted a bit when Tori let out a stifled screech.

'Are you trying to give me a heart attack?' She grimaced, turning pale then puce and back again. 'I just needed to check something on my phone.'

'At this hour?' I frowned.

'Yes,' she said, sucking in her lower lip as her dark eyes widened. 'I think I might have made a mistake, Em.' It wasn't the first time I'd heard her say that. 'I've done something in good faith but I think it's going to backfire on me in a way I hadn't bargained for. I knew it might cause trouble, but . . .'

I puffed out my cheeks as her words trailed off. In the past, she'd have the mother of all meltdowns about maxing out her credit cards at the start of the month, then her father would pay the bills or up her allowance limit and that would be that, but that clearly wasn't the sort of thing this early morning tizz was about.

'What have you done?' I hissed, pulling her into my bedroom as Alex moved again.

'It's to do with—' she started to say, but then Rachel wandered in before I could close the door and Alex gave a frustrated groan.

'It's Sunday,' he grumbled, when Rachel asked what was going on. 'Why are you all awake and what are you all whispering about at this ungodly hour?'

'Are we whispering?' said Rachel at a volume that was definitely not a whisper.

Alex groaned again.

'What's the craic?' Rachel asked, turning back to us and rubbing her hands together in anticipation of gossip.

'There is no craic.' Tori shrugged, still looking pale.

'You've been spending too much time with Connor,' I said to Rachel. 'Hasn't she, Tori?'

'I don't know,' she said, heading to the bedroom. 'I'm going back to bed.'

'Oh no,' said Alex, flinging the covers off. 'No one's going back to bed. You've woken me up now and it took me ages to nod off, so we're having coffee and then we're going for a walk around the lake.'

'You can't tell us what to do,' Rachel laughed at his bluster and bonkers bed hair which confirmed he'd been tossing and turning.

'Yes,' he said, manically trying to flatten the bouffant, 'I can. Get the kettle on and your coats ready, because we're going for a hike.'

Even with Tori's toes covered in plasters to minimise the blister risk, she still grumbled as we strode around the lake and Alex looked as if he was regretting bossing us around even before we'd made it through the woods. Rachel was looking bleary-eyed and I was too worried about what disaster Tori thought she had set in motion to really enjoy the fresh air.

I tried to collar her a couple of times to ask, but Rachel was always within earshot and she just nervously shook her head and hung back to wait for Alex. I supposed I would have to wait it out and see what, if anything, kicked off.

We had plans to go to the pub that evening. Connor was holding another book-lovers' quiz night and as Tori hadn't been with us for the last one, we decided to go along. But only after I'd made Rachel promise to leave the mixology to the landlord.

'I will,' she said slyly, loud enough for the other two to hear. 'But only because we don't want a repeat of what happened last time, do we?'

'Oh, I don't know,' Alex confused me by saying, accompanying the unexpected comment with a suggestively raised eyebrow.

'Why?' Tori gleefully pounced, sensing scandal. 'What happened last time?'

It was the first time she'd looked anywhere near like herself all day but I wasn't about to furnish her with the details and I was shocked Alex had hinted that something had happened.

'Never you mind,' I said dryly.

'Let's just say, I underestimated the impact of double measures,' Rachel put in with a mischievous wink.

'Triple,' Alex and I said in unison, then grinned even though I tried not to.

Tori looked between us and I didn't linger to enjoy the camaraderie with Alex or further feed the moment. Given that I had persistently tried to claim that I wasn't interested in the man who was now paired up with one of my closest friends, I had just failed dismally to rein my feelings in when they received even the merest hint of encouragement.

'I'm going to go and start getting ready,' I said, even though it was way too early.

Tori still seemed to be in a less jittery frame of mind by the time Alex had driven us to the pub. She was looking very glam for a night in The Drover's but then she always looked glam whenever we went out. It felt like forever since we'd met in The Flamingo and she'd dropped her bombshell about not being able to join us on the holiday, but the scent of her perfume kicked off a whole host of Friday night drinks memories.

It felt as if we were all living entirely different lives now. Which in a way, I supposed, given everything that had happened to each of us during the last few weeks, we were and that, of course, was perfectly in keeping with the plot of the book. My Passion for Patchwork business had launched, Rachel was moving in with Jeremy, Alex had fulfilled Gracie's wishes and further assimilated his grief and as a result, he and Tori were now partners. I shoved that last twist in the plot firmly and as far away as I possibly could.

'I'll get the first round in,' offered Alex, leaning past me and assaulting my senses with a full-on close-up waft of the same aftershave he'd been wearing at the last party.

I'd got a whiff of it in the car, but not close to and I felt every erogenous zone light up before I could take a step away.

'And I'll find us a table.' I swallowed, dragging Rachel along with me.

'What's up?' she asked.

'Nothing,' I said, shaking the impact of Alex's aftershave off the further I moved away from him. 'I'm fine.'

'Good,' she said, looking back to where Tori was standing at the side of the bar scrolling on her phone and not taking any notice of the attention she was drawing. 'I'm pleased one of us is because Tori has been in the weirdest mood all day.'

I didn't hear a word of what Rachel said after that as I watched Tori, thinking she must be completely besotted with Alex if she was capable of not responding to the admiring looks and attention she was getting.

'Don't you think?' Rachel nudged, when I didn't respond.

'I don't know.' I shrugged, hoping she had still been talking about Tori's weird mood. 'I haven't noticed.'

'Not you too,' she tutted.

'Here we go,' said Alex, coming back with a loaded tray. 'Connor reckons these have got so little alcohol in them, they're practically mocktails.'

I raised my eyebrows, feeling sceptical.

'His words, not mine.' Alex beamed, making my insides fizz again as he put down the tray and held up his hands.

'Well,' I said, feeling half-drunk already, in spite of the fact that I hadn't tasted a drop. 'Let's hope he's right because you're driving us home.'

'I'm not actually,' he said, handing me a glass and not letting go as my fingers closed around it. 'I've booked the taxi and I'm leaving my car here, so we'd better watch out.'

My eyes flicked to his and I wondered what he was doing. He couldn't possibly be flirting with me when Tori was almost in earshot. In fact, he shouldn't be flirting with me, wherever she was. I got a grip on myself and looked away, embarrassed that I had read too much into what he had said. Of course, he wasn't flirting with me. I was delusional to even think that let alone for a moment believe it.

He had just finished handing out the rest of the drinks when Tori shot across the pub and almost knocked the whole lot for six.

'What the hell's the matter with you today, Tori?' Rachel tutted, as she used a paper napkin to mop up the spillage. 'You're doing my head in.'

'Come on,' I said, wondering if her speedy second change of mood was related to whatever it was that she had snuck out so early to do or if it was connected to what had just beguiled her on her phone. Or were they even both the same thing? 'Sit down and have one of these. It'll settle your nerves.'

'I'm not nervous,' she said, downing the drink I handed her in one huge gulp.

Alex looked at her and frowned. 'I'd better get another round in then,' he said, heading off again.

'Make them doubles!' Tori shouted after him.

Having drunk a couple more cocktails and come second in the quiz, Tori seemed to settle down, which helped the rest of us relax. I wasn't sure if she was feeling genuinely soothed or if the alcohol had knocked the worst of her jitters off, but whichever it was, I was grateful for the transformation. However, the evening didn't stay settled for long.

We had just started to discuss what we were going to do the following week to keep the *Hope Falls* momentum going when an argument broke out at the bar. I'd never heard Connor shout before and his infuriated Irish lilt made me flinch.

'What the hell?' Alex frowned, quickly jumping up and racing through the packed pub to his new friend's aid.

It was then that the shouting really cranked up and it sounded like a fight, *a real fight* (as Tom in *Bridget Jones's Diary* had so ecstatically declared), had broken out. The three of us took one look at each other and then rushed in the direction Alex had headed.

'Oh my god!' Rachel practically screamed and Tori burst into noisy sobs as we waded through the crowd of onlookers. 'Jeremy!' Rachel yelled, grabbing his shirt sleeve before he swung his fists again. 'What the hell are you doing here?'

Alex was bent double and when he straightened, there was blood pouring from his nose and the beginnings of a black eye blooming.

'Alex,' I said, rushing to his side as Connor manhandled a

swearing and very ugly-looking Jeremy towards the door. His face was horribly contorted with fury. 'Here,' I said, grabbing a tea towel and steering Alex towards a seat.

'Was that who I think it was?' he choked.

'Pinch the end of your nose,' I commanded, handing him the towel. 'And lean forward. Can you do that?'

He nodded and did as I had instructed.

'Tori,' I then said. 'Come and help Alex while I go and find Rachel.'

Tori was still sobbing and I guessed the nasty little scene which had just played out had something to do with her, but we would get to the bottom of that later.

'Tori!' I said more sharply because she hadn't moved. 'Come and sit here with Alex.'

The kitchen staff had already shut Siddy behind the bar and were picking up the glasses which had got knocked over and smashed in the one-sided scuffle. The expressions on the faces of the customers were a mixture of appalled and enthralled.

'I take it you know this feckin' eejit?' Connor asked me the moment I stepped out of the door and found him, Rachel and Jeremy in a silent stand-off.

Connor looked pretty wild, but then given that Jeremy, the ultimate feckin' eejit, had just ruined a wonderful night in his pub, I was hardly surprised.

'Unfortunately,' I said, giving Jeremy a look of pure loathing, 'I do, yes. Are you all right, Rach?'

The look she gave me was withering.

'Of course, you're not,' I responded, shaking my head. 'Sorry.'

I didn't think I'd ever seen her looking so angry, not even when Tori and I had tried to make her see sense over Jeremy's

behaviour before and she had vociferously defended him, her misplaced annoyance turned squarely on us.

'We need to talk,' Jeremy had the gall to boisterously say to her. 'Alone.'

'You need to shut the hell up,' said Connor, pushing him roughly back down on the bench he'd dumped him on, when he tried to stand up.

'It's okay, Connor,' Rachel said, her softer tone at odds with the look in her eyes. 'Really. Jeremy's right. We do need to talk.'

Jeremy shrugged off Connor's grip on his shoulder and re-arranged his shirt, looking triumphant.

'But we won't be alone,' she then said, which made Jeremy's smile falter. 'Em, will you stay, please? I want a witness to what I'm going to say.'

'Of course,' I said. 'Whatever you want.'

Connor shook his head and didn't budge.

'You need to go and sort things in the pub,' Rachel insisted. 'We'll be fine.'

He looked at her for a long moment and she nodded.

'You'd better behave yourself,' he then said to Jeremy, through gritted teeth. 'Em,' he added, turning to me. 'One wrong word out of him and you come and get me.'

'I will,' I said, thinking what a pleasure that would be. I felt like thumping Jeremy myself and I'd never thumped anyone. 'Will you ask Alex if he wants to press charges?'

'I'm going to call the police,' he told me. 'So, they'll ask him that.'

Jeremy didn't look quite so cocky all of a sudden.

'Good idea.' I nodded.

Giving Jeremy another hard stare, he reluctantly went back

inside and Jeremy immediately opened his mouth to speak. I would have been interested to hear how he was going to attempt to justify his behaviour, but Rachel didn't give him the opportunity.

'No,' she said, pointing a rigid finger in his face. 'I'm going to talk and you're going to listen. You can answer my questions, but that's the only time you get to speak. Do you understand?'

I shook my head in disbelief as Jeremy had the audacity to roll his eyes. I would have thought by then he would have been contrite and wheedling for forgiveness but there didn't appear to be a hint of remorse in a single bone of his body.

'Question one,' Rachel began, holding up her thumb. 'What are you doing here?'

He took a moment before answering. 'I was looking for the cottage,' he said tersely. 'I couldn't find it, but your phone led me here, anyway.'

I shook my head again, realising his words confirmed that Tori had been right about him having a tracker app connected to Rachel's phone.

'I should have known you and the other two would be out partying,' he then said, throwing me a look of pure disdain.

In return, I rolled my eyes.

'And here you all are.'

'Your opinion isn't necessary,' Rachel said with far more tolerance than I could have mustered under the circumstances. 'Just stick to answering the questions. Question two,' she carried on, holding up the finger next to her thumb. 'Why have you come here now, when we'd agreed a few weeks back that you would stay away?'

He looked at her and ground his jaw, a spark of his former

aggression reigniting. I wondered if I was going to have to shout for Connor sooner than expected.

'Because I saw the photos that snooty cow, Tori, posted online and after first cosying up with that Connor bloke, I couldn't believe that you'd been shacked up with a guy all this time and not said a word,' he half-shouted in a furious rush. 'You let me assume Alex was a woman and when I saw those photos—'

'You saw red,' I neatly finished for him and he fired another look of hatred my way.

So that's what had got Tori jittery. She'd posted the photos to taunt Jeremy and been panicking ever since, and with good reason, about what his reaction to them might be. I bet I knew which ones she'd shared. There were a fair few she'd taken of the four of us, laughing at the lake, and I daresay she had cleverly cropped a couple to fit her purpose.

'For fuck's sake, Jeremy!' Rachel shouted, making me jump. 'Given what you've just done in there, is it any wonder that I didn't tell you?'

'I was hurt,' he said, sounding pathetic. 'If you'd told me from the start . . .'

'You would have dragged me straight home,' Rachel raged on.

'I'll feel better when we're living together,' Jeremy said, making my mouth fall open. 'When you've moved in, I'll feel more secure.'

'This isn't about feeling secure or anything like it,' Rachel laughed without humour. 'This is about you being a control freak and an abuser.'

Jeremy flinched at the word, but I felt a huge rush of relief to hear her say it. The scales had finally dropped.

'My friends have always been able to see that your so-called

protectiveness was actually jealousy and manipulation,' she further said, 'but it wasn't until I met Connor—'

I saw the muscles in Jeremy's arms tense up.

'It wasn't until I spent a decent amount of time with him,' Rachel continued, ignoring Jeremy's reaction, 'that I realised exactly how off-kilter and screwed up our relationship is. I've been tying myself up in knots these last few days because I knew I was going to break things off but I didn't know how best to do it. Thankfully, although my poor friend Alex and his bloody nose probably wouldn't agree with me, I don't have to find the words now because you've just done it for me.'

So, that explained Rachel's strange mood. Not only was she worried about how to handle the break-up, she was most likely also fretting over the fact that Tori had said she'd move in when Rachel moved out. The complications with the flat didn't matter though. All I cared about, and all Tori would care about, was that Jealous Jeremy had, at long last, been issued his marching orders.

'You're breaking up with me?' Jeremy gaped.

I had to stop myself from laughing at the incredulity in his tone. He really was deluded.

'Yes,' said Rachel. 'Well done, Jeremy. You've got it. I'm breaking up with you and you're in real trouble because that assault you've just carried out, in front of witnesses, was premeditated. The police won't see this as a common assault because you singled Alex out.'

I watched with interest as the colour drained from Jeremy's face. 'But I was just trying to protect you.' He swallowed.

'From what?' Rachel shrugged. 'My friends? Newsflash, Jeremy. Men and women can be friends. Just friends.'

'But he's in love with you,' he said, his nostrils flaring. 'You only have to look at those photos.'

I sensed movement behind me and turned to see Alex and Tori coming out of the pub. Alex's face was still covered in blood, but his nose had stopped bleeding. Tori's complexion was as white as snow. She was clearly terrified to see the result and repercussions of her well-meant interference, but I was beginning to think she deserved a congratulatory slap on the back. That was, as long as Alex had suffered no lasting damage, of course.

'Are you all right?' I asked him.

'I'll live,' he said, sounding as though he'd got the head cold from hell. 'No thanks to this cretin.'

Jeremy went to stand, but then thought better of it. It was beginning to look like the fight had finally gone out of him.

'He's in love with you, Rach,' he said again, in one last-ditch attempt to justify what he no doubt considered to be chivalrous behaviour in his screwed-up head.

'Jeremy!' Rachel screeched. Clearly, she still had some frustration left to vent. 'Alex is not in love with me. He's in love with . . .'

At this juncture she pointed her thumb over her shoulder in the general direction of where the three of us were standing.

'She means you,' I said to Tori, who then, even though I wouldn't have believed it possible, turned another shade paler.

Rachel spun around at my words with a deeper frown etched across her already troubled brow.

'No, I don't,' she said, sounding irritated. 'I meant you, Emily.'

I felt my knees go weak and wondered if she'd had a blow to the head too. No wonder Tori was still looking more ashen than a hint of white paint chart. No one wanted to hear that

their partner was smitten with someone else and in this instance it absolutely wasn't true.

'No,' I stuttered. 'You're wrong.'

'No,' said Alex, stepping away from Tori and closer to me. 'She's right. It is you I'm in love with, Em.'

Chapter 29

When someone you're utterly enamoured with reveals in no uncertain terms, leaving not one inch of opportunity for misinterpretation, that they're in love with you, you should, in theory, be on the ultimate high. Yes?

Um, that's what I had always thought, too. However, that's not quite where I found myself when Alex declared his feelings for me, because the second he uttered the magical words, the sound of police sirens assaulted my ears and Jeremy tried to make a run for it which meant that Connor, who had only just joined us again, had to wrestle him to the ground in a rugby tackle which might also have involved a bitten butt cheek because Siddy had broken free of the bar and thought her beloved master was in trouble.

The next few minutes were a blur, which saw us all denying that we'd seen Siddy do anything, and by the time we were able to leave The Drover's and head back to the cottage, I had convinced myself that Alex hadn't said anything even remotely like, 'I'm in love with you, Em,' in spite of the many loaded glances he threw me as Rachel drove us back, the taxi trip abandoned.

'Are you sure you're feeling okay?' she asked him for the ump-teenth time. 'Not sick or anything?'

'No,' he said with a wry smile. 'If anything, I'm on a bit of a high. I think my nose was flattened for a very worthy cause tonight and I have just the thing stashed away at the cottage to celebrate that ... amongst other things.'

Tori sat in the back of the car next to me. She looked to be in a total daze and hadn't uttered a word for ages. I couldn't bring myself to ask if she was all right. She certainly didn't look in the mood for a celebration and her apparent upset did make me wonder again if I had heard Alex right, after all.

I was still feeling all at sea when we arrived back at the cottage and ducked out on the pretence of changing into my pyjamas and Rachel and Tori did the same. With my emotions in such a muddle and my recollection of what had happened at the pub hazy at best, I would have much preferred to hide away for the entire night, but Alex wasn't going to allow that and it was hardly fair on Rachel.

'Come on, you three!' he called, loudly clapping his hands and I realised it wasn't only me who was taking my time. 'I've cleaned myself up, lit the wood-burner *and* I've got fancy crisps. Where are you all?'

Rachel and I stepped out of our bedrooms at the same time.

'Oh, well.' She smiled, looking more like herself again. 'If fancy crisps are on offer.'

'Where's Tori?' I asked.

'Still getting changed,' she informed me, but didn't get the chance to say anything else, even though I could tell she was about to, because Alex carried on.

'And there's this as well as the crisps,' he said, holding up

a bottle of Elderflower and Rose Gin Liqueur from Lakeside Liqueurs. 'I was saving it,' he told us, flipping open the stone swing top with a flourish, 'for the week we were due to leave. I knew we'd all be down in the dumps and thought this would give us a lift, but I'm in the mood for it now. And not because I'm down in the dumps,' he elaborated with a huge smile at me.

'Did someone say liqueur?' asked Tori as she finally joined us.

Like the other two, she was also smiling and looked fine again as she sat next to Rachel on the sofa. I hadn't been expecting her to reappear looking so happy and couldn't take my eyes off her as I plonked myself down on the footstool and Alex commandeered the armchair, as usual.

'Sit here,' Rachel said to me, nodding at the space next to her, as she reached for the crisps and Alex poured the liqueur which was prettily pink. 'There's plenty of room.'

'I'm all right here,' I said, the words sticking in my throat as I tried to work out the altered group dynamic. 'I'll warm up quicker next to the fire.'

'Cheers, everyone,' said Alex, handing out the glasses filled with generous measures and holding on to mine as he passed it to me until I had no choice but to look at him. 'Cheers,' he said again, but softly and just loud enough for me to hear.

'Cheers.' I swallowed and he finally released the glass.

The tender look in his eyes had me questioning whether I was right to dismiss what I had thought he'd said back at the pub. I didn't much like the way my heart lifted at the thought, given that Tori was going to be hurt in the potential fallout, even though she was suddenly looking happier, and they were words I had yearned to hear.

'And here's to an evening of further revelations,' he added, holding his glass up higher and prompting us to toast.

I could have sworn Tori winked at him when he said that but didn't have time to properly puzzle her reaction out, before I had swallowed the deliciously floral tasting treat and realised that Rachel was crying.

'Oh, Rach,' I said, as I put my glass down and rushed to the space she'd already suggested I should fill. 'It's okay. It's going to be okay.'

She shook her head as I put an arm around her and pulled her close and it was then that I realised she wasn't crying, she was laughing and on her other side, Tori was tittering too.

'I really am forgiven then?' Tori further giggled.

'Of course, you are,' said Rachel, wiping her eyes. 'Posting those photos was a masterstroke, Tori. I can't get over the look of shock on his face as I stood up to him. That was priceless!'

Clearly, explanations regarding Tori's involvement in the evening's events had been made in the bedroom while they were changing and Tori's change of mood was the result of Rachel's understanding and, if her laughter was anything to go by, gratitude. It was cheering to see her in such high spirits again, even though my own emotions were now further spread all over the place.

'I obviously wouldn't have forgiven you just a few weeks ago,' Rachel carried on. 'But I meant what I said about my time with Connor putting my relationship with Jeremy into perspective. His completely overblown and irrational reaction to those photos was just the thing I needed to give him his marching orders. Although I'm still sorry your nose was punched before I had the chance, Alex.'

'As am I,' Tori vehemently agreed. 'You getting assaulted hadn't been part of my plan, Alex. I really am sorry about that.'

'It's all right,' he said, tentatively touching his nose. 'It's still attached to my face, thankfully, so no harm done.'

The three of them laughed again and I began to feel like I was walking through a dream where everyone other than me had read the script. Alex couldn't possibly have said he was in love with me then because if he had, Tori wouldn't have cheered up to this extent, no matter what Rachel said.

'And given what I know about your relationship, Rachel,' he then more seriously said, 'I'm happy to have borne the brunt of Jeremy's temper if it helped free you from him.'

'Thank you.' Rachel nodded.

'So, I really am off the hook?' Tori smiled.

'You are,' Rachel confirmed.

'And the locals are going to love you even more after tonight.' Alex grinned at her. 'You've given them something to talk about for months!'

'That's true,' she said, biting her lip to stifle another giggle. 'Did you see their faces? So, all's well, that ends well.'

'Absolutely,' said Alex. 'Although, it does now leave you in a conundrum about the flat. If Tori's moving in—'

'Oh, don't worry about the flat,' Tori cheerfully cut in as if she hadn't a care in the world. 'I'll just carry on at Dad's if I can't talk him into signing the new lease on my place.'

Given her continued breeziness and Alex's almost blasé tone when addressing her, I was further convinced that I really had misheard what he'd said. The pair of them couldn't possibly carry on as they currently were if they'd just broken up.

'I can't believe I let him take me in for so long,' Rachel then

huffed, sounding frustrated. 'The pair of you tried to warn me so many times,' she tutted. 'And when I think about how I reacted . . .'

'Don't think about it,' Tori said resolutely. 'It's done now and we can all move on.'

'Yes,' Rachel agreed. 'You're right. We can.'

I took another sip of the liqueur.

'You're very quiet, Em,' Alex softly said to me.

I swallowed and looked up at the three pairs of eyes now trained on me.

'I guess I'm still trying to process everything,' was all I could manage to falteringly say.

'I can give you something else to mull over if you like?' he offered.

'No,' I said, shaking my head. 'You're all right.'

'Well, I'm going to,' he said, ignoring my request not to. 'I can't not after what I said back at the pub, can I?'

My eyes focused on his face. He had said something then.

'That was probably the concussion talking,' Tori grinned and Rachel gave her a nudge, ramping my confusion up another notch and making me feel even more like I was the one who had received a blow to the head.

'It wasn't concussion,' he said, his eyes never leaving mine. 'Or anything like it. I was a fool to think that after our kissing gate moment that I could go back to being just your friend. I don't want to give you up, Em.' He carried on, 'I can't. And I don't think you want to give me up either. Not really. Not deep down.'

'Alex,' I burst out, unable to keep my thoughts in a moment longer. 'Stop. How can you say all of this when Tori is sitting right there?' I leant around Rachel to point at her. 'You're really

not the man I thought you were if you think you can treat us like this. It's only five minutes ago that Rachel and I walked in on you in each other's arms, for pity's sake!'

Rachel let out a gasp and Tori jumped up. 'No, no, no,' she said, pointing at one of us and then the other. 'Oh my god, oh my god, oh my god!'

She looked squarely at Alex and some thought transferred from her brain to his and as a result his eyes widened and his mouth fell open.

'No,' he said, looking from Tori to me.

'Yes.' She vehemently nodded.

'No,' he said again.

'Will someone please tell me what's going on?' Rachel exasperatedly asked. 'I thought that hug . . .'

'I don't believe it,' Alex cut in, as he put down his glass and ran a hand through his hair. 'Did you really think—'

'If someone doesn't put me straight, right now,' Rachel demanded, thumping the cushion next to her and narrowly avoiding me.

'Em,' said Alex, jumping out of the armchair, handing my glass to Rachel and kneeling in front of me. 'That day, when you walked in on us, I'd just told Tori about Gracie.'

'And I'd just told Alex about losing my mum,' added Tori.

'And that's why we were hugging,' Alex further said.

'It was a comfort hug,' Tori finished up. 'Nothing more.'

'Oh.' I swallowed.

'And when I said that you and Rachel had introduced me to a potential new partner,' he carried on, sounding desperate, 'I meant business partner. Not life partner.'

I looked from him to Tori.

'We're going to be working together,' Tori carried on. 'That's why I went with Alex to Manchester. We needed to further discuss our idea and didn't want you or Rach to find out about it until we'd got it more sorted.'

'Until we'd ironed out a few of the wrinkles,' Alex said, squeezing my hand.

'So, you're not a couple then?' I whispered, feeling lightheaded.

'No,' said Alex.

'And we never have been!' Tori said.

'I don't know what to say,' I breathed, as relief rushed through me with the power of a storm force gale.

'Don't say anything then.' Alex smiled.

'But . . .'

'No, I mean it,' he said. 'I'd rather you took the time to think about what I said than rush into giving a response that you might later regret. I'd honestly rather have no hope than false hope because I've put you on the spot as a result of a post-brawl adrenaline rush.'

I laughed at that and was itching to throw my arms around him but respected his request and held myself back. Just.

'With your new business to focus on,' he said kindly, 'I know you've got a lot on your plate, and given that we've called a halt on things between us once already, I'm happy to wait for the right answer.'

I wasn't sure I was going to be capable of waiting or further thinking, but I could see the sense in what he was saying.

'All right,' I said, giving him a look which I hope offered some indication as to what my final response was going to be. 'If that's what you really want.'

'It is,' he said, kissing the back of my hand.

'You two!' Rachel groaned. 'I really wish you'd just get on with it, but I'm not going to interfere. Given my relationship track record . . .'

'You weren't the problem,' Tori firmly reminded her.

'I suppose.' She shrugged. 'So, come on then,' she carried on, letting Alex and me off the hook. 'If this pair aren't about to immediately head off into the sunset, tell us what's the plan, Tori?'

'Well,' she excitedly said, as Alex stood up again and refilled our glasses. 'It was all Alex's idea really.'

'No, it wasn't,' he corrected, her words stopping him from staring down into my eyes again with an intensity that had me aching to kiss him, which was probably just as well given his request that I should take my time and think things through. 'You should take the credit, Tori.'

'All right,' she conceded. 'It was *our* idea.'

Alex raised his glass to that and went back to his armchair. I was tempted to follow him.

'And in a roundabout kind of way,' Tori continued. 'Dad's too because when he cut me off, he said that if I spent half as much time establishing a career as I did messing about on my phone, then I'd be at the top of the corporate ladder by now.'

'That was a bit harsh,' Rachel tutted.

'No,' said Tori. 'It wasn't. It was true, and his words, combined with the success I've made of launching Em's business and Alex pointing out a few things, has helped me to realise that messing about on my phone, as Dad put it, could actually become my career.'

'I don't understand.' Rachel frowned.

'That's because you're knocking that liqueur back too quickly.'

I smiled, noticing her glass was empty again. 'I get it,' I said, giving Tori my full attention. 'You're going to help businesses develop their online presence, aren't you, Tori?'

'Yes.' She nodded.

'Got it in one,' Alex confirmed. 'And even though we won't be business partners in the true sense of the word, we're going to operate a sort of combined consultancy package. I often get asked if I know someone who can take on the branding I create and maximise its impact, especially online.'

'And I'm bound to find clients who will want rebranding before they launch, or re-launch, online,' Tori chimed in. 'Or even clients who I recommend a rebrand to and can then introduce to Alex.'

'Now I see.' Rachel smiled.

'I think it's a genius idea,' I said, looking at them both.

'You do?' said Tori, sounding a little unsure.

'I really do,' I told her. 'This is the perfect role for you. No one knows the tricks of the getting-noticed-online trade like you do and you're always one step ahead. You were right at the front of the line when TikTok became a thing. You're really going to be in demand.'

'I certainly hope so,' she said, biting her lip.

'We're putting together a business plan for Tori to present to her father after the holiday,' Alex further explained.

'He could certainly do with refining his branding and upping his online game,' Tori said, shaking her head.

'He could be your first official client,' I suggested.

'Oh my god!' she gasped. 'Can you imagine?'

'I can actually,' Alex said thoughtfully.

'And of course, Alex is in charge of my branding.' Tori

grinned. 'Although I do have some ideas about how I want everything to look.'

'Crikey,' I said, raising my glass to them both. 'I'm both impressed and relieved.'

'Relieved?' Tori frowned.

'Yes,' I laughed. 'I'm relieved you helped me launch Passion for Patchwork before you went public. I'm pretty certain I wouldn't be able to afford your fees now.'

'Don't worry,' she laughed back. 'I would have offered you mates' rates.'

'I've already got Tori one client,' Alex said. 'And along with what she's done for you, Em, that will prove to her father that the time spent on her phone could be very lucrative indeed.'

'And he'll love that,' Tori said, draining her glass. 'Dad's all about a healthy bottom line. That might even convince him to take me on.'

'Crikey.' Rachel smiled, puffing out her cheeks. 'This really is turning out to be a transformative getaway, isn't it?'

'I told you I was a changed woman,' Tori laughed. 'But I am sorry about what you've been through tonight, Rach.'

'Well, I'm not.' She beamed. 'I'm well shot of Jealous Jeremy. Although I do wish your face hadn't been on the receiving end of his fist, Alex.'

'Rather mine than yours,' he pointedly said, gingerly touching his slightly swollen nose again.

'He never laid a finger on me,' Rachel said. 'But I suppose there was no telling where we might have ended up after one row too many, was there?'

'Exactly,' Alex said. 'You really are well shot of him.'

'I am,' she said again. 'And with Tori and Em finding their

business feet and you honouring your promises to Gracie, I'm certain all our wishes for this wonderful summer have come true.'

'Almost all,' said Alex, looking at me, and making my heart thump and my cheeks flush. 'But I'm happy to wait to hear the outcome of my most recent one.'

Chapter 30

I didn't really expect to sleep that night, but I went out like a light and stayed slumbering until I was woken by a rare streak of sunshine which found its way through a tiny gap in the curtains and eventually across my face.

I stretched out in the bed, luxuriating in the warmth where the sun had already been and playing over the events of the day before, which rivalled even the most thrilling Friday night drinks session.

Rachel was finally free of Jeremy, Tori had at long last discovered her niche and I had launched my own bespoke business *and* had the love of a good man. And Alex, I realised, had played a huge part in all of those things. He had taken one on the nose for Rachel (literally), he'd guided Tori along the path to work and he'd encouraged me to become self-employed. He'd also said he was in love with me and, as yet, the poor guy didn't know for certain if I was in love with him. In spite of the promise I had made to take my time to think it over, I made it my thrilling mission for the day to rectify that.

'Oh, look who finally woke up,' tutted Tori, but with a grin as I arrived in the kitchen at the exact same moment she and Rachel

came in from outside, laden down with bags. 'I reckon the only thing that would make that double bed more comfortable would be to have a decent bloke in it.'

I rolled my eyes and filled the kettle.

'What do you think, Rach?'

'Perhaps,' she said. 'But to be honest, I'll stick to having one side of my bed empty for a while.'

'Just as well,' Tori said cheekily, putting the bags she was holding down. 'Especially as we're currently sleeping in single divans.'

'What on earth have you got there?' I frowned, ignoring the pillow talk as Rachel put her bags down too.

'Never you mind,' she mysteriously said.

'It's a surprise.' Tori winked and Rachel groaned.

'It's *supposed* to be a surprise,' she said sardonically. 'You're not to go in the fridge today, Em, or mine and Tori's room. Got it?'

'How am I supposed to eat without going in the fridge?' I laughed, wondering what the pair of them were cooking up that I wasn't allowed to know about.

'Tori will keep you fed and watered today,' Rachel firmly said. 'Won't you, Tor?'

'I'll do my best,' she promised.

Knowing her culinary repertoire was even more limited than mine, I wouldn't be eating three courses.

'So, what is this surprise?' I quickly asked, hoping to catch one of them off guard.

'Nice try,' said Rachel, in her trademark teacherly tone. 'Now, go back in your room until we've sorted this lot and then Tori will scramble you some eggs.'

Tori wrinkled her nose. 'Tori will *try* to scramble you some eggs,' the assigned chef amended.

'Where's Alex?' I asked, noticing that the pull-out had been put away and his pillows and blankets were folded on one of the window seats.

'He's at the police station where they kept Jeremy overnight,' Rachel said, with a sigh. 'Connor came and told Alex earlier this morning that his presence was required.'

'Jeremy has been in a cell all night?' I frowned. 'That's not normal procedure, is it? I thought they would just have a word and send him on his way, for the time being at least.'

Not that I had an in-depth knowledge of police procedure, but that had been the lie of the land when we came back to the cottage.

'That's what I thought too.' Rachel nodded. 'But the idiot got all cocky again after we'd left. Apparently, he kicked off big time and ended up punching one of the attending officers.'

'No way!' I gasped.

'It's true,' said Tori. 'Lakeside is buzzing with it. Mrs Timpson is doling out the goss to all and sundry.'

'But she wasn't even there,' I pointed out.

'Not directly on the scene,' Tori sniggered. 'But she was hanging out of her bedroom window which is right opposite the pub, so she had a bird's eye view of the aftermath even though she didn't see the first punch.'

'And she recorded it all on her phone,' Rachel said, shaking her head. 'So, the evidence against Jeremy is pretty damning.'

'What a knob,' I muttered.

'Always was,' said Rachel, ushering me back into the bedroom, 'always will be. And talking of phones, I'm ditching mine and having a new one with a new number and everything. That way, I'll be certain the knob isn't still tracking me.'

'Excellent idea,' Tori and I agreed, feeling grateful that Jeremy had dropped himself further in it by confirming that he had been.

After a very late breakfast of extremely dry scrambled eggs and charred toast, I decided to walk down to the village. Not to get the latest lowdown on Jeremy's fate – as far as I was concerned, they could throw away the key – but to clear my head and check in on Passion for Patchwork courtesy of The Drover's Wi-Fi.

Not surprisingly, the pub was abuzz and Connor was making the most of the till ringing. Sundays were always busy with people stopping for his legendary lunches but the world and his wife seemed to be in either the shop or the pub and on occasion switching between the two and back again that afternoon.

'Any sign of Alex?' Connor asked, when he spotted me among the throng.

'No,' I said. 'No sign. No word. What do you think the police wanted him for?'

'To convince him to press charges I should think,' he said, in a low voice. 'The officer Jeremy punched won't let him off lightly and Alex adding the weight of what happened to him to the cause will get the idiot further into trouble.'

'It's no less than he deserves,' I said, feeling especially uncharitable.

I was generally easy-going, but not where he was concerned.

'I agree.' Connor nodded. 'What on earth did Rach ever see in him?'

'I have no idea.' I shrugged, not wanting to get into it. 'But I know she values your friendship deeply, Connor,' I was willing to say and which made him blush. 'She said that her relationship

with you had flagged up just how wrong hers was with Jeremy, so we're all extremely thankful for that.'

'Well, you know how I feel about her,' he whispered. 'And that's not going to change. I hope she'll stay in touch when the time comes for you to . . .'

'Don't,' I winced. 'I can't bear to think about it.'

He smiled and nodded. 'Same,' he agreed. 'I never usually have all that much to do with whoever's staying at the cottage, but you four have been different.'

'We've been that all right,' I laughed.

'In a good way,' he grinned.

'I should hope so.'

'And what about you and Alex?' he then asked. 'Is he going to have a happier ending to your dream getaway than I am?'

'I think I should tell him that before you, don't you?' I grinned.

'Fair enough,' Connor laughed. 'But I hope you don't keep him waiting too long. He looked like a tortured soul when I came to the cottage this morning.'

'Don't worry,' I said, further forgetting the promise I had made to think everything through now I knew he was suffering. 'I'll put him out of his misery soon.'

'Say no more.' Connor winked. 'Now, what can I get you? It's on the house.'

It was noisy inside the pub and, as the sun was still shining, I sat out front at one of the picnic tables. The change of position didn't afford me much privacy, but thankfully the Wi-Fi stretched that far and I was able to keep my head down and get through what I needed to do without too much disruption.

There were further dress enquiries and dozens more likes and comments on what I'd already uploaded and, thanks to Tori's

foresight, I had more photos to share. Consistency was key, she had told me, when she set the accounts up and that if I didn't want the initial interest to tail off, then I needed to keep on top of responding and make sure there was always something new to look at. Looking at the results of what she'd started, I had every faith that she would make a huge success of her business.

As I made one last check that I'd made notes of everything I needed to, I scribbled down a few extra words about an idea I'd had for some bespoke bags. I couldn't wait to make one up and as much as I was dreading my book-lovers' adventure coming to an end, at least I knew I had something exciting to start on when we left. And I had Alex too, of course, no matter what I decided to say to him, because he was going to be working with Tori.

Who was I kidding? I laughed to myself, making a couple of passing hikers give me a wide berth. The decision was already made, it had been for weeks, all I had to do now was find a way to present it in the most romantic way possible. I thought that after everything he'd been through, Alex deserved that and actually, so did I.

The cottage was empty when I arrived back but there was a note from Rachel and Tori pinned to the door.

We're at the lake. ~~Don't~~ come down.
R and T
X

'What are they up to?' I muttered, as I unpinned the note and went in.

There was no sign of Alex either so I headed into the

bedroom to look through the bags of fabric to see if I could cobble something bag-like together from the material I hadn't yet used. I hadn't planned to properly start the new idea, but I was itching to see if it might work and I soon lost track of time. My neck was horribly stiff from having sat in one position for so long when I heard the cottage door open and close and looked around.

'Ow.' I winced, gingerly moving my head from side to side to reduce some of the tension which had built up.

When I started sewing full-time I would have to schedule alarms to remind me to get up and have a jig and a stretch every now and again.

'Em?'

'Alex,' I said, abandoning the stretches and jumping up. 'You're back.'

I rushed from the bedroom and found him pulling off his shoes.

'I am,' he said. 'At bloody last. What a waste of a day.'

He sounded tired and crotchety and I could hardly blame him. None of what had happened was his fault and yet he was well and truly caught up in it.

'Do you want to talk about it?' I asked.

'Not really,' he said, rubbing his eyes. 'I'll only get wound up.'

'In that case, maybe I can cheer you up?' I suggested, giving him a smile.

'If anyone can,' he smiled back, 'you can.'

With three quick strides I was across the room and in his arms, ready to give him the news that his feelings were reciprocated and that they always had been. Not that my reaction to seeing him could really have left him in any doubt.

'No, no, no, no, no!' shouted Tori as she burst in through the back door.

'Yes, yes, yes, yes, yes!' Alex retorted, holding me tighter and making me laugh.

'Rachel!' Tori yelled at the top of her voice. 'Hurry up! They're almost doing stuff!'

Rachel then bounded in and Alex groaned. He released me, knowing it was impossible to carry on. It wouldn't have been the grand romantic moment I had been hoping to conjure, but had we not been disturbed we would at least have now been reading from the same page. Not that my rushing into his arms could have really left him in any doubt as to what I was going to say.

'Em,' Rachel primly admonished. 'I thought you were supposed to be taking time to think through your response to Alex's public declaration of amour?'

'I am,' I said defensively, then realising how the situation looked, added, 'I was.'

'We were just in the nick of time,' tutted Tori. 'Just a few seconds later and it would have all been wasted.'

'Do you have any idea what she's talking about?' Alex asked me.

'Not a clue.' I shrugged. 'But that's not unusual. You'll learn that as you get to know her better.'

Alex shook his head.

'Come on,' said Rachel, sounding bossy. 'Grab a jumper or a jacket and follow us.'

I really did have no idea what the pair of them were up to, but did as I was told. I pulled on a jumper while Alex put his shoes back on and then we followed them, crocodile style, out of the cottage and through the woods down to the lake.

'There,' announced Tori, giving Alex and I a little shove

towards the end of the path. 'Now you can properly carry on doing or saying whatever you were just getting into back at the cottage.'

'And we'll see you later.' Rachel waved, pulling Tori quickly away.

Alex and I watched them go, giggling as they went, then we turned back to one another.

'I'm still none the wiser,' said Alex.

'Me neither,' I laughed, heading for the pebbled shore. 'Come on.'

Just a few seconds later, however, we were both in the know. I no longer had to worry about how to create the most romantic moment to tell Alex the outcome of my brief musings because Rachel and Tori had gifted me one.

'Is this?' Alex gasped, looking around.

'It is.' I swallowed, feeling choked that my friends had gone to so much trouble.

'It looks exactly like we've just walked into the book,' Alex said, sounding choked.

'I know.' I smiled, blinking back tears. 'I think that's the idea.'

One of our favourite scenes, one of everyone's favourites scenes to be precise, was set at the side of the lake on a clear evening exactly like the one we were experiencing. It was a pivotal point in the book, the very moment that Heather allowed her formerly broken heart to be healed, the second she embraced hope again and declared her love for the kind and gentle man who had so tenderly helped put her back together again.

The seats were arranged identically to the scene in the film, around the campfire which had also been lifted straight from the pages and there were throws over the chairs, a packed picnic

hamper, champagne to celebrate, candles in jars, hurricane lanterns and even the film soundtrack playing from somewhere.

'I really hope your friends haven't misinterpreted what your reaction to my still being in love with you might be, Em,' Alex said, with a slightly apprehensive smile. 'Because if they have, this could be really awkward . . .'

'Alex,' I said, moving to stand in front of him and so close again that there could be absolutely no room for misunderstanding.

'Yes.' He swallowed.

'Stop talking.'

'Okay . . .'

I silenced him with a soft kiss on the lips, my eyes never leaving his.

'Given my reaction back at the cottage just now, you must know that I'm still in love with you too,' I whispered. 'How could I not be?'

I kissed him again, for longer that time.

'So.' Alex smiled. 'My unexpected wish for this summer really has come true.'

His hands found my waist and he pulled me close again, the next kiss reaching the passionate heights we'd climbed to after cocktail hour and it wasn't until the song played through for the third time that I realised just how long we'd been kissing for. We both took a breath and I rested my forehead against Alex's.

'My wish has come true, too,' I told him. 'I didn't expect anything like this to happen on this holiday.'

'Of course, you didn't.' Alex grinned. 'Because you thought I was going to be someone else for a start.'

I let out a breath as I remembered the first few days after our arrival.

'I thought your being here was going to bugger everything up,' I told him.

'I know,' he said, also reminiscing. 'I remember.'

'But actually, you've made it a million times better.'

'And you've made my time here a million times easier,' he told me. 'You all have, but you especially, Em. All this time we've been waiting to come here, all these years we were on Catriona's list and then we end up at the cottage together, right at the same time.'

'It was serendipity,' I whispered, moving to kiss him again.

'I love serendipity,' he whispered back.

'Me too.'

'It was written in the stars,' he added, punctuating each word with another kiss.

By the time we sat down and opened the champagne, I was beginning to see stars.

'You have the best friends,' said Alex, opening the picnic and finding that even the food was the same as that featured in the book.

No wonder it had taken Rachel and Tori all day to put the surprise together. This was pure magic.

'You have them as friends now too,' I reminded him. 'We're both equally blessed.'

I thought back to what I'd arrived on the holiday with – a head packed full of tangled thoughts – and compared it to what, in just over a week, I would be leaving with. A treasure trove of special memories, a thrilling future and a fine romance. It wasn't a bad effort for just a few weeks.

'Penny for them?' Alex asked, as we snuggled under a blanket and got comfortable to wait for the real stars to appear.

'I was just thinking how wonderful this summer has been,' I told him.

'And it's not over yet,' he reminded me. 'We've still got more time here to enjoy.'

Now that Alex and I were officially a couple, the thought of that was even more thrilling than before.

'That we have,' I said, snuggling into his arms. 'And I want to savour every single moment.'

Chapter 31

When we eventually returned to the cottage that evening, Rachel and Tori had tactfully turned in for the night, but they were both up with the lark the next morning to make up for their former discretion.

'What's he doing on there?' Tori hissed and pointed, when we met in the kitchen and she spotted Alex sound asleep on the pull-out. 'You didn't turn him down, did you?'

'Tori,' Rachel shot back. 'You can't ask Em that!'

She then gave me a look so loaded with inquisitiveness that I knew I had no choice but to say something by way of explanation if only to shut the pair of them up.

'Come into my room,' I said, hoping Alex really was asleep and hadn't heard what Tori had just asked.

'So?' she squealed, bouncing up and down on the bed the second I'd shut the door and climbed back under the duvet.

'So,' I repeated. 'First off, I want to say thank you both so much for what you did last night. The whole set up was incredibly romantic, utterly perfect down to the last detail and it totally set the scene for me to tell Alex . . .'

'Yes,' Tori and Rachel gasped, as they moved closer together, clutched hands and leant in.

Surely, they could have no misgivings about what I'd told him, given that I had just thanked them for the dreamy tableau they had created, but then, finding Alex sleeping alone had seemed to throw Tori a curveball.

'That I was in love with him, of course,' I laughed. 'What did you think?'

'I told you, Tori!' Rachel beamed, letting go of Tori's hand and flinging herself across the bed to give me a hug.

'Well, I wasn't completely sure,' Tori admitted, also getting in on the hugging action.

'And I know partly why,' I laughed with a nod to the sitting room. 'But Alex was the perfect gentleman and we went our separate ways at bedtime.'

'How very civilised,' Rachel commented. 'Were you disappointed?'

'No,' I said, shoving her away but still laughing.

'What about before bedtime?' Tori asked, suggestively waggling her eyebrows. 'Tell us everything.'

'Tori,' Rachel tutted. 'She doesn't have to tell us anything, let alone everything. Unless she wants to,' she hopefully added.

I told them enough to satisfy their curiosity.

'I still can't believe he's on the sofa,' Tori said disbelievingly once I'd shared most of the details of our romantic evening under the stars. 'Are you sure he didn't leave you in the early hours?'

'No,' I said, throwing a pillow at her. 'He did not. I think I'd remember if he'd been here in my bed, don't you? Don't answer that,' I hastily added.

She still didn't look convinced but Rachel did.

'If it was going to be my first time with a fella,' she succinctly said, 'I wouldn't want to be going for it with you two in the next room.'

'Bloody prude,' Tori teased.

'We don't all have zero inhibitions.' Rachel grinned, but then her face dropped. 'Not that I'm suggesting . . .'

'I know,' Tori said, whacking her with the pillow.

Having already been on the receiving end of some truly searing kisses, I was very much looking forward to getting to know Alex more intimately than I already did, but Rachel was right. That was going to be impossible while we were at the cottage with her and Tori watching our every move.

'Don't worry,' said Rachel, giving me a nudge. 'I know exactly what you're thinking and we've come up with a solution to that.'

'I'm not sure the weather here in Lakeside is compatible with al fresco lovemaking,' I giggled as the rain began to drum on the cottage roof.

'Have no fear.' She winked. 'My plan leaves you in no danger of exposing any goose pimpled flesh in the great outdoors and it will benefit us as much as you.'

'Well, well, well,' said Alex, making us screech as his head appeared around the door. 'What have we here? Or shouldn't I ask? I hope I'm not the main topic of conversation this morning.'

'Absolutely not,' Tori said cheekily as she hopped off the bed and squeezed around him.

'Your name hasn't come up even once.' Rachel grinned, also disappearing.

'Now you've said that, I don't know whether to be relieved or disappointed.' Alex smiled, flopping down on the duvet. 'God, I've missed this bed.'

'I don't believe it,' I gasped, chucking the pillow I'd previously aimed at Rachel at his head. 'You're only really interested in me for my feather filled mattress, aren't you?'

'Damn!' he cried. 'The cat's out of the bag. You've sussed me.'

I leant over him and before I had a chance to kiss him, he flipped me over and pinned me down, one hand either side of my head. He looked deep into my eyes and I felt my body relax as he slowly lowered his lips to mine. Things were just about to get interesting when Rachel started bossily shouting about us joining her and Tori for a breakfast meeting.

'You could never doubt what she does for a living, could you?' Alex sighed, reluctantly releasing me.

'Absolutely not,' I said, feeling hot all over and more than a little frustrated. 'I gave her a Little Miss Bossy mug for her birthday last year in the hope that she'd take the hint and tone it down, but if anything, it's made her worse. The damn thing's a constant reminder and I'm sure she strives to live up to the title every time she drinks out of it.'

'The first time I come to your flat,' Alex whispered, 'that mug might go missing.'

I couldn't wait to welcome Alex to the flat, but quickly banished the image of him there because that would mean the holiday would be over and, even though I was excited to get stuck into my business plans, I wasn't anywhere near ready to leave Lakeside. The same, however, could not be said for Tori and Rachel.

Over a breakfast of coffee and eggs, Rachel shared the plan she and Tori had come up with while Alex and I had been canoodling by the lake the evening before.

'But that's just five days away,' I groaned. 'And a whole

five days ahead of the proper end of our holiday. You can't leave then.'

I might have been craving some alone time with Alex, but not at the expense of finishing our getaway without her and Tori.

'But remember, term starts on the sixth,' Rachel said for the umpteenth time. 'And I have so much prep to do . . .'

'Since when?' I huffed. 'The original plan was for us to leave here at stupid o'clock on the sixth and for you to go straight to school in time for first registration. You'd even cleared it with the head.'

I had always thought forgoing the two days planning in school ahead of the start of the autumn term was a bit bonkers because I knew how much she usually got done in that time, but she had insisted that, just this once, she could manage without it. And now, she'd had a total turnaround and was trying to convince me that she couldn't.

'You were the one who always said that was a mad idea,' she reminded me. 'And if I'm being honest, I only really came up with it because it meant I could have a few extra days away from Jeremy.'

'Oh, Rach,' I said, feeling relieved that she didn't feel obliged to give Alex and me some time, but also choked to know what had been her real motive before. 'But you were going to move in with him.'

Alex reached for my hand.

'Sometimes,' he said, sounding wise beyond his years, 'we can't see how wrong something is until we're completely free of it.'

'Exactly,' Rachel shudderingly said. 'Now Jeremy's out of the picture, I've got an entirely fresh perspective and I can see as clear as day all of the things that were so wrong in our relationship and further than that, my life.'

I supposed that was the silver lining to her leaving ahead of schedule.

'I'm going to miss you, Rach.' I swallowed. 'I know it's only going to be a few days, but this place won't be the same without you in it.'

'Will you miss me, too?' Tori then piped up.

'Not you as well,' I groaned.

'I'm going to stay with Rach, until you get back,' she explained. 'Just in case Jeremy turns up and makes a nuisance of himself.'

'I think that's a good idea,' said Alex, and I couldn't disagree.

I didn't like the thought of Rachel staying in the flat alone so soon after the punch up at the pub. At least if Tori was there and Jeremy did show up, there was safety in numbers.

'And while Rachel is getting to grips with her prep,' Tori carried on, 'I'm going to be honing my business plan and contacting a few people ahead of presenting Dad with my idea and proving to him that I really have got my life together.'

I couldn't object to that either. Until just a few weeks ago, the only thing Tori had appeared to be interested in focusing on was having a good time.

'In that case, I'll get the train back,' I said, as the practical as well as emotional implications of their early departure sank in. 'But I'm not sure how I'll manage with all my stuff. There's my sewing machine for a start.'

'That's no problem,' Alex insisted. 'I can drive you back.'

'Are you sure?'

'Yes,' he said, then sombrely added. 'It will mean the holiday doesn't end when we put the cottage keys back in the security box.'

'Thank you,' I said, kissing his cheek and forcing myself not to think about the end of anything as I looked at Rachel and Tori. 'And if you two have made up your minds . . . .'

'We have,' they confirmed.

'Then we'd better make the most of these last few days here all together, hadn't we?'

The four of us had a fabulous time traveling further about, visiting the pub, rowing on the lake and of course, reading scenes from the book aloud, and watching the film – this time, pointing out how cleverly Tori and Rachel had set up the lakeside picnic – but the biggest highlight of the lot, we all agreed, was heading back to Archer's Force for the day.

'I'm still gutted Star Shine Falls was such a let-down,' Rachel tutted as we packed up Alex's car for the journey, 'but at least we managed to find an alternative.'

'An extremely beautiful alternative,' I added. 'And all thanks to Charlie, the security guard.'

'Have you got your skirt, Em?' Tori asked, as she checked we'd packed up as much as we could carry.

She had insisted that I should take the fern skirt so she could photograph me in the exact spot that had inspired the design for it. Her clever marketing strategy was inspired and further proof that she had the right head for the business she had chosen to go into.

'I have,' I told her. 'And have you got the plaster pack? It's a bit of an uphill hike to reach the falls.'

'And I won't be giving you a piggyback,' Alex laughingly added.

'My boots are fine after all the extra walking we've done this week,' Tori told us both and I hoped she was right.

The last leg of the journey and the road up to the falls was as daunting as the first time we'd navigated it, but that could have been because I was now sitting in the front and Rachel was in the back with Tori. When we eventually arrived at the car park, however, we found it entirely empty so traversing the treacherously tight roads a second time had been totally worth it. I couldn't believe we were going to have the place to ourselves again, but we did and, on that occasion, with extra wildlife to make it even more memorable.

'I don't believe it,' I whispered, my voice filled with emotion as I watched a red squirrel scampering nimbly through the branches of the trees which lined our path down to the falls. 'It really is Squirrel Nutkin.'

The sight of the bushy tailed creature sent me spiralling back through time and I imagined myself tucked up in bed with Nanna and Grandad sitting at the side of my bed and reading the tale, along with all the others, aloud to me. My love of books had been instilled long before Grandad introduced me to *Hope Falls* and I was so grateful for that.

'Are you sure it's not Twinkleberry?' Alex asked, also watching the little red's progress.

'No,' I said as the creature slipped silently out of sight. 'That was definitely Nutkin.'

As soon as the falls came into view, Tori fell into raptures just as we all had on our first visit. She keenly scrambled up and down, her cheeks flushed as she tried to pick out the best spot to photograph me wearing my skirt.

With the sun thankfully shining, the waterfall and verdant ferns were every bit as beautiful as the first time I'd set eyes on them. Familiarity hadn't taken away any of the magic of the place

and I really wouldn't have been surprised to discover some spell had been cast over the place.

'Here,' announced Tori, pointing at a boulder right next to where the falling water splashed into the pool. 'This will be perfect.'

Rachel helped me out of my practical trousers and jacket and into my skirt. I was already wearing a floaty cream blouse and was grateful the day wasn't too cool, although it still felt a bit chilly with fewer clothes on.

'Barefoot will be perfect,' Tori insisted, looking me up and down, before positioning me in the spot she thought would best showcase my outfit.

'You can look now,' Rachel said to Alex who had chivalrously kept his back turned while I undressed and re-dressed.

'Are you certain?' he teased. 'I don't want to catch Em in her undies again.'

'Are you sure about that?' Rachel teased and Tori insisted she was told what the in-joke was.

My toes were feeling chilly by the time she was happy with the photos she had taken on her phone but looking over her shoulder as she scrolled through the images, I could see the few goose pimples I'd succumbed to had been completely worth it.

'You'll be able to write a lovely narrative to go with this,' she said, as Rachel helped me back on with my socks and Alex poured champagne we didn't know he'd picked up into the tin mugs we'd brought with us from the cottage. 'Your clients will love reading about the background behind the skirt.'

'Especially if you tell them how one disappointment then turned into something so memorable,' Rachel suggested, harking back to our first trip to admire a waterfall.

'A bit like me really,' Alex laughed as he handed out the mugs, his considerably less filled than ours, and we all snuggled together on the rocks next to the falls.

'You were never a disappointment,' Rachel shot back.

'But you are extremely memorable.' I smiled, leaning over to kiss his cheek.

He turned his head just at the right moment and my lips landed on his.

'It just goes to show, doesn't it?' Tori wistfully said as a breeze softly ran through the branches above us and the water sparkled even brighter.

'Show what?' Rachel asked, when Tori didn't carry on.

'That sometimes in life,' she eventually continued, 'something unexpected, which might seem like a complete disaster, can turn into something wonderful.'

'You're right,' I agreed.

I had once thought Alex was going to ruin my book-lovers' getaway, Tori had believed her father's actions were going to stop her finding her purpose and Rachel had realised she was trapped in a ruinous relationship. However, each of us had found ways around and through the challenges we faced and come out the other side carrying something life-enhancing and fabulous. Even Alex, whose life had been so engulfed by grief, had been able to move forward and find a way through the darkness.

'We really have done Heather, Rose and Laurie proud, haven't we?' Alex smiled. 'They all came to the cottage for the summer with problems to work through and so did we.'

'Our time here really has turned out to be about so much more than just taking the *Hope Falls* book-lovers' tour, hasn't it?' Rachel laughed.

'It certainly has,' I sighed happily. 'And I'm so pleased we've been able to come here all together.'

The four of us smiled and put our mugs together to toast our future as well as our recent past.

'Unshakeable and unbreakable,' said Tori and Rachel in unison.

'Unshakeable and unbreakable, for life!' Alex and I added.

Alex had decided to forgo his days in Manchester once the countdown to going home began in earnest, but not even the change in routine had the ability to stop the sand slipping through the timer and before we knew it, it was time for Rachel and Tori to leave.

'I'll call you when we're in the pub Sunday afternoon,' I tearfully said as we got ready to wave them off.

Typically, it was a gloriously sunny day, quite possibly the warmest we'd enjoyed since we arrived and the irony of that wasn't lost on any of us.

'Don't spend the whole afternoon indoors,' Tori said cheekily. 'Now the sun's properly shining you should go for a swim.'

We had talked about skinny-dipping the evening before, but Rachel reckoned her toes were still suffering from frostbite and insisted that jumping naked into the lake was the one and only *Hope Falls* tradition she was happy to miss out on.

'Oh yes,' she said as she turned the engine over, knowing she was now completely safe from getting pushed in at the deep end. 'There's still time for you two . . .'

'Off you go then,' I said, patting the roof of the car, before she fixed the idea too firmly in Alex's head. 'See you next week.'

Amid shouts, laughter and waves, Rachel released the handbrake and they were off.

'So,' said Alex as the car turned the corner and they disappeared out of sight. 'What now? It is pretty hot for once.'

'I can think of something,' I said, grabbing his hand and pulling him back through the gate. 'And it doesn't involve any UV risk whatsoever!'

I had no plans to tell Tori that we didn't see the light of day, let alone the sunshine, for the next twenty-four hours, but I knew, given the reason, she wouldn't have scolded us too severely for missing out on the warm weather.

'It's just as well we're heading into Lakeside today,' Alex said, treating me to a lovely glimpse of his wonderfully toned body as he slipped into the bath I was already in and very nearly caused a flood in the process.

'Why's that?' I asked, looking admiringly at his broad shoulders and wondering if my own muscles were going to get a chance to relax before we put them through their paces again.

We were deep in the honeymoon phase and even though I had been upset when Rachel and Tori had decided to leave, I was now feeling grateful for the privacy their departure had gifted us.

'Because without my weekly top-up shop,' Alex explained, 'stocks and supplies are running low.'

'Oh yes,' I said, stifling a yawn. 'I hadn't thought of that.'

'Mrs T is bound to have everything we need to get us through the next few days.' He smiled. 'And I'm sure Connor can help out if there's anything she hasn't got.'

I couldn't imagine there would be anything she hadn't thought of, but he was right.

'In that case,' I said, standing up, 'let's head to The Drover's now. I'm looking forward to calling Rachel and Tori and I've worked up quite an appetite.'

'Me too,' he said seductively, also standing up and then demonstrating quite wonderfully just how famished he was.

With groceries to buy and feeling exhausted after many hours spent getting to know each other better, Alex said he'd drive us to Lakeside, rather than walk and given how satisfyingly worn out I felt, I didn't object.

'You can tackle Mrs Timpson while I call Rachel and Tori, can't you?' I hopefully suggested as he parked up just around the corner from The Drover's.

'Coward,' he teased and I flashed him a smile. 'Oh, go on then.'

I gave him a long kiss as a thank you.

'But only if you're going to be bragging to the girls about my prowess as the perfect partner,' he insisted, flexing his arms, muscle-man style. 'Make sure you let them know I was worth the wait.'

'Believe me,' I laughed, as I went to climb out, 'we won't talk of anything else.'

'Don't you dare!' he gasped, leaning across me so I couldn't move. 'I was only kidding.'

'Well, I wasn't,' I said, finding his most ticklish spot so he couldn't keep me trapped a second longer. 'Take your time,' I told him. 'I have a lot to tell them.'

He shook his head and I was still laughing when I walked into the pub.

'Someone's happy,' said Connor, wiping down the bar. 'I thought you and Alex might call in last night for the karaoke, but I'm guessing you were otherwise engaged.'

'You could say that,' I said, unable to rein in the smile which stretched from ear to ear.

'I'm really pleased for you both,' he said kindly. 'I don't think there's ever been a cottage romance before.'

'Has there not?'

'No,' he said, thinking for a moment. 'Most people are either in friendship groups like you, Rach and Tori or holidaying as a couple. I'm pretty sure you two are a first.'

'I love that,' I said, thinking that made mine and Alex's romance even more special.

'Me too.' He nodded. 'And I also love that Rachel called me last night and has promised to come and visit in October half-term,' he added, with a shy head duck.

'Has she now?' I beamed, wondering if there was hope for her and Connor after all.

'She's going to stay in my spare room for a couple of days,' he said. 'And help out with the Halloween party on the Saturday night.'

'I might have to see if we can all make that trip.' I nodded, imagining myself partying in a witchy orange and black patchwork creation. 'There's bound to be a bed and breakfast somewhere around here that could put the rest of us up.'

I made a mental note to think about seasonal adaptations for my dresses, skirts and potential bags, too.

'It would be great if all of you could be here,' Connor said. 'The party is always a laugh and then there's bonfire night and Christmas . . .'

'Are you trying to turn us into Lakeside residents, Connor?' I asked, cutting him off.

'Maybe,' he laughed.

I loved the thought of living either in or near the village. I could imagine myself in a tiny cottage, with a blazing fire and a cat curled up next to it while I worked away at my sewing

machine. If Passion for Patchwork really took off, I could single-handedly keep Mrs T's post office afloat!

'Can I get you a drink?' I heard Connor ask as I drifted out of my Lakeside fantasy.

'A Coke, please,' I told him. 'Alex will be here in a sec, so I'm going to quickly call the girls.'

Once the video call connected, I gave Tori an instant warning.

'I'm in the pub,' I told her, 'so no squealing and certainly no questions of an intimate nature. Right?'

She looked disappointed, but Rachel laughed.

'Everything all right though?' she asked with emphasis.

'Everything *very* all right,' I told her. 'Thank you for asking.'

'Well,' Tori said, 'you certainly look happy.'

'What are you talking about?' Rachel objected. 'She looks knackered.'

'Exactly,' said Tori, giving Rachel such a shove, she nearly fell off the sofa.

I tried to keep my laughter under control and ended up giggling instead.

'Oh, good grief,' Rachel laughed along. 'She's got it bad.'

'I really have,' I was happy to confirm. 'But never mind me, how are you two getting on?'

We were still chatting when Alex joined us.

'Here he is,' Tori said loudly. 'The man responsible for Em's eyebags.'

'Shush,' I admonished, but Alex stuck out his chest looking like a prize rooster.

I half expected him to crow, but he kissed my cheek instead.

'Ah,' said Rachel. 'Come on, Tori, let's leave the lovebirds to their nesting.'

'And their lunch,' Tori said naughtily. 'After all that shagging, they must be ...'

I cut the call off and messaged them some outraged, laughing and shocked emojis.

'I think she was going to say starving.' Alex grinned, picking up the menu.

'But that's the thing about Tori.' I grinned back. 'You can never be sure.'

Chapter 32

Whenever I had fantasised about my *Hope Falls* inspired dream holiday, I had always shied away from imagining what the end of it would feel like on the assumption that there would be nothing but negative emotions attached to it. However, given the number of surprising, unexpected and transformative things which had happened during my six weeks' stay at the cottage, the reality couldn't have been more different.

The book-based pilgrimage had been a total joy and had ended up exceeding expectations in every conceivable way. That in itself was a miracle because not only had it got off to such a rocky start, I had also put it on such a pedestal of perfection for so many years, it could have easily fallen short, but ultimately it hadn't, not in any respect.

My relationship with both Rachel and Tori had gone through some testing times as had each of our lives, but I felt (and I knew they would agree with me) that we were all the better for it. We had, each of us, shed and gained so much during the last couple of months and as a result our sisterly bonds were bound even tighter.

And then, of course, there was my other relationship. My cheeks flamed when I thought of how I had objected to and

resented Alex's presence when we first arrived. Had someone told me then how we were going to end up, I never would have believed them. I felt immensely grateful for both the changes our relationship had gone through and for the opportunity Alex had found at the cottage to both grieve for Gracie and heal.

Last, but by no means least, there was my new business. I had left home with the intention of thinking about it, mulling it over and trying to decide if I was brave enough to take it on. However, not only had I made the decision to go for it, but with Tori's expertise and my friends' support and encouragement, I had already launched it! Consequently, I had reached the end of my time at the cottage having finally sent off the email to turn down the data analyst job, and I felt excited about my future, was looking forward to the challenges to come and ready to embrace every fresh opportunity with open arms.

Never mind Passion for Patchwork, I was feeling passion for *everything*! I felt as though a light had been switched on inside me and the bulb which lit up as a result was burning bright and shining out into the world.

On our last evening at the cottage, Alex and I walked hand in hand down to the lake. We had spent the day talking and planning while we packed our bags so that what we were doing didn't feel quite so final.

We had plans to see each other every weekend. What with the train journey for me being only an hour each way and less time for Alex in the car, it was doable and it would ensure our working week was uninterrupted and we stayed focused and committed to helping our businesses grow. We had both agreed that we wanted our lives to have the right balance and that, for now at least, felt like the best way to achieve it.

However, during our last night under the stars, we focused only on the moment and each other. Not the past, or the future but the present. It was all that mattered, it was all that we were living and breathing for.

'Are you sure you want to do this?' Alex asked, as we arrived at the end of the jetty.

'Absolutely not,' I said, pulling Gracie's hoodie over my head and unzipping my jeans.

'Me neither,' he said, puffing out his cheeks as he pulled off his trainers and socks. 'But we owe it to Gracie.'

'And ourselves,' I insisted. 'I know we'll regret it if we don't.'

'Even undies?' he asked, wrinkling his nose as we stood almost naked, but not quite.

'Even undies.' I nodded, looking about before I unclasped my bra.

'Sure?' Alex grinned, twanging the waistband of his trunks.

'Yeah,' I quickly said, stepping out of my knickers before I chickened out of going the whole hog, 'I'm sure.'

'Okay,' he laughed as he hastily joined me in the raw.

He pushed his pile of clothes to the side of the jetty with his foot and I did the same with mine, making sure I didn't knock them in.

'I think I'm going to need a run up,' said Alex, already shivering. 'Is it deep enough for that?'

'Yes' – I swallowed, looking over the edge – 'it's definitely deep enough for that.'

'Come on then,' he said, reaching for my hand and pulling me along with him. 'On three we start running.'

There was no time to back out.

'One, two, three!' Alex yelled.

We set off still holding hands and we both jumped as high and as far as we could when we reached the end of the jetty.

'Here we go!' I squealed and Alex laughed.

I braced myself knowing that the water I was about to plunge into was going to be bitterly cold, but the sensation would be exhilarating too, and best of all, Alex was going to be there, ready to pull me into the safety of his arms and that made me feel secure and very happy indeed. As I hit the icy water and let out a screech, I felt ecstatic in the knowledge that my life had turned a page and I was starting a thrilling new chapter.